AYN RAND HATES TUSCALOOSA

...AND YOU TOO, JOPLIN!

BY GEORGE KELLEY

ISBN-13:
978-0983997436
ISBN-10:
0983997438

One single candle
www.onesinglecandle.com

contents

ACKNOWLEDGEMENTS

This book would not be possible without the inspiration and support of so many. I must begin with my parents, George and Emma Kelley, who instilled in me a strong sense of right and wrong that remains in me today and even though I have not always lived to that mark, it is the motivation of this book.

I would also like to thank those who acted as a combination sounding board/editorial committee/focus group and read what I wrote, rewrote, and listened to my ideas as I had them; whether the ideas or writing were worth discussing or not. Jim Jones, Stephen Kelly, Chris Border, Andy Akin, my cousin Alan Palmore, my boss Russ Cheatham, Randy Verma, Mark Edwards, Murphy Mullican, my lifetime friends Wade Wiggins and Jon Parsons have been invaluable for their input and support. I appreciate every email you returned and every phone call you answered.

My sister-in-law Alison Hunter with her editing kills has provided the structure I need, but do not possess. Her keen eye and editing have saved me much embarrassment and allowed me to express myself in proper English- that is not something that naturally flows from me in my writing or my conservations. Please note that I have elected to keep some phrases intact, as I thought them to be clever. Any butchering of the language that is present in the text is in high probability just as I wrote it.

The credit for the book's cover belongs to two talented and creative individuals: Sarah Schork and Donkey Hotey. Sarah provided the design and much needed creative input on the book and website, you can find her at http://www.sarakathryndesigns.com. Mr. Hotey-his friends call him Donkey-provided the out of the park caricature of Ayn Rand. His artwork is unbelievable. Check him out at www.donkeyhotey.com.

My longtime pal Hank Lambert has been an incredible asset for me in this venture. Even as he conducts his life on the left coast in LA, he finds time to help set up my web presence, advise me, coach me, direct me, and manage me in this venture. Hank is truly an indispensable part of this process. I can't imagine being at this point without him.

My two wonderful stepchildren William and Hannah are especially thanked, as they tolerated my messy stacks of papers, books, magazines and my mood swings while writing. Hannah in particular is appreciated for her copy editing for me. Details are not my strong suit, having her insert corrections in long manuscripts saved me some major stress. She did confidently what I can only do gingerly.

The biggest thanks goes to my partner and best friend, my wife Rosemary. Besides the obvious support of a roof over my head and food on the table, she provided the strength, inspiration and courage for me to attempt this project. She has consistently pushed for the perfect job for me; with perfect being defined as the one that made me most happy. She had the clarity and confidence to nudge me to becoming a full time writer. I could have never taken that step without her. I am not sure that I could even be standing here at all without her. She has given me life, she has given me hope, she has given me happiness, and she has given me a reason to want to follow my heart and to do it to the best of my abilities. I love you sweetheart. This book, as is my life, is dedicated to you.

FORWARD: MARLEY'S GHOST

The Ghost, on hearing this, set up another cry, and clanked its chain so hideously in the dead silence of the night, that the Ward would have been justified in indicting it for a nuisance.

"Oh! Captive, bound, and double-ironed," cried the phantom, "not to know, that ages of incessant labour by immortal creatures, for this earth must pass into eternity before the good of which it is susceptible is all developed. Not to know that any Christian spirit working kindly in its little sphere, whatever it may be, will find its mortal life too short for its vast means of usefulness. Not to know that no space of regret can make amends for one life's opportunity misused! Yet such was I! Oh! Such was I!"

"But you were always a good man of business, Jacob," faltered Scrooge, who now began to apply this to himself.

"Business!" cried the Ghost, wringing its hands again. "Mankind was my business. The common welfare was my business; charity, mercy, forbearance, and benevolence, were, all, my business. The dealings of my trade were but a drop of water in the comprehensive ocean of my business!"

ebenezer scrooge and jacob marley
"a christmas carol", 1843

GEORGE KELLEY

ALLOW ME TO INTRODUCE MYSELF...

I've entertained the idea of writing a book for some time now, even going as far as to do a good bit of research on various subjects. This wasn't my first idea for a book, but it had the most sticking power.

My wife had listened to all my grand schemes and wonderful ideas that always seemed to fall by the wayside. It is certainly understandable to expect eye rolls after many starts that withered on the vine.

But this idea was different; it was relevant because it was so personal. When the devastating tornado hit Tuscaloosa I was heart sick and fretted for my friends who lived there. After all of my circle were accounted for, it became obvious that Tuscaloosa would never be the same physically in addition to emotionally. The bitter irony of the disconnect between the needs of the people of Tuscaloosa (and any other town that suffers tragedy of this magnitude) and the political preferences disturbed me.

Here Tuscaloosa sat in rubble, crying for help to the very government so many there claim to despise. The governor, Robert Bentley, had campaigned on the "Tenth Amendment" meaning he refused to yield any power to the federal government that wasn't strictly enumerated in the constitution. Yet there he was asking for help from FEMA and other agencies, which are not justified by the Tenth Amendment.

One can overlook his immediate hypocrisy, but it would be foolhardy to ignore the rhetoric coming from the conservative movement in the United States. They aren't as hypocritical and their sincerity poses a danger to all of the future Tuscaloosa's out there, along with any other component of the downtrodden.

That's when the idea for the book hit me. The hook was obvious to me; the political loyalties of Tuscaloosa and the rest of red state America was to the Republican Party, and the Republican Party's loyalty was to Ayn Rand.

I was very familiar with Ayn Rand, having read "Atlas Shrugged" about twenty years ago. I found it hard to understand, as her writing style was obtuse to say the least, but the parts I did understand disgusted me.

That in and of itself wouldn't surprise someone who didn't know me except through the context of this book, as I identify myself as a somewhat liberal voter. But to those who have known me all of my life, including almost all in Tuscaloosa who know me, there ought to be an element of shock.

I was as extreme right wing as a person could be, up until 2007. I was not a casual conservative; I found Rush Limbaugh too shallow and redundant. All he ever did in my mind was read the editorials I had already read. His analysis left a great deal to be desired in my mind. I wanted the hard stuff. I read every book by Milton Friedman I could find (and understand). I subscribed to the National Review for about 15 years, the Wall Street Journal for about half that long.

When I turned 18, I mourned the fact that my birthday fell too late for me to vote for Ronald Reagan's first term. I did celebrate the fact that I helped to give him the huge landslide over Walter Mondale in 1984 with my vote.

I have never in my life voted for a Democrat as president, including in the last election. I voted for John McCain, in spite of the not insignificant reservations about McCain's ability to lead us through the financial mess and of course, Sarah Palin. I still had enough Republican in me to vote for him and his service to our country in Viet Nam was something I valued highly and I felt it reflected well upon his character.

I now regret my vote, not because my vote made any great difference in the grand scheme, but because I realized shortly thereafter that I could no longer justify internally all of my previous votes for conservative principles.

There is no small amount of embarrassment in me confessing this, but at one time I was a fan of Pat Buchanan, as I felt he was one of the few true conservatives in the public eye. I still feel more confident that Pat Buchanan is the purest conservative, but it is no longer a selling point with me, it's a reason to avoid him.

I cannot attribute my conversion to a more progressive worldview completely to the events of the day, namely the financial crisis of 2008. That certainly played a significant role in my transformation, but it was not *the* turning point. Events in my private life drove my change of heart more than what I read in the newspapers did.

I was attending the University of Alabama around that time as I was taking graduate courses in political science while working at the Mercedes Benz production facility in Vance, Alabama concurrently. I worked for a contractor as a manager, despite the fact that I knew little or nothing about automobile production and after three years working there I probably know even less. I did become aware of the lives of my employees; almost all of them were extremely poor and uneducated. I saw the lives of people up close and realized that the blame for their lives that myself and all good conservatives assign to the poor wasn't really justified.

I witnessed the working poor at the most personal level, as most had no insurance or chances at it. Within my first month of working at Mercedes, one of my employees died of a heart attack at 40 years old. She had complained during our lunch hour every night about chest pains, but couldn't afford to see a doctor. I understand that her family had to wait two to three weeks to bury her because of financial difficulties. Donations had to come from her extended family to help with the cost.

I also found out that one of my employees, one of my favorites had been living in a trailer for four months with no power. If you spent any time in Alabama in the summer, you would know that it is almost unbearable *even with* power and air conditioning. This man and his family lived in a trailer with no power and cooked on the dirt outside with cans of Sterno.

A friend and I paid off the electrical deposit and I arranged the power hook up. The employee did not even have the wherewithal to arrange it himself, as he was baffled by the system. He also didn't know how to apply for food stamps, with which I assisted him.

I then realized that not all of the poor on welfare were gaming the system. Sure, there was, is and always will be fraud, but many are not educated enough to take advantage of loopholes. Many are actually honest! I found this to be the most surprising counter to my previous prejudices.

About this time the bottom dropped out of the economy, and I saw the Republican Party's solution to be...well, I wasn't sure what it was. Tax cuts were involved, I do remember that. Tax cuts cure all in the world of the Republicans. I am pretty sure the Republicans believe that diabetes, cancer and AIDS can all be cured with enough tax cutting.

The idea of bailouts disgusted me, but I felt strongly that the doomsayers were correct; the entire system would collapse without capitalization through the injections of massive amounts of money. I knew enough history of the Great Depression to hope for capital injections; and I hoped that they would be followed by massive regulations of the financial industry such as Franklin Roosevelt brought with Glass-Steagall Act.

The Republicans turned out to protest the bailouts and then also the regulations that would reduce the chances of more bailouts. They complained about the fire, but refused to put the matches out of reach for the arsonists.

Republican governors refused stimulus money for unemployment benefits for purely political reasons while "true conservatives" cheered them. All of this happened as I saw friends at Mercedes by the hundreds lose their jobs in the financial crisis. Most of these people had enthusiastically embraced their jobs as "good jobs". Indeed they were at one time, as they were a chance for poor, relatively uneducated Alabamians to achieve middle class status.

13

But I also witnessed Mercedes go from a good job to borderline exploitation. Mercedes came to Alabama because of millions of dollars worth of tax credits. Economists say that Alabama paid $177,000 per job to Mercedes.

I know hundreds who have worked and still work there, and I have been told this by too many to discount it. The pay rate while Mercedes was still beholden to the state of Alabama was phenomenal. The job carried full benefits and a top wage rate of slightly less than thirty dollars per hour. This was to demonstrate that unions were not necessary and that it was possible to have good jobs without collective bargaining.

But as the contractual agreement with the state of Alabama expired, Mercedes shifted its hiring of employees from the state's employment office to a temporary employment service. All new employees were required to be vetted through the temp service. They had no rights, no insurance to speak of, and could be dismissed for any trivial reason.

The temp status was one that was limbo, lasting several years for some. All temps start at approximately $14 hour or so; more than ten bucks per hour less than their full time counterparts. The temp agency is contracted three years at a time, and when it rolls over, the temps lose any seniority and start over again at day one as far as Mercedes was concerned.

Mercedes temps do the same jobs that the full timers do, with much lower pay, less job security, almost zero health coverage, and the risk of repetitive stress injuries among other workplace hazards (which are certainly real, based on personal observations). Who needs unions?

Mercedes aggressively worked to buy out the old timers, giving them generous buy outs to leave. Then they could move temps up into their slots for much less. As the old timers leave through retirement or attrition, no full time people are hired to replace them.

This is the good job that lures locals desperate for work. Life for the contractors is much worse. The pay rate is much less, and the work conditions are less than accommodating. I witnessed many practices that violated my conscience. As a manager, I had some flexibility in protecting my employees. For example, it is customary in the auto industry to deny holiday pay if a worker is absent for the shift before or after the holiday. This is to prevent massive call-ins so the workers might take an unauthorized extra vacation day.

As we prepared for Thanksgiving shutdown one year, I was told that the home office wished to send any extra workers home to save labor.

I was also told that once that happened, the home office would dock the holiday pay of the worker, as they had not fully worked the shift before. This in the name of profit for the company, but at the expense of those who struggled to feed families on $9 per hour. Other managers and myself found work for all our people to do, which might have included sitting at a table talking to me about football.

Incidentally, Mercedes has never had a vote for union. It's a moot point now as the only ones that can effectively unionize, the old timers, won't as they have great benefits; while those who need unions, the temps, have absolutely no way to do so. They are completely expendable. Which is the way Mercedes wants it. This is only anecdotal, but everyone I have asked who works at Mercedes tell me they would vote union if they had it to do it all again.

I came to realize that this was the way that most all businesses want it. Lower wages and a "traumatized" workforce. The expression traumatized is in quotations because it was a term promoted by Alan Greenspan. He celebrated the notion of a traumatized worker that had too much fear to ask for a wage increase. Alan noted that the tradeoff between full employment and inflation had now been made obsolete. In the old days, it was thought that if employment were close to 100%, all the good workers would shop around and ask for mo' money. That would drive inflation. But in the eighties, Greenspan noticed that fears of outsourcing, the destruction of unions, and technology made every worker traumatized and in fear of his or her job, no matter how crappy it was.

Who does this benefit? The corporations, with the corporations strictly being defined as shareholders-not necessarily the people who make up the corporation. It benefits those on Wall Street who invest and speculate, as it boosts profit margins.

Meanwhile wages for the little guy drop and drop and drop. Mercedes Benz in Vance, AL is a small example of what has taken place across America. Now you have no chance at a comfortable life, college for your children, and even basic healthcare unless you have a white-collar job. Chances are if you have a white-collar job you were lucky enough to be born into a family of white collars. It's a destructive cycle and it is more than a little disheartening to see it happen to people you know and love.

But those people vote against their interest, as they identify themselves as conservative and believe what Fox News tells them about the glories of capitalism. The average working man can't define socialism, but he knows it is bad, and best he can tell, based on what Fox News and Rush tell him, socialism is anything that interferes with business. It is the classic frog in the water. He never feels the temperature rising and by the time it is boiling; he's dead.

The tornado should drive this point home, but I don't see any evidence of it in Tuscaloosa. The average person identifies himself as a "conservative" and therefore he or she is resistant to anything that challenges the status quo. Which is exactly what Mercedes, the Republicans and Ayn Rand want. The status quo is being run in a manner where the little man is of no consequence, but only the wealthy who create these low paying jobs.

So for whom is this book written? Allow me to break down society in five compartments by political leanings. The world isn't just right and left; or even right and left and middle. There are five categories:

1) Strongly liberal- will vote liberal in all things

2) Mostly liberal- will vote liberal for his/her interest.

3) Independents/Neutrals- the largest group typically disinterested, uninformed and cynical about the whole process.

4) Mostly conservative- will vote conservative for his/her interest

5) Strongly conservative- will vote conservatives in all things

I would love to change everyone's mind, but that is a fantasy. Political views are deeply and strongly held and people such as me are rare. Not many people change political views in their forties; particularly going from right to left.

So as a former number 5, I can tell you the hard-core conservatives will not change, notwithstanding my own conversion. Therefore I wish to reach the 3's, the people who are detached. They are the most important people in the world now. I truly believe we are at a cross roads for this country and if the system is to work there has to be more input from the number 3's.

So with that in mind, I write for the middle. I hope that the writing is effective, and to be effective in my mind it has to entertain as well as educate.

I've tried to enlighten and illuminate with multiple sources, all of them linked if possible. I have tried to do it in a style that is non-threatening and colloquial. So you will notice this isn't exactly an academic work. That doesn't diminish the importance of my intended purpose, it is merely my attempt to motivate the audience that our country needs at this point.

To you who are truly open to new ideas, all I ask is for you to read and examine my points. Every day there are fresh stories in the news that should disturb you.

As I am writing this, the Occupy Wall Street movement is in its second month or so. These people completely independent of me have noted the same things I have in this book. They are taking action the best way they know how.

Don't be put off by pierced noses or drum lines and just dismiss them as weird. Read my book and listen to what we all say. If you think my words aren't factual or logical, then go back to your previous condition. If you happen to come to believe things are worse than you thought, then join me in this fight to take back our country.

george kelley
nashville, tennessee
november 9, 2011

CHAPTER 1: THE MOUTH OF HELL
& THE CHURCH OF SATAN

"I want to just make a commitment to the communities here that we are going to do everything we can to help these communities rebuild.

We can't bring those who have been lost back. They're alongside God at this point. We can help, maybe a little bit, with the families dealing with the grief of having a loved one lost.

But the property damage, which is obviously extensive, that's something that we can do something about.

And so we're going to do everything we can to partner with you, Mr. Mayor, with you, Governor. As the governor was pointing out, this community was hit as bad as any place, but there are communities all across Alabama and all across this region that have been affected, and we're going to be making that same commitment to make sure that we're doing whatever we can to make sure that people are okay.[1] "
president barack obama
tuscaloosa, april 29, 2011

On April 27, 2011 Hell arrived in Alabama and made its presence known in the most violent and destructive way possible. It took the form of an F5 tornado, which is a measurement on the "Fujita Scale", the official classification system for tornado damage.

According to the scale, tornados are classified by intensity, wind speed, and damage. The range consists of six levels: F0 (gale force), F1 (weak), F2 (strong), F3 (severe), F4 (devastating), and F5 (incredible). The Fujita Scale takes in account wind speed and damage in its classification. F5's, according to the scale, do not damage the structures as much as they blow them away.[2]

19

The tornado entered Tuscaloosa through Greensboro Avenue and 35th Street, which is one of the poorest areas of town. It has a high African American population and it is the address of the public housing project, Rosedale Court. After viewing the monster tornado as it traveled towards her, one Rosedale Court resident commented, "it opened up like the mouth of Hell"[3] If Hell is an appropriate metaphor, then one can say things went to Hell in a hurry. The tornado moved forward at speeds in excess of 60 mph. When it was over, it averaged a speed of 73 mph. This tornado was the biggest one of 58 tornados that swept through Alabama that day, killing over 200 and injuring thousands.[4]

If you can, imagine a residential district accustomed to 30 mph speed limits. Now picture a monstrous funnel cloud with internal wind speeds over 260 mph, moving towards you at 60 mph, with its mass being in some parts a mile wide.

Climatologist Brent McRoberts of Texas A&M University says that most tornados stay on the ground for less than 5 miles, and it is extremely rare for them to stay on the ground for more than 10 or 20 miles.[5] This one is said to have stayed on the ground for 300 miles, all the way to Georgia.

For those not familiar with Alabama geography, Tuscaloosa is on the west side of the state, only 60 to 70 miles away from the Mississippi border, depending from where one starts.

As of April 30, 2011, there were reports of over 400 papers, photos and personal items of Tuscaloosa citizens being found as far away as Birmingham (approximately 60 miles away) and Gadsden (approximately 125 miles). A Facebook page has been established with almost 40,000 members designed to reunite victims with their personal documents and photos.[6]

Given these incredible statistics, one can imagine the destruction that resulted. Television reports, snapshots, satellite photos and personal YouTube videos posted online have documented the destruction, but as witnesses have told me, they just don't capture the scope of it.

I can certainly believe it. It is impossible, for those who did not know Tuscaloosa as the locals did, to fully comprehend how bad things are now. The points of reference are weak for the stranger to Tuscaloosa. The images of rubble, splinters, and destruction are horrific enough, but those piles of debris were once fixtures in the every day lives of all the citizens. Seeing pictures on the news and internet of Sixth Avenue East to the viewer unfamiliar with the town is shocking for sure, but inadequate. The untrained eye sees destruction that one would associate with a tornado, such as destroyed buildings and rubble.

But those who live or have lived in Tuscaloosa would not recognize the location if they did not know what had been there before. This particular street, Sixth Avenue East, separated McDonalds from Taco Casa, a local restaurant chain.

The locals know that after you crossed Sixth Avenue East past Fifteenth Street, you could drive through a neighborhood called Cedar Crest, passing along the way the Hokkaido, a Japanese steakhouse, and Express Oil Change on the left and right corners of Sixth and Fifteenth respectively.

You would drive through approximately 4 blocks of modest homes in the neighborhoods, with trees and shrubs in almost every yard, then veer to the left as you cross railroad tracks (and the street inexplicably turned in to Fifth Avenue East), finally coming to the intersection of Paul Bryant Drive and Fifth Avenue East. On the right would be the city's only hospital, Druid City Hospital, DCH to the locals. On the left you could see The University of Alabama's law school, and beyond that Coleman Coliseum, the home of the University's basketball teams.

It is bittersweet to note that the tornado barely missed **DCH**, as the hospital was only 3 blocks away from this massive force. Also, there is some consolation that The University of Alabama, which had at the time over 30,000 students/employees/teachers on campus at the time, was spared.

But how do you measure the potential tragedy as being worse than the literal tragedy that became reality? Do you put an extra modifier of "really" and change it from "really bad" to "really, really bad"? It's like adding the extra volume measurement on "This Is Spinal Tap", where the pain and destruction here actually goes up to 11. I can visualize so very easily the destruction and the ramifications. I need no briefing on the landscape and the neighborhoods. I know Tuscaloosa and I love Tuscaloosa.

I was born in a small town near the Florida border, Andalusia, Alabama, and I currently reside in Nashville, Tennessee. But in between those two destinations I have spent an awful lot of time in Tuscaloosa, over twenty years. I have a canned line I always say when asked about my hometown. I say, "My hometown technically is a little town called Andalusia, but emotionally it is and will always be Tuscaloosa"

Because of my education at the University of Alabama, I am able to do what I truly love, and that is teaching, and in my particular case, teaching political science.

Tuscaloosa has given me so much in my life. It has been instrumental in my becoming who I am today, for better or worse. Out of civility, I'd ask you to refrain from commenting if Tuscaloosa is worse for having me there.

I can't claim a unique connection to the town, although my path through there certainly was unique and special. It is a major part of the state's life and consciousness. It houses The University of Alabama, home of the beloved Crimson Tide.

Sports fans across the country know Tuscaloosa from their exposure to its sports teams, most notably the football team. The state, to put it mildly, is football crazy. It is not unreasonable to say that every citizen knows where Tuscaloosa is, much like they know where Auburn is, our most emotionally charged rival. I would not claim that all of the state knows where Montgomery is, the state capital.

Millions have passed through Tuscaloosa in their formative college years, and return for games and reunions, and donate generously to the University. The love affair with Tuscaloosa begins early and stays late, lasting a lifetime.

This is not to neglect the locals, the indigenous people of the area. They know no other life than Tuscaloosa, their families work for the University, the Goodrich plant, the Mercedes Benz production facility, and hundreds of locally owned businesses. Many of these businesses are no more or at best, are severely damaged. This is a blow to all of us who currently, formerly, or will always call Tuscaloosa home.

I wept several times watching the coverage and viewing the horrific videos of the tornado. I frantically contacted all of my friends still there, and breathed a sigh of relief when I knew they were safe, although a few I know sustained damage from light to "everything one owns". I share this to establish my bona fides. I love Tuscaloosa; I have a tremendous bias towards it.

One of the most passionate desires I have at this time is to see the rebirth of the town. I want the place I love to be repaired, I want it to be restored. Of course, any restoration will be partial. Nothing can replace the human lives lost. Nothing can remove the scars, both physical and emotional. Money will help, but there will still be financial burdens for all involved, no matter what level of assistance they get. That's life. So then, what is my purpose with this book?

Go back in your mind to the Facebook page mentioned earlier, the one established to post photographs and assorted keepsakes whisked off to other counties, and perhaps other states.

23

The website devoted to lost mementos is telling. There are random tattered photos, invitations, drawings, receipts and hosts of other documents, both official and personal.

Recently, a blog devoted a page to highlight several select pictures. The significance of each memory reflected in each photograph was heartbreaking. [7]

One showed a woman in a black and white photo, most likely from the fifties or sixties, in a party dress. Perhaps she was someone's mother from her younger days?

Another showed two happy African American teenage girls, standing with broad grins with numbers pinned to their evening gowns, as if they were participants in a pageant. There is no way of knowing if they won the pageant, or won just some congeniality consolation designation. But whatever the outcome, they were quite pleased and happy to be there that night, and it doesn't take too much of an imagination to envision that the photographer, who could very well be the owner of this lost photo, was just as happy.

Still another photo showed a group of men, all dressed in desert cammo, smiling for the camera and waving at someone thousands of miles, a couple of oceans away. Were they in one of the Iraq wars? Or maybe they were in Kuwait, or Afghanistan? Were they safe and sound back in Tuscaloosa, or did they just not make it home from the scene of that desert photo?

That mystery adds to the painful poignancy even more. Someone held that photo because someone in it mattered to him or her, they may have held it very tightly because the person of interest in it may be forever precluded from holding them. Memories like these are what one hangs on to as life moves on. They are photographic benchmarks of a time where everyone was happier, thinner, younger, and living.

The "Hell" storm destroyed the present for Tuscaloosa, no doubt, as it displaced tens of thousands and traumatized at least a hundred times more. All activities and ambitions were put on hold to better facilitate survival. The future, on that day, was reduced to the next breath, as citizens faced the terrifying reality that even that was not promised, regardless of health, wealth, or choice of shelter. All focus in the here and now concentrated on just hoping to survive, here and now.

With the loss of the photos, these moments in time that cannot be replaced or even effectively reproduced with frail human memories over the years, the past was destroyed. Irreplaceable precious moments were stripped from their fingers, more prized than any item that can be bought, lost and bought again. Odds are very low that the wealth of loving mementos will ever be restored to the rightful owners who safeguarded them the best way they knew how. It's not known if those who lost the photographs and memories were even found themselves; the lost photos could very well be metaphors for their owners who were removed from the loving protection of their families, never to be returned or found.

So it isn't a stretch to say that along with the destruction of the present, the here and now, we also have a stripping of the past, one memory at a time. In the most violent and deadly way, the things that matter most to people after the accumulation of a lifetime of living, working, and loving, were destroyed.

It is tragic enough that the present was rudely and viciously interrupted, but we all have an universal acknowledgment that the arbitrary nature of nature could reach out and touch any of us, from Tuscaloosa, to Joplin, Missouri with tornados; or with hurricanes directed to New Orleans, or maybe an earthquake in San Francisco. That's the cost of doing business on planet earth. We are at its mercy and subject to its sometimes-deadly outbursts.

Those are tragedies that are hard-wired into our existence. "Man is born to trouble as surely as sparks fly upward",[8] as it has been said by the Old Testament's Job, a man knew suffering well.

That's bad enough and we all should feel, pray, and volunteer for the sake of those whose time has come in that matter. It should be our duty to do so.

So we resign ourselves to the sudden loss of the present and the past, and grieve with them who suffer. But we all can affect the future, and should contribute as brothers and sisters to our fellow man when the future is taken from those left behind. When someone is kicked and forced down by tragedy of this scale, through no fault of his or her own, do we not need to take stock of our priorities and decide that we owe it to them to assist them on the way back up? If ever the phrase "there but for the grace of God" means anything, it should resonate loud and clear with respect to disaster relief.

To be clear, the outpouring of brotherly love is staggering when events such as these take place, not just in Tuscaloosa but also on foreign shores, for example, Haiti and Japan.

Americans of all races, creeds, religions, and of course, all political persuasions are loving and giving, rolling up their sleeves to give blood, sweat and tears until they can't anymore. That is the way it should be. Who could argue, or even attempt to argue, with that as being a good thing?

Ayn Rand, that's who. She stated forcefully, by words both spoken and written throughout her life, that she thought we owed no duty to anyone but ourselves. She went so far as to write a book she called "The Virtue of Selfishness". [9]

It wasn't merely a hook that she explained away. She really meant it. She stated as a central tenet of her philosophy that charity and altruism were evil; she even despised the religion(s) that promoted such mischief as living for others, loving your neighbors as yourselves, and serving instead of being served. She derisively called them "mystics", as if they were nothing more than supernatural fables from witchdoctors, used to mollify ignorant villagers. [10]

Which begs the question, who is Ayn Rand? (Not pronounced as Ann, as people most often do, but as "ine", as in "mine") It's an appropriate pronunciation, as she preached as the highest virtue, a lifetime of shrieking "mine, mine, mine!"

It shouldn't shock anyone to consider that Ayn Rand hates Tuscaloosa, AL, Joplin, MO, sick children with cancer, the mentally retarded, coal miners who die for no other reason than safety measures cost too much; or anyone else whose existence stands in the way of a profit. Subsequent examination of her very words, and her life will bear this out.

Ayn Rand valued one thing as far as measuring one's worth, money. If you have it, you are good. If you don't, you may not be necessarily evil, provided you know your place of course, but you do need to know that you do not have a moral claim on anything, not even life.

Note the verb tenses used. I said "Ayn hates Tuscaloosa " present tense, and other losers of life's lottery, but said "Ayn valued" money, past tense. The latter is technically correct, as Ayn is now enjoying her eternal reward, wherever that might be. She passed in 1982, of heart failure, a remarkable fact, given one could easily believe that her heart failed decades before, based on the cold callous philosophy she espoused.

So you caught me. Ayn Rand doesn't really hate Tuscaloosa. She probably never even heard of it, and it is doubtful that she is staying abreast of current events wherever she is. I'd like to think I've effectively used the type of argument, known as a "straw man", in this example.

A straw man is a device used in an argument, to score cheap points, by creating a false argument so offensive that no one could disagree with it.

Of course the argument has never been presented or advocated, but the creator of the straw man wants you to veer off the course of the debate and defend a proposition that you can't defend, that you wouldn't want to defend, and that you really never even suggested.

I've qualified my use of the term by saying "I'd like to think it is a straw man". But, as noted, to qualify as a "straw man", it has to be a mythical creature that no one wants to associate him or herself with.

Everyone runs from an association with this demon, refusing to taint their moral cause with one that is obviously so loathsome. But I have doubts to whether or not Ayn is a "straw man," as too many refuse to run from her, but instead rush to embrace her.

Ayn Rand built a straw man with her life's work, in particular a mammoth novel called "Atlas Shrugged". As a novel for entertainment's sale, it falls short of the mark, although not because of a lack of effort on her part. It weighs in at 1084 pages, most of it very dull and tedious reading.

If I were giving book recommendations to a friend on a trip and I had to choose between "Atlas Shrugged" and the Manhattan Phonebook, there is no question I would heartily endorse the phone book. The plot in the white pages is repetitive, to be sure, but it captures and holds your imagination much better than Rand's novel does.

My critique of it as an entertainment vehicle is not to be construed as a dismissal of its importance. This book is widely popular and influential, so popular, according to a survey conducted by the Library of Congress in cooperation with the Book of the Month Club, it is considered the second most life changing book of all time, second only to the Bible. [11]

In spite of that, I have to wonder how many actually read the whole thing through given its boring, pedantic style. If any book calls to mind Mark Twain's famous quote *"A classic is something that everybody wants to have read and nobody wants to read"*[12], it would be this one.

I've talked about this book with people who have read it, or claimed to, and I can honestly say I have never heard any one praise it as entertainment unless they had another agenda; in other words, they loved the philosophy of the book and their appreciation for the theme made the style much more palatable.

I admit my opinion on artistic value is completely subjective, and any anecdotal evidence offered by me as to my opinion of any readers' motives is useless in a debate, which is as it should be. My contempt for the novel stems from Ayn Rand's philosophy and Ayn Rand herself, not her prose that flows like sewer sludge through a garden waterfall. The narrative is not crucial to understanding the message, although those who love her swear they see parallels between it and today's world in the riveting storyline presented by Ayn Rand.

The story can be briefly described as follows: a dystopian world exists in the future where there are two types of people, first the producers who create wealth for themselves, and jobs for the little people, and second those who steal from the producers by use of the government and distribute to all the leeches who sit on their asses and draw government checks.

The narrative describes the moocher class as being defended and enabled by the evil government workers, and the even more sinister "mystics", who push some tomfoolery about a Higher Power that demands that the better class take care of the blind, crippled and crazy.

You need not read the whole book to get the gist of what she says. The plot is only incidental to finding out what it is all about. The very first line of the novel is "Who is John Galt?" He is the hero and he organizes a strike, if you will, of the wealthy. The metaphor is of the mythical Atlas; tired of holding up the rest of the world, so he finally shrugs, and boots the whole sorry bunch. In this novel, the rich take their ball and go home, and Galt stays back to taunt the leeches at the end, telling them that basically they are tired of feeding "the least of these".[13]

When he finally gets around to telling off the freeloaders, he gives a long, and brother, I mean long, speech towards the end of the book, in which he answers that question. The speech begins on page 936, and ends on page 993. A Rand website (thousands of them exist) asks: "How long would John Galt's speech last if spoken?" They proudly note that it would take over three hours for a speaker to ramble through this sermon.[14] Based on the fluidity of the prose, three hours for the speaker would translate to twelve hours or more to the listener.

This three-hour monologue isn't an easy read either, although it is easy enough to unmistakably see her point. You don't have to slog through the plot and story to get to the point, it is laid out clearly (ok, perhaps not always clearly, she was just a wee bit verbose) in Galt's monologue.

It is the essential part of the book, it is the core of what the novel was about, and it is what makes Republican and Libertarian's hearts go aflutter. It is just as warming to the true Republican/Libertarian believer as violin music played at a table in a French restaurant.

As I said, the book's narrative has 1084 pages. On page 1085 of my copy, there is a note, "About the Author" written by Ayn Rand. The first sentence from her is printed here verbatim:

> "My personal life is a postscript to my novels; it consists of the sentence: 'And I mean it' I have always lived by the philosophy I present in my books, and it has worked for me, as it has worked for my characters. The concretes differ, the abstractions are the same"[15]

So it is fair to say that to love Ayn Rand's books is to know her. Consequently, if you dislike the book, not just because she bores you, but because she offends you to your core and you find the underlining philosophy repugnant and evil, then you might take a pretty dim view of Ms. Rand.

What if one thought that the book was anti Christian? What if one thought it was distorted and could be the stuff of which totalitarianism was made? Would it be enough to condemn Ayn as a person? What if you thought that it was just as dangerous for the good of mankind as Communism or Nazism were? Those aren't really my words, although I don't really dispute them, they are the words and thoughts of Whittaker Chambers, a giant in the conservative movement.

He was famous as an anti-Communist, he ratted out Alger Hiss, a Communist spy who worked in the highest levels of government. Whittaker had the goods on Alger, because he used to be a spy himself. After his conversion to Christianity, he devoted his life to fighting and exposing Communism.

Whittaker Chambers risked his reputation and stood upon his principled beliefs, to better defend what he just recently held dear: to wit Christianity, and the freedom of the capitalistic system in the United States that he had previously sought to destroy.

After his experiences, he wrote what is considered a classic in conservative literature in American politics, "Witness"[16] Like "Atlas Shrugged"; I own it and have read it. Unlike "Atlas Shrugged", I found this book to be an outstanding read.

On one level it is an amazing autobiography that anyone would enjoy. On another level, it is an example of an artist with the written word at work. He was a very talented and gifted writer and intellect.

Whittaker Chambers was so well respected by the conservative movement, that William F. Buckley recruited him to write for his fledgling magazine, "The National Review", which would become the most influential conservative publication in America. Chambers also influenced a passionate FDR Democrat to become a Republican, an actor named Ronald Reagan. Ronald Reagan was so moved and inspired by Whittaker Chambers that he would often recite whole passages from "Witness", and cross out suggested lines in speeches in favor of quotes from Mr. Chambers.[17]

31

It should be pretty obvious that Whittaker Chambers was, and is still highly thought of in conservative circles, based on the two previous examples. This should remove all doubts as to his antipathy for the left, particularly socialists and collectivists. It should also be noted that his editor William F. Buckley tasked Chambers to review "Atlas Shrugged" when it was released, back in 1957.

One would think that the conservatives of 1957 and the conservatives of 2011 would be arm in arm, sharing common opinions of philosophers.

After all, the implied nature of conservatism is resistance to change, therefore philosophy would have an eternal, rock steady consistency as it honored the wisdom of the ages and such a philosophical disposition would be resistant to any radicalism.

But Chambers spoke differently of the novel than his counterparts in 2011's Republican Party do. He wrote a scathing review called "*Big Sister is Watching You*" in the December 28, 1957, issue of the "National Review" in which he flatly states:

> "*From almost any page of Atlas Shrugged, a voice can be heard, from painful necessity, commanding: "To a gas chamber - go!*""[18]

Pretty strong words indeed, but if one takes Ayn Rand at face value, one could easily see how that outcome would occur. Sadly, very few who know of Ayn run from her. The average person knows very little of her, else she would be roundly condemned, with the same type of rhetoric.

But it should be made clear that Ayn Rand lives even today, thirty years after her death, and not as a villain, but as an exalted heroine to a very powerful group in these United States. Her legacy isn't something these wealthy and influential fans flee, far from it. They worship her as a goddess who has delivered a new morality unto them, where faith in God is to be mocked, charity is to be condemned as the ultimate evil, and selfishness promoted as the only worthwhile goal of mankind, Tuscaloosa, Joplin, Missouri or any other soul in need be damned.

This in and of itself isn't that shocking. Dysfunctional sociopaths have existed and will exist as long as we have people.

Heck-fire, pun intended, society possesses those who willingly seek to be possessed, more or less, in Satanists.

You can visit the official Church of Satan website at www.churchofsatan.com should you doubt this assertion.

You'll note when you arrive that the homepage pays tribute to the church's founder here on earth (the home office is located elsewhere I believe), Magus Anton Szandor LaVey (1930-1997). Anton LaVey founded the Church of Satan in 1966 and wrote its un-holy scripture, the Satanic Bible. [19]

It wasn't good enough for Anton LaVey just to break the Ten Commandments, while pretending to strictly follow them, like the rest of us do. He had to go and write his own version of them, and he only needed nine. He called his the Nine Statements. As one might imagine, the Nine Statements were offered as a new paradigm to replace the old morality brought to us by the Judaic and Christian tradition. Who would really expect Satan to have an adultery clause or taking the Lord's name in vain prohibition? It was certainly ambitious of him to overturn both the Judaic and Christian tradition in nine simple bullet points, when the former by itself had to be established in ten. LaVey had to exhibit some economy of prose in producing the ultimate anti-God creed. Just changing all of the "Thou shalt not's" into "Thou shalts" wouldn't do the trick, he had to show some imagination.

When finished with his scripture, Anton LaVey had done a Hell of a job of blasphemy with his written rejection of every tenet of Judaism and Christendom. His statements insisted that this was the only material reality, so let's all live it up. No greater love hath a man than for himself, do unto others as you damn well please; I'm paraphrasing of course.

But alas, like with all great religions, schisms occurred. Some Satanists viewed Anton LaVey as a huckster and tried to distance themselves from their alleged founder.

On a website called SatanismCentral.com, where one can find the real truth about the prince of lies, myths about Satanism are put to rest. The legend that Anton LaVey wrote the Satanic Bible as scripture for the flock is addressed with this straight scoop:

> *"REALITY: The Satanic Bible was conceived as a commercial vehicle by paperback publisher Avon Books.*
>
> *Avon approached [Anton LaVey] for some kind of satanic work to cash in on the Satanism & witchcraft fad of the late 1960s.*
>
> *Pressed for material to meet Avon's deadline, [Anton LaVey] resorted to plagiarism [.] ...The [Satanic Bible]'s" Nine Satanic Statements", one of the Church of Satan's central doctrines, is a paraphrase, again unacknowledged, of passages from Ayn Rand's Atlas Shrugged.*[20]

What? Are we to believe that the Satanic Bible is not legitimately demon inspired but instead merely lifted from a dull novel titled "Atlas Shrugged"?

It's bad enough being a devil worshipper, but plagiarism is truly an unforgivable sin. It's not that the competing Satanists factions object to the ideas behind the statements, it's the lack of footnotes that bother them. The only thing that could possibly be worse would be to find that their scriptures were copied straight from Wikipedia.

Not to worry, one has to take what one finds on the internet with a grain of salt, even when the truth is revealed on such a distinguished site as Satanism Central; established by John Allee, self proclaimed freethinker and devil's advocate.[21]

What better referee for this dispute than a refereed journal? In case you aren't familiar with the term, a refereed journal is also known as a "peer reviewed journal". To quote the website of the University of California-Polytechnic State University's Library Services:

"Peer-reviewed journals (also called refereed journals) are scholarly journals that only publish articles that have passed through this review process. The review process helps ensure that the published articles reflect solid scholarship in their fields."[22]

So we go now to a scholarly journal, written by experts in their field, for experts in their field, reviewed and edited to the strictest standards by experts in their field.

I now present to you the "Marburg Journal of Religion", devoted solely to the research and study of religion, and is edited by a consortium of religious scholars.

In Volume 7, Issue No. 1, published in September 2002, Professor James R. Lewis of the University of Wisconsin-Stevens Point, an esteemed member of the Department of Philosophy and Religious Studies, corrects the slanders on the academic integrity of Satanist Anton LaVey.

Professor Lewis notes that while some say that Anton LaVey lifted the unholy "Nine Statements" from "Atlas Shrugged", it is unfair to say it was cut and pasted, so to speak. He asserts that although the themes are very similar,

"It would be more proper to say that he was inspired by [Ayn] Rand rather than to assert that he paraphrased her work."[23]

Lewis goes even further in his defense, declaring that Anton LaVey plagiarized nothing! He acknowledged fully his inspiration. He quotes LaVey as saying to those of us who might be skittish about Satanism, not to worry, his religion is "just Ayn Rand's philosophy with ceremony and ritual added"[24] Whew! So if one takes away the black mass, the blood pentagram on the floor, the midnight sacrifices to the dark lord, all you really have when you strip it down is a Republican Party gathering.

The last line, while full of sarcasm, was not a joke. Because once you strip out the ritual of Satanism, and you just go straight to the inspiration and overall theme, all you have left is the current permutation of the Republican Party.

Not all of the party of course, certainly not the millions of good people who give generously to their churches, communities and fellow men.

Certainly not the millions of faithful and earnest Christians, who value service to God and follow the example of His son with service to the least of these.

Nothing like the spirit of Ayn Rand lives in these people who compose the bulk of the party's base. Those people are the not only the heart and soul of the party, but they represent the bulk of the citizenry of thousands of American towns, including Tuscaloosa. I know this with certainty. I lived there too long, and know too many wonderful loving people to believe otherwise.

But what of the party they vote into power? Tuscaloosa has steadfastly been a conservative town, in a very conservative state, that votes Republican. But here in lies the conflict, as there is a not insignificant portion of the party that has fallen prey to the Cult of Ayn Rand.

As Tom Cruise is to L. Ron Hubbard's Scientology, Wisconsin's Paul Ryan is to Ayn Rand and her "new morality". Paul Ryan has stated on many occasions that Ayn Rand is the reason he is in politics. He was inspired so much that he requires his staff to read Atlas Shrugged, which smacks of a workplace safety violation, as drowsy staff members possibly could require stitches when their heads hit their desks face first. One of Paul Ryan's favorite sayings is

> *"Rand more than anyone else did a fantastic job of explaining the morality of capitalism, the morality of individualism...It's that kind of thinking, that kind of writing that is sorely needed right now."*[15]

It's good to know that Paul Ryan keeps a level head and rejects all the ceremony of Satanism and opts only for the theology. I feel similarly when I attend Episcopalian services with my wife, the fellowship is wonderful, but I can take or leave the hymns and liturgy. It's not the blood sacrifice and conjuring up of demons that turn him on, it's the morality of it that he loves.

Paul Ryan is now the face of the Republican Party's alleged fiscal sanity. He authored a budget resolution, embraced by the Republican Party titled "A Roadmap for America's Future".

It's featured prominently on the webpage of the Republican members of the House of Representatives, with nice graphics, and it displays a picture of Paul Ryan looking earnest and very handsome with his million-dollar smile. I'm not sure if that is his disposition or that he just saw a kitten fall into a blender.

The title is represented as a highway sign, and utilizes the image of a federal highway sign that says "US 21", for the 21st century.[26] The House of Representatives, controlled by Republicans, passed his budget resolution. It did not make it through the Senate, with not nearly enough votes to pass it given the procedure rules there. But in the House, it passed with almost all Republicans voting for it. Only 4, out of 239 voted against it. No Democrats voted for it. It was a straight partisan vote. The right wing of the party is pissed at three of the four for not making it a shutout. These three are Denny Rehberg of Montana, Walter Jones of North Carolina and David McKinnley of West Virginia. They all could face serious Tea Party activism in their next primary election, for "selling out to the liberals". Ron Paul, as the fourth GOP dissenter voted no on principle, as it wasn't harsh enough to suit him.[27]

While passing the House, it failed in the Senate, by a vote of 57 to 40. Every Democrat voted no except Chuck Schumer of New York, who wasn't there to vote. Based on his long career and consistent liberal voting record, it is safe to say that he would not have voted for it.

All but five republicans voted for it, those voting against it on the GOP side were Senators Scott Brown (R-Mass.), Susan Collins (R-Maine), Lisa Murkowski (R-Alaska) and Olympia Snowe (R-Maine). Sen. Rand Paul (R-KY.) followed in his Daddy Ron Paul's footsteps and voted against it because it was too liberal.[28]

The most controversial notion in the Republican blessed Ryan budget was the elimination of Medicare, as we know it. It also included massive cuts in FEMA and the NOAA. Everyone should know FEMA, the Federal Emergency Management Agency, but perhaps not the NOAA, the National Oceanic and Atmospheric Administration. The obvious mission of the NOAA is hurricane monitoring, which is not a little thing, even in Tuscaloosa. I lived in Tuscaloosa at the time, and I recall very clearly the impact of Hurricane Katrina.

The NOAA also provides satellite-assisted forecasts of weather conditions including tornados. With the help of the NOAA, thousands of lives were saved in Tuscaloosa due to the early warning system given by them and the National Weather Service.

When I first heard about the tornado after the fact my heart sank and I felt panic. I knew the tornado went down 15th Street, one of the busiest commercial districts in the town. I knew it happened right at rush hour, approximately 5:15 P.M. On most days 15th street is bumper to bumper at this time.

When I called a friend who lived through the storm, I asked if it was made worse by the rush hour timing? He told me no, that there had been ample warning where people stayed off the streets, many businesses had closed, and people had gone home. The streets were empty, thank God.

And also thank the National Weather Service, for it provided the warning that so many people heeded, saving thousands of lives. The Paul Ryan budget plan cuts the National Weather Service by 30%, as Republicans have stated it is a waste of money.[29]

We cannot afford the NOAA, Paul Ryan says. Well, maybe we might be able to afford it if it were considered a priority. Because the Paul Ryan proposed budget also cuts taxes for the top income tax group, those making over 250k per year, and also for corporations.

In the Paul Ryan written, GOP blessed budget, both groups get a whopping ten percent cut from 35% to 25%. [30] Paul Ryan, in the spirit of Ayn Rand believes those that really matter, the wealthy and big corporations, deserve to take home more wealth, and those who stand in the path of killer tornados need to just pray, merely a figure of speech of course, because Ayn Rand tells us there is no God.

But I write this book, with these documented facts about Ayn Rand and her followers, the Satanists and Republicans, to explain that my values are not Ayn Rand's, and that I know for a fact that they aren't Tuscaloosa's values either.

They aren't the state of Alabama's values or any states' in this union. I truly believe that. I see great, loving, caring, giving till it hurts, God fearing conservatives that I know and love.

I see these people pouring open their hearts, their time, their prayers, and their love, all for people who were strangers the day before. I see volunteerism unlike I have seen before and for that I am grateful. Thousands of volunteers have confirmed my optimism. I never doubted the goodness of the rank and file conservative.

The original intent of this book was to establish who Ayn Rand was, what she stood for, and show case by case how her fanatical followers (Paul Ryan, et al) don't even care if they destroy the very people that need the government the most, all the while receiving overwhelming support from those said people!

I had in mind a punch line to this book, wherein I made a bold prediction at the end that one day, the same people with the same warped worldview would say "we just can't afford it" when the next Tuscaloosa happened and refuse to ask the corporations, the wealthy, or any privileged citizen to chip in and pay for services that little people need.

I wondered as to how I could pull this rhetorical trick off, as I thought it might seem too far-fetched for the average, non-political junkie to swallow.

Well, the Republicans did not disappoint when life surprised me with how rapidly my internal prediction came to fruition.

Less than three weeks after the absolutely worst tornado I have ever witnessed, a more horrific one hit Joplin, Missouri. This monster storm killed over 130 people in this one town alone.

But the Republicans, true to the spirit of their muse, refused to commit to aid for Joplin, MO. Eric Cantor, the second in command for the House of Representatives, said on   CBS' Face the Nation:

> "When a family is struck with tragedy -- like the family of Joplin ... let's say if they had $10,000 set aside to do something else with, to buy a new car ... and then they were struck with a sick member of the family or something, and needed to take that money to apply it to that, that's what they would do, because families don't have unlimited money. And, really, neither does the federal government."[31]

Eric Cantor had no compunction about holding aid hostage, as we couldn't afford it otherwise.

Please note that by "not affording it", Cantor meant we couldn't afford it while still being able to cut the tax rates for the biggest corporations and wealthiest Americans, including those who make multimillion-dollar salaries per year. Cantor refuses to consider just not cutting their tax rates down to 25%, not even at the cost of Joplin's recovery.

Just put off buying a car, Joplin. Put off buying a fire station, school, hospital and whatever else you foolishly left out in the path of the tornado. Silly rabble, you need to take responsibility instead of whining to the government.

To further document Eric Cantor's deep conviction and passion, he made this statement less than 24 hours after the tornado destroyed the town, when all victims had not even been accounted for. Talk about a rapid response.

The purpose of this book is not to condemn "conservatism" per se, with conservatism being defined as prudent, limited government, and an aversion to radical change. There are some valid points to be made about the scope and size of the government, and that debate is currently needed.

The purpose of this book is to condemn, as loudly and with as many documented examples as possible, the warped priorities of selfishness, the contempt of charity, and the refusal to acknowledge a moral responsibility for all of us, even the wealthy, to society.

This is what the widespread worship of Ayn Rand has gotten us. You will see exactly how widespread and pervasive this is in subsequent chapters. It has infected a once great party and the party refuses to take care of anyone but the highest net worth citizens at the expense of the sick, the elderly, the wounded, and those who lost every material possession and loving memory in a tornado in places such as Tuscaloosa and Joplin.

This book isn't necessarily about the tornados, nor is it necessarily about   Tuscaloosa and Joplin, although they are certainly are at stake now. This book is about   standing up against an evil, masquerading as stewardship and responsibility. It is about educating those good, wonderful people that make up my home state and city that I love dearly and showing them that the people and policies that they vote for aren't really concerned with their well being, or even their survival.

I don't expect all reading this to vote Democratic straight ticket. I know it will not happen. But I do wish that my conservative friends out there would listen to what I am saying and note the malicious, systematic attempt to destroy all functions of government; not merely stopping at cutting waste, but working to make the government so small you could drown it in a bathtub. That bathtub analogy is a direct quote from a very influential man who heads one of the most powerful and well funded special interest groups in Washington. You will learn about him later, I promise you.

This book is at its core about philosophy, not in the study of the Greeks and Enlightenment thinkers, but at a base level where you ask and answer "What should the government do?" It is also about policy, which is the implantation of the philosophy, and politics, which is the mechanism for policy to take root.

And at the core, this book asks over and over: where are your priorities and values and where are the priorities and values of your party? Mine aren't with Ayn Rand; I intend to explore hers at length going forward in Chapters 2 and 3.

Then in Chapter 4, I will demonstrate that one needs not claim to be a disciple of Ayn Rand to follow her; in fact she has co-opted the conservative Christian movement.

Chapter 5 will show how Ayn owns the entire Republican Party, from the federal to the state level.

Chapter 6 will show the base level of Ayn's support; the corporations and big moneyed interests. It is their worldview that is promoted, and they have had amazing progress in pushing it forward.

In Chapter 7, I indulge myself with a mock up of Ayn's sacred text, as I answer the infamous question "Who is John Galt" with a question "Who is George Kelley?" In this chapter, I intend to show the ramifications of such a worldview, a world of multiple monopoly powers, with all of us little guys just one tornado, just one unemployed spell, or one catastrophic illness from landing on a loaded Boardwalk or Park Place. It would not be a happy world for 95% of us, and we are going too fast towards it.

I know too many good people, good people who happen to be conservative, to believe that their values are the same as hers, the same values that inspired Anton LaVey. Is it not troubling to good God fearing Christians to support a party that drinks from the same intellectual well for inspiration as the Church of Satan?

SOURCES CONSULTED FOR CHAPTER 1

[1] Statements by President Barack Obama in Tuscaloosa April 29, 2011. Available from http://www2.alabamas13.com/news/2011/apr/29/president-obamas-remarks-tuscaloosa-ar-1781931/

[2] The Enhanced Fujita Scale.; Available from: The National Oceanic and Atmospheric Administration (NOAA) Website

[3] Zucchino, R.F.a.D. "Survivors tell tales of horror". Los Angeles Times Date April 30, 2011 Available from: http://articles.latimes.com/2011/apr/30/nation/la-na-tuscaloosa-tornado-20110430.

[4] CBSNews.com. "Tornado experts: How complacency kills". Date May 31, 2011 10:08 AM]; Available from: http://www.cbsnews.com/stories/2011/05/31/scitech/main200 67509.shtml#ixzz1Q3yMepUH.

[5] McRoberts, B. "Today's topic: Time of Tornadoes on the ground". [Texas A&M News & Information Services] ; Available from: http://tamunews.tamu.edu/2011/04/27/today's-topic-time-of-tornadoes-on-the-ground/.

[6] Ligon, L. "Tornado Facebook Page". Available from: http://www.fox10tv.com/dpp/only_on_fox10/daily_dot_com/tor nado-facebook-page.

[7] D., D. "25 Photos Found After The Alabama Tornadoes" Buzzfeed.com Available from: http://www.buzzfeed.com/donnad/photos-found-after-the-alabama-tornadoes.

[8] Job 5:7 Yet man is born to trouble as surely as sparks fly upward

[9] Rand, A., *The Virtue of Selfishness* 1964, New York, New York: Signet.

[10] Rand, A., *Atlas Shrugged* 1957, New York, New York: Signet Books. P. 941, of many

[11] Jones, D. "Scandals lead execs to 'Atlas Shrugged'" USA Today September 23, 2002 Available from: http://www.usatoday.com/money/companies/management/20 02-09-23-ayn-rand_x.htm.

[12] Twain, M. Available from: http://thinkexist.com/quotation/a_classic_is_something_that_e verybody_wants_to/216803.html.

[13] Matthew 25:41 He will reply, 'I tell you the truth, whatever you did not do for one of the least among you, you did not do for me.'

[14] Lawrence, R. *Objectivism Reference Center*. Available from: http://www.noblesoul.com/orc/books/rand/atlas/faq.html#Q5.1

[15] Rand, A., *Atlas Shrugged* 1957, New York, New York: Signet Books. P. 1085

[16] Chambers, W., *Witness* 1952: Random House (NY).

[17] Kengor, P., *"The Intellectual Origins of Ronald Reagan's Faith"*, in *Heritage Lectures* 2004, The Heritage Foundation. Available from: http://www.heritage.org/research/lecture/the-intellectual-origins-of-ronald-reagans-faith

[18] Chambers, W. *"Big Sister Is Watching You"*. National Review Date. 28, 1957 Available from: http://www.nationalreview.com/articles/222482/big-sister-watching-you/flashback?page=3.

[19] Author Unknown. *Home Page Church of Satan*; Available from: www.churchofsatan.com

[20] Allee, J. *"Anton LaVey: Legend and Reality"*; Available from: http://www.satanismcentral.com/aslv.html.

[21] Allee, J. *Home Page and Description of Owner*; Available from: www.satanismcentral.com.

[22] Library Services, R.E.K.L.C.T. *"Finding Peer-reviewed or Refereed Journals"*; Available from: http://lib.calpoly.edu/research/guides/peer.html.

[23] Lewis, J.R., *"Diabolical Authority: Anton LaVey, The Satanic Bible and the Satanist "Tradition" "*. Marburg Journal of Religion, 2002. **7**(1) Available from: www.uni-marburg.de/fb03/ivk/mjr/pdfs/2002/articles/lewis2002.pdf.

[24] Ibid.

[25] Beam, C. *"The Trouble With Liberty"*. New York Magazine Date Dec 26, 2010 Available from: http://nymag.com/print/?/news/politics/70282/index1.html.

[26] Ryan, P. *"Roadmap to Prosperity"*; Available from: http://www.roadmap.republicans.budget.house.gov.

[27] Moody, C. *"Paul Ryan's budget passes House, but GOP nearly falls for Dem trick on conservative alternative"*. The Daily Caller Date 2:22 PM 04/15/2011 ; Available from: http://dailycaller.com/2011/04/15/paul-ryans-budget-passes-house-but-gop-nearly-falls-for-dem-%20trick-on-conservative-alternative/#ixzz1LD9nvpGU.

[28] Bolton, A. "Rand Paul will vote against budget deal; calls cuts negligible" The Hill 04/11/11 03:21 PM ET Available from: http://thehill.com/homenews/senate/155299-rand-paul-to-vote-against-budget-deal-slams-cuts-as-negligible.

[29] Goldenberg, S. Can Hurricane Irene batter Republicans into a U-turn on NOAA cuts? Guardian News Blog; Available from: http://www.guardian.co.uk/world/blog/2011/aug/28/hurricane-irene-natural-disasters

[30] Chait, J. "Yes, Paul Ryan Does Cut Taxes For The Rich" TNR/blog/Jonathan Chait; Available from: http://www.tnr.com/blog/jonathan-chait/87123/yes-paul-ryan-does-cut-taxes-the-rich

[31] Madison, L. *"Cantor: Funds for tornado victims will be offset"*. Face The Nation Date ; Available from: **http://www.cbsnews.com/stories/2011/05/29/ftn/main20067183.shtml.**

PART ONE: THE GHOST OF AYN RAND PAST

During the whole of this time, Scrooge had acted like a man out of his wits. His heart and soul were in the scene, and with his former self. He corroborated everything, remembered everything, enjoyed everything, and underwent the strangest agitation. It was not until now, when the bright faces of his former self and Dick were turned from them, that he remembered the Ghost, and became conscious that it was looking full upon him, while the light upon its head burnt very clear.

"A small matter," said the Ghost, "to make these silly folks so full of gratitude."

"Small!" echoed Scrooge.

The Spirit signed to him to listen to the two apprentices, who were pouring out their hearts in praise of Fezziwig: and when he had done so, said,

"Why! Is it not? He has spent but a few pounds of your mortal money: three or four perhaps. Is that so much that he deserves this praise?"

"It isn't that," said Scrooge, heated by the remark, and speaking unconsciously like his former, not his latter, self. "It isn't that, Spirit. He has the power to render us happy or unhappy; to make our service light or burdensome; a pleasure or a toil. Say that his power lies in words and looks; in things so slight and insignificant that it is impossible to add and count 'em up: what then? The happiness he gives, is quite as great as if it cost a fortune.

ebenezer scrooge
& the ghost of christmas past
"a christmas carol", 1843

GEORGE KELLEY

CHAPTER 2: WHAT IS THE OBJECTIVE OF OBJECTIVISM?

"Of all the vices which degrade the human character, Selfishness is the most odious and contemptible. An undue love of Self leads to the most monstrous crimes; and occasions the greatest misfortunes in States and Families. As a selfish man will impoverish his family and often bring them to ruin: so a selfish king brings ruin to his people and often plunges them into war."
william makepeace thackeray
"vanity fair", 1848

Washington D.C., as the power center of the United States, quite possibly the world, attracts ambitious people. Ambition will corrupt for sure, and the pursuit of power is a taint on men and women's character. Polls bear this perception out, as politicians rate low among voters' idea for an honest profession. Because of this, hypocrisy is the rule not the exception as dishonest people are constantly trying to put an honest mask over a dishonest face.

Think back to the days of Richard Nixon. His world imploded and all of the accomplishments of his career, and there were a few, were lost forever due to the indelible stain of Watergate and "Tricky Dick".

The name Richard Nixon will immediately conjure up dishonesty, fairly or unfairly. An endorsement in the form of a quote from Richard Nixon will at best produce chuckles, at worst eye rolls and an immediate loss of credibility, at least with out major qualifications and caveats.

However, an amazing irony is that an honest and almost universally respected man exists, in Washington D.C. of all places. Add to the list of improbable factors, this man is a veteran of Nixon's administration, once called his "evil genius". He boasted that he would "run over his grandmother to get Nixon reelected".[2] This man's name is Chuck Colson.

Chuck Colson didn't have to harm his grandmother as a re-election ploy, but he did just about everything else. He sought to hire Teamster thugs to beat up anti-war protestors, he plotted to raid or firebomb the liberal Brookings Institution, a think tank on the left of the political spectrum that was highly critical of the Nixon administration's policies, all of these things while serving in the capacity of his White House position. Some people actually had the gall to call this an abuse of power.[3]

Colson was brought to justice in more ways than one, however, when he was caught, arrested and convicted for conspiring to defame Daniel Ellsberg, who was on trial for his part in the infamous "Pentagon Papers". His plan was to violate Daniel Ellsberg's constitutional rights by poisoning his reputation and denying a fair trial, thereby ensuring a forthcoming vengeance enacted upon an enemy of his president.[4]

A conviction did result from the trial, but not for Daniel Ellsberg, but Chuck Colson. Colson was sentenced to federal prison for seven months in 1973. His career in politics ended. His name was immediately smeared and discredited, and his "ex-con" status would surely hinder any opportunities going forward.[5]

Which might cause some readers some confusion, as they try to reconcile Colson's fate with the initial claim; that is, Colson is an almost universally respected man, and one who is considered honest too.[6]

It is easy to clarify as his life didn't end then, it really began. In fact, he documented his change in a best seller called "Born Again".

Colson experienced a deep spiritual awakening, and became a "born again" Christian in prison. At first the critics snickered, which was to be expected, given his previous incarnation as the meanest man in D.C. The saying was, "when the going gets tough, the tough get religion". Cynicism is natural and time bears out the true story as the fruits of his new life would be on display in a high profile way. There were many enemies who longed for his fall from grace and a discrediting of his conversion.[7]

But to everyone's surprise, it became obvious that he was sincere. When released he wrote the aforementioned book and used the royalties to start a ministry, Prison Fellowship Ministries. He has devoted his life to this ministry ever since its inception in 1976. In one way, he was sent to prison, and never left, and seems more free than ever.[8]

Colson's purpose is straightforward and driven by his faith. He aims to serve the least of us, the lowest on the American food chain, and love them. His emphasis isn't rehabilitation as much as it is spiritual reconstruction. He has worked out of the darkest and most despair ridden prisons to good effect. It is not an exaggeration to say that he is the nation's most successful prison reformer. His organization is 50,000 volunteers strong, and is active in almost all of the prisons in this country. The services provided are more than just spiritual. Colson serves prisoners' other needs including pen pals for slightly less than 30,000 inmates and psychological counseling on all matters.[9] The organization even provides Christmas gifts to hundreds of thousand of kids with a locked up parent. I know this for a fact as I have witnessed two of the finest people I've ever known, my parents, contribute to this cause for almost as long as it has been active.

Colson's organization has stayed scandal free and has a reputation of honesty and, beyond that, statistics show that his prison programs avoid recidivism. Liberals love his social consciousness as he walks the walk across the board advocating for prisoners rights in all areas. He also works with the conservative side of the aisle to lessen overly harsh sentencing. Conservatives are thrilled with him, partly due to the evangelical nature of his work. Also he is conservative with respect to fiscal and social policy.

Colson hasn't traded in his partisan nature, although even his critics agree that he isn't as vicious as most partisans. He speaks to issues based on deep conviction with consistency. I myself disagree with him on many political issues but I do not question his motives. He is an honest man, and he, like myself and all others in this country, is entitled to his own opinions.

Never has Colson's integrity been so on display than April 2011, when the movie adaptation of "Atlas Shrugged" was set to premiere. A very intense strategic marketing campaign was underway to build buzz for this film and the whole conservative movement was on board to build momentum. The Tea Party was instrumental in creating the perception of demand as the plot played into their worst nightmares about the direction of the country. Fox News and other right wing media outlets took a very active role in promoting the film.[10]

The film had been anticipated with Pavlovian drooling by the Randites since its release as a novel in 1957. There were many obstacles to its development, Ayn Rand being a huge one. As a control freak she insisted on her way or the highway. She was verbose and every precious syllable had to be inserted. After she died, the movie rights were sold to businessman John Aglialoro in 1992 and he has worked for years to generate momentum for the movie.[11]

Then, a dream came true for Ayn Rand-fans. The economic world collapsed. The Tea Party, not the most restrained bunch, became vocal in the demand for this modern day parable as they saw it as prophecy and truth. The Ayn Rand Institute noted that "Atlas Shrugged" sales spiked in 2008 when Barack Obama was elected president. The hard core Randites saw him as the ultimate big government mooch; with mooch being the pejorative word of choice used by all Rand true believers to describe basically all of the non-billionaire faction of society.

So, Aglialoro scrambled to make the film, which was to be made in three parts to cover the good parts of Ayn Rand's book. (In my opinion, this would leave plenty of screen time for two full films and 4/5ths of a third film). He ended up financing this film himself. As a true believer he wanted the message spread, so much so that he put $20 million into the project by his own estimation. Part One of the movies was going to play to libertarian awareness by being released on traditional tax day, April 15, 2011.[12]

Several key conservative voices were on board to praise and promote the film. The trailer was shown at the Conservative Political Action Committee (CPAC) convention of 2011.[13] The CPAC is the hardest right wing of the Republican party, and as limited government passionate believers they are a fertile ground for recruitment into the Ayn Rand cult.

Ayn Rand would have loved that show of economic force and unity, as it fit her worldview. So, what better place to unveil the trailer of this long awaited masterpiece? The CPAC crowd responded with glee. The ball started rolling and conservative blogs were all abuzz with anticipation. One blogger noted that it was awfully suspicious that President Obama announced a high-speed rail plan exactly two years to the day BEFORE the movie release and the liberal press would hype it to steal attention from this "must see masterpiece".[14]

Fox and Friends declared it "A victory for capitalism". Sean Hannity called it the "film that liberals do not want you to see",[15] and a special screening was set up for current Speaker of the House John Boehner and commentator Andrew Breitbart. Freedomworks, one of the groups that founded the Tea Party, was heavily promoting the film. (Former Congressman Dick Armey, R-Texas, a hard rightwing disciple of Ayn Rand founded Freedomworks) His organization was tasked with printing promotional posters entitled "Who is John Galt", among other tasks.[16]

With so much emphasis being placed on this movie and with obvious political motives in mind, the conservative movement all chipped in and promoted the movie. Box office success would translate to the casual observer as a widespread mandate for St. Ayn's Gospel of Greed. So with this backdrop, Chuck Colson felt compelled to offer commentary on the upcoming masterpiece.

His commentary was put out on his website, www.colsoncenter.org in a video called "Two Minute Warning". He makes the most of the two minutes, flatly saying to avoid the movie and to avoid anyone that promotes Ayn Rand. Quoting Colson:

> A "silly" and "bumptious" novel can have destructive and lasting power...and then it finds new life as a movie. Viewers beware because the new movie Atlas Shrugged is an adaptation of Ayn Rand's novel, which peddles a starkly anti-Christian philosophy."[17]

Colson did not mince words and he had no qualified condemnation or anything positive to say about the book, the film, or the author. It's safe to say, he is not a fan.

Which begs the question, why? Why go against your own political interest? Colson has almost consistently endorsed Republicans.

He was so partisan during his early political life that he broke federal laws so he could smear a political enemy of his boss, Richard Nixon. He has shown his conversion to be true, based on his good works, but his political endorsements since then have almost always been the Republican candidates that have promoted the Republican family values agenda. One would think at first glance that the practical strategy would to be to hold one's nose and then let momentum build for one's party, in this case, the very conservative Republican Party.

No, this is a case of conscience trumping the pursuit of power. Chuck Colson is to be praised for his integrity, as he could have gone along with the crowd, his crowd, his base, and promote this film. No one would have singled him out for condemnation. Instead he stood against the popular passions and offered a stinging rebuke, and framed it in the most serious of language. What did Chuck Colson see in "Atlas Shrugged" that disgusted him so?

Chuck Colson recognized a dangerous and poisonous worldview, one that springs from Ayn Rand's vision. This vision is stated perfectly in "Atlas Shrugged", and it serves as the driving intellectual force for her millions of disciples. The purpose of this book is to go even deeper into the problematic nature of Ayn Rand's worldview, so the reader may judge for himself. The root of the problem starts with Rand, an ill-tempered and arrogant immigrant who had difficulty all her life in both making and keeping friends. It expands with her cult, an obsessive compulsive multitude that worship her musings, live her philosophy, and devote their lives to raise millions of dollars for the cause of her perverted gospel.

It is currently manifested in Paul Ryan; at face value a seemingly nice young man who happens to be the rising star in the Republican Party. Ryan alleges a devotion to fiscal sanity, and uses Ayn Rand as cover for limited government, but it's deeper than that, as he has fully embraced Ayn Rand, as a teacher of the new morality.

The Republicans party's energy is all channeled his way as he has led the way on all domestic agenda items. When criticism of him has occurred, it has doubled down on the passion for Ryan. For proof of this, see Newt Gingrich. He angered the entire base of his party, and effectively derailed his chances of nomination for president within the first week, because he referred to Paul Ryan's plan as "radical" and "right-wing social engineering". Newt quickly backtracked, given the loud backlash. The Republicans have elected to live and die with Paul Ryan.[18]

Because of Paul Ryan's zealotry for Ayn Rand, I say he must be rejected. Anyone who agrees with Ayn's worldview, much less worships her to the point of devoting their life to her message, should be rejected from leadership and roundly condemned. I am quite certain that many readers are perplexed at this blanket statement due to their unfamiliarity with Miss Rand or her signature novel. Fair enough, it's one of the purposes of this book to try to convince you of this statement.

By the end of this chapter any reader will have more than enough evidence to render a verdict on the fitness of Ayn Rand for inspiration. I will state unequivocally, that anyone who endorses Rand as a person, or as a prophet of a "new morality" (words used by both Ayn Rand and Paul Ryan), is not a good person. I base my notions of good and evil, right and wrong, on certain principles.

It will soon be clear that Rand does also, but her principles will never coincide with mine. I hope not with yours either. Also, I mean to show that what Rand wanted wasn't a celebration of capitalism as her ultimate goal, but the creation of a "new morality". These are her very words, and they are repeated throughout every thing she wrote and said.

This is the most important point to make, because too many uninformed people are cowed and bullied into supporting the agenda under the guise of protecting capitalism.

Ayn Rand wasn't as interested in protecting capitalism as much as she was interested in protecting wealth, and the greater idea of promoting selfish virtue to get it.

Former Egyptian President Hosni Mubarek lived his life in Egypt under the principle promoted in the works of Ayn Rand, although it is doubtful he ever heard of her. He was driven by selfishness; he stole billions of dollars from his people and inflicted poverty and injustice along the way.

Ayn would say that selfishness should be constrained by the law, but Hosni broke no law. Please note that the hard-core acolytes of Ayn Rand these days profess a love for *THE LAW* as an abstract but they will systematically list a whole host of individual laws that they wish to be gone.

Every one of these laws that they wish to purge protects society from abuses.

It doesn't give me much comfort to know the most powerful people respect *THE LAW* as long as it is there, but use their wealth and influence to destroy every component that stands in their way.

Pay attention to the words spoken and written by Ayn, Paul Ryan, and indeed all of her wealthy and powerful cultists that devote their lives to spreading this dangerous ideology with more passion than any missionary.

It ought to be pretty clear by the end of this and the next chapters how vile, dangerous, widespread, aggressive and influential this belief system is. And verification for my claims is only one Google search away. It's all out there. These are bold, judgmental words on my part, but to justify my rash assertion, allow me to quote none other than Ayn Rand herself:

> *"One must never fail to pronounce moral judgment.*

> *Nothing can corrupt and disintegrate a culture or a man's character as thoroughly as does the precept of moral agnosticism, the idea that one must never pass moral judgment on others, that one must be morally tolerant of anything, that the good consists of never distinguishing good from evil.*[9]

Well, there you have it. She has effectively given me permission to condemn her, her life, and legacy. I feel comfortable in the challenge and relish the opportunity to type the words that I know will follow. A morality death match if you will, with my values, and what I believe to be America's values versus Ayn's. Choose your side, and ask yourself: "are these my values, my priorities, and how I define good and evil?"

This chapter isn't as much a biography chapter on Ayn Rand, as it is an exposition of her beliefs and documentation of her sincerity. I feel there is no better place to begin than to define her philosophy/religion, Objectivism. It's the central theme in all of her writings. Also, if you choose to closely examine her biography, you can see it evolve as she progresses.

Specifically, Objectivism is represented in "Atlas Shrugged", which encapsulates everything about her philosophy within its covers.

To refresh or to educate, depending on your level of prior Rand-ness, its message can be received loud and clear in the voice of the mysterious hero, John Galt.

To briefly summarize, "Atlas Shrugged", if doing anything briefly is possible with this clunker, John Galt is a strike organizer of the wealthy, the "producers". He and the upper class have just about had it and decide that the party is over for the "freeloaders", or lower classes, hence the disappearance of the power elites.

He makes his dramatic speech around page 900, after hijacking a radio transmission. This speech, as noted previously, lasts about three hours.

Quoting yet another pro Rand website, on the three hours of Galt's speech:

In the three hours that follow, Galt tells the world about the strike and his reasons for it. He reveals the philosophical meaning and cause of the world's crisis and the cure: "We are on strike against self-immolation. We are on strike against the creed of unearned rewards and unrewarded duties. We are on strike against the dogma that the pursuit of one's happiness is evil. We are on strike against the doctrine that life is guilt." Damning the ideas of mysticism, altruism, and collectivism, he outlines the basis for a new morality: a morality of rational self-interest.[20]

I have to admit, this fan-boy site quoted here does a much better job of summarizing Galt's message than Rand does, but if you were familiar with anything of Ayn's, then you wouldn't be surprised.

This summary, in a nutshell, tells you everything you need to know about Ayn's worldview. She coined her own special term, Objectivism.

It was a new aged religion, disguised as pure reason. Critics misinterpret its goal, as they merely look at the natural outcome, economic and capitalistic success, and mistake those for its core value.

To be sure, capitalism plays a big role in it, but as a reward, not the driving force. This is an important distinction, which shall be examined later in this chapter.

To be even more concise, Objectivism is founded on the principle that the objective reality is the only reality. That is, if you can't see it, touch it, taste it, or reason it, it can't exist. Sorry, no room for deities here, unless we are talking about Ayn. She builds a case, step by rational step, for self-interest. Her reasoning, more or less, follows:

• Our existence and reason and logic are the only reality. Therefore, our "self", the individual, is the highest power.

• The opposite of individual is evil, which is collectivism. Ayn went so far as to refer to democracy as collectivism, as she believed it was the mob stealing from the individual.

• To serve one's self, is the highest goal. Selfishness therefore becomes the purpose for our existence. The flip side is that altruism, or charity or sacrifice for others is evil. Not just inefficient, but evil. (Ayn bent over backwards to stress this).

• Reason is the pathway to all knowledge; therefore the antithesis of reason is faith. Just as she presented selfishness/altruism as dual concepts, (in other words good and evil), she did the same for reason and faith.[21]

That was Ayn's way, everything had to be black and white. She had no value in any idea that you could not carry to its further conclusion. She got off on absolutes, as per this quote from her:

> *"Reality is an absolute, existence is an absolute, a speck of dust is an absolute and so is a human life. Whether you live or die is an absolute. Whether you have a piece of bread or not, is an absolute. Whether you eat your bread or see it vanish into a looter's stomach, is an absolute."*[1]

I am reasonably sure that it made her absolutely furious to see some looter urchin munching on a piece of her bread.

Let's distill this even more, and examine it point by point. Ayn believed in absolutes, her absolutes, and she demanded strict adherence. The only reality is what you know from experience or reason and that led to these six principles listed above.

The self is the highest power or authority, or lets call it "the individual". Therefore, any force that denied the individual was evil, and needs to be purged from society. The masses that vote for policies such as Social Security, the G.I. Bill, or even tornado relief, are thieves. She called them exactly that in almost everything she wrote. It is mentioned over and over in John Galt's writings as seen in "Atlas Shrugged". This should be blatantly obvious in the quote from John Galt above. She disdainfully called the majority, "The Collective", a highly emotionally charged word that conjures up visions of Marxism. "The Collective" wanted to crush the individual, through forcing guilt, pity, or a sense of duty. Therefore "The Collective" was and still is, in the mind of her followers, evil. There is no worse example of this than democracy.

The ramifications of this view are staggering. Democracy is nullified as a moral good in her view, where the average person has no right to vote or rule.

The foremost disciple of hers today, out of millions in this world, is a man named Leonard Peikoff. She actually left her estate to him when she died in 1982. Not surprisingly, she didn't leave it to charity. Peikoff holds the keys to the vault, which contains millions of dollars from royalties, which he administers to causes that promote Objectivism. In a lecture given in 1976 called "The Philosophy of Objectivism" Peikoff unequivocally states:

> *"Democracy, in short, is a form of collectivism, which denies individual rights: the majority can do whatever it wants with no restrictions. In principle, the democratic government is all-powerful. Democracy is a totalitarian manifestation; it is not a form of freedom .*[23]

Be not deceived with all the warm fuzzies you may get from talks by objectivists' on the beauties of the U.S. system of government, the wealth and jobs created, and how much we are better for it.

They have contempt for the "little man" if he or she dares goes against any of their viewpoints. For example, Social Security, Medicare, or governmental safety regulations should not exist. The individual trumps society, the only moral arbiter to an Objectivist is power, might, or money. Which, in our society, all mean the same thing.

Ayn Rand stated that building on the "first principle"-that the self is all that matters and represented all that was good; it followed that selfishness, a complete desire to serve only one's passions, wants, and lusts, was the highest moral choice to make.

It was more than a choice; it was a commandment in her view. To her, charity and altruism was the tool of the "collective", that is in the sense that the masses that could vote themselves the right to steal from the deserving.

Oh yes, I forgot, mankind was divided into two classes, the producers and the moochers. The active and the passive. That's the whole plot line of "Atlas Shrugged", where the good and noble titans of industry are just about fed up at the intrusion of government, and on top of that, they are sick and tired of feeling guilty because they are successful.

In "Atlas Shrugged", Ayn writes of the beggars on the street, preying on the good nature of the capitalists. This is a figure of speech, of course, as the "true good" is the denial of any material aid to these people.

If Ayn's diatribe full of obtuse and incomprehensible jargon isn't clear to you, all you have to do is go to any of her disciples' websites. Some examples are the Ayn Rand Institute and The Atlas Society, which tend to talk as pretentiously as their matriarch did. How about a regular guy's view, just someone who read her book as a youngster and had his life changed by it?

Check out the website, www.whoisjohngalt.com (Who Is John Galt?) The site has been active since February 2009. The author's first post answers that question in a post appropriately titled as such.

He explains that Galt is the hero of the novel but he is more, he's the world's hero now. The author was so inspired by reading the book, he changed his views on everything. He found it inspirational in its foundation of a new morality; the moral basis for individualism. Quoting:

> ""Atlas Shrugged" was rated by readers as the second most influential book (after The Bible) in a 1991 survey co-sponsored by The Book-of-the-Month Club and The Library of Congress. It's a lengthy read, but it's well worth the time for anyone who wants to understand why the ideas of the political left are so destructive and irrational, or for anyone seeking a moral basis for individualism."[4]

Every post on the blog is an angry screed about the direction of our country, against Obama, liberals and those who want to do charity.

After a while he has had enough and he posts a rant about liberals and their call for "giving back".

> "On a news report this morning, I heard a talking head describe charity as 'giving back.'

> *I have something to say about this. First, it isn't giving back. It's giving. Giving back implies something that was taken from someone else. When you get a tax refund, that's giving back. The government gives back money that belongs to you. But charity? That's a gift....*
>
> *Charity is conditional. Charitable organizations turn away applicants who just want support. Charity is about getting beneficiaries to live by the values of donors, not because of some power trip, but because those are the very values that create the gift itself...*
>
> *...And, finally, when someone else says they're interested in "giving back," consider asking them: Why? Did you steal something?"*[25]

That's about as clear as he can make it, and to give him credit; he summed up very well what Ayn meant about allowing charity.

She excused it if it were given with no cost or sacrifice to you. If you were hurt giving anything then you have committed evil, as you shouldn't sacrifice.

Ayn endorsed charity that was used as a carrot in the carrot and stick way, as it would be just a mechanism for getting your own selfish desires. That kind of charity was acceptable. But never, ever, give because of need. Let's back up that claim with a couple of quotes from Grandma Greed herself:

> **Ayn quote 1:** *"There is nothing wrong in helping other people, if and when they are worthy of the help and you can afford to help them. I regard charity as a marginal issue. What I am fighting is the idea that charity is a moral duty and a primary virtue."*
>
> **Ayn quote 2:** *"The proper method of judging when or whether one should help another person is by reference to one's own rational self-interest and one's own hierarchy of values: the time, money or effort one gives or the risk one takes should be proportionate to the value of the person in relation to one's own happiness.*
>
> *To illustrate this on the altruists' favorite example: [T]he issue of saving a drowning person. If the person to be saved is a stranger, it is morally proper to save him only when the danger to one's own life is minimal; when the danger is great, it would be immoral to attempt it: only a lack of self-esteem could permit one to value one's life no higher than that of any random stranger. "*

Ayn quote 3: *The small minority of adults who are* unable *rather than unwilling to work, have to rely on voluntary charity; misfortune is not a claim to slave labor; there is no such thing as the* right *to consume, control, and destroy those without whom one would be unable to survive.* [86]

You are really doing yourself a disservice if you take me at my word, and abstain from going to the links provided. The above quotes from Ayn, come from three different original sources, none of them being "Atlas Shrugged", but all of these thoughts summarized by John Galt.

The first one was a quote from a Playboy interview. The second one is from her landmark book, revered and studied by her followers, entitled "The Virtue of Selfishness", where Ayn instructs us on the only acceptable times we can save a drowning man.

The third one is from her book entitled simply, "Capitalism", in which she describes her views as to what capitalism is all about.

Her capitalism requires us to avoid taking care of those who are "unable to work rather than unwilling to work". No mentally retarded, no elderly who don't have the means, no one at all who cannot work. She hated welfare mamas to be sure but she viewed any who were disabled and incapable as being blights, with no "*right to consume, control, and destroy those without whom one would be unable to survive.*" [87] Just in case you don't understand her, she's talking about those who are physically or mentally unable to survive without assistance.

But I didn't have to spend much time consolidating those quotes, they were all laid out for me on a wonderful site called the Ayn Rand Lexicon (www.aynrandlexicon.com) Don't misunderstand me, I didn't find this after I scoured the net until I found a nest of Ayn haters. This is one of their sites devoted to the study of her words and meaning. All three quotes appear under the entry "charity" when you click on it. The site owners felt that those quotes were representative of her philosophy.

You can go to the "About the Lexicon" portion and see a glowing note and dedication from Leonard Peikoff, who I mentioned earlier as her only heir. He's the protector and benefactor of her estate. He closes his warm endorsement with this:

> "The Lexicon is a welcome addition to the growing Ayn Rand Library, of which it is Volume IV. It is going to be extremely helpful to me personally, and I am happy to recommend it to anyone interested in the thought of Ayn Rand. She herself, I know, would have been pleased to see it become a reality."[88]

As noted before, John Galt's famous speech contains everything you wanted to know about Ayn Rand's worldview, but were afraid to ask.

Her view was that with reason being the highest source of knowledge, the biggest threat to man's advancement was faith. Quoting John Galt, who was actually channeling Rand:

> "The alleged short-cut to knowledge, which is faith, is only a short-circuit destroying the mind."[89]

Therefore, the intent of Ayn's life work, according to her, was the establishment of a new morality, one that denies any service or sacrifice.

Capitalism was just one manifestation of this morality, but any type of indulgence was encouraged, if you truly wished for it and were strong enough to make it happen.

In Ayn's world, you must pursue the ultimate good, selfish desires, at any cost, and avoid evil, charity and sacrifice, at all cost.

Galt's most famous line is the oath he required of the working stiffs in the Billionaires Union, before they went on strike. It was:

> "I swear by my life and my love of it that I will never live for the sake of another man, nor ask another man to live for mine."[90]

This conflict with Jesus Christ was not problematic for Ayn, as she had already determined that religion and faith were for suckers and looters anyway.

This oath, called the striker's code, sums up the doctrine of rational self-interest. Rand believed that individuals have an inalienable right to pursue their own happiness based on their own values and that they must have complete liberty to pursue their own self-interest anyway they choose. Under this system, no one has any obligation to anyone else beyond the general obligation to honor the freedoms and rights of other self-interested people.

Ayn is perfectly clear about altruism, or charity:

> *"Even though altruism declares that "it is more blessed to give than to receive," it does not work that way in practice.*
> *The givers are never blessed; the more they give, the more is demanded of them; complaints, reproaches and insults are the only response they get for practicing altruism's virtues (or for their actual virtues). ... Altruists are concerned only with those who suffer—not with those who provide relief from suffering, not even enough to care whether they are able to survive. When no actual suffering can be found, the altruists are compelled to invent or manufacture it.*[31]*"*

She nails exactly what is wrong with charity in the world, altruists are only concerned with those who suffer, and they just don't care enough about those who give the relief. Are you getting the sense of her twisted worldview?

This has to be made clear: Ayn's number one goal was a new morality, not a more efficient capitalism. Capitalism was a means, not an end. Total acceptance of the self was her goal. What better way to demonstrate fealty to her thinking than to gather tremendous wealth at any cost?

For Ayn, her dream world was the ruthless world of the turn of the twentieth century where children died in coal mines, factory workers burned to death because the cost of sprinklers was too high, rancid meat was sold-regardless of the waste and filth ground into the meat for all the little children to eat and enjoy. Or perhaps the world of today where dictators can steal a country's wealth for personal benefit, while their people starve. In her mournful screed titled in complete seriousness with absolutely no sense of irony, "America's Persecuted Minority: Big Business", Ayn writes:

> *Evading the difference between production and looting, they called the businessman a robber. Evading the difference between freedom and compulsion, they called him a slave driver. Evading the difference between reward and terror, they called him an exploiter. Evading the difference between paychecks and guns, they called him an autocrat. Evading the difference between trade and force, they called him a tyrant. The most crucial issue they had to evade was the difference between the earned and the unearned.*[32]

Let's see, a society where the boss can work me to death, and pay me as little as he wishes; I can't vote for anyone to represent my interests; no mercy from the well-to-do, unable to count on someone pulling me out of a lake if I fall in and were about to drown? Sign me up right away!

It's hard to imagine why one would willingly follow such a person. Let me backtrack, its not hard to imagine how a billionaire or captain of industry would love it. Ayn sings their song for sure, but the average guy? What's in it for him?

I'm not talking what's in it by way of a pay check, what's in it for him as far as a quality of life, a voice in government, a chance to overcome a bad start, a chance to survive a catastrophe like the tornados that almost destroyed Tuscaloosa and Joplin?

Why would anyone vote for this platform? Would anyone that wanted a society with the safety net of FEMA, other disaster relief agencies for Tuscaloosa, Joplin or any other ravaged community want this world?

Yet, here we have Paul Ryan, the new face of the Republican party, trying to do just that. He's not alone, he's got plenty of support in Congress itself, and you better believe that the big money "fat cats" love him in spite of his Ayn Rand-like sour personality.

It's my gut feeling, and my sincerest hope, that people from places like Tuscaloosa and Joplin, and Atlanta and Dallas, are voting for this ideology out of ignorance because they don't know about the details. But no one is lying about the goal. Ayn said it, Paul Ryan says it, and colleges now teach it as the only rational choice...it's a new morality, its not just dollars and sense.

So why embrace Ayn Rand's view? Is this the only defense of capitalism? Why not Adam Smith? Not too long ago, Smith was considered the father of Capitalism. Had a lot of fans in the old Reagan administration. Many of his people would wear Adam Smith ties.

Since 1776 Adam Smith has been taught to school kids and studied as the father of capitalism. Ayn did not invent self-interest, or the profit motive. Those were his ideas. So why not him, instead of her as the face of the free market? Why not embrace the actual father of it?

Maybe because Adam Smith believed in a progressive tax, where the rich paid a higher percent, as that was his notion of "fair". In his landmark work, "The Wealth of Nations", if you check out Book V: On the Revenue of Sovereign or Commonwealth, and read Chapter II: On The Sources of the General or Public Revenue of the Society, Part II On Taxes, (just in case you doubt me) Smith lists four conditions of taxation needed, the first one is fairness, with fairness being described as the rich paying more.

> "The subjects of every state ought to contribute towards the support of the government, as nearly as possible, in proportion to their respective abilities; that is, in proportion to the revenue which they respectively enjoy under the protection of the state.
>
> The expense of government to the individuals of a great nation is like the expense of management to the joint tenants of a great estate, who are all obliged to contribute in proportion to their respective interests in the estate. In the observation or neglect of this maxim consists what is called the equality or inequality of taxation."[63]

Whoa! "*As nearly as possible, in proportion to their respective abilities?*" Sounds a lot like, "*From each according to his ability, to each according to his need*". Has Adam Smith gone pinko on us?

Actually, the concept of fairness as defined this way can be demonstrated in Jesus' parable of the "Widow's mite".[34] This notion goes against the current battle cry of the radical Republicans with their call for a "fair tax" which of course lowers taxes on the rich.

Maybe the disciples of Ayn Rand avoid Adam Smith because he had an aversion to monopolies. He stated that the government should do what it could to prevent price fixing and control of an industry.

The Objectivists and their ilk probably dislike his belief that government had a legitimate role, to produce "public goods" for every one's sake.

Perhaps it was because he wrote a long theory as prelude to his "Wealth of Nations" where he explained his motives? He wanted what was best for everyone. His prelude was called "The Theory of Moral Sentiments" in which he talked about the old morality; the one that Ayn and Paul Ryan want to abolish.

For the sake of you youngsters who were raised in this era of Facebook, texting and Ayn Rand's landmark "Virtue of Selfishness", let me share with you some words from the guy we old timers had to study when we studied capitalism.

> "*The wise and virtuous man is at all times willing that his own private interest should be sacrificed to the public interest of his own particular order or society. He is at all times willing, too, that the interest of this order or society should be sacrificed to the greater interest of the state or sovereignty, of which it is only a subordinate part.*
>
> *He should, therefore, be equally willing that all those inferior interests should be sacrificed to the greater interest of the universe, to the interest of that great society of all sensible and intelligent beings, of which God himself is the immediate administrator and director.*[35] "

Somebody somewhere is calling something capitalism when it ain't really capitalism, at least not in the eyes of Adam Smith, the founder of capitalism. Ayn Rand tells us that above all, we must embrace capitalism. She also said there are no contradictions. I therefore must reject Ayn as anything remotely resembling capitalism, at least Adam Smith's version.

It is instructive for the sake of the narrative to note that Ayn was born in Russia, as Alisa Zinov'yevna Rosenbaum in 1905. Alisa was part of a relatively well to do Jewish family that lived in Saint Petersburg. They were Jewish by heritage only, as the family was largely non observant.

Her father was a successful pharmacist who rose to a level of success by owning his own pharmacy and even the building in which it was housed.[36]

Her father lost his pharmacy after the Bolsheviks confiscated it in 1917. The family had to subsequently flee to Crimea, which is where she later recalled that she determined that she was an atheist and she developed an appreciation for reason above   any other human attribute. After graduating from high school, she returned with her family to Petrograd (which was Saint Petersburg) where the family suffered greatly, coming close to starving.[37]

It's not clear that any time in Alisa/Ayn's childhood was fun. Her father worked hard, being a self-made/up by the bootstraps sort of fellow. Ayn's mother was from wealth. When her maternal granny needed a tissue, she never got it herself, she just pressed a button and had an underling bring it to her. Ayn's mother, Anna, was very competitive with her sister, who had "married up", and Ayn's father had to work for what he had. Consequently, Ayn was constantly being compared with her cousins, most often in a negative way.[38]

Anna, Alisa/Ayn's mom, would brag on Alisa/Ayn in front of the extended family, then berate her at home for being such an awkward kid. The nagging was constant, "Why don't you have any friends? Why don't you play with others?" Surprisingly, this tough love did little to bring the young genius out of her shell.[39]

Anna also had anger issues. She would explode and do loving things like tearing the legs out of Ayn's dolls, and once she sadistically ripped up a photograph of Ayn's hero, Alexander Kerensky, who irony of ironies was a political leader of a socialist persuasion.[40]

There is something symbolic about the destruction of a socialist's photograph. Perhaps gentle hands from mother could have at least worked up sympathy for Social Security later from Ayn?

The greatest show of maternal love and care from Anna came from the constant reminder to the girls that she had never wanted children, and she hated caring for them and only did it because she had to, not because she wanted to. I have no training in psychology, but maybe this was a factor in the development of a "new way of morality" that stressed selfishness above all things, even the family?

Later in life, after fine-tuning her Objectivist mantra, Ayn stated that it would be immoral for a person to sacrifice for anyone else in any circumstance, even a child. Ayn with razor sharp logic rationalized that if there were only one child, and one parent, the parent had a duty to keep himself/herself alive, because they had to be there for the kid, as the kid would be screwed anyway if he were the only one that survived.[41] A trickle down theory of child care, if you will.

Ayn had witnessed her dad refusing to work for the Soviet authorities, which provided the inspiration for her "Going Galt" strike in Atlas Shrugged.[42] She went to University, which wasn't common for Jews or women at the time, and she was introduced to all manner of philosophies and philosophers. The Soviet authorities purged her shortly before her graduation, that is to say expelled for political reasons because she was part of the "bourgeois". However she was allowed to return to finish her studies.[43]

This may come to a shock to everyone, but oddly enough the woman who made it her mission to demonize charity was not, by almost all accounts, a nice person, and by "almost all", I mean everyone except the most starry-eyed sycophants.

As a child, she would not make friends, and she could not keep the ones she stumbled onto. One of the few non-Objectivist biographers, (which ironically means she was the most objective), Professor Jennifer Burns of the University of Virginia notes that Ayn never maintained a serious steady friendship in her life.

She was always "too different...uncomfortable with gossip, games or the intrigues of popularity".[44]

Later in life she broke off every friendship she had fostered and alienated her closest friends, many times because they dared to disagree with her.

Ayn had an inflated opinion of herself despite not getting a second to that motion and a move for all in favor of the proposition voting on her self-assessment. Ayn didn't need democratic functions to validate herself. She later expressed extreme contempt for the notion of any type of democracy. As to her notion of philosophers that matter, she told journalist Mike Wallace, who interviewed her in depth in 1959 on television, "If anyone can pick a rational flaw in my philosophy, I will be delighted to acknowledge him and I will learn something from him."[45] Until then she noted that she was forced to consider herself "the most creative thinker alive". Her modesty kept her from claiming the number one position of all time, and she humbly yielded that to Aristotle.[46]

In 1923, Ayn got a tourist visa to visit relatives in the United States. Around this time she adopted her literary name "Rand" and the first name "Ayn". She picked Rand off of a Remington-Rand typewriter. She felt that Rand sounded better.[47] What might have been if she had chosen the other one, Remington? Chances are she still would have been the Republican pin-up doll, only as Ayn Remington, darling of the NRA and defender of gun rights.

She arrived in New York, and ultimately ended up in California. Just as her visa was about to expire she conveniently married her American, Frank O'Conner and avoided deportation.

Her marriage to Frank O'Connor was a strange one. Frank was a mousy little man who let Ayn openly humiliate him. They stayed married for 50 years until his death. Ayn had met Frank in Hollywood.

Ayn was a big movie fan, and ended up in Hollywood writing scripts. She actually has one movie credit to her name as an actor, listed on the Internet Movie Database, IMDB. She was an extra on Cecil B. DeMille's classic silent film, 'The King of Kings", a movie about Jesus.[48] There is more than enough fodder for an ironic observation about this fact.

Let me interrupt with what would seem to be an out of context anecdote, but will prove to be another bit of humorous irony to anyone but Rand fans. Ayn knew she was special in the field of philosophy at an early age, when she learned of syllogisms. That's a fancy word for the building upon logic with facts. A famous one always used to demonstrate this: All men are mortal, Socrates was a man, and therefore Socrates was mortal.[49]

Ayn recounts the moment that changed her life, where she first encountered the path to truth:

> "The first syllogism made an enormous impression on me. It was like a light bulb going off in my mind. The syllogism was 'All cats have tails, this is a cat, therefore it has a tail. My first reaction was: That's wrong; when people say, for instance, that all Frenchmen are no good, they don't really mean every one of them, it's just an expression. Then I grasped, as a revelation, that when you say 'all', you must really say 'all'[50]

Now, my first impulse is to mock her with a sarcastic "duh" to a word meaning what it actually means. She is correct and the imprecise nature of word usage causes miscommunication and even deceit more often than most people realize.

Even in the context of this book, for example, the idea of imprecise language rings true.

71

If I were to say I am concerned that the poorest and most dependent on government are in danger of dying off because they could lose their government support or stress places such as Tuscaloosa or Joplin must have the help of the federal government to survive; there is always one pat answer.

The reflexive response from the well-intentioned conservative is "NOBODY wants that to happen, we are just concerned about waste and excess".

That is patently false if the word "nobody" has any meaning. I have demonstrated that Ayn felt that way, and that her followers feel that way. As you proceed in this book, you'll see it more and more. With the Ayn Rand mindset, there can be no expenditure for the public good that isn't inherently wasteful. There is no good government versus bad government; to those who live in the world of Ayn Rand, it is all-bad.

But, giving Ayn the benefit of the doubt, it is amusing that she used this philosophical anecdote to follow up and say that at that moment she became acutely aware of the need for precision in language, and made it her life's calling.

Ayn's recollection of her first meeting Frank, in her own words, reveals either an unspoken or unacknowledged faith that would shock us all. Or maybe it reveals that she wasn't as clever as she said she was? Maybe she should drop down to number 13 or so on the greatest philosophers of all time list, instead of being ranked at her self-assigned number 2 position?

Quoting Ayn about that fateful day where the Objectivist met the object of her heart's desires:

> *"He was magnificent!* (speaking of her future husband)...*I spent the next three days just staring at him on the huge, crowded set, watching his every move, and trying to figure out how to meet him...I was following him like a camera...I sat beside him, staring at him, but he didn't turn; and I didn't have the courage to talk to him...*
>
> *...By the fourth day, I had decided what to do. They were filming a big street scene in Jerusalem, Christ was carrying the cross to the Crucifixion, surrounded by a mob, the extras were to mill about chaotically, some shaking their fists and yelling insults at Christ, others weeping and pleading with the Roman officials."*[1]

Don't get caught up in Ayn swooning over her husband to be, that's not the point of the quote. Examine the queen of precision's description of the title character: Christ. Ayn referred to Him by his title, the description given by His followers, Christ, which means "anointed one" or "messiah", which bestows upon Him the recognition of divinity as the one sent by God.[52] Jesus was His name. Surely Ayn was too smart to have made that error in semantics?

Nevertheless, romance bloomed between her and Frank. She was smitten, they dated, and were married. Along the way they moved to New York and back again to California where she wrote a blockbuster novel well received by critics and fans alike, called "The Fountainhead". This was a huge commercial success and established the origins of her large following, the cult of Ayn Rand.

Ayn had had her bit of success as a writer. She wasn't as successful in her social life. Biographer Jennifer Burns quotes an acquaintance saying "My first impression is that this woman is a freak". Ayn knew better. If Ayn were a freak, she was a freakishly brilliant woman. Ayn knew with such conviction that she was so awesome that she had to keep herself focused on the tasks at hand. One entry about this time had Ayn telling herself: "Stop admiring yourself – you are nothing yet!"[53] Tough words, spoken out of love, but needed to make Ayn the best Ayn she could be.

She finally felt she had cracked the code of the secret of life. This became the basis of her new religion/philosophy Objectivism. She noted: "The secret of life: you must be nothing but will. Know what you want and do it. Know what you are doing and why you are doing it. Every minute of the day. All will and all control. Send everything else to hell!"[54]

At face value this mantra is somewhat innocuous; it could be any motivational speaker saying that. But Ayn carried things to extreme. She held the view that a principle wasn't valid unless you observed it all the time.

She believed with her cold, dark heart that will and control were all that mattered. Selfish ego stomping on the world to get your way. This is most often thought of as an endorsement of wealth at any cost but it is far more sinister, far more evil.

This was an endorsement of a worldview that would justify even the death of a child. And of course there are flip sides to all of her axioms. If the individual is right above all others, then the masses have no right to judge him. They are not fit to sit in judgment of anyone that has a strong enough will. Even if you have to destroy a child and everyone that loved, nurtured and adored this child.

This wickedness I speak of is laid out in all of its ugliness, provided again by her cult, who offer it for the historical record. I am speaking of her journals where she would jot down observations of life, philosophy and ideas for books and plays. These journals were released in a book appropriately titled "The Journals of Ayn Rand". [55] This book was released by the Ayn Rand Institute, with Leonard Peikoff her anointed one and sole heir to her estate, listed as author. He owns these papers. Another follower, David Harriman, is listed as an editor.

In 1928, Ayn had a memorable set of observations about one William Hickman, which are recorded in the aforementioned book "The Journals of Ayn Rand".

However, a couple of background points are in order before I present these entries. First, the diaries included commentary by an editor when they were released, presumably to explain and give context.

What the reader should know is that the editor, David Harriman, is an Objectivist, a follower of Ayn's philosophy. The Ayn Rand Center for Individual Rights website lists him as a contributor with specialties in history and philosophy of physics, and "the development of Ayn Rand's ideas as reflected in her journals".[56]

So remember that he isn't exactly neutral as you read his description of the William Hickman entry.

Quoting from Harriman's commentary preceding the Hickman entries, as he describes her basing a character Danny Renahan in a novel she didn't finish on William Hickman:

> "Some of Danny's characteristics are based on an actual nineteen year old boy, William Edward Hickman, who was the defendant in a highly publicized murder trial that had just taken place in Los Angeles. Hickman was accused of kidnapping and murdering a young girl. He was found guilty and sentenced to death in February 1928 and he was hanged on October 20, 1928.
>
> Judging from the newspaper accounts of the time, Hickman was articulate and arrogant, and seems to have enjoyed shocking people by rejecting conventional views. The public furor against him was unprecedented. For reasons given in the following notes, Ayn Rand concluded that the intensity of the public's hatred was primarily "Because of the man who committed the crime and not because of the crime he committed." The mob hated Hickman for his independence, she chose him as a model for the same reason.[57]

Let us examine the record of Hickman and see if the "mob" overreacted. Consider the editor's description and ask yourself if he seems to be soft-pedaling. To give Mr. Harriman the proper benefit of the doubt, I shall go to the newspapers of that day and judge for myself whether or not the reaction was surprisingly overdramatic and see if it was his sassy independent spirit that enraged all of the jealous wanna-bes.

The New York Times offers archives of its papers to subscribers, or for a fee for individual requests; going all the way back to 1851.

The New York Times found the William Hickman story newsworthy enough to devote several articles to it; from the original crime to his execution.

The basic facts of the case are this: Hickman kidnapped a 12 year old girl by checking her out of school under false pretenses on December 15, 1927. He held her for ransom; hoping to get $1500 from her father, who happened to be a successful banker. Marion Parker was the victim, a 12-year-old child. Marion Parker was one of twin daughters of the banker Perry Parker. Hickman had originally chosen another girl, another daughter of a banker, but decided she was too young. He particularly chose Marion because she appeared to be her father's favorite.[58]

Marian's father, Perry, was double crossed on the exchange, as Hickman took the money, but only gave Parker the corpse of his daughter in return. After a massive manhunt he was caught in Pendleton, Oregon; offering a confession after being taken into custody. The New York Times printed his confession in full on December 22, 1927.[59]

Well, not exactly in full. Hickman's initial confession was there was an accomplice, a mysterious chap with a nasty disposition named Andrew Cramer. Andrew was the truly evil one of the conspirators, as he actually did the nasty business of killing as Hickman was only in it for the money-so he could attend college, of all things.

In an article bylined from "*On Board Hickman Train, San Jose, Cal.[sic] Dec. 26*" the New York Times reports:

> In giving his version of the crime Young Hickman remained calm until he mentioned the name of the slain girl.
> "Marian and I were good friends." He sobbed, "and we had a good time when we were together and I really liked her. I am sorry that she was killed"
> He said he had not been cruel to her and that she was murdered and dismembered by Andrew Cramer, an alleged accomplice. He related how he had treated the child gently and had become friendly with her and how he had taken her to a motion picture show the night before she was slain.[60]

Hickman recounted that he and Marian got along fabulously, with discussions about how cool show-and-tell at school would be once she returned back to everyday life. Hickman quoted Marian as saying:

> *"I wonder what the school kids will say when I go back to school*[?] *They will want to know what I did and everything"*[61]

Hickman also told of Marian's calm and compliant demeanor. Hickman even took her to the movie, and they had a wonderful time. But Andrew Cramer went and ruined it for everyone. When Cramer found out that Mr. Parker had contacted the police, it pushed him into acting rashly and he murdered Marian as an act of retribution. Hickman claimed to have brought the body to dad, because Hickman figured one way or another, he'd want his daughter back.[62]

Hickman continued with his confession:

> *And if there had not been any detectives he* [Marian's father] *would have gotten her back. And if this fellow* [Hickman's alleged accomplice Cramer] *had not killed her it would have come out all right, as we had planned, because I am sure she didn't want to die, because when she was me she said:*
>
> *"I wonder what the school kids will say when I go back to school. They will want to know what I did and everything"*
>
> *I am terribly sorry she was killed myself, because I sure liked her*[63]

At this point, the reporter who received and transcribed the confession inserted the comment below Hickman's statement:

> *(Hickman wept here)*[64]

But detectives charged with escorting Hickman back to Los Angeles didn't quite believe his confession, particularly the part of an accomplice who did all the dirty work. Hickman confessed that his first confession was a bit inaccurate; there was no accomplice and it had been all of Hickman's doings. It didn't help Hickman's case that the "fiend"[65], as described by Hickman, was actually in jail at the time in Los Angeles, two-thirds through a 200-day sentence.[66]

Hickman revised his confession and acknowledged that he was the sole actor in this gruesome tragedy. The word gruesome is used because the worlds kidnapping and murder are too generic and plain. Hickman killed the girl by strangulation, then cut her arms and legs off. He gutted her body, and wrapped her entrails up in towels. He planned to later spread her internal organs and limbs all over Los Angeles. He did.

He relaxed after his crime at the movie, and when he took the armless, legless corpse of Marian to her father, he pried her eyes open with piano wire to give the appearance of being awake.

The New York Times from December 27, 1927:

Hickman killed Marian by strangling her with a towel in his room at the Bellevue Arms Apartments. He knotted it about her throat and pulled tightly for two minutes before she was unconscious. Then he dismembered the body.

He then arranged the eyes to make the girl appear to be alive, when he took the body to the father and got the ransom.

Hickman said he wrote the "last chance" note to Parker. He went to a theatre in the afternoon after slaying the girl.

He returned to his apartment about 5:30 P.M., took all parts of the body down to his car, which was parked by a side entrance, hurried out Sunset Boulevard and turned into Elysian Park, where he disposed of the limbs....

When he saw Mr. Parker he showed his sawed-off shotgun and told the father to keep quiet. He raised the head of the girl and asked for the money.

Hickman said he drove ahead and left the body. He then drove to Park and Grand Avenues, where he parked the car. He then went to Leighton's cafe, and he had a meal and cashed the first of the $20 notes he received from Mr. Parker.

Hickman had killed Marian the day he had instructed her to write a letter to her father. Here's the note that Marion wrote to her father, the last communication he ever received from his daughter; the daughter taken because it was believed to be his favorite.

Dear Daddy and Mother,

I wish I could come home. I think I'll die if I have to be like this much longer. Won't someone tell me why all this had to happen to me. Daddy please do what this man tells you or he'll kill me if you don't. Your loving daughter, Marion Parker.

P.S. Please Daddy I want to come home tonight. [67]

She was right. Daddy didn't even have to do anything wrong, and this loser still killed her and took in a movie to unwind after a hard day's work.

Back to the introduction by Mr. Harriman, the follower of Ayn Rand who is so enamored with her brilliance that he devotes his life to studying her. Could he have given a just a little bit more detail in his description of the context, instead of the plain vanilla one he used to introduce this episode?

Harriman quickly backs up Ayn's assertion that the mob was hating on this guy, just because he was a bit different. With that, he agrees with Ayn.

How about the description that the "mob", which really wasn't a mob but public outrage, had an "unprecedented reaction?"

Not sure if you noticed or not, but the abduction happened on December 15, and capture on December 22. I fully understand that to the God-hating, greed-promoting, self-worshipping Objectivist bunch, Christmas isn't that big a deal. Maybe the melodramatic outburst of the peasants had to do with their holiday cheer being disturbed by such a gruesome act?

Did Mr. Harriman, the scholar and physicist, feel that perhaps the people of Los Angeles needed a little perspective, and not blow this out of proportion?

But more to the point, this book is about Ayn and HER reaction to the crime. After all, Harriman was just an editor. It's pure coincidence that he is an Objectivist, a member of Ayn's cult that she founded, and quite coincidentally he is a full time researcher and fellow at the Ayn Rand Center for Individual Rights. He's just writing commentary so we don't take her thoughts the wrong way.

As you can see here, Harriman really shouldn't have worried. There is no way anyone jumped to the wrong conclusion with regards to Ayn's take on Hickman:

> *"The boy is a perfectly straight being, unbending and uncompromising. He cannot be a hypocrite. He shows how impossible it is for a genuinely beautiful soul to succeed at present; for in all modern life, one has to be a hypocrite, to bend and tolerate.*
>
> *This boy wanted to command and smash away things and people he didn't approve of.*
>
> *He could not compromise with that which he despised and knew he had a right to despise. All life is compromising, at present. A man that could not compromise."*[68]

OK, so if we understand Ayn, Hickman is a beautiful soul; so maybe he overreacted just a wee bit, but he had to just to stay true to his principles.

Personally, I'm conflicted. Should I celebrate that Hickman didn't bow down to "the man", or should I be glad that "the man" finally caught him and executed him for taking a family's daughter from school, chopping off her legs and arms, gutting her innards, gouging her eyes out, propping them open with chicken wire to stay open, and finally tossing the parts throughout LA on his way to the picture show? I am leaning towards the feeling that I'm glad "the man" won this one.

Harriman appears to have missed all of these details. But he was honest enough to concede that perhaps Hickman was a bit too arrogant when he taunted with his ransom notes signed "Death", "Fate", and "The Fox". Individuals with a strong sense of identity do that, and the little people "aren't sophisticated enough" to admire the chutzpah of someone like William Hickman.

Continuing with the words of Ayn Rand, the creator of the new morality as espoused by the current Republican goddess, {all emphasis and quotation marks are Ayn Rand's} :

> "*The first thing that impresses me about the case is the ferocious rage of the WHOLE society against ONE man. No matter what the man did, there is always something loathsome in the "virtuous" indignation and mass hatred of the "majority.""*

> "*One always feels the stuffy bloodthirsty emotion of a mob in any great public feeling of a large number of humans. It is repulsive to see all those beings with worse sins and crimes in their own lives, virtuously condemning a criminal, proud and secure in their number, yelling furiously in defense of society"*[69]

A couple of points deserve attention at this point. First, Ayn is gobsmacked by the notion of a pissed off population; which based on his comments, apparently her intellectual heir Harriman is too. To be honest, I can't speak to the 1928 reaction to the murder and horrific mutilation of an innocent. But nowadays we all kind of overreact. So, in fairness to Paul Ryan's fairy godmother, perhaps they were a bit cooler with the notion then.

Secondly, Ayn is quite indignant to the idea of some bunch of hooligans, fresh from their churches, work days at the factories, and families all converging to harass an iconoclastic hero. Nice touch also, adding the sarcastic "yelling furiously in defense of society". Silly worker drones. The real threat is from a too high capital gains tax.

Let's continue, shall we?

> "*This is not just the case of a terrible crime. It is not the crime alone that has raised that fury of public hatred. It is the case of a daring challenge to society. It is the fact that a crime has been committed by one man, alone; that this man knew it was against all laws of humanity and intended it that way; that he does not want to recognize it as a crime and that he feels superior to all. It is the amazing picture of a man with no regard whatever for all that society holds sacred, and with a consciousness all his own. A man who really stands alone, in action and in soul"*[70]

81

Isn't that just like the masses? Getting their panties in a wad for boys just being boys and exercising human butchery on children?

Are you getting the picture as to why the Satanists love this chick so much? I can't figure out though the attraction for Fox News, Newt Gingrich, Dick Armey, Clarence Thomas (yes, he is one too), and lover-boy Governor Mark Sanford of South Carolina.

Skipping over more rants about the injustice of mob anger, we go to these nuggets of wisdom, continuing from Ayn:

> *"Worse crimes than this have been committed. No one has ever raised such furious indignation."*[1]

Here is where I begin to be just a tad skeptical. Ayn was convincing me of this lad's status as the true victim until this, but even I can't rationalize this one. I think if the masses made a habit of this activity, or worse, we would have heard about it.

> *"Why? Because of the man who committed the crime and not because of the crime he has committed. Because of Hickman's brazenly challenging attitude"*[2]

There are about ten more pages of more of the same, much of it worse. I won't continue copying, but I do want to drive this point home, lest you think this was just a freak outburst. Which is: this was a sustained sermon in defense of this guy. The parts excluded talked of his strength, and the "hata's being hata's", keeping him down with their silly rules.

Ayn also shows pure disgust at the media, which mocked the brave boy because he broke down in hysterical fear when he faced the gallows. She blamed society for not allowing him his dignity. What were her thoughts on the jury that oppressed him?

> *"Average, everyday, rather stupid looking citizens. Shabbily dressed, dried, worn looking little men. Fat overdressed, very average, "dignified" housewives. How can they decide the fate of that boy? Or anyone's fate? If a man has to be judged, why can't he be judged by his superiors, who alone would have a right to?"*[3]

Excellent question Ayn! Why can't a vicious, barbaric animal like Hickman be judged by his superiors, rather than the filthy common working folk?

She did praise some things about the incident however, Hickman's dashing humor, joking about the victims during the trial, she also noticed that
> "*[H]e looks like a bad boy with a very winning grin*" and "*that he makes you like him the whole time you are in his presence*"[4]

Ayn was particularly offended by
> "*[T]he depravity of pastors who try to convert convicted murderers to their religion*"[5]

Again, quoting Ayn:
> "*The fact that right after his sentence Hickman was given a Bible by the jailer. I don't know of anything more loathsome, hypocritical, low and diabolical than giving Bibles to men sentenced to death.*"[6]

And finally, this really pissed her off, and was one of the top disgusting things she saw in this whole sorry affair:
> "*The twelve year old little girl, who wrote a letter to Hickman, asking him 'to get religion so that little girls everywhere would stop being afraid of him'*"[7]

I'm hoping you get the picture here. If not, I've used less than half of her comments pertaining to Hickman, you can go look up more to your heart's content.

I had no difficulty at all finding shockingly, bizarrely, perversely offensive passages that reflected her starry eyed hero worship of this murderous misfit.

Her thoughts the same thing over and over. It was all society's fault. She saw worthless common people oppressing a free thinker. Too many disgusting cretins with Bibles trying to torment this man before his death. And the audacity of the little child who begged for him to find religion so that little girls everywhere would stop being afraid. How dare she. Children should neither be seen, heard, or comforted. I had no difficulty at all finding such. I did not want an isolated sentence. I felt it important to instill in the reader a sense of how much Ayn wrote, how strongly she felt about this and where her values were.

One thing I never found though, was one single mention at all for the victim. Well, let me correct that. I did see where she was mentioned as "the child" in that plain vanilla description given by the Rand cultist that tried to whitewash Ayn's hero worship. I'd like to have known Ayn's thoughts on the child. After all, Marian's daddy was a banker, so she must have been worth something.

It's a relief that Ayn's dead now, but in a way she is immortal. It is puzzling to me how Harriman can sanitize her feelings on this, but I suppose it shouldn't surprise me. After all, he devotes his life to the study of her work at an institute that bears this woman's name. He's an idealist who adores Ayn for what she brings to our culture; much like the great, serious thinker Paul Ryan, the hero of Fox News and good, Christian Republicans everywhere, the type of people that weren't worthy to even sit in judgment of William Hickman.

If you "Google" the phrase "defense of Ayn Rand William Hickman" you will find as one of the top returned sites, which reflects one of the highest concentrations of traffic that way, a blog called The Right Guy Show,[78] "The Right Guy Show" is a reference for a radio show.

The show, "The Andre Controversa Show", is described as a "Conservative Libertarian Radio Talk Show". Jim Lagnese co hosts the show with Andre Controversa, whose actual name is Andre Traversa,

The "Controversa" name makes the title a play on words as he likens himself to a bull in a china shop that spreads controversy wherever he goes by sticking up for conservative principles against the liberal masses. If you are interested, the Facebook page for "The Andre Controversa Show" has a picture, which uses the cover of "Atlas Shrugged" as its profile picture.[79]

In this particular post, cited here[80] with full link, Jim Lagnese wants to put a controversy to rest to clear the air about a previous show when he was not there to assume his co hosting duties apparently. He said he wasn't really trying to defend Ayn Rand with respect to her love of Hickman but he wanted to clear up some misrepresentations that the previous guest had made about the incident.

He spends the whole lengthy post with a very well written and thoughtful listing of the things that he admired about Rand, including the Objectivist belief, while acknowledging that sometimes Ayn wasn't so nice to people around her.

He closes with this last paragraph, which I will offer here in its entirety so I do not mischaracterize his thoughts. I will say they are consistent with every defense I have seen made of Rand by her followers. Almost all of them know of the Hickman incident but they rationalize her fawning over Hickman, like she was a teenager writing a love letter to Justin Bieber, with arguments like this one.

I accept his explanation, not as moral justification for Ayn but as a gateway to understanding those who would study every word of her lifetime of writing and speaking as if it were the Gospel and they were St. Paul with no other choice but to spread it.

Quoting Lagnese fully with not exclusion or editing, all punctuation and spelling are in the original:

> *"Now, as far as William Hickman goes, Joe Carter was trying to disparage and dismiss Rand based on some infatuation she had with a sociopath when she was very young. We all do stupid things, and if Mr. Carter is the christian he says he is, may be he could find some compassion in his heart for her, instead of using it as an a priori argument against Objectivism, in my opinion, primarily because it is at opposition to many belief systems, including his own.*
>
> *I can also tell you that while I have tried to integrate rational and objectivist systems with christian beliefs. So far I have to say it's a no go. One of them is incorrect. Ayn Rand herself said there are no contradictions, only incorrect premises. So which one is incorrect? The one where we know what we know, or the fairytale? Thomas Jefferson wrangled with the same arguments and came to some interesting conclusions with which I tend to agree.*[81]

That's fair enough. Ayn was young, a kid of 23, incidentally four years older than Hickman who committed his noble deed, and eleven years older than the child who would remain throughout eternity at that age.

Is this relevant to the discussion? Should any of us hold this against Ayn? After all she was only 23, a mere child, and she had not perfected her philosophy of "Objectivism". Heck when I was 23 I had a mullet. I certainly wouldn't want that resurrected. Her apologists, and it might shock you as to how many try to minimize this misplaced affection, all say she was wrapped up in the philosophy of Friedrich Nietzsche, this was just a phase she went through.

Friedrich Nietzsche, in case you aren't familiar with him, was the radical philosopher who declared God dead and inspired another charismatic leader, Adolph Hitler. Nietzsche began a "Campaign against Morality" and referred to himself an "immoralist". He called the establishment of moral systems based on a dichotomy of good and evil a "calamitous error" and wished to initiate a re-evaluation of the values of the Judeo-Christian world.[82]

Ayn always got really defensive when she was compared with Nietzsche. She wanted to make sure we knew she thought of all his ideas first, never mind the fact he passed away five years before her birth. You may draw your own conclusions from the fact that he died in an asylum after going insane.

She's right in the sense that she can take credit for this one, not Nietzsche. If you are an Objectivist, you have no reason to apologize for worshiping Hickman. He fulfills the requirements to the core as living a virtuous life. Selfish? Check. Self centered? Check. Living out his most base and selfish whims with no regard for the masses or their values, or notion of self-restraint? Big check here.

William Hickman was born fifty years too early. Had he been around in the 1970's, he could have done a "twofer" and picked up the Ayn Rand Merit Badge for Selfishness and Deification in the Church of Satan in one simple act of butchery.

One quick look at the Ayn Rand inspired Nine Statements of Satanism shows Hickman pretty much hit for the cycle. The Nine Satanic Statements are as follows:

1. Satan represents indulgence, instead of abstinence!

2. Satan represents vital existence, instead of spiritual pipe dreams!

3. Satan represents undefiled wisdom, instead of hypocritical self-deceit!

4. Satan represents kindness to those who deserve it, instead of love wasted on ingrates!

5. Satan represents vengeance, instead of turning the other cheek!

6. Satan represents responsibility to the responsible, instead of concern for psychic vampires!

7. Satan represents man as just another animal, sometimes better, more often worse than those that walk on all fours, who, because of his "divine spiritual and intellectual development, has become the most vicious animal of all!

8. Satan represents all of the so-called sins, as they all lead to physical, mental, or emotional gratification!

87

9. Satan is the best friend the church has ever had, as he has kept it in business all these years![83]

I haven't seen an official ruling yet but I'd say Hickman deserves nine for nine in this checklist, including the last one. I imagine his adventure caused a great many people to seek comfort in the church after reading of his beautiful soul that made Ayn swoon so.

Every tenet, every value of Objectivism is on display here where one lives for the self, denies nothing, and crushes anyone that stands in his or her way.

It's the morality of doing whatever one wishes, for whatever selfish desire he or she craves with no regard for anyone else; as long as they have the power, the means, and the strength enough in willpower to follow it through.

It's the morality of a new age: proposed by Nietzsche, perfected by Ayn Rand, plagiarized by Satanists, and propagated by the Republican Party as policy. Paul Ryan states that he is in politics for one reason, which is the influence of Ayn Rand. He repeats over and over to anyone that will listen, and I quote:

"Ayn Rand, more than anyone else, did a fantastic job of explaining the morality of capitalism, the morality of individualism. And this to me is what matters the most."[84]

Nietzsche called for a new morality. Ayn's apologists insist loudly that he only talked of it and Ayn actually had the guts to invent one. There is no condemnation of Nietzsche from Objectivists unless you count their sneers that he did it half assed and didn't finish the job.

Think that's just hyperbole on my part? Consider this scathing review of historian Jennifer Burns' book on Ayn Rand. As I have noted, Jennifer Burns was not a fan of Rand, but she presented the truth of Rand's life, warts and all, in her book "Ayn Rand: Goddess of the Market". If you feel need to research Ayn any more, get this book. It is well researched, scholarly, and not tied to or associated in any way with Ayn Rand's followers or organizations; per chance you might have moral qualms about putting more money in their pockets.

The scathing review, written by one Edwin Locke, is proudly featured on his website. He lists it at the top so you can't miss it. He's not ashamed to say he is a follower of Rand. His latest book is based on Ayn Rand's theories of romance. The title is called "The Selfish Path to Romance".[85] I'll wait for the movie.

But, back to the review. It is 27 pages and contains 51 objections to Burns' book, which included plenty of details about Hickman. Locke had one praise for Burns' book, but 51 objections.

The praise is a pat on the back to Burns for recognizing and acknowledging that her *"book contains many correct statements about events in Ayn Rand's life (based on my knowledge), including her great popularity as a speaker and guest on TV shows."*[86] That was the only praise.

The negatives, all 51 of them, can be summarized thusly, as he did in the second paragraph. Quoting again:

> *"The most critical errors Burns is guilty of are superficiality and misrepresentation, specifically the failure to understand and present the essentials of Ayn Rand's total philosophy as an integrated whole."*
>
> *"More fundamentally, Burns does not really take ideas seriously. A recurring theme of the book amounts to: "Why couldn't Rand be less rigid, less focused on consistency and just get along with people?" (examples are given below). Most people's philosophies are a random collection of bromides, half-digested ideas and unanalyzed emotions. However, this is not true of Ayn Rand. You cannot understand her at all without understanding her philosophy. She is her philosophy—she meant it and lived it.*[87]

So, if we understand Locke's beef with the book, it's not because of any factual errors but because of the author's lack of appropriate shock and awe for Ayn's greatness.

Locke proceeds with a 51-point tirade because Rand wasn't treated with the seriousness she deserved. Note that Locke never mentioned Hickman at all. The closest reference you might contort to being about Hickman was Locke's reference about Nietzsche.

In the following passage, Locke responds to
Professor Burns' recounting the claim of one of Ayn's
cousins made that Nietzsche beat Ayn Rand to all her
ideas. Locke lays this lie to rest six feet deep with a shovel
full of dirt in its face. Quoting from Locke's review:

> "Burns cites a quote from a cousin of Ayn Rand's
> who said: Nietzsche "beat you to all your ideas." But Burns
> does not mention here that the claim was not true. Even later
> in the book Burns indicates she does not get it (p. 303-4,
> Note 4).
>
> Ayn Rand's view of Nietzsche was made clear in
> her introduction to the 25th anniversary edition of The
> Fountainhead. For a time when she was younger she admired
> Nietzsche, but as she developed her own philosophy, she
> came to totally reject Nietzsche's philosophy, because was it
> mystical and irrational—the complete antithesis of her own
> philosophy. She admired certain quotes from Nietzsche such
> as "the noble soul has reverence for itself."
>
> Ironically, such a quote could not even be rationally
> defended without Ayn Rand's philosophy at its base.
> Nietzsche's alleged individualism had nothing in common
> with Ayn Rand's which was based on reason.[88]

Note the last paragraph. This scholar did not
condemn the association with Nietzsche based on a
revulsion to the ideas. No, he just considered Nietzsche a
mere poseur. Observe Locke's scornful, "Nietzsche's
alleged individualism had nothing in common with Ayn's
philosophy", as if Nietzsche were all hat and no cattle.
Locke continues with the last line:

> Nietzsche may have called for a new morality, but
> he did not provide one. Ayn Rand did.[89]

Don't dismiss Edwin A. Locke as just some
lunatic. He could very well be a lunatic, I grant you that,
but he has some respect in the world of thinkers. His
website has his vita linked within the link to this review. In
it one may find all of his academic papers that he has
published, and links where one might buy all of his books.
He has recorded lectures on all sorts of wisdom for you to
download.

Locke also has an opening paragraph, where he
introduces himself, on the off chance that you haven't
heard of him:

Edwin A. Locke, Ph.D., is Dean's Professor
(Emeritus) of Leadership and Motivation at the R.H. Smith
School of Business at the University of Maryland, College
Park. He received his BA from Harvard in 1960 and his
Ph.D. in Industrial Psychology from Cornell University in
1964.[20]

Edwin is a serious academic , a graduate of
Harvard and Cornell with 12 books under his belt, he has
"published over 290 chapters, notes and articles in
professional journals, on such subjects as work motivation,
job satisfaction, incentives, and the philosophy of science"[91]
Locke has been *"elected a Fellow of the American*
Psychological Association, the American Psychological
Society, the Academy of Management, and has been a
consulting editor for leading journals.

He was a winner of the Outstanding Teacher-
Scholar Award at the University of Maryland, the
Distinguished Scientific Contribution Award of the Society
for Industrial and Organizational Psychology, the Career
Contribution Award from the Academy of Management
(Human Resource Division), the Lifetime Achievement
Award from the Academy of Management (Organizational
Behavior Division), and the James McKeen Cattell Fellow
Award from the American Psychological Society.

He is a writer and lecturer for the Ayn Rand
Institute and is interested in the application of the
philosophy of Objectivism to behavioral sciences.[92]

What should impress you the most is that Locke
is a Professor Emeritus at the University of Maryland in
the School of Business in "Leadership and Motivation",
although it does make one wonder if his method of
motivating underlings is consistent with Ayn's philosophy
and less like today's pampered workforce and more like
Simon Legree's? But nevertheless, that's quite impressive.

Dr. Locke is a professor emeritus at the number 4 ranked business school in the U.S., according to the Financial Times. His field, Management, is only #15 in the country in prestige, according to the Wall Street Journal.[93] These rankings are from 2010, so things possibly could have changed if word got out about his worship of Rand. But somehow I doubt that her influence bothers many business schools today.

Shocked at how revered Ayn is by this gentleman? You shouldn't be. Ayn Rand studies are required in most prestigious business schools in this country including some backwater schools you might have heard of such as the University of Texas, the University of North Carolina, and my wife's alma mater, Duke University.

Ayn Rand's followers are very wealthy and they include John Allison, the former CEO of the mega bank, BB&T. John Allison is a devout Objectivist. He has donated hundreds of thousands of dollars to Ayn Rand's foundation. No, make that millions. Here's a gushing account linked on a forum for Ayn Rand fans appropriately found at an Ayn Rand message board. It includes a link to the official press release from the University of North Carolina, Greensboro, boasting of Allison's generous gift:

> "A $1 million gift from the BB&T Charitable Foundation to the Bryan School of Business and Economics at UNCG will strengthen students' understanding of the moral foundations of our economic system.
>
> The gift will establish the BB&T Program in Capitalism, Markets and Morality. The program will offer undergraduate and graduate students from disciplines across UNCG the opportunity to examine the ethical and philosophical basis for free market economies.
>
> "Unfortunately, we find that many students who graduate with business degrees while understanding the 'technology' of business, do not have a clear grasp of the moral principles underlying free markets," said John Allison IV, chairman and executive officer of BB&T Corporation.

> *"This program matches our shared interests in giving students a fair and balanced perspective on capitalism and free markets and in giving students across the UNCG campus a better understanding of our economy and greater ability to make meaningful contributions to our world," said Dr. James K. Weeks, dean of the Bryan School of Business and Economics.* [94]

So much here to take in. Take a moment and read this again. The title of the program he created? "Capitalism, Markets, and Morality" created by a $1 million donation from a man who identifies himself as an "Objectivist." Does this bother you?

How about this quote from Allison:

> *"Unfortunately, we find that many students who graduate with business degrees while understanding the 'technology' of business, do not have a clear grasp of the moral principles underlying free markets,"* [95]

That is so awesome! It's about time we had colleges and universities teaching young, uber-ambitious Gordon Gekko wanna-bes that there has to be morality in business. I hope that they stress the dangers and the evils of unadulterated greed, as it leads to a world of Enron, Bernie Madoff, and Wall Street circa 1929 and 2008.

Do you think they will, particularly since "Atlas Shrugged" is required reading? Just for giggles, go to the site linked below that is run by Clemson University. Clemson University received a major donation from Allison's old bank BB&T for its tax exempt charity, which is devoted to spreading the morality of capitalism. It's an informative link called the Capitalism Resources Home, and it notes that "the BB&T Charitable Foundation has created sixty programs at colleges and universities around the country to study the moral foundations of capitalism. Although each of these programs differs in its composition and mission, all are united by a commitment to teaching and research on the moral foundation of capitalism" [96]

You can find this direct quote, as to their goals, at this site along with all of the major colleges that teach Ayn Rand's new morality. I bet you recognize quite a few names.

All this time you thought that colleges were only corrupted by the liberal professors, didn't you? You thought that the only threat to little Johnny and little Ann were from fat, pony tailed, aging hippy liberals, who sanctimoniously preach about solar energy and no nukes.

Nope, the business schools, as servants of business, are all about true American values; or should I say value in the singular, greed?

However, it's worse than you think. The Rand disciples are so aggressive and you don't even know it. No need to worry that little Johnny and little Ann turn commie, the real fear should be that they will change their names to little Johnny Galt and little Ayn.

The capitalists are coming for your kids. Be very afraid. Ayn stated clearly she wanted a new morality; she had Paul Ryan from hello with that. A blogger such as "The Right Guy" might not be sophisticated enough to know the mission, but a highly educated, widely respected scholar like Dr. Locke certainly gets it. He has studied her, read her, and he knows how to grind her philosophy through the rigors of critical analysis.

In Dr. Locke's attack on Professor Burns for not taking Ayn Rand seriously, he speaks with absolute clarity about Ayn's goals; just as Ayn did and just as Paul Ryan is currently doing. It's not about capitalism, it's about something greater. To return briefly to Locke's review of Jennifer Burns' book:

> *"p. 63: Burns says that Ayn Rand viewed capitalism as "the solution to all ills." Clearly, Burns is taking conventional literary license here, but again, it is a careless formulation.*
>
> *What Burns should have said here is that Ayn Rand held that capitalism is the solution to poverty or, more broadly, the only means of large-scale wealth creation. (Of course, more fundamentally, Ayn Rand regarded it as the only moral economic system.) The closest thing to a solution to all ills would be her entire philosophy."[7]*

The philosophy that is Ayn Rand's? With selfishness being the highest morality, charity being pure evil. With no support for any of life's downtrodden.

Democracy must never stand in front of the individual, so disenfranchisement is an option; correction, make that the only solution.

No assaults on reason are to be allowed so God would have to die, that is if Ayn Rand had not killed Him first.

There are two levels of people, the virtuous rich, and the rest of us. According to Ayn Rand, the rest of us weren't even fit enough to judge William Hickman.

I'll leave the last word in this chapter to my intellectual better, Dr. Edwin Locke, and acknowledge his point. He is correct.

"The closest thing to a solution to all ills would be her entire philosophy.[98]*"*

SOURCES CONSULTED FOR CHAPTER 2

[1] Thackeray, W.M., *Vanity Fair* 1848: Boston, Fields, Osgood & Company. P. 165

[2] Plotz, D. *"Charles Colson: How a Watergate crook became America's greatest Christian conservative"* Slate Friday, March 10, 2000 Available from: http://www.slate.com/id/77067/.

[3] Ibid

[4] Ibid

[5] Ibid

[6] Ibid

[7] Ibid

[8] Ibid

[9] *Prison Fellowship Programs; Available from:* http://www.prisonfellowship.org/prison-fellowship-programs.

[10] *Search_Results. "Fox News & Atlas Shrugged". Fox News Website; Available from:* http://www.foxnews.com/topics/entertainment/movies/atlas-shrugged.htm.

[11] *McNary, D. "Cameras roll on 'Atlas' Production ends 30-year trek to bring pic to screen" Variety Mon., Jun. 14, 2010 Available from:* http://www.variety.com/article/VR1118020578?refCatId=4026.

[12] Ibid

[13] *Argetsinger, R.R.a.A. "Read This: "Atlas Shrugged" Movie Promoted at CPAC" Washington Post 02/12/2011 Available from:* http://voices.washingtonpost.com/reliable-source/2011/02/read_this_atlas_shrugged_movie.html.

[14] *Hash, T. "Atlas Shrugged, The Obama High-Speed Rail Promotion Movie" 02/12/2011 Red State Electric 02/12/2011; Available from:* http://redstateeclectic.typepad.com/redstate_commentary/2011/02/atlas-shrugged-the-obama-high-speed-rail-promotion-movie.html.

[15] *Hannity, S. "Stossel: Why Hollywood Was Against the "Atlas Shrugged" Film" March 9, 201 Fox News Insider March 9, 2011; Available from:* http://foxnewsinsider.com/2011/03/09/stossel-why-hollywood-was-against-the-"atlas-shrugged"-film/.

[16] *Kibbe, M. "A Movie For The Tea Party" April 12, 2011 Why Freedom Works April 12, 2011; Available from:* http://blogs.forbes.com/mattkibbe/2011/04/12/a-movie-for-the-tea-party-movement/.

[17] *Colson, C. "Atlas Shrugged and So Should You". Date May 11, 2011; Available from:* http://www.colsoncenter.org/twominutewarning/entry/33/17003.

[18] *Hernandez, R. "Gingrich Calls G.O.P.'s Medicare Plan Too Radical" New York Times May 15, 2011 Available from:* http://www.nytimes.com/2011/05/16/us/politics/16gingrich.html?_r=1.

[19] *Rand, A. "Moral Judgement"; Available from:* http://aynrandlexicon.com/lexicon/moral_judgment.html.

[20] Bidinotto, R.J. *"Synopsis of the Plot of Atlas Shrugged".*; Available from: http://www.atlassociety.org/synopsis-plot-atlas-shrugged

[21] Rand, A. *Introducing Objectivism.*; Available from: http://www.aynrand.org/site/PageServer?pagename=Objectivism_intro

[22] *Rand, A. "Absolutes". Ayn Rand Lexicon; Available from:* http://aynrandlexicon.com/lexicon/absolutes.html.

[23] Peikoff, L., *The Philosophy of Objectivism*, L. Peikof, Editor 1976. Available from: http://aynrandlexicon.com/lexicon/democracy.html

[24] *"who is john galt".* Date 02/09.09; Available from: http://www.whoisjohngalt.com/2009/02/who-is-john-galt.html

[25] "who is john galt". Date 02/09.09; Available from: http://www.whoisjohngalt.com/2009/05/giving-back.html
[26] Rand, A. "Charity". Ayn Rand Lexicon; Available from: http://aynrandlexicon.com/lexicon/charity.html
[27] Ibid
[28] Peikoff, L., "About the Lexicon, H. Binswanger, Editor January 1986, Available from: http://aynrandlexicon.com/book/intro.html
[29] Rand, A. "Faith". Ayn Rand Lexicon Date; Available from: http://aynrandlexicon.com/lexicon/rationality.html#order_2
[30] Rand, A., Atlas Shrugged 1957, New York, New York: Signet Books. P. 993
[31] Rand, A. "Altruism". Ayn Rand Lexicon Date; Available from: http://aynrandlexicon.com/lexicon/altruism.html#order_1
[32] Rand, A. "Political Power versus Economic Power". The Ayn Rand Lexicon Date; Available from: http://aynrandlexicon.com/lexicon/economic_power_vs_political_power.html#order_2
[33] Smith, A., The Wealth of Nations (1776). Available from: http://www.online-literature.com/adam_smith/wealth_nations/
[34] Luke 21: 1-4 "As Jesus looked up, he saw the rich putting their gifts into the temple treasury. He also saw a poor widow put in her two mites. "Truly I tell you," he said, "this poor widow has put in more than all the others. All these people gave their gifts out of their wealth; but she out of her poverty put in all she had to live on."
[35] Adam, S., R. David Daiches, and A. Macfie, The theory of moral sentiments 1759; Available from: http://www.ibiblio.org/ml/libri/s/SmithA_MoralSentiments_p.pdf
[36] Burns, J., Goddess of the market: Ayn Rand and the American right 2009: Oxford University Press, USA. P. 9
[37] Ibid; P. 11-12
[38] Ibid; P. 9
[39] Ibid, P. 10
[40] Ibid.
[41] Ibid; P. 82.
[42] Ibid; P. 13.
[43] Ibid; P. 14.
[44] Ibid; P. 11.
[45] Ibid; P.1
[46] Walker, J., The Ayn Rand Cult 1999: Open Court. P. 1
[47] Branden, B., The Passion of Ayn Rand 1986: Doubleday. P. 71.
[48] Internet Movie Database listing The King of Kings 1927
[49] Aristotle's Logic Stanford Enclyclopedia of Philosophy
[50] Branden, B., The Passion of Ayn Rand P. 35
[51] Branden, B., The Passion of Ayn Rand 1986: Doubleday. P. 80-81.
[52] Definition: the Messiah prophesied in the Old Testament (used chiefly in versions of the New Testament). Greek chrīstos anointed, translation of Hebrew māshīaḥ anointed, Messiah. Available from: http://dictionary.reference.com/browse/christ
[53] Burns, J., Goddess of the market: Ayn Rand and the American right P. 21.
[54] Ibid; P. 22.
[55] Rand, A., D. Harriman, and L. Peikoff, Journals of Ayn Rand 1999: Plume Books.
[56] David Harriman Biographical Information. Date; Available from: http://www.aynrand.org/site/News2?id=5256
[57] Rand, A., D. Harriman, and L. Peikoff, Journals of Ayn Rand 1999: Plume Books. P. 22

[58] Gado, M. *"My Baby is Missing!"* Criminal Mind; Available from: http://www.trutv.com/library/crime/criminal_mind/psychology/child_abduction/6.html.
[59] The Associated Press, Text of Hickman's Confession The New York Times December 23, 1927 Available from: Text of Hickman's Confession New York Times Archives (Pay Access)
[60] End of the Long Chase New York Times December 22, 1927 Available from: Hickman Captured New York Times Archives (Pay Access)
[61] Ibid;
[62] Ibid;
[63] Ibid;
[64] Ibid;
[65] Ibid;
[66] Ibid;
[67] Photocopy of original note. Available from http://i196.photobucket.com/albums/aa47/flower_child67/crime/MarianParker/mariannote.jpg
[68] Rand, A., D. Harriman, and L. Peikoff, *Journals of Ayn Rand* 1999: Plume Books. No page number, ebook Kindle edition Location 730 of 13849.
[69] Ibid, Location 899 of 13849.
[70] Ibid;
[71] Ibid, Location 916 of13849
[72] Ibid;
[73] Ibid, Location 959 of 13849
[74] Ibid, Location 1043 of 13849
[75] Ibid;
[76] Ibid;
[77] Ibid;
[78] www.therightguyshow.com
[79] The Andre Controversa Show Facebook page available from http://www.facebook.com/pages/The-Andre-Controversa-Show/190403097655211
[80] Traversa, A. Ayn Rand, William Hickman and other idiots September 05, 2010; Available from: http://www.therightguyshow.com/2010/09/ayn-rand-william-hickman-and-other.html
[81] Ibid
[82] *Nietzsche's Moral and Political Philosophy.*; Available from: http://plato.stanford.edu/entries/nietzsche-moral-political/
[83] Available from http://www.churchofsatan.com/Pages/NineStatements.html
[84] Beam, C. *"The Trouble With Liberty"*. New York Magazine Date Dec 26, 2010 Available from: http://nymag.com/print/?/news/politics/70282/index1.html.
[85] http://www.edwinlocke.com
[86] Locke, E.A., *Comments on Jennifer Burns's Goddess of the Market: Ayn Rand and the American Right*, 2011 Available from http://www.edwinlocke.com/Edwin_A_Locke_Comments_on_Burns.pdf
[87] Ibid
[88] Ibid
[89] Ibid
[90] http://www.edwinlocke.com
[91] Ibid
[92] Ibid
[93] *Fast Facts & Rankings.* ; Available from: http://www.rhsmith.umd.edu/about/facts.aspx

[94] http://forums.4aynrandfans.com/index.php?showtopic=4887
[95] Ibid;
[96] Available from ___
http://www.clemson.edu/capitalism/capres/bbtp/bbtp.html
[97] Locke, E.A., *Comments on Jennifer Burns's Goddess of the Market: Ayn Rand and the American Right*, 2011 Available from
http://www.edwinlocke.com/Edwin_A_Locke_Comments_on_Burns.pdf
[98] Ibid.

GEORGE KELLEY

CHAPTER 3:WHO IS JOHN GALT'S MAMA?

> *In the infatuation of the moment, Wolfgang avowed his passion for her. He told her the story of his mysterious dream, and how she had possessed his heart before he had even seen her.*
>
> *She was strangely affected by his recital, and acknowledge to have felt an impulse towards him equally unaccountable. It was the time for wild theory and wild actions. Old prejudices and superstitions were done away; everything was under the sway of the "Goddess of Reason."*
>
> *Among other rubbish of the old times, the forms and ceremonies of marriage began to be considered superfluous bonds for honorable minds. Social compacts were the vogue. Wolfgang was too much of theorist not to be tainted by the liberal doctrines of the day.*
>
> *"Why should we separate?" said he: "our heart are united; in the eyes of reason and honor we are as one. What need is there of sordid forms to bind high souls together?"*

washington irving
"the adventure of a german
student", 1824

Merriam-Webster defines art as "the conscious use of skill and creative imagination especially in the production of aesthetic objects",[2] or you might be able to simplify the definition as merely *creating from imagination*. What separates good art from bad art? That is subjective, as good art, as is beauty, is in the eye of the beholder.

If I may be so bold, I'd like to offer my definition of good art, and consequently its antithesis, bad art. I think the most precise definition of good art would be art that conveys truth.

To be precise, art can be anything that is created, such as a painting, sculpture, a novel, or even a situation comedy. Good art, as defined by the truth standard I am presenting, is art that reflects a truth in life we all see and recognize.

If you look at a basic example, one could see the artistic merit in Norman Rockwell, as his paintings are so realistic that they represent true moments in time, or at least moments the viewer can relate to. Any work by Michelangelo would meet this truth standard, as his works appear to be snapshots of life, all created by his hand.

This is not to say that only the hyperrealist styles contain truth, it can be found in abstract art also. Those who appreciate it recognize emotions and moods, which reflect a different reality. Art need not be considered highbrow to invoke truth; one can appreciate "Dogs Playing Poker" and imagine a bulldog having the audacity to put an extra ace in his paw.

Movies require what is called a suspension of disbelief in order to work with the audience. That is to say, the audience is required to suspend its disbelief in order to accept the fantasy storyline.

When this device works, it works well. Even a movie such as "King Kong" works, if one can visualize real people reacting the way the people in the movie do if real people were to face the possibility of a giant ape on the loose in New York.

The eternal debate of Mary Ann versus Ginger on "Gilligan's Island" assumes the viewer has enough real world experience to have a preference for either the girl next door or a high maintenance model type. This preference will be decided based on the individual's concept of truth, as it relates to the type of girl you find hot enough to live with on a humid tropical island.

So with respect to Ayn Rand and her cult, which consists of her actual disciples in her lifetime along with today's generation of sycophants, one should realize the influence of Ayn Rand's art on them and examine it to determine if it does contain a recognizable truth. The reality for objectivists, their truth, is in "Atlas Shrugged", supplemented with Ayn's other works. It is their Bible. They justify their worldview based not only on the theme of the book, but also on the characters and their thoughts, sayings and reactions. The believers look hard in the real world for the archetypes of these truths. It goes without saying that they will *ALWAYS* contort reality to suit their egocentric view, where they will be the heroes of Ayn Rand land, and their adversaries, which is anyone that challenges their selfish worldview, will be the villains of "Atlas Shrugged". Ayn Rand's bad guys are always portrayed with the nuance of Dudley Do-Right's Snidely Whiplash. For the Objectivists, the world is sharply defined between the good and bad, the producers and the leeches, between the individual and the collectivists.

This view is the view of a fundamentalist doctrinaire believer, which is dangerous in almost any setting. All of us have witnessed the damage to society from fundamentalists of all stripes; be they religious fundamentalists such as Islamic terrorists or murderers of abortion doctors, or political fundamentalists such as Timothy McVeigh.

The problem with fundamentalism is that the fundamentalist always knows the answers before any question is given, which will result in a refusal to examine any other worldview, option, or perspective.

Objectivists certainly fall into this category, as they view only one solution to the world's ills, Ayn Rand's new morality, as evidenced by Professor Locke's statement presented at the end of the last chapter. Ayn created, or at least took credit for creating, her philosophy and new morality through a lifetime of writing and proselytizing.

As we shall soon see, this proselytizing continues even today, more aggressively than she ever did, and with a huge financial backing from book sales and wealthy believers.

Ayn Rand's philosophy of Objectivism was perfected in "Atlas Shrugged", but everything she published up till then contained most elements of it. An astute reader can easily see the consistency and evolution of her thought throughout her life. For instance, with respect to her delightful infatuation with the barbaric animal, William Hickman, mentioned in the previous chapter, Ayn never got over her first love.

Ayn maintained a love for the so-called virtues she saw in Hickman, and developed them in a more sophisticated way.

She had originally planned on modeling a character named Danny Renahan after Hickman, and hoped to feature him as the hero in an unfinished novel she called "The Little Street". [3] But even after she abandoned that project her love for her old flame burned on.

Novelist Michael Prescott on his website finds a couple of interesting entries in her journals, where she wrote about the character of her character Howard Roark, the hero of "The Fountainhead".

This novel became her first major commercial success and served as a magnet for the young, hungry intellects that became her cult. Ayn had used many of the same descriptive phrases that she used for the butcher Hickman, verbatim at times, in describing her new fictional hero Howard Roark. Quoting Prescott:

"In her early notes for *"The Fountainhead"*: "One puts oneself above all and crushes everything in one's way to get the best for oneself. Fine!" (Journals, p. 78.)[citations in original]

Of *"The Fountainhead's hero, Howard Roark*: He "has learned long ago, with his first consciousness, two things which dominate his entire attitude toward life: his own superiority and the utter worthlessness of the world." (Journals, p. 93.)[4]"

I should add that Ayn instilled in Howard Roark's personality another trait she found admirable, that of a rapist. Roark has a famous, or infamous, scene in the novel, where he rapes his love interest, Dominique Francon. Don't take this the wrong way, because as you will soon see, she loved it.

Here is a funny, both "ha-ha" and ironic funny, defense of the act by an Ayn sycophant on a website called www.braincrave.com, which I found via Google search. Let me tell you about braincrave.com. Its members "crave brains", not in a Hannibal Lector kind of way, although no doubt Hannibal would have loved "Atlas Shrugged" and Ayn Rand would have surely reciprocated.

The website is a dating site for people who are really intelligent and crave really intelligent people. Notwithstanding the fact that there are reasonably bright people on other dating sites such as eharmony.com, or even available in real life to meet. The ridiculously intelligent among us seem to require targeted marketing. Some have found themselves to be way too clever for the common every day *hoi polloi*, so extra diligence is necessary in matchmaking.

As you can very well imagine this type of self-awareness requires maximum self-esteem. So who would be best suited for this type of extraordinary courtship? The know-it-all, egocentric, virtuously selfish members of Ayn Rand's cult, the Objectivists, that's who. These people have already secured ultimate knowledge and are fully qualified as Rand Storm Troopers to combat anti-reason and anti-individual forces wherever they may encounter them, even in a TGIFriday's bar during a first date meeting. Loaded potato skins and frozen margaritas can go a long way in establishing objective reality and revealing mutually agreed upon selfish desires. Before consummating their selfishness, you could imagine randy Randites taking time to scold the management about the "G" in TGIFriday's, while they sneer at the chain's adherence to mysticism.

Anyhow, this site was founded for the Ayn Rand types, by one of their own. An examination of the LinkedIn profile of creator and CEO Brian Lovett reveals his interests listed right off the bat as "reading, Ayn Rand (e.g., The Fountainhead, Atlas Shrugged)"[5] If you snoop around a bit at the profiles on his actual site, you will see many references to individualism, freedom, and selfishness, just the type of buzzwords one would expect from a Rand inspired dating site.

There is intrinsic humor in the existence of a dating site for brainiacs and not just brainiacs, but the self-aware super geniuses that are too brilliant for the rank and file single person. It also gives us a generous dose of irony.

One distinguishing feature of this service is that members of this site have a blog, in order to better express themselves through the written word and what better way for high IQ Romeos to seduce their soul mates than with a writing sample?

The excerpt below really showcases this ironic humor with some super nerd using his blog space to express his brilliance through a written defense of rape written in order to project his desirability for a date. Talk about a first date icebreaker.

The member named "bindependent" shares his thoughts on the "alleged" rape in the novel "The Fountainhead". He explains to us it isn't really rape if she enjoys it after the fact. Quoting "bindependent" and his explanation of the act, along with his cut and paste of the relevant passages in "The Fountainhead":

"I think Dominique did consent to the sex, wanted it, and even encouraged it through her actions. Within the scene, there are multiple facts to support my contentions. (There are even more if you include other passages surrounding the scene and overall character development.)

For example, Ayn Rand writes, "She fought like an animal. But she made no sound. She did not call for help." (bottom of p. 216).

She goes on: "He did it as an act of scorn. Not as love, but as defilement. And this made her lie still and submit. One gesture of tenderness from him - and she would have remained cold, untouched by the things done to her body. But the act of a master taking shameful, contemptuous possession of her was the kind of rapture she had wanted." ...

In fact, after Roark leaves, Ayn Rand writes (middle of p. 219): "She could accept, thought Dominique, and come to forget in time everything that had happened to her, save one memory: that she had found pleasure in the thing which had happened, that he had known it, and more: that he had known it before he came to her and that he would not have come but for that knowledge. She had not given him the one answer that would have saved her: an answer of simple revulsion - she had found joy in her revulsion, in her terror and in his strength. That was the degradation she had wanted and she hated him for it."

When Dominique is reading a letter from Alvah Scarret: "She read it and smiled. She thought, if they knew... those people... the old life and that awed reverence before her person. I've been raped... I've been raped by some redheaded hoodlum from a stone quarry... I, Dominique Francon... Through the fierce sense of humiliation, the words gave her the same kind of pleasure she had felt in his arms."[6]

The beauty of being a Rand cultist is that since your only reality comes from the works of Ayn Rand, you can defend anything by quoting the thoughts of her imaginary characters and you can therefore exonerate, or even elevate Ayn. For the record, Ayn Rand features rape in other works as well and never in a negative light. The biographer Jennifer Burns quipped, quite cleverly I must say out of envy, that in Ayn Rand's world, "Lovers don't hold hands, they hold wrists".[7]

But I do not want to give you the impression that I am typecasting Ayn as a one trick pony who is only interested in the glorification of violent sociopaths. The fascination with violent sexual crimes was just a hobby; her true love was always the real master of selfishness, the white-collar criminal.

The inspiration for one of her characters named Bjorn Faulkner in her play "Night of January 16" came from the Bernie Madoff of her day: a smooth talking, Ponzi-scheme promoting Swede named Ivar Kreuger.

Kreuger ran a massive con that bilked investors by making promises of creating monopolies in matches. Not in the braincrave.com way, but in the creating of fire by tiny chemically altered sticks.

Kreuger was called the "Match King" of Sweden, as he owned the market there with a monopoly. He persuaded investors that they too could strike it rich with matches if only they invested in his scheme to expand his empire.

Everyone wanted a piece of this action, so much so that his stock became the most widely held stock in the world during the 1920's. He was paying out a whopping 20% return per year in cash through dividends.

But alas, if it seems too good to be true, it probably is. It became known that he was burning through cash at a faster rate than he would if he had taken one of his matches to his money.

In 1932, just as he was about to be arrested for securities fraud, he shot himself in the heart and extinguished the burning flame of life, most likely leaving the faint smell of smoldering sulfur just as his matches would as a foreshadowing of his next destination.

The good old days when shame -or at least the threat of meaningful prison time-would drive high rent thieves to self impose a metaphoric Chapter 7 bankruptcy-where the damaged entity just dissolved out of existence-are sadly no longer around.

These days, we prefer the Chapter 13 bankruptcy reorganization metaphor, where debts are restructured; the losses are socialized so the little guy can feel like a big capitalist, or at least feel like a big capitalist SHOULD feel when he fails.

We now restructure the fraud so that we all can feel broke, dejected with a huge fine levied-in the form of taxes to pay for the excesses of capitalism. Kreuger should be commended for actually successfully piercing his heart, as it surely presented too small a target to hit without a scope and kudos to him for having enough courage to take the coward's way out.

Some scholars suggest that Kreuger was the biggest single influence upon the passage of government oversight of the markets,[8] and for that he could indeed be considered a hero.

It is doubtful that Ayn would have glamorized him had she connected those dots. Instead, she focused on the real foundation of his character with her fictionalization. She writes her character Faulkner as a ruthless businessman, but also as a victim in the truest sense, as he is dead at the beginning of the play and therefore the object of the plot. He had been a hard-nosed businessman who attempted to corner the world's gold market, and just for fun, he had raped his girlfriend, a character named Karen Andre.[9]

It seems Ayn never really got too far away from that theme. Karen reacted to her rape in a manner perfectly consistent with the truth in Ayn Rand's world; she fell in love with her rapist.

Someone had murdered him, or perhaps they didn't? The play was a whodunit, with Karen Andre as the prime suspect, and the audience serving as a jury. It was actually a clever concept; Ayn wrote two endings that satisfied either of the jury's verdicts.

Ayn used this play as a social laboratory experiment with the audience as the lab rats. The theme of the play was that individualism would drive the perception of morality; Ayn would pepper the dialogue with dog whistle type cues - silent non-obvious signals to reach subconscious allies - that promoted the superiority of individualists.

Karen Andre was a perfect Ayn Rand honey/heroine: she was an atheist, just like Ayn. She was driven by personal greed and her own morality, just like Ayn. She had contempt for societal values, just like Ayn. She was smoking hot and sexy, just like...uh, never mind. Nevertheless it was Ayn's contention that the more the audience/jury valued individualism, the more likely it would be that they would acquit Karen Andre.[10]

As I said earlier, it is pretty easy to justify anything if you create your own morality. Which begs the question as to whether the corporate sponsored "Morality of Capitalism and Ayn Rand" programs at colleges includes a sexual harassment in the workplace block of study, or do they just assume that the successful Radian will have enough money to compensate their victims for having the courage to come forward and admit that they loved it all along? Dominique Strauss-Kahn, the former head of the *International Monetary Fund*, could have learned a few things from Ayn Rand. Or maybe he did, given the outcome of his case?

This play, "The Night of January 16th", was somewhat successful and it inspired in her to answer a new calling, one better suited for her natural abilities as a towering intellect, which was to become the greatest philosopher of the past two millennium. She began a philosophy journal, and in it she acknowledged that it was merely "the vague beginnings of an amateur philosopher", but she quickly came to realize that she knew where she was going: "*I want to be known as the greatest champion of reason and the greatest enemy of religion".*[11]

Ayn felt that religion was public enemy number one to all the thinking men and woman out there. Mostly because established an impossible standard of behavior and was too abstract, it wasn't real world enough to suit her, it was a fantasy that could never be achieved.[12]

The foolishness passed off as morality in ancient myths contradicted her reality where criminals are heroes and rape victims gush "You had me at hello" to their attackers.

But on a lesser scale, Ayn detested religion because it promoted belief in unseen spirits and forces. I feel it relevant to note that Ayn had no problems believing in UFO's; as she reported nonchalantly to a friend she had seen one and knew for a fact it was an alien ship. [13] Some things can be accepted more easily than others.

But with the moderate success of the play in hand, she worked towards her long-term goal, which was to possibly capture financial success in the same net as she did philosophical purity.

Which brings us back to "The Fountainhead". Here, as noted before, she had refined a hero, Howard Roark, and she included in him all of the swell things about Hickman, without the distractions produced by the internal conflict that always results from the murderous creep/heroic individual dichotomy. She spared the reader the tension and doubt that all of us had with Hickman, where we all wondered if Hickman deserved to be charged with his ambiguous crimes.

This time, she had her hero in this book arrested and put on trial for an act without the moral uncertainty of the murder and dismemberment of children.

Ayn constructed a crime perpetrated by the hero in defense of his right to be an individual that would not and should not alienate any American. In fact, it inspired outrage in decent people everywhere who were incensed that such an act would be considered illegal to begin with.

In Ayn's book "The Fountainhead", Roark did not get arrested for murder, rape, or cornering the gold market, all of the little things we accept as basic issue in the toolbox of capitalism these days, but for the ridiculous "crime" of dynamiting a public housing project for poor people[14].

It is a testament to Ayn Rand's influence and just how far we have evolved morally in such a short period of time, where nowadays we laugh at the absurdity of anyone considering *THAT* wrong.

Howard Roark was therefore a more civilized manifestation of William Hickman, and Ayn planned on John Galt becoming the most perfect evolution of the singularly focused individual.

Her tweaking of the Hickman influences of Roark worked perfectly. Ayn was savvy enough to realize that an independent architect with a proud adherence to his creative principles would be received more favorably and sell more books than a leading man that was a demented child mutilator.

She did include the sexy-rapist-with-integrity personality quirk to her character to display the bad boy side of him and to entice her readers to swoon, just as she did in 1928. Ayn spoke of the rape as being "by engraved invitation"[15] and said that while it was sexy that Roark did what he wanted with no regard for morality and convention (much like Hickman); his victim, for lack of a more romantic word, actually liked it after all the dust and DNA had settled. Hickman never had that going for him.

Roark beats the rap for this housing project silliness by going to trial, and speaking to the jury on his own behalf. Roark sat through the entire trial, while he sneered at the prosecutor, and then asked to speak on his own behalf at the summation portion. Roark's delivery was paleo-John Galt, meaning it was a short, abbreviated, primitive beast that would later develop and grow into the refined eloquence that can only be achieved in a 70 something paged monologue.

Roark's speech is peppered with references to individualism where he tells the jury and we the readers these truths: that no creative person ever collaborated in creating, and that no collective minds have ever created, creativity only comes from individuals, the singular mind.

Therefore, if it is your ball, or low rent housing project for the poor, you can take it and go home (or blow it to smithereens as the case may be) anytime you wish. You made it, you can break it, kind of like the "you break it, you buy it" rule in reverse.

Notwithstanding the patently false premise present here, as that right doesn't exist in our world, the real one, (Ayn always did tell us to check your premise when we faced a moral dilemma) Roark hit a home run.

Roark's appeal to his own selfishness won the day and validated the morality of destroying the homes of the poor for ego driven purposes. Which suggests a possible inspiration for the most recent Wall Street destruction of the entire housing industry.

No man should ever compromise on his work for any reason. He created it, and he owns it, Hell yeah! When you boil it down to its basic form, it is the gospel of selfishness, just not as straightforward as what John Galt brought down on tablets from Mt. Ayn, but the same thing at its core.

"The Fountainhead" was in every way a success, bringing wealth to Ayn and her timid and mousy husband John O'Connor, and it inspired a movie that starred Gary Cooper and Patricia Neal.

This fame brought her adoration from people from all over the world, as they gushed over the portrayal of individualism they observed in the book and/or movie. [16] Ayn Rand created this reality for them, an artistic truth that they could latch on to and pattern a new way of living. She was more than glad to assist these searchers for truth and reality and point them in the right direction, which was towards her.

Just off the top of my head, one minor problem comes to mind, which is this reality comes strictly from Ayn Rand's twisted, drug addled mind.

I may have forgotten to mention, Ayn had quite the drug habit. She went through most of her adult life addicted to amphetamines. Her strange manic energy was a thing to behold, particularly for the people who did not know of her dependence upon pills.

Her cult, "The Collective" would marvel at how she could stay up all night lecturing them with more energy and alertness than even her young pups had who sat at her feet. [17] Ayn Rand's pill popping fetish explains perfectly Rush Limbaugh's adoration of her, birds of a feather and what not.

Medical experts say that long term or excessive use of amphetamines, which in Rand's case, both were present, can result in mood swings, a sour temper with a hair trigger, distorted judgment and paranoia. [18]

Thank goodness Ayn was able to avoid those nasty side effects, as she claimed the drugs only made her a better Ayn. One must assume the mood swings, the sour temper with a hair trigger, the distorted judgment and the paranoia that Ayn possessed were already there before she started popping pills from the figurative Pez dispenser. It might be that she had Charlie Sheen's "tiger blood" pumped through her veins by her cold, black heart, immunizing her to the dangerous effects that mere mortals would feel.

Besides, she noted, that if she really didn't need the pills, a doctor would not have prescribed them. [19] Apparently doctors had a higher degree of professionalism back in her day, long before they allowed self destructive celebrities such as Elvis and Michael Jackson unlimited access to their prescription pads.

But she kept on popping, and she kept on collecting a cult of youngsters along the way. She had a strong effect on teenagers, as they tend to be susceptible to flattery, or anything that would validate their typically self indulgent worldview. [20]

Who better to understand the morality behind the question "why should I help the poor?" than the segment of the population that has the philosophical curiosity to constantly ask "why do I need to go to bed so early?" or "why do I have to clean my room?" Objectivism is tailor made for teenagers, or any other immature personality that may view itself as the center of the universe.

This is where Ayn's story really gets weird. It's not like the signs weren't there before. But with success came fame and money and a bizarre group of followers emerged; a tribe of young, social misfits who fancied themselves intellectuals and sat at her feet, soaking up her wisdom. The youngsters weren't that impressive to adults and/or outsiders. Murray Rothbard, the economist, ceased attending Ayn's get-together because he became increasingly annoyed with the *"posturing, pretentious, humorless, robotic, nasty, simple-minded, ...dazzlingly ignorant people."*[21]

A case in point, two very influential members of her cult, husband and wife Nathan and Barbara Branden, fell hard for Ayn after reading "The Fountainhead" at fifteen.

Barbara and Nathan had met in Canada, their home country, as kids. They both read "The Fountainhead" over and over, and found it changed their lives.[22] Seeing as how that both were only fifteen at the time, I am pretty sure that their lives weren't really firmly established anyway.

The Brandens, Nathaniel (who preferred the nomenclature Nathan) and his wife Barbara, give you more than enough information to pass judgment upon Objectivism.

Let's first establish that Branden is a married name. Barbara's maiden name was Weidman, as in Barbara Weidman. Nathaniel's maiden name was Blumenthal, as in Nathaniel Blumenthal.

They both celebrated their marriage, with Ayn and Mrs. Ayn (Frank O'Connor) present and they changed both their surnames to Branden, which possessed in it, the word "Rand" with the remaining letters unscrambled to spell "Ben", which means "son of" in Hebrew, as any good Jewish boy such as Nathaniel could tell you.[23]

Mr. and Mrs. "Son of Rand", which appropriately sounds like a sequel to a bad horror movie, both came to Ayn as young, single high school student (him) and a young single college freshman (her, as she was a year older). Both had gone to the effort of contacting her after "The Fountainhead" movie came out. They were huge fans of it and of course, the written version.

They contacted her in California; she and Mrs. Ayn (Frank O'Connor) had lived in New York for a few years, as she wrote "The Fountainhead" novel there. Ayn and the "missus" (Frank O'Connor) moved back to California for the movie version, with her writing the script.

Ayn, staying true to form, found something to complain about in California. I am not making this up, and it delights me to report that Ayn found the sunshine in California "disgusting".[24] I have no explanation as to why, but can only speculate that perhaps the absence of smog implies the lack of virtue on the part of the community, as businessmen aren't exploiting the environment as thoroughly as they could? Anyhow, Ayn and Frank moved back to California reluctantly, and struggled with the inclement sunshine of the Golden State, while wistfully longing for the soothing climate of New York City.[25]

Ayn had encountered a bit of difficulty in developing a following of the mature New York intellectuals. By this I mean she pissed them all off with her hardheadedness, and the more accomplished ones thought she was full of herself, or full of crap, or both.

But with success of "The Fountainhead", Ayn had a new, younger, more gullible following. Ayn found that younger minds would receive her message in a more unconditional manner, immediately recognizing Ayn as the most brilliant person they had ever been around,[26] which most likely reflected their lack of social mingling more than it did Ayn's abilities.

Barbara Branden in her biography of Ayn Rand, "The Passion of Ayn Rand", tells us how Ayn just adored the youngsters. They were all just full of energy and Ayn just loved to teach. Barbara also states that older acquaintances of Ayn's would be less likely to unconditionally surrender intellectually, so Ayn sought out young acquiescent minds who were fresh enough to accept radical truth when presented with it.[27] I believe the latter to be a more accurate assessment than the former.

Also in Barbara's biography of Ayn, she marvels in awe, even to this day, at how Ayn kept her distance. She states in her book that Ayn never referred to them as "her children", but as "the children".[28] Barbara came to realize later, that this was the highest compliment. Ayn believed blood families were overrated, in fact not of any value at all. She felt that families should be formed by choice, not by biology.[29] Maternal instincts were not Ayn's strong point.

Nathan Blumenthal wrote Rand in 1949, and gushed about "The Fountainhead" and how it changed his life. She was not very impressed at first, and considered him to be uneducated, with no inclination on her part in bringing him up to speed.

He was an 18-year-old high school student from Canada, who had dreams of studying psychology. His girlfriend, his future wife, Barbara was in college, studying philosophy. He was not deterred by Ayn's standoffishness, and kept persisting.

Finally Ayn agreed to talk to him on the phone, and from there he and Barbs moved to California. [30] No records exist to my knowledge as to what they thought about the sunshine there.

Ayn had already been aggressively seeking out college kids, speaking to political science classes when she had a chance, and inviting interested young minds to her house – with the caveat that communists need not show up.

Those who did show up were soon part of the Ayn Rand posse, so to speak, who came over to her house just to sit at her feet and learn.

When Nathan Blumenthal finally arrived at Ayn's place he remarked, "I'm home". Barbara was even more impressed. She said when she gazed into Ayn's eyes, she felt they *"seemed to know everything, [they] seemed to say that there were no secrets, and none necessary"*[31]

As you will see further that with respect to Barbara and Nathan's married life, this is quite the ironic bit of foreshadowing.

Barbara and Nathan became frequent fliers at the ranch, as both progressed though college, Nathan in psychology and Barbara in philosophy. Ayn became not only their spiritual and intellectual mentor; she became a wise older friend who counseled them on love and relationships.

Nathan was a bit obsessed with Ayn, by the time he actually got to meet her; he had "The Fountainhead" memorized. Even though "The Fountainhead" could be considered slim relative to "Atlas Shrugged", it still has over 750 pages. But Nathan could back up his claim, if you gave him a sentence from the book, he could tell you the preceding and following ones.[32] He didn't get out much.

He didn't do much socially. He was a bit of an outcast in high school, and found solace in drama; reading close to two thousand plays in his high school years.

Digesting huge chunks of "South Pacific" and "Death of a Salesman" can help with the pain of solitude, but it doesn't do much on developing social skills.

When Ayn acknowledged him finally, he responded by calling her every day, several times a day, and he was there every Saturday night. Ayn on the other hand, was by now very impressed with Nathan. She thought him to be bright, and energetic with much potential.[33] Ayn also felt he was drop dead hot, as he possessed a thick head of hair, a strong chin, and a tall athletic body, which didn't hurt his chances with her.

Ayn had developed a mentor relationship with both of them. She had come to respect the brilliance of Nathan, as she actually enjoyed having her introduce her to the field of psychology, a field she had previously dismissed as quackery.

Ayn liked the way Nathan took her principles and integrated them into therapy, reducing therapy to just a matter of building self esteem.

What is particularly amazing, given the historical brilliance of Ayn Rand, is that Nathan tutored Ayn in the principles of psychology when he was in his mid twenties and she her late forties. Ayn was smitten by the intellect of a college senior and from him learned all one needed to be an expert in psychology.[34]

The intellectual and emotional attraction was mutual. Nathan referred to Ayn as himself with more feminine traits. This took some working up to, as it wasn't his immediate perception.

Nathan dedicated a letter to the editor he wrote to his mentor Ayn. He inscribed, "*To my father, Ayn Rand, the first step*".[35] Ayn was overjoyed, particularly at the part where she was addressed as "his father".

Ayn had been referred to as a man before and enjoyed it just as much. Famed economist Ludwig Von Mises called her "the most courageous man in America".[36] She had asked for clarification, as in "did he really say that?" When told yes, she beamed with pride. One can only assume Nathan's inscription to his "father" brought her the same pleasure. Her gender confusion only adds to the mystery that was Ayn.[37]

The letter that Nathan wrote to the UCLA student paper was an attack on a literary critic, F.O. Mathiessen, who taught at Harvard. What made this attack noteworthy is that he had just died, by suicide. Mathiessen had some associations from his past who were communists, and he suffered guilt through association. It effectively destroyed his career, and he spiraled into a deep depression, resulting in his suicide.

Leftist academics mourned him, as a man, and as a symbol of the tragedy of blacklisting. Nathan wrote his letter to correct them. He basically said why be surprised when a man kills himself because his ideology isn't working? He went on to say that Mathiessen deserved no pity but deserved "to be condemned to Hell". Nathan was widely criticized and shunned by everyone but Ayn Rand, who beamed with pride, particularly since he did it for her, his father.[38]

This should strongly suggest that Barbara and Nathan held Ayn in such high esteem, as to base their reality on her work. Both wrote memoirs about Ayn, twice. They collaborated on one in the early sixties, which surprisingly was nothing but a puff piece. Then, after they were expelled for reasons to be disclosed later, both wrote more honest portrayals of her, but still fawned over her intellect and character.

Barbara's book gives many fantastical stories that an objective, non-Objectivist type might find dubious.

For instance, Barbara recalls the following anecdote from Ayn's younger years, which took place in Russia before the birth of Barbara, so there can be no doubt as to Barbara's source.

Barbara tells the story of Ayn in a Professor Losky's course on philosophy, back in 1924. Professor Losky's was one of the toughest courses, and Ayn was nervous prior to an examination. Ayn recalled that she had prepared and hoped for a question on Aristotle, but instead was given a question on Plato, who she loathed. According to Barbara, who is obviously recounting Ayn's version:

> After a while, although she had not stated any estimate, Professor Losky said sardonically: "You don't agree with Plato do you?"
>
> "No, I don't," she answered.
>
> "Tell me why?" he demanded.
>
> She replied, "My philosophical views are not part of the history of philosophy yet, but they will be."
>
> "Give me your examination book," he ordered. He wrote in her book and handed it back to her. "Next student," he said.
>
> He had written: "Perfect"[189]

Barbara Branden gives this story with no critical examination, or even any hint of skepticism. Of course, she wasn't there, and I certainly wasn't. But, given Ayn's history of embellishment and her tendency to over inflate her own worth, I'd not be surprised if it were a fib. But, this anecdote reflects more on Barbara's gullibility than it does Ayn's duplicity, as far as I am concerned.

I had already formed my opinion on Ayn's integrity; this story reinforces that conclusion and it gives me new data on Barbara's ability to discern fantasy from reality.

So Nathan and Barbara met and fell in love as kids, in their pre-Branden days, and found their love for Ayn Rand naturally led to another type of love, of the Eros type.

Barbara was the first for Nathan, [40] and it apparently was enough of a test drive for him for him to decide he wanted to purchase the vehicle, if I may frame this delicate subject as a euphemism. Barbara, on the other hand, didn't really want to purchase right away. She liked shopping around, test-driving a wide variety of cars, all makes and models.

She might have considered a lease arrangement, but that idea discouraged Nathan, as he was intent on buying his dream car immediately. Enter into the arrangement the sales manager, Ayn Rand, willing to negotiate a deal that all parties could agree upon, where they could all enjoy driving for the sake of driving. [41]

The heroic traits of Nathan were so obvious to Ayn that she could not comprehend why Barbara rejected him. Ayn didn't have room in her theories of life for emotions as they violated the principle of rationality.

Ayn devised her own theory of sex, where she said that a person's sexual attraction is a signal for what the person values on a rational basis. [42]

So, if a superior intellect like Nathan had the hots for Barbara, then she should be honored and reciprocate else it would reflect a lack of intellect and reason on her part.

Ayn even confided in Barbara, that she saw Dominique from "The Fountainhead" in Barbara, and because of that she had the strength to do the right thing. Barbara understood this to be the truth, but she struggled with the idea, because mysterious feelings of uneasiness came from deep inside her.

Barbara worked hard, because she believed she had a character flaw in herself, because a truly rational being would love Nathan also. [43]

Nathan as a prodigy in psychology helped Barbara sort through her confusion. He helped her realize that the only rational thing to do was to love him back.

Barbara also notes that while she wasn't quite sure of her love for Nathan, she realized she was beginning to love Ayn. [44] For her, Ayn's warmth and love were irresistible. It was all time well spent, because there came finally, a breakthrough:

> "Through long discussions with Ayn and Nathaniel, I came to accept Ayn's theory of sex. And I made a decision. Nathaniel appeared to embody the values I cherished. The difficulty had to lie in me, in psychological problems I had not dealt with. I must continue growing, I must continue learning, I must work to resolve my unidentified problems, and the day would come when I would respond to Nathaniel as I should and wanted to respond. The road would be cleared and I would be free to live my life rationally."[45]

One has to admire Barbara and her willingness to accept responsibility with respect to her flawed character. And even more praise should be given to Ayn and Nathan, for both having the patience required to coach her through her muddled period of her life.

In 1951, Barbara had graduated and elected to go all the way across country to New York University to study philosophy in graduate school there. Nathan, as a rational thinker, reasoned it was the logical thing to do to transfer during his junior year and follow her. Ayn was devastated, and she cried as they left. She had begun to recognize the heroic character of John Galt in this youngster and she realized how much she'd miss him. [46]

Ayn then insisted that the Rands move back to the Big Apple, and they were all reunited in New York, but things didn't go that smoothly. Barbara left the auto lot and test-drove a couple of other cars while in New York, and Nathan felt confused. [47]

Ayn advised him to keep counseling her and to reject her foolish non-rational ways. Barbara did try, and worked hard to deny her unreasonable side. [48]

Finally, Barbara came to her senses and agreed to the only rational solution, which was to marry Nathan. Their old lives and surnames were cast aside, and the new derivative Rand name were embraced.

So the Branden kids got married in 1953, with Ayn and Frank as best man and maid of honor, respectively.[49] But in spite of all of the positive and rational signs, this was as about as good as it got in this marriage for Mr. and Mrs. "Son of Rand".

But for Nathan's father, Ayn, things got much better. She was able to begin writing again in New York, she loved the city life. Frank had been fond of the country home, and missed it, but as a loving husband who knew where his bread was buttered, he agreed this was the best move.

But Ayn would not be deterred and now that she had experienced financial success, she was in a position to live anywhere she wished to live. And she decided she wished to live in New York City. Frank on the other hand, did not.

He was very happy in California. He had a flower garden, and he would go out and pick mums and dip them in paint to make pretty corsages while Ayn and the kids talked deeper stuff. He didn't want to move. But Ayn gently reminded him who wore the pants in the household, who was Atlas holding up the other spouse, in other words.

Frank just shrugged and agreed. [50] It was in some ways, a bizarro "Green Acres" with the heavily accented wife forcing the husband to go back to the city. This version of Green Acres even had a swine that tried to act human, but he was named Nathan, not Arnold.

This turned out to be good for both of them. Frank found a job in a flower shop[51] and Ayn quickly developed another intellectual following, her self-named Collective.

The Collective were a small, and young, cadre completely devoted to stamping out communism and irrationality wherever they imagined it to be. [52]

123

Expanding on the art as truth meme mentioned earlier, I believe the case can be made of Ayn being's Nathan's father, as in Don Corleone to Nathan's Michael Corleone. Ayn established the family business, became the Godfather that everyone pandered to. Nathan was the son who found himself in the business, protecting the family and becoming more and more ruthless as he grew. He would destroy those who went against the family, and even destroyed his own family with his ruthless single-minded focus.

Nathan and Barbara were in prime position as the closest to Ayn to be in her inner circle. Which made a hierarchical structure, with Ayn at the top, followed by Nathan and Barbara, in that order, then the rank and file of the "Collective". [53]

The economist Murray Rothbard had a brief flirtation with the Collective, before finally split with Ayn Rand and her group, after he witnessed a group of high school students verbally attack someone who had the nerve to dispute one of her theories.

He concluded that "*the adoption of her system would be a soul shattering calamity*", [54] particularly with the young and impressionable. This is from the man who wanted to dissolve practically all government; he knew extremism when he saw it.

Rothbard basically summed them up as kooks and labeled them a cult, even calling them dangerous. [55] He was advised to divorce his wife because she was a Christian. He declined.

He fell out with Nathan Branden, who by this time had become Ayn's second in command, her intellectual heir (as declared by her), and the object of her affection to whom she dedicated her masterpiece "Atlas Shrugged", but to Rothbard, he was "*the same pompous ass, the same strutting poseur and mountebank, the same victim of his own enormously excessive self esteem*". [56]

Rothbard later wrote a blistering piece titled "The Sociology of the Ayn Rand Cult" in which he point by point establishes what traits cults possess, and then identifies them in the world of Ayn Rand with numerous examples. [57]

In the afore mentioned essay by Murray Rothbard, "The Sociology of the Rand Cult", he documents the structure of cults in general, and it becomes obvious how this applied to the Collective. Quoting Rothbard, with his remarks on the Ayn Rand Cult:

> *"Another method was to keep the members, as far as possible, in a state of fevered emotion through continual re-readings of Atlas.*
>
> *Shortly after Atlas was published, one high-ranking cult leader chided me for only having read Atlas once. "It's about time for you to start reading it again," he admonished. "I have already read Atlas thirty-five times."*
>
> *The rereading of Atlas was also important to the cult because the wooden, posturing, and one-dimensional heroes and heroines were explicitly supposed to serve as role models for every Randian.*
>
> *Just as every Christian is supposed to aim at the imitation of Christ in his own daily life, so every Randian was supposed to aim at the imitation of John Galt (Rand's hero of heroes in Atlas). He was always supposed to ask himself in every situation "What would John Galt have done?" When we remind ourselves that Jesus, after all, was an actual historical figure whereas Galt was not, the bizarrerie of this injunction can be readily grasped. (Although from the awed way Randians spoke of John Galt, one often got the impression that, for them, the line between fiction and reality was very thin indeed.)"* [58]

In my opinion last paragraph quoted here are the most interesting, and telling. For those without a thesaurus handy, "bizarrerie" is a real word and it is defined as a grotesque oddity. Rothbard witnessed first hand what I have been screaming for the last 25 pages or so, which is that the Ayn Rand cultists have only one reality, and it is hers.

To summarize Rothbard's observations in his essay:

> • A cult has a defined hierarchy, with the leader closest to him/her the longest serving members.

- There is a strict discipline imposed, where no other texts besides the leaders can be considered, unless the leader approves
- Psychological pressure is placed on members for discipline, often in a cruel way
- The ultimate punishment to the cultist is excommunication.
- The only reality these people know is the reality of Ayn's books[59]

All of these things, and more, were present in Ayn Rand-land. Nathan became an enforcer in the cult, and he shielded Rand from any outside critics. Critics inside the cult were nonexistent, thanks to the hard work of Nathan Branden.

Nathan embraced the Ayn Rand lifestyle, and it paid off in spades. First of all, he and Barbara were given status as original members, and they were worshipped by the newbies as heirs to the throne. Nathan was literally heir to the throne, Ayn Rand herself identified him as her "intellectual heir"; many times to whoever would listen.[60]

He and Barbara came to know her before and during her writing of "Atlas Shrugged" and they would sit and eagerly listen to every snippet of her writing that she would share with them, as she wrote it.

The whole Collective was formed around Ayn as she perfected her new morality through the words of John Galt. Ayn's hardest time emotionally was when she wrote the lengthy John Galt rant; it took everything out of her. I can certainly understand, I had the same emotional experience reading it; there were times I did not think I could finish.

But Nathan was there for her, in more ways than one. Barbara was the beauty of the Branden partnership, but obviously not the brains. She started getting suspicious one day when she noticed Ayn and Nathan canoodling in the back seat of Frank's Cadillac, as they were joy riding.

Frank and Barbara were in the front seat, Nathaniel and his father, Ayn Rand, were in the back, and obviously enjoying each others company. Excessive giggling went on, holding hands, lingering embraces, and kisses that made everyone just a little bit uncomfortable.

Finally, it dawned upon Barbara what was up. After they stopped at their motel room, as it was an overnight trip, Barbara confronted Nathan with this outburst:

> *"She's in love with you! And you're in love with her!* [61] *"*

Nathan, not being as emotional as Barbara, responded just as a superior intellect would do when faced with a non-rational accusation. He lied:

> *Nathaniel stared at me with a look of stunned disbelief, as if I had suddenly gone mad. "What in hell are you talking about?"*

> *I told him what I was talking about-I stumbled out the words-I shouted and paced the room as tears of rage and pain streamed down my face-while Nathaniel listened and watched as if paralyzed with incredulity.*

> *"She's in love with you!" I said, "And you are in love with her! I KNOW what I saw! I KNOW what it means!"*

> *"For God's sake, I love YOU!" he replied, as his own eyes grew wet. "She- she's twenty-five years older than I am!"* [62]

Nathan was mathematically correct. He was twenty-five, Ayn was fifty. Not withstanding the emotional moment, Nathan calmly invoked the theories of Marx to settle her; no, not the Marx who represented all the evil in the world for Ayn Rand, but Groucho Marx, who has been attributed as saying "Are you going to believe me, or your lying eyes?"

But a few days later, Ayn and Nathan called their respective spouses in and they all four sat as Ayn spoke. Quoting Barbara as she recounted what Ayn said, she and Nathan had fallen in love, and

> *"It was no longer the love of a teacher and her student, it was no longer the love of intellectual comrades, it was the love of close friends. It was the romantic, sexual love a man and woman.* [63] *"*

127

Ouch! The cat was out of the bag, now the question remained, what are we going to do about it? Ayn presented it as a no-brainer; there was no other solution. Ayn calmly, rationally, logically, and selfishly to the point of being virtuous, told them:

> *"You know what I am, you know what Nathan is...By the total logic of who we are - by the total logic of what love and sex mean - we HAD to love each other...It's not a threat to you, Frank, or to you, Barbara. ...It's something separate, apart from both of you and from our normal lives...Nathan has always represented the future to me-but now it's a future that exists in the present...Whatever the two of you may be feeling, I know your intelligence, I know you recognize the rationality of what we feel for each other, and that you hold no value higher than reason...There's nothing in our feeling that can hurt or threaten either of you...There's nothing that alters my love for my husband, or Nathan's love for his wife..."*[54]

You can guess the reactions of Frank and Barbara as they received the message. Yup, they acted like they had not one ounce of logic in them.

They were actually resistant to the idea of Ayn and Nathaniel being honest with each other, and resented their attempt to be honest with them. Both Frank and Barbara stamped their feet and pouted as children might, and basically said in their petulant way "we will not stand by why you have an affair!"

Barbara and Frank weren't really listening; Ayn and Nathan weren't suggesting an affair. The insecure spouses with their non-rational worldview only heard what they wanted to hear. Ayn stepped up to the plate and calmed all concerns. Continuing with the words of Barbara Branden, from her book:

> *Ayn's husky voice -hadn't it always been the voice of logic, of reason, of morality? -continued as if no one had spoken, and her marvelous eyes seemed to probe into Frank's brain and mind. "We're not suggesting an affair. Both of you must understand that...We want it, but too much is at stake, and it's not the only important thing...Besides, the age difference is far too great.... We've decided that we need to spend time alone, one afternoon and one evening a week, we want time together, for ourselves...That's all..."*

> *Frank turned to look at me, a faint touch of relief*
> *on his face. They weren't talking about a sexual affair...not*
> *yet. This was something we could live with, perhaps. We*
> *could try. There was a long, heavy silence. Then I nodded*
> *my head. "I'll agree to that." Ayn turned to her husband.*
> *"Frank?" "I agree," he answered.*[65]

That should have settled it. A rational, selfish solution that was agreed upon and all parties had full disclosure, it was just like a free market contracts between businessmen and customers should be; rational full disclosure and agreed upon terms. You didn't need a government to interfere with free commerce. This parallel extended itself even further as just as it often happens when an unregulated businessman contracts with a consumer, someone will end up screwing someone, with one of the parties completely unsuspecting it.

Shock upon shock happened when a mere few weeks later, Barbara was faced with the unthinkable. The affair, that really wasn't an affair, had gone the distance and Ayn and Nathan were literally giving full disclosure to each other. I'll let Barbara continue as she explains how she dealt with this unexpected turn of events:

> *The four of us sat in Ayn and Frank's apartment, as*
> *she discussed all the reasons why she and Nathaniel could no*
> *longer keep their original agreement – and all the reasons*
> *why Frank and I should understand their desire for a sexual*
> *relationship, and accept it – and all the reasons why Ayn and*
> *Frank and Nathaniel and I could and should remain,*
> *respectively, loving husband and wife. As we talked hour*
> *after hour, there were moments when it seemed as if all of us*
> *had stumbled into a home for the insane – and there were*
> *other moments when Frank and I remembered that this was*
> *Ayn, her magical eyes had not lost their tenderness, and this*
> *was Nathaniel, and we knew who and what they were, they*
> *were sane and reasonable and just, they were the people we*
> *loved, and this quiet living room in New York City, where*
> *Frank was serving coffee and Frisco (the Rand/O'Connor cat,*
> *named for an "Atlas Shrugged" character of course) was*
> *tumbling across the floor with his ball, was not a chamber of*
> *horrors.*[66]

This plays out oh-so-clear in my mind's eye. I imagine this domestic scene unfolding calmly, with Frank, ever the gracious hostess, serving coffee while they discussed their next solution.

I can imagine him there, with his frilly apron, trying to maintain dignity, with his hands nervously gripping each other over and over.

I can see his nervous laugh, sometimes awkward, and then I can see him occasionally bursting into tears and running back into the kitchen, after slinging his kitchen towel down on the coffee table.

I can see Ayn, stiffening up with her broad shoulders pulled back, walking to the kitchen, maybe even leaning back on one foot and kicking the swinging door open and then forcing him to turn around and look into her strong eyes with his tear filled ones.

Then the kiss, as he dug his head into her shoulder and sobbed, "I love you", and she replied, "I love you too, but what else am I supposed to do? I've got selfish rational needs, you know?" At least, that's how I visualize it.

Barbara doesn't elaborate on this scenario, and I concede, it may not have played out exactly as I described. Barbara just recounts Ayn's rational argument, which was a sexual relationship isn't forever. It would be one thing if she and Nathan were the same age, but they weren't. Continuing with Barbara quoting Ayn:

> "This isn't intended to be forever," Ayn kept saying. "Perhaps a year or so, that's all. If Nathan and I were the same age, it would be different. But we aren't the same age. An affair between us can only be temporary...This is something out of space and out of time. If the four of us were lesser people, it could never have happened and you could never accept it. But we're not lesser people...It's right and rational that Nathan and I should feel as we do for each other. Bit it's right and rational that a sexual affair between us can last only a few years. I could never been an old woman pursuing a younger man..." [187]

Barbara handled this in the most mature and rational way possible, and so did Frank for that matter. They shouldered all the blame for forcing Ayn and Nathan to fall in love, by being inadequate for their respective partners. Barbara explains thusly:

> *"Nathaniel had no power to resist the force that was Ayn Rand. Her passion for him was a triumph beyond any he had ever dreamed. It was a triumph that ennobled him, it was the proof of his worth, of his virtue, of the greatness that was to be his future-and he knelt as if before a queen to receive the gift of knighthood. It was more than knighthood, it was a morganatic marriage, and he was raised high to sit on the throne beside her."...* [68]

> *"I cannot judge the precise extent to which my sense of guilt toward Nathaniel aided in forming my decision, except to know that it was significant. Since our marriage, although I had fought to change whatever in my psychology was preventing me from giving him the response he had and a right to expect, I had failed. Nathaniel was painfully unfulfilled."* [69]

Frank's motive, according to Barbara, was the same, with some slight variations:

> *Frank's motivation seemed to be almost identical with mine. He, too, revered Ayn; he, too, believed that the love between Ayn and Nathaniel was inevitable; he, too- the man who rescued sick chickens and left his peacocks free to fly- could not bring suffering to the woman he had married.*

> *And he too, was tormented by the guilt of failure, the guilt of not being the hero he believed Ayn deserved- the man of productive achievement, of limitless ambition, of unique, self-generated intellect-the hero who would match her heroism.* [70]

She quotes Frank after an outburst years later:

> *"I want to leave her, he said his voice a hiss of rage and despair. "I want to leave her!" ...His hand fell from my arm, and I could barely hear his words as his voice dropped and he turned his face away to look into a void. "But where would I go...What would I do?"* [71]

It obviously was a weak moment for Frank, as Ayn had always said that she loved him because she saw in him John Galt, the perfect rugged, individualistic and heroic man. This type of sniveling sounds like one of the mooches in "Atlas Shrugged", the type of "second-hander" that pissed off Howard Roark so much that he had to teach the poor a lesson by blowing up their homes.

But, nevertheless, Frank had more time to let his peacocks fly freely, and Ayn did the same.

Frank adapted very easily to his stool at the local bar, but Barbara would backslide time and time again, as she did not have the emotional maturity of someone like Frank, and did not know how to self medicate with booze. That's an advantage that age will bring you, knowing exactly how to cope with challenges.

Meanwhile, the cult never knew this. Ayn gave her three conspirators strict instructions to keep it on the down low, and just keep things on a professional level. After all, she was working on "Atlas Shrugged" and she didn't have time for the drama. All three complied with her wishes, and the Collective were none the wiser.

Nathan was able to carry out his duties unhindered by any guilt or awkwardness. In fact, he devised a perfect manifestation of Ayn Rand's philosophy. He came up with a way to make a buck or two off of Ayn.

Nathan created the Nathan Branden Institute, and it was a force for good in the world, with good being defined as Ayn Rand's good, along with the good of Nathan's bank account. [72]

Nathan would practice psychology with an Objectivist flavor, he would cater to Objectivists that suffered from the most deadly of all maladies in their world: low self-esteem. Nathan Branden made a very financially successful career out of counseling, teaching and writing about self-esteem.

I challenge you to go to Nathan's Amazon page as an author; [73] you'll find any aspect of self-esteem covered you wish. His titles on Amazon include the following works, which impressively show his diversity of intellect and scholarship:

"Honoring the Self" (1983)

"How to Raise Your Self Esteem"(1988)
"The Power of Self-Esteem" (1992)
"The Art of Self Discovery" (1993)
"The Six Pillars of Self-Esteem" (1995)
"Nathaniel Branden's Little Blue Book of Self-Esteem" (1995)
"Nathaniel Branden's Self-Esteem Every Day" (1998)
"The Art of Living Consciously" (1999)
"The Psychology of Self-Esteem"(2001)

The most intriguing title, given that Nathan wrote it, is "Taking Responsibility" (1997). Lest you think the well has run dry with him, he also wrote, although I cannot find these on Amazon.com these additional books: "A Woman's Self Esteem" and "Self Esteem at Work", both published in 1998. I suppose all he has left to write are the books "The Self Esteem Cookbook" and "Self Esteem For Dummies".

When he wasn't busy writing or boinking Ayn or ignoring Barbara, Nathan was giving lectures at the NBI (as it came to be known) on topics such as the "destructiveness of the concept of God". [74]

The NBI grew and grew, and Ayn was cautious about how she managed her brand. She did not own the NBI, although she adored Nathan and supported it. Nathan in fulfillment of her wishes announced that no one would be allowed to refer to themselves as Objectivists. From this point on, only Ayn, Nathan and Barbara could wear that crown; all others would be referred to as "students of Objectivism."[75]

Nathan worked hard to make sure no one exploited the good name of Objectivism for a profit, excluding himself of course. Ayn was very aggressive in making sure her works weren't exploited.

Ayn was invited to the University of Virginia to speak at the Ayn Rand Society conference, with speakers, a banquet and social functions. The club reached out to her with their promotional literature and she immediately noticed them using a John Galt phrase on their stationary without her permission.

She was furious and demanded a removal of the quote. The president of the club had to apologize and he wrote a letter explaining

"I have cut the bottoms from all of our stationery I have, and have issued instructions and anyone else who has any of our stationery shall do likewise"[76]

Damn moochers. The parasites were everywhere, even within the Ayn Rand cult.

On Saturday nights, it was back to normal with the ever-expanding Collective. Nathan would impose strict discipline on those who dared challenge Ayn, or even read anything that Ayn disapproved of. If someone was discovered to be disloyal to Ayn or Objectivism, then a hearing would take place, an actual trial where Nathan would be the inquisitor, and Ayn would sit in judgment.

Barbara, who was awfully forgiving and worshipful of Ayn was even shocked at some of the sadistic methods used by her husband and her father-in-law, Ayn Rand. Quoting Barbara as she describes the inquisition of a twenty year old girl who had developed doubts in herself, and in Objectivism:

> That evening, Ayn exhibited a lack of human empathy that was astonishing. As Nathaniel, who conducted the conversation-it had the aura of a trial, except that the accused had no defense attorney- was pointing out the young woman's psychological deficiencies, he occasionally made some especially compelling point, succinct and well-phrased. Each time, Ayn chuckled with appreciation and clapped her hands in applause"[7]

It should also be noted that Nathan ran a side business as a therapist, as a psychologist. He viewed his mission as teaching Objectivism, rather than allowing inferior thoughts to prevail. He would go as far as to disclose matters discussed in his sessions at the trials, to better prove his point.

It would also be helpful to the reader to note that Nathan one day received a request from the California Board of Psychology asking him to no longer refer to himself as a psychologist, due to the tiny technicality that he did not have a psychologist's license.

His Ph.D. actually hindered this goal, as he acquired it from the not so prestigious California Graduate Institute, which struggled and failed in its attempt to get accreditation as it did not have a sufficient number of full-time staff or a library deemed worthy of a graduate school.

It appears that they did not even demand a dissertation from Nathan, as Jeff Walker notes in his book "The Ayn Rand Cult". It seems that they accepted a collection of recorded lectures on love and romance, the Ayn Rand way, to suffice as research.[78]

Nathan complied and editions going forward of his books would list him as a "psychological theorist." Therapy, he says, is just another method of research, and he never minded sharing his research with his true love, Ayn Rand and the Collective.[79]

With this backdrop, it is easy to see why everyone would be happy. Ayn was writing the greatest novel of all time, Nathan was strutting around like a vicious and overly proud peacock, Frank was walking to the bar and stumbling back after letting his peacocks fly freely, and Barbara was safe and sound at home, secure in the fact that Nathan loved her, as did Ayn, and whatever happened as four hairy legs intertwined was merely the result of logical, rational, positive self interest.

It was too good to last. Barbara, as you might have guessed, didn't have the greatness required to live this life. She was quite distressed, suffering from anxiety attacks, walking the streets and wondering about what it all meant.

Finally, she showed her true colors, and dared to disturb her husband as he was in private sex time with his 25-year senior father figure.

Oh of course, she will claim she really tried, and made the effort to accept this as an absolute good and moral thing, but talk is cheap. She says

> "One absolute was that I must accept my husband's love affair with Ayn, that it was right, it was rational-the other was the absolute screaming silently within me that "I cant."[80]

She obviously had no intention of rationally working this out, so she opted for the way of a much lesser person; the way of someone without a reason based high self-esteem (and this was before Nathan wrote his "Self Esteem for Women" book, so one could argue that she didn't have the tools needed to cope). She broke down and called Nathan while he was alone with Ayn. I'll let her describe it for you:

> *"There was one night I shall never forget - the worst of all those years and of the years to come. It was about eleven o'clock, I had been walking all evening; the anxiety was building to a pitch greater than ay I had ever experienced. I began to grow frantic; I believed that my mind might collapse from the bombardment of so great a terror. I had never called Ayn's apartment when she and Nathaniel were together; but that night, I stopped at a pay phone and dialed Ayn's number. When she answered, I told her what was happening, and that I wanted to come over to talk."*[1]

Pathetic. After all Ayn, and Nathan too, had done for her, she wanted it to be about her. Disturbing Ayn as she was bonding with Nathan. I picture a whiney puppy that needs a ticking alarm clock to sleep with, as it is not strong enough to make it through the night without whimpering.

Lucky for Barbara, Ayn was strong enough to see through all of the emotion and talk to her on a rational level. Continuing with Barbara's account of Ayn's reaction:

> *Her explosion made the telephone drop from my hand - and a moment later I felt her voice pursuing me as I hurried away from it as from the cold clasp of hatred. "How dare you! Do you think only of yourself? Am I completely invisible to you? I don't ask anyone or help! There's your whole problem in the fact that you called - if you want something, that's all you know or care about! Don't dare to dream of coming here!"*[2]

Barbara goes on to say she understood Ayn's angst, as she was going through a stressful time, she had been right smack dab in the middle of writing the greatest portion of the greatest novel: John Galt's speech.

In that context, Barbara would have done the same thing. Besides, later accounts show that Ayn was always asking Nathan about his feelings, asking if he loved her too. She had to scold him several times when he would mention his wife to her, so much that she had to forbid his mentioning her when Ayn and he had time alone.

Nathan and Ayn's physical connection later fizzled, and Ayn concentrated on finishing her life's calling. When it was released, she went into a deep depression because she received reviews that Barbara Branden referred to as "savage." There were many ugly reviews, including one previously mentioned by Whittaker Chambers, where he suggested that Ayn's worldview might lead to gas chambers.

Ayn had a loyal cult member write the New York Times to loudly denounce the ridiculous and hateful accusation and establish that it was not a book like that at all. This wasn't a typical starry-eyed teenager; this was a successful economist who would grow up to be the most powerful man in the world as Chairman of the Federal Reserve, Alan Greenspan. Perhaps you've heard of him?

In his response to Chambers in the New York Times, Greenspan was measured, logical, and emphatically explained to the readers what was the true nature of Ayn Rand's masterpiece. "Atlas Shrugged" celebrated life, and it was a positive book. Greenspan wrote:

> " 'Atlas Shrugged' is a celebration of life and
> happiness. Justice is unrelenting. Creative individuals and
> undeviating purpose and rationality achieve joy and
> fulfillment." [83]

That was a typical Greenspan, reducing the argument to cold hard facts, with no inflammatory talk.

He did however, feel the need to follow up with this sentence. Given this statement by Greenspan, it is clear that Whittaker Chambers was way off the mark when he suggested "Atlas Shrugged" commanded people to go to gas chambers. Further quoting Alan Greenspan from his very next sentence, from a 1957 letter to the New York Times:

> *"Parasites who persistently avoid either purpose or reason perish as they should."*[4]

Nathan did his best to shield Ayn from the ugliness of the critics, and even though the affair had gone non sexual for a while, he showed his love by persecuting, ridiculing, and excommunicating any member of the Collective that didn't give Ayn her due.

But Ayn would not stay down for too long, she decided in 1966 to rekindle the spark she had with Nathan. She has already seen him grow up into the money making machine, and she had written him in her will as her heir, and even dedicated "Atlas Shrugged" to him, along with Frank, her husband of course. Ayn was ready to get frisky, in the most rational way, with Nathan again.

Yet Nathan was strangely passive. He showed no interest in her. Ayn was puzzled, as she said sexual desire meant that it reflected the highest values of the rational individual, therefore Nathan dang well better respond to a great thinker like her with the hots for him. But still, no spark came forth. Ayn would seek out Barbara for comfort and guidance, after all, she was Nathan's wife and she would be able to explain why her husband would not have sex with her.

Ayn would ask Barbara every question one could imagine, save for "Does this dress make me look fat?" Barbara recounts Ayn's distress:

> *"The more Nathaniel and I talk," she said, "the less I understand. And I have the feeling that nothing I say or discover will be heard, that I'm working harder on his psychology and I care more about it than he.*

Why is he able to think brilliantly about theoretical problems of psychology or morality, but not about personal problems? He'll seem to understand something one day - then it's gone the next day. He's warm and loving with me one day, he'll" kiss me in a way that's sexual, he'll tell me he can't live without me, and I'll feel that something magnificent is possible between us, and then that's gone the next day..."[85]

Ayn emphatically and passionately asked this question of Barbara, and to no avail:

"Doesn't he know that the great proof of my love for him is that I chose him despite a happy marriage and the difference in our ages? Doesn't he know that an exclusive commitment for life is impossible?"[86]

I wonder if these problems ever arise on braincrave.com?

Barbara just sat in silence, she wondered

"What had happened to the two giants of the intellect I had known, now lost and helpless in the morass of their emotions"[87]

It was puzzling to Ayn, but perhaps a piece of the puzzle illuminates the total picture that being the fact that Barbara and Nathan were on the verge of splitting up. Go figure.

And Nathan had a cute little gal named Patrecia, who had come to him as a student at the Nathaniel Branden Institute, and ended up in his bed.

He was telling Ayn he was too tired, intimidated, and afraid every time she confronted him. She would ask point blank, "Is it my age?" as she was 63 and he was 38, and Patrecia was 20, to which he flatly denied. To complicate it more, but not really by much as this was only a technicality, Patrecia was married also.[88]

Long story short, after much anguish and begging, Nathan fessed up to Ayn. Oh my, it hit the fan.

She accused him of lusting after a person beneath him, and could not understand why he would choose her over him. She had a famous yelling session at him as she banished him in the presence of Barbara, which both recount verbatim:

*"IF YOU HAVE AN OUNCE OF
PSYCHOLOGICAL HEALTH, YOU'LL BE IMPOTENT
FOR THE NEXT TWENTY YEARS! AND IF YOU
ACHIEVE ANY POTENCY, YOU'LL KNOW IT'S A
SIGN OF STILL WORSE MORAL DEGRADATION!"*[89]

Then she slapped him three times and that was that. She excommunicated him and Barbara, for her part in deceiving her. She had Alan Greenspan draw up the statement, saying they were both expelled for violating Objectivist principles. [90]

Oddly enough, in my view selfishness seemed to be his driving force, so I don't know what she meant, perhaps there was more to the story. Her followers were forbidden to mention either Branden, she disassociated herself from the Nathan Branden Institute. She changed her will, and then she changed the dedication in "Atlas Shrugged" to the barest minimum, her husband.

As a final act, she took in Nathan's misfit cousin, Leonard Peikoff, who actually had been excommunicated before and had worked his way back, and declared him her heir, both intellectually and physically. Peikoff now owns her estate.[91]

The split, to put it mildly, was not amicable. She never reconciled with Nathan, and hated him until she died. She issued a smear piece of both Brandens, which they both responded to. He didn't own up to the affair, he just framed it as her wanting him but him saying no. A split in the family occurred and enemies rejoiced. William F. Buckley mocked the Ayn nerds, laughing at the fact that they expected the rest of us to follow them to Nirvana when they couldn't even manage their own lives.[92]

The Godfather metaphor runs full circle here. The Godfather, Ayn, passes the torch to young Michael Corleone, Nathaniel, who ruthlessly enforces discipline against anyone that goes against the family, stopping at nothing to consolidate power and becomes more corrupt. Then the final act has Ayn starring as Michael, yelling a curse to Nathaniel's little "Fredo", telling Nathaniel and it specifically, you are dead to me, and I hope you are dead forever.

This should have killed the cult, as it caused a rift and most not even knowing why. But it survived and came back from the dead, mostly thanks to one man, Alan Greenspan. For that we thank you Alan. Well, not really.

In order to paint the portrait that is Alan Greenspan, I request your indulgence as I refer to the truth of a fictional story; a novel written by Jerry Kosinski in 1970 entitled "Being There". [93]

My apologies for the heretical act of straying from the Ayn Rand canon for my truth, but I felt it had relevance to the subject at hand, although I concede this could be a subjective burst of irrationality on my part.

This novel is a short one, with approximately 160 pages. This brief novel packs a disproportional punch with its satirical bite. It was so widely appreciated that it was made into a very good movie of the same name in 1979, with Peter Sellers in the lead role, which would turn out to be his last.

Sellers was nominated for an Academy Award as Best Actor that year, but he lost to Dustin Hoffman in Kramer vs. Kramer. But for his performance as the powerful millionaire businessman, named by a complete coincidence as Ben Rand (Another son of Rand?), Melvyn Douglas won his second Academy Award for Best Supporting Actor, and Golden Globe Award for Best Actor in a Supporting Role.

Roger Ebert wrote two reviews of the movie, the first one written as the movie was released in which he presented it with four out of four stars, and the second one written to be included in his book, "Great Movies, II."[94] It was very good, but not so good to be in his first book I suppose, we had to wait for the sequel. Nevertheless, the book and movie were very well received.

The plot is simple, yet clever and it works. It was basically a Forrest Gump type film, where an idiot stumbles through life. Peter Sellers plays an imbecilic gardener named Chance; no last name is ever given.

In the book we learn that an old man had raised Chance, and he never had any other name, or any papers. Chance was the old man's gardener for decades and devoted his life to two activities: gardening and watching television.

Chance's only expertise was in gardening, and his only education was from his television. He couldn't even read or write.

The book begins with the death of the old man. Attorneys discover Chance as they are working to clear the old man's estate after his death. They tell Chance that he cannot stay there, and Chance compliantly leaves with all of his possessions in one suitcase, walking around town aimlessly with his possessions until fate strikes him down.

To be precise, it was fate in the form of a limousine. The young trophy wife of a wealthy man (his business or his actual net worth were never disclosed, but let's just call him a billionaire industrialist) is being driven around by her chauffeur, and this trip results in the accidental contact with Chance.

Chance is slightly injured and unperturbed, but the accident upsets the billionaire's wife, who is named Eve Rand. She is overwhelmed by guilt and she insists on him coming to the house to recover. She asks Chance his name, to which he replies, "I am Chance, the gardener." She misunderstands him to say "Chauncey Gardiner" and so begins the adventures of Chauncey as he accidentally rises to power.

The old man, Ben Rand, is intrigued by Chauncey, as everyone knows him from this point on. He considers Chauncey stoic and wise because of his silence, while in reality it is just Chauncey being an idiot and not knowing what to say. Billionaire Ben Rand inquires about what type of business Chauncey does and if he had obligations elsewhere, to which Chauncey replies:

> "It is not easy sir," he said, "to obtain a suitable place, a garden, in which one can work without interference and grow with the seasons. There can't be too many opportunities any more...I've never seen a garden. I've seen forests and jungles and sometimes a tree or two. But a garden in which I've planted in it grow..." He felt sad"[85]

While Chauncey was speaking literally, the billionaire heard what he wanted to hear, that is that Chauncey was speaking metaphorically as an entrepreneur, and he was looking for investment opportunities, but was with great sadness commenting that regulations and difficulties made him wonder if capitalism had ever been attempted. Rand responds:

> *"A gardener! Isn't that the perfect description of what a real businessman is? A person who makes a flinty soil productive with labor of his own hands, who waters it with the sweat of his own brow, and who creates a place of value for his family and for the community. Yes Chauncey, what an excellent metaphor!"*[196]

I need not point out the obvious John Galt quality of this observation. Beyond the obvious, you have the interpretation by the fictional Rand in "Being There" that capitalism hasn't really been tried, while in the real world, our Rand promotes the very same idea.

The uncanny similarity goes even further when you learn that Alan Greenspan was listed as an author along with Ayn Rand, Nathaniel Branden, and another Objectivist named Robert Hessen on a book of essays that they titled: "Capitalism, The Unknown Ideal."

This book is a collection of whines and complaints about how government has allowed the little guy to keep the man down and how oppressed capitalists have been through the ages.

Chapter eight is called "The Effects of the Industrial Revolution on Women and Children." I'll save you the trouble of reading it and go ahead and spoil the ending: it was good for them. Long hours, low pay in dangerous conditions was just what they needed.

GEORGE KELLEY

One of Ayn's contributions is "America's Persecuted Minority: Big Business." I am assuming you can guess the theme of that one. I was ready to contribute to a charity for starving CEO's after reading it. Greenspan's contributions are two chapters, one on Antitrust legislation (hint: he's against it) and "Gold and Economic Freedom." If you can get past the dull prose in all these essays, the book makes for some good humor, provided you take it as a joke. Sadly, reality hits us in the face and reminds us the authors were serious when they wrote this.

But one part of it is very funny; I don't care who you are, if I may paraphrase my intellectual muse, Larry the Cable Guy. The introduction by Ayn is some good comedy. Sure, it flows like all of her other stuff, and she up-fronts her message; the first two lines say *"This book is not a treatise on economics. It is a collection of essays on the MORAL (emphasis hers) aspects of capitalism"*[97] Ayn is very good at staying on message. Yeah, yeah, we get it; it's about the new morality. Paul Ryan has told us all about it. But that's not the humorous part. If you can make it through, or better yet, skip over the infomercial-like content of her boring introduction, you can get to the punch line, her last paragraph:

> *"Now a word about the contributors to this book. Robert Hessen is presently completing his doctorate in history at Columbia University, and is teaching in Columbia's Graduate School of Business. Alan Greenspan is president of Townsend-Greenspan & Co., Inc., economic consultants."*
> *-Ayn Rand*
> *-New York, July 1966*[98]

Notice any omissions? Perhaps this direct quote can clue you in if you missed it. Taken word for word on the same page, it is printed in the book one inch below the previous:

> *P.S. Nathaniel Branden is no longer associated with me, with my philosophy or with "The Objectivist."*
>
> *A.R. New York, November 1970*[99]

144

Back to "Being There". Chauncey meets the president through Rand, he impresses him with his statements on the seasons, cold winter makes the garden die, and then it grows in spring; yada, yada. The president takes this as calming statement on the self-regulating cyclical nature of the economy. He goes in front of the American people and relays Chauncey's words, and he gives attribution to Chauncey. The American people heartily respond, and they clamor for more Chauncey.

Chauncey is interviewed on television, he goes to the UN and meets the Soviet Ambassador, who believes him to be fluent in Russian and an expert on Russian literature, all the while saying nothing but idiotic, meaningless drivel.

The end of the book finds the president in a quandary because his vice president had to resign because of scandal, and all other candidates are unclean with possible corrupt ties to business (I'm inferring the president was a Republican here). The book ends as they decide on the perfect veep for the president, the unknown but widely popular Chauncey Gardiner. A very biting satire in a wonderful book. It's hilarious...or maybe not, I guess you had to be there.

Don't think I'm finished with the Alan Greenspan comparison to Chauncey, I have not yet begun to bite, with my wit with respect to Greenspan, that is. First of all, we see Chauncey, praised as a wise oracle, when in reality he is a fool. We see Greenspan, whose whole career had him praised as an oracle, while in reality he was...a fool?

Like the fair and balanced Fox News, I report, you decide. Consider this. When Alan Greenspan met Ayn Rand, he was a moral relativist, which is a fancy way of saying there were no absolutes, not only no absolute ideas of right and wrong, but he wasn't sure about the existence of things he saw, touched, or even was. He would tell people, "*I think I exist. Actually, I can't say for sure anything exists*"[100]. Seriously.

145

Ayn put the rational smack down on his goofy ass and said, *"And by the way, who is making that statement?"* [101] BOOM. OH NO SHE DI'INT! Greenspan was flummoxed, he had no retort, and he had fancied himself clever. But with Ayn, he found his Yoda to his young Jedi self. He was never the same after that. He ran to Nathan Blumenthal immediately after this humbling and said "Guess who exists?"[102] This had to be a proud moment for the thirty something year old intellectual.

Greenspan would warn anyone that was foolish enough to try to verbally combat Ayn that

> *"Many are the people who laughed at my description of her dialectical invincibility, only later to try their hands and join me among the corpses on the Randian battlefield."*

Greenspan was forced to admit that before meeting Ayn Rand, he was *"intellectually limited"* and concedes that he was *"a talented technician, but that was all."*[103] It takes a big man to admit his smallness.

Greenspan was successful before he met Ayn, and on his way to becoming very rich, if not already. He is a mathematical genius, no sarcasm here at all. He is a whiz at crunching numbers and has a superb talent at scanning data and interpreting it.

But that is a function of intelligence, which allows you to pull facts out of data. Facts do not convey truth. Truth comes from piecing together facts, and drawing conclusions that reflect reality.

Think of the scientific process, where facts are accumulated and tied together to form what? An academic theory. Science is even humble enough to admit that the best one can do with facts is theorize, you can not find truth empirically. You may have a general perception of the truth, but as Ayn Rand would say, "check your premises." Two people can watch the same movie and come away with differing truths.

If you will, examine the link cited in this paragraph, which is to an Ayn Rand discussion board.[104] Here, the Objectivists are sharing their opinions on the beautifully made sentimental Christmas classic, "It's a Wonderful Life". The consensus here is to label it as a poisonous and toxic film. Why? Because Jimmy Stewart's character, George Bailey, had to give up his dream of traveling the world and settle for marrying a smoking hot Donna Reed and siring four beautiful children that loved him.

To the Objectivists, it's natural to applaud the fact that George Bailey was miserable enough on the bridge to off himself, as he realized the natural consequence of denying one's selfish desires; but the Objectivists despise the artificial ending that has him realizing that his life isn't so bad at all, in spite of his business failures and financial struggles.

The Objectivists have watched the same movie that we all have, but they have come up with wildly different reactions than most of us have. Or another way of expressing this: because of the values of Objectivists, their notion of truth is distorted.

This can't be overstressed. It's their truth that drives policy these days nationally, and this truth becomes the basis of the laws and policies of the land, at least as far as the Republicans can influence them.

It's not consistent with my understanding or belief as to the nature of the truth of this life; and the primary object of this book is to challenge the reader to evaluate their understanding of truth and values, and compare them against what is being promoted by the individuals and party that receives their votes.

147

Truth isn't a function of intelligence. This is not to say that intelligent people cannot find the truth, they certainly can. Truth and intelligence are not mutually exclusive. Intelligence, to a certain extent, is a necessary, but not sufficient condition for the truth. You can't double up on the intelligence part of the recipe at the expense of including another ingredient, wisdom. It will fail like a cake without flour. Wisdom gives you the truth, based on experience and observations of reality, not just facts. This is lost on too many people. The antithesis of a wise man is a fool. A fool draws improper conclusions, which leads him to say and do stupid things. You draw your own conclusion as to whether Greenspan is a fool or not. I offer this: a wise man would never question whether or not he existed.

But to be clear, the problem with Greenspan wasn't with him being goofy. He was goofy and he was destructive. Think of a giant wrecking ball going through the economy with reckless abandon, and imagine it with Coke bottle glasses and a lame comb over. Terrifying. I guess we can now say, lucky for us, the nightmare is over, now we are cleaning up the mess that this dork left us with. Not so fast, my friend.

How about a quick recap of the legacy of the man who did not know he existed? Matt Taibbi is the political reporter for Rolling Stone, and he is a heck of a journalist and an even better writer. You should seek out his work, and start with his expose on Goldman Sachs. He has an excellent book, called "Griftopia: Bubble Machines, Vampire Squids, and the Long Con That Is Breaking America."

Warning, this book is obscene. No, not because of the occasional "F-word" Matt drops, that is mild relative to the true filth here. The obscenity lies in the facts he brings to the table, how the wealthiest in our country are exploiting our system, ripping off taxpayers and destroying our middle class, infrastructure and safety net in one fell swoop. I suggest if you read his book and think the offensive part is in his occasional R-rated vernacular, I have to wonder where your priorities are. Some things need to be cursed.

Matt has a whole chapter devoted to Greenspan, his second chapter titled "The Biggest Asshole in the Universe." He attacks Greenspan like a pit bull would an unattended toddler. My complaint with this chapter is that I felt he let Greenspan off the hook a little too much, but I have a bias. Matt shows in case after case how Greenspan was the biggest con man to ever run the world, and if you don't think the Chairman of the Federal Reserve runs the world, given that he controls the supply of every U.S. dollar in circulation, then you need a basic civics and econ class to catch up. Greenspan was wrong about every prediction he ever made.

Taibbi recounts when Greenspan "saved" Social Security in the 80's by almost doubling the taxes on the poor and middle class, while exempting the rich. Then he stood by as the Reagan, Bush, Clinton, Bush administrations stole the surplus that it accrued and gave it to the wealthiest billionaires. Now he calls for the elimination of Social Security, as the trust fund is almost all gone.

The book recounts how Greenspan systematically destroyed or blocked regulations that the country needed. Oh boy did we ever need them.

Why would he do that? Because he believed that silly balderdash he and Auntie Ayn promoted, where the garden would grow and bloom and die with the changes of the season. It is as silly in real life as it sounds in the book.

No better example of his being a "Being There" doppelgänger than Greenspan's record on derivatives.

Derivatives are complex, in every aspect, from their structure, their valuation, and even their definition. That's why they are hard to explain; for the listener and the one doing the explaining. The simplified definition is that they are special financial instruments that derive their value from some underlying, or real asset.

For example, you can own gold physically. You can buy derivatives on gold in many forms, such as a contract to buy gold in a future at a set price.

For example, the price of gold at the time of this writing is around $1800 per ounce. If one chose to do so, he could contract to buy 1000 ounces of gold a year from now at $1900 per ounce. The $1900 is called the strike price. The price of the contract in the future is determined by several factors, one is the current market price of gold; along with interest rates, time to maturity and the volatility of gold.

Now obviously if this contract is made, the purchaser who obligates himself to buy at that price is expecting a run up in gold.

If gold becomes even more of a precious metal in the next year, and rises to $2000 per ounce, then the purchaser of the gold futures contract (as this particular derivative is called) may buy it at a bargain.

Consequently, the contract holder is screwed if gold drops below the strike price. So derivatives in a nutshell are opportunities to wager large sums of money for a huge payoff. It's a form of leverage, and as you might have inferred, a dangerous form of leverage.

This is not to say that derivatives don't have a positive use and a responsible application. They can be used to hedge wildly volatile prices. Consider the risks FedEx takes if it negotiates a two-year contract with the government, or a mega corporation such as Wal-Mart. They propose to deliver packages for x amount per year, and that is based on the assumption of a certain price of jet fuel. Chances are they neutralize this risk by purchasing futures contracts for jet fuel.

But hedging isn't what got us in to our current mess; it was raw speculation and greed. Add to this toxic mixture the complexity of the subject matter.

My first masters' degree was in finance, specifically majoring in risk management; the theory and structure of derivatives. I am not ashamed to say that I was completely baffled while trying to understand some of the complex models I saw. I was the intellectual runt of the litter, as far as my relation to my extremely bright classmates (some of which are successful in the financial field, even on Wall Street).

But my insecurity is lessened, at least by a little bit, by the fact that major money players have admitted bafflement with derivatives. Note: my intellectual density in derivatives and many other matters is still overwhelming with respect to the soon to be quoted billionaires and my brilliant classmates from years past. I only feel ever so slightly better about my lack of comprehension.

Felix G. Rohatyn was and is one of the most powerful men on Wall Street. He began at Lazard group (one of the most prestigious investment houses in the world) in 1949 and rose to the position of senior partner and managing director during the course of his fifty years there.

How wealthy did that make him? Let's put it this way, while anyone walking through New York can be subjected to a panhandler asking "brother can you spare a dime?", Mr. Rohatyn got hit up by the actual city of New York.

He responded by raising billions of dollars, which saved New York City from bankruptcy in 1975. [105] He knows a bit about investing, to understate the obvious. What is his take on derivatives? He doesn't use them; he refers to them as financial "*hydrogen bombs*". [106]

Billionaire George Soros avoids derivatives "*because we don't really understand how they work.*" Warren Buffett, who is sometimes the richest man in the world, or sometimes the second or third, depending on the day, has famously called them "*financial weapons of mass destruction.*" [107]

Alan Greenspan believed in the complex instruments so much he thought they could regulate themselves. The buyers and sellers worldwide would do the right thing. It's not like derivatives snuck up on us in 2008; many have called for tighter regulation for twenty years, while specifically warning us about a scenario like we are living through now.

In 1987, the stock market experienced the largest one day drop in history. The day came to be known Black Monday: October 19, 1987. The Dow Jones Industrial Average fell over 500 points that day, and to put it mildly, a panic ensued. Many factors were at play in causing this meltdown, but one new financial device had a disproportional impact; the derivative instrument known as portfolio insurance.

Portfolio insurance was designed to work as a hedge, just as it was described above, one that just covered stocks.

As a simplified explanation of it, think of it as hedging the whole index, for instance the 500 stocks in the S&P 500. If you managed a huge mutual fund, and owned a large collection of stocks, you really couldn't guard against each individual stock losing drastic value. So portfolio insurance was designed to fix that little problem.

It required the money manager to purchase a contract to sell their stocks at a value predetermined, to hedge against losses. For example that morning of Black Monday, the S&P 500 was at 282. Billions of dollars in stock were hedged at many different prices for the index.

Hypothetically, a fund manager had an option to sell his index at 270, to better avoid catastrophe if the S&P plunged to 225, which incidentally did as the day closed. As the price went down, a computer program would trigger the sell off and he would minimize his losses. The problem is, many funds had such a structure, and they all rushed for the exits, all at the same time.

It should be intuitive that when billions of dollars of stocks are being sold, the prices will drop, and drop, and drop some more.

Which they did and the markets devolved from an efficient democratic function of buyers and sellers into a stampede; which is the democracy of frightened beasts.

President Reagan tasked Nicholas Brady-who would later serve Reagan as Treasury Secretary and George H.W. Bush also in that capacity-to head a commission to investigate the causes and possible remedies of that panic. This report had the formal name "Report of the Presidential Task Force on Market Mechanisms" and was submitted to the President, the Secretary of Treasury, the Federal Reserve, and Congress.

One of the commission's observations was that investors in portfolio insurance didn't have to have actual stock to buy it, or put up any significant margin for collateral.

In other words, naked speculation ran rampant. Quoting the Brady Report, as it has become more commonly known:

> For example, on October 19, a professional market participant, who is classified as a hedger, could have taken a position in the equity market by purchasing an index futures contract with an underlying value of $130,000 (500 times the index value of 260) by making an initial investment of $7,500, or approximately 5.8 percent of the contract's value.
>
> In order to purchase $130,000 worth of stock, such a participant would have to make an initial investment of about $35,000, or about 25 percent of the value of the stock.
>
> Although the futures investor only has to come up with $7,500, the entire $130,000 stock equivalent may be transmitted into the stock market through index arbitrage. Similar leverage is possible on the short side of the market. [108]

Plain English: When it doesn't take much skin to get in the game, betting big is bound to happen. Brady and company had the radical suggestion of raising margin requirements so that losses could be minimized, and installing "circuit breakers" to halt trading when things moved too fast. [109]

Alan Greenspan was new to his job as Chairman of the Federal Reserve; but not to worry, he had no shyness about expressing his opinion to this prestigious panel's recommendation.

The New York Times article's title in February, 1988 says it all: "Greenspan Opposes Brady Plan". [110] He felt the market could take care of itself in this matter. He begrudgingly accepted the need for circuit breakers as

"The least bad of all the solutions" to activity that might lead to a panic. He added, "The choice is not between good and bad, but between bad and worse."[111]

Alan Greenspan stated his position that he would hold for the next twenty years. Whenever a calamity happened because of derivatives, or was nearly averted, his response in the press and Congress was to effectively say "we don't need your stinkin regulations".

In 1994, Orange County, California went bankrupt because of derivatives. Its hotshot treasurer lost about $1.6 billion by betting the wrong way on interest rates. Whoops!

As might be expected, collectivists everywhere were shouting down the Ayn Rand supporters by calling for tighter regulations of derivatives. But alas, it was to no avail, as the Chairman of the Fed was a citizen of Ayn Rand's world. I shouldn't have to summarize the article printed in the papers after the smoke cleared titled "Greenspan warns against harsher derivatives laws"[112].

In 1998, a firm called "Long Term Capital Management" imploded, losing about $4.6 billion in less than a month when their fancy-schmancy derivatives betting strategy backfired. Whoops, the sequel!

Long Term Capital Management was like the Superfriends of finance, with almost superhuman investment wizards running it. One of the brightest minds on Wall Street of all time, John Merriwether, created the firm and he enlisted as senior partners two winners of the Nobel Prize in Economics, Myron S. Scholes of Stanford University and Robert C. Merton of Harvard University.

Under normal circumstances superior intellects such as the above-mentioned can overcome a $4.6 billion hiccup. But things were exacerbated by the fact that Long Term Capital Management had accumulated over $100 billion in debt; borrowing from all of the major Wall Street banks that threw money at them because of Long Term Capital Management's starting lineup.[113]

Greenspan continued his insistence upon the self-regulation of the derivatives market, but added a new act to his repertoire. He bailed the players out.

Because all of the major players on Wall Street had so recklessly lent money to this foolhardy group of geniuses, he felt he had no choice but to corral all of the CEO's and have them pony up a few billion to bail out Long Term. He told Congress in no uncertain terms that they were too big to fail.

> "Had the failure of L.T.C.M. triggered the seizing up of markets, substantial damage could have been inflicted on many market participants, including some not directly involved in the firm, and could have potentially impaired the economies of many nations, including our own,"[114]

Oh sure some folks complained, saying Greenspan set a bad precedent.

The negative Nancy's were all uptight over some far-fetched future scenario where Wall Street would act recklessly, knowing full well their asses would be wiped with billion dollar checks the next time they pooped on the economy with stupid bets.

Thank goodness that hasn't happened.

Greenspan, true to his Objectivist principles, calmly lectured the lesser beings in government that regulation never solved, or prevented, anything:

> Mr. Greenspan, however, stuck to his position that it would be difficult or even counterproductive to impose more direct regulation on hedge funds. Regulating the funds, Mr. Greenspan said, would drive them to operate from other nations with looser regulations, undermining the ability of the United States to monitor them even indirectly through their lenders and investors.
>
> The best way to rein in gambling by those firms, Mr. Greenspan said, is to encourage their lenders to assess rigorously the risks they are taking and deny credit to those whose bets become unwise. In that way, he said, banking supervisors and other regulators can act as a second line of defense by pushing lenders to make sure their risk assessments are adequate.
>
> Under questioning from members of the panel, Mr. Greenspan acknowledged that same approach had failed in the case of Long-Term Capital Management.
>
> But he said that such failures were inevitable in markets, that he had been surprised at how few had occurred in the last five years and that he expected more of them in the future. Moreover, he said, if the financial system is unwilling to assume risks, the economy's ability to grow will be impaired.

'Let's not presume that the ideal outcome is more regulation," Mr. Greenspan said. [115]

Too bad that Greenspan's worst fears weren't validated, which we were in a reality where he didn't actually exist.

Because in spite of his genius, in spite of his blind, dogmatic faith in the efficiency of the market to take care of business in the best way possible, the system crashed; yet again because of derivatives-this time in the housing market, and we are still feeling the pain.

Yes Virginia, there is an Alan Greenspan and he exists. We see his footprint with every foreclosed house, every shut down business, every lost retirement, every failed bank, and every insanely wealthy Wall Street jerk who ever bankrupted a company.

With apologies to Billy Joel, Alan didn't start the fire; he just poured a volatile mixture of kerosene, gasoline, and rocket fuel upon it.

The ultimate chutzpah on his part may have been when he faced Congress on October 22, 2008. He was asked does he still think the market self regulated? His response, "there is a flaw in the theory." [116] No kidding? Thanks Alan, we will miss your genius. Enjoy your retirement and your rest of your life away from work. I only wish millions of the rest of us could go back to work.

But now Greenspan is retired; Ayn is dead, and in a just world we would be grateful for both of these events and feel secure in our recovery.

But we can't celebrate, because the cult that should have died when Nathan divorced both his wife and mentor/lover/father and got excommunicated for his trouble lived to fight another day. It should have been tossed in the ash heap of history after Ayn croaked, but it did not. It bounced back to flourish and it is more powerful today.

The cult is well funded; BB&T is one of the biggest banks in the world and it devotes millions of dollars to teach Ayn Rand's morality to hyper competitive arrogant grad students who feel led by the god of mammon to pursue MBA's at places like Duke, University of Texas and North Carolina, to name a few of the sixty programs that teach this propaganda. [117]

The Ayn Rand Institute is alive and well, and they boast that they send 400,000 free copies per year to the top Advanced Placement high school students in the U.S. [118] 400,000 **PER YEAR**. Did you get that? Our best and brightest kids are being injected with Vitamin Ayn.

I'm sure an exceptionally bright 15 year old will be level headed enough to ignore some pseudo intellectual literature that tells them that he or she has been right all of their lives; there isn't really any good reason to share toys or help someone up off the playground.

Did I say 15 year olds? Oops, my bad. The Ayn Rand Institute reaches out to youngsters from the eighth grade on. There are essay contests, where the concept of good and evil are discussed with respect to money. There are grants to teachers to encourage them to teach it. A quick look at the site and you will see resources for schools under these menu headings: Essay Contests, Student Website, Student Clubs, and Debate Resources. [119] The last one is very important, so that the little Objectivists can verbally smack down the belligerent parent that dared to correct them with some mystical claptrap.

And please stretch your memory back to the early pages of this long chapter, where I discussed Ayn Rand's glorification of rape. Recall that? Do you recall "The Fountainhead" having its hero rape his gal, just to show her he cared? The Ayn Rand Institute promotes a high school study, complete with free lesson plans, on "The Fountainhead."

No need to fret, most likely the kids won't notice the rape; the little rapscallions never pay attention anyway. Except for the inconvenient fact that the Ayn Rand Institute includes essay questions for teachers that take their free goodies. Uh oh, looks like it's on the test, so they better learn it. Here's an interesting question, cut and pasted:

> At the granite quarry, Dominique is deeply attracted to the redheaded worker who stares at her insolently. She pursues him aggressively, but resists him in the moment of her triumph.
>
> Given that Dominique is eager to make love to Roark, why does she physically resist? Ayn Rand once stated regarding this scene that, if it is rape, " then it is rape by engraved invitation." What does she mean? Is this actually rape, i.e., is Dominique an unwilling victim?[120]

That's some outstanding moral guidance for our high school students and what better lesson for them to learn? However, I am a little nervous that our religious right has forbidden sex education, save for abstinence.

How will the teachers teach abstinence is the gal is sending signals, engraved invitation signals as Ayn describes it, that subtlety say she really wants it, no matter what she might verbalize?

"No" means "hell yes, I want it now!!" for the junior Objectivists. Parents, do you wish the schools would give out condoms now to the kids, now that you know that the Republican party endorsed Objectivists are pushing a pro rape agenda?

It's happening right under your very nose. Prom night will be special in the Republican districts; they will bear the brunt of the rape rallies. Inner city schools aren't as fertile a hunting ground for young minds because poor dark kids aren't as keen on materialism as the white suburban spoiled ones are, and the Aryan Ayn lovers know this.

What would your reaction be if someone sent Darwin's "Origins of the Species" to every student? You'd go ape. Remember when some right wing lunatics were pulling their kids from school in 2009, when Obama wanted to speak to them and tell them to stay in school and study hard? Conservative talk show hosts were calling for a skip day for students, lest they learn the wrong message. How's this quoted section grab you for hypocrisy?

> The chairman of the Florida Republican Party is condemning Obama's speech as an attempt to "indoctrinate America's children to his socialist agenda."
>
> "The idea that school children across our nation will be forced to watch the President justify his plans for government-run health care, banks, and automobile companies, increasing taxes on those who create jobs, and racking up more debt than any other President, is not only infuriating, but goes against beliefs of the majority of Americans, while bypassing American parents through an invasive abuse of power," Chairman Jim Greer said in a press release. [121]

Well, not to worry, there is no code here, its about as straight forward as you can get. I understand perfectly now, Republican values are rape = good, and health care for the poor = bad.

I can only assume it pleases you, as it is all in the name of capitalism, a value you hold higher than anything God asked of you.

For those who say you don't approve, that you are as disgusted as me-prove it. Talk is cheap.

Does it bother you enough to demand your party change? Does it bother you enough to even consider pulling your support? Does it bother you enough to vote them out of office? For some of you, I believe it may.

For many, I believe you to be just as corrupted. I am looking at the evangelical Christians when I say this. You may say that you don't approve, or that you find these things contemptible, but know this: you do not have to be an Objectivist to do their bidding.

Many self-proclaimed Christians do the bidding of the people who would destroy them; along with the poor they give lip service to caring about.

It's all in your party, it's throughout your political agenda, and it is driven by the biggest concentration of wealth this country has ever seen. If you don't believe me, stick around. The things I present in the chapters going forward are even worse. I can excuse your culpability up to this point, but after this you should be reevaluating your priorities and see if your party is in line with what you envision as a good and just society

I transition this chapter into the next one with this question, why did you not know about this? I read Ayn's book twenty-five years ago as a Republican and even then she made me uneasy. There were enough Republicans around like William F. Buckley for me to feel relieved, where I could believe in the rhetoric of the free market and not loathe the poor and celebrate selfishness. Name one conservative today, save for Chuck Colson who has warned you about Ayn Rand?

If you are a conservative offended by this you should realize it is your own fault this value system has corrupted the party.

This warped new morality has taken over the right wing evangelical Christian movement, which shall be documented in the next chapter.

It now dominates the current GOP at both the federal and state level. It's not the liberal media, academics, or swear words on TV that have brought this upon us.

I leave you with this truth, found in this quote from William Shakespeare, who was considered literature back in the day, before our standards dropped to Ayn Rand:

> Men at some time are masters of their fates:
> The fault, dear Brutus, is not in our stars,
> But in ourselves, that we are underlings.

SOURCES CONSULTED FOR CHAPTER 3

[1] Irving, W., *Adventure of the German Student*. Tales of a Traveller by Geoffrey Crayon, Gent: p. 32-36.

[2] Definition of art available from: http://www.merriam-webster.com/dictionary/art?show=1&t=1292602796

[3] Burns, J., *Goddess of the market: Ayn Rand and the American right* 2009: Oxford University Press, USA. P. 25

[4] Prescott, M. *"Romancing the Stone-Cold Killer: Ayn Rand and William Hickman"*. ; Available from: http://www.michaelprescott.net/hickman.htm

[5] LinkedIn Profile of Brian Lovett; Available from:http://www.linkedin.com/in/brilovett

[6] Author Unknown "Sex in The Fountainhead - The Rape of Ayn Rand" www.braincrave.com ; Available from: http://www.braincrave.com/viewblog.php?id=14.

[7] Burns, J., *Goddess of the market: Ayn Rand and the American right* P. 86

[8] Flesher, D.L. and T.K. Flesher, *"Ivar Kreuger's contribution to US financial reporting"*. The Accounting Review, 1986. **61**(3): p. 421-434

[9] Burns, J., *Goddess of the market: Ayn Rand and the American right* P. 28

[10] Ibid; P. 29

[11] Ibid; P. 29

[12] Ibid; P. 29

[13] Heller, A.C., *Ayn Rand and the World She Made* 2009: New York: Random House. P. 233

[14] Rand, A. and L. Peikoff, *The Fountainhead* 2005: Plume Books.

[15] Burns, J., *Goddess of the market: Ayn Rand and the American right* P. 86

[16] Heller, A.C., *Ayn Rand and the World She Made* 2009: New York: Random House. P. 161

[17] Heller, A.C., *Ayn Rand and the World She Made* P. 305.

[18] Ibid, P. 146

[19] Ibid, P. 174

[20] Walker, J., *The Ayn Rand Cult* 1999: Open Court. P. 11

[21] Walker, J., *The Ayn Rand Cult* 1999: Open Court. P. 28

[22] Branden, B., *The Passion of Ayn Rand* 1986: Doubleday. P.232

[23] Heller, A.C., *Ayn Rand and the World She Made* P. 254.

[24] Burns, J., *Goddess of the Market: Ayn Rand and the American Right* P. 99

[25] Heller, A.C., *Ayn Rand and the World She Made* P. 161.

[26] Rothbard, M.N. and C.f.L. Studies, *The Sociology of the Ayn Rand Cult* 1990: Center for Libertarian Studies. Available from: http://www.lewrockwell.com/rothbard/rothbard23.html

[27] Branden, B., *The Passion of Ayn Rand* P(xi Introduction).

[28] Ibid, P. 241

[29] Heller, A.C., *Ayn Rand and the World She Made* P. 225

[30] Branden, B., *The Passion of Ayn Rand* 1986: Doubleday. P.

[31] Burns, J., *Goddess of the Market: Ayn Rand and the American Right* P. 136

[32] Ibid, P. 137

[33] Ibid

[34] Burns, J., *Goddess of the Market: Ayn Rand and the American Right* P. 135

[35] Burns, J., *Goddess of the Market: Ayn Rand and the American Right* P. 137

[36] Ibid, P. 114

[37] Heller, A.C., *Ayn Rand and the World She Made* P. 249

[38] Burns, J., *Goddess of the Market: Ayn Rand and the American Right* P. 137

[39] Branden, B., *The Passion of Ayn Rand* P. 42

[40] Heller, A.C., *Ayn Rand and the World She Made* P. 222.

[41] Ibid, P. 226.

[42] Branden, B., *The Passion of Ayn Rand* P. 248

[43] Ibid, P. 238.

[44] Ibid;

[45] Ibid, P. 249

[46] Heller, A.C., *Ayn Rand and the World She Made* P. 233.

[47] Ibid;

[48] Burns, J., *Goddess of the Market: Ayn Rand and the American Right* P. 138

[49] Ibid; P. 146

[50] Ibid; P. 138

[51] Heller, A.C., *Ayn Rand and the World She Made* P. 238.

[52] Burns, J., *Goddess of the Market: Ayn Rand and the American Right* P. 241

[53] Walker, J., *The Ayn Rand Cult* 1999: Open Court. P. 25.

[54] Burns, J., *Goddess of the Market: Ayn Rand and the American Right* P. 152.

[55] Walker, J., *The Ayn Rand Cult* 1999: Open Court. P. 49.

[56] Ibid, P. 169.

[57] Rothbard, M.N. and C.f.L. Studies, *The Sociology of the Ayn Rand Cult* 1990: Center for Libertarian Studies. Available from: http://www.lewrockwell.com/rothbard/rothbard23.html

[58] Ibid;

[59] Ibid;

[60] Burns, J., *Goddess of the Market: Ayn Rand and the American Right* P. 214.

[61] Branden, B., *The Passion of Ayn Rand* P. 256

[62] Ibid, P. 257.

[63] Ibid, P. 258

[64] Ibid, P. 258-259.

[65] Ibid, P. 259

[66] Ibid;

[67] Ibid, P. 259-260.

[68] Ibid, P. 261.

[69] Ibid, P. 262.

[70] Ibid, P. 262-263.

[71] Ibid, P. 263.

[72] Burns, J., *Goddess of the Market: Ayn Rand and the American Right* P. 214.

[73] Amazon page for Nathaniel Branden Available from http://www.amazon.com/Nathaniel-Branden/e/B000APCVE8/ref=sr_ntt_srch_lnk_1?qid=1315853444&sr=8-1

[74] Burns, J., *Goddess of the Market: Ayn Rand and the American Right* P. 215.

[75] Ibid, P. 217.

[76] Ibid, P. 221.

[77] Branden, B., *The Passion of Ayn Rand* P. 271

[78] Walker, J., *The Ayn Rand Cult* P. 155.

[79] Ibid, P. 158-159.

[80] Branden, B., *The Passion of Ayn Rand* P. 277.

[81] Ibid;

[82] Ibid;

[83] Rubin, H. "Ayn Rand's Literature of Capitalism" New York Times September 15, 2007 Available from: http://www.nytimes.com/2007/09/15/business/15atlas.html?scp=1&sq= Parasites%20who%20persistently%20avoid%20either%20purpose%20 or%20reason%20perish&st=cse

[84] Ibid.

[85] Branden, B., *The Passion of Ayn Rand* P. 337.

[86] Ibid;

[87] Ibid, P. 338.

[88] Ibid; P. 336-337.

[89] Ibid; P. 347.

[90] Burns, J., *Goddess of the Market: Ayn Rand and the American Right* P. 241.

[91] Heller, A.C., *Ayn Rand and the World She Made* P. 383.

[92] Burns, J., *Goddess of the Market: Ayn Rand and the American Right* P. 243.

[93] Kosinski, J., *Being there* 1983: Black Swan.

[94] **Amazon Link Great Movies II**

[95] Kosinski, J., *Being there* P. 39

[96] Ibid;

[97] Rand, A., et al., *Capitalism: The unknown ideal.* Vol. 4795. 1967: Signet Book. P. 6.

[98] Ibid, P. 8.

[99] Ibid;

[100] Taibbi, M., *Griftopia: Bubble Machines, Vampire Squids, and the Long Con That Is Breaking America* 2010: Spiegel & Grau. P. 54.

[101] Burns, J., *Goddess of the Market: Ayn Rand and the American Right* P. 149

[102] Woodward, B., *Maestro: Greenspan's Fed and the American boom* 2001: Touchstone Books. P. 56.

[103] Burns, J., *Goddess of the Market: Ayn Rand and the American Right* P. 150

[104] Forum For Ayn Rand Fans: Topic It's a Wonderful Life

[105] Fried, J.P. "Metro Business Briefing; Rohatyn's New Venture" New York Times April 24, 2001 Available from: http://www.nytimes.com/2001/04/24/nyregion/metro-business-briefing-rohatyn-s-new-venture.html?scp=6&sq=rohatyn&st=Search

[106] Goodman, P.S. "Taking a Hard New Look as a Greenspan Legacy" New York Times October 9, 2008 Available from: http://www.nytimes.com/2008/10/09/business/economy/09greenspan.ht ml?scp=1&sq=%22taking%20hard%20new%20look%20at%20a%20gre enspan%20legacy%22&st=cse

[107] Ibid;

[108] A full copy of this report is available from the Department of Treasury's web archive, in multiple formats including for all ebooks, pdf, word, or viewing on web. Available from: http://www.archive.org/details/reportofpresiden01unit

[109] Ibid;

[110] Kilborn, P.T. "Greenspan Opposes Brady Plan" New York Times February 2, 1988 Available from: http://www.nytimes.com/1988/02/03/business/greenspan-opposes-brady-plan.html?scp=1&sq=alan%20greenspan%20and%20brady%20report&st=cse

[111] Ibid;

[112] "Greenspan warns against harsher derivatives laws" The Financial Post (Toronto, Canada) January 6, 1995.

[113] Truell, D.F.a.P. "Long Term Capital: A Case of Markets Over Minds" New York Times October 11,1998 Available from: http://www.nytimes.com/1998/10/11/business/long-term-capital-a-case-of-markets-over-minds.html?scp=1&sq=long+term+capital+management&st=nyt&pagewanted=all

[114] Stevenson, R. "Fallen Star: The Regulators; Fed Chief Defends U.S. Role In Saving Giant Hedge Fund" New York Times October 2, 1998 Available from: http://www.nytimes.com/1998/10/02/business/fallen-star-the-regulators-fed-chief-defends-us-role-in-saving-giant-hedge-fund.html?scp=3&sq=long+term+capital+management+moral+hazard&st=nyt

[115] Ibid;

[116] Andrews, E.L. "Greenspan Concedes Error on Regulation" New York Times October 23, 2008 Available from: http://www.nytimes.com/2008/10/24/business/economy/24panel.html

[117] Available from ___ http://www.clemson.edu/capitalism/capres/bbtp/bbtp.html

[118] Ayn Rand Institute Available from http://www.aynrand.org/site/PageServer?pagename=about_ari

[119] Ibid;

[120] Ayn Rand Lesson Plans Available from http://www.aynrand.org/site/DocServer/lessonplans.pdf?docID=124

[121] Henderson, N.-M. "Right blasts Obama speech to students" Politico 9/3/09 Available from: http://www.politico.com/news/stories/0909/26711.html.

PART TWO: THE GHOST OF AYN RAND PRESENT

"Spirit," said Scrooge, with an interest he had never felt before, "tell me if Tiny Tim will live."

"I see a vacant seat," replied the Ghost, "in the poor chimney-corner, and a crutch without an owner, carefully preserved. If these shadows remain unaltered by the Future, the child will die."

"No, no," said Scrooge. "Oh, no, kind Spirit! Say he will be spared."

"If these shadows remain unaltered by the Future, none other of my race," returned the Ghost, "will find him here. What then? If he be like to die, he had better do it, and decrease the surplus population."

Scrooge hung his head to hear his own words quoted by the Spirit, and was overcome with penitence and grief.

"Man," said the Ghost, "if man you be in heart, not adamant, forbear that wicked cant until you have discovered What the surplus is, and Where it is. Will you decide what men shall live, what men shall die? It may be, that in the sight of Heaven, you are more worthless and less fit to live than millions like this poor man's child. Oh God! to hear the Insect on the leaf pronouncing on the too much life among his hungry brothers in the dust!"

ebenezer scrooge
& the ghost of christmas present
"a christmas carol", 1843

GEORGE KELLEY

CHAPTER 4: OH BROTHER, WHERE ART THOU?

"I proposed a national system of health insurance in 1946 and I have urged it repeatedly since that time. There is no other way to assure that the average American family has a decent chance for adequate medical care. There is no other way to assure a strong and healthy nation...

The plan I have proposed does not disturb the traditional relationship between doctor and patient-except that the doctor will be paid more regularly for his services. Nor is this any more revolutionary than any other form of insurance. It is 100% American. It is just a way to collect the cost of medical care on a pay as you go basis.

What did the Republicans do with my proposal for health insurance? You can guess that one. They did nothing. All they said was – "Sorry. We can't do that. The medical lobby says it's un-American" And they listened to the lobbies in the Congress.

I put it up to you. Is it un-American to visit the sick, aid the afflicted, or comfort the dying? I thought that was simple Christianity. Does cancer care about political parties? Does infantile paralysis concern itself with income? Of course it doesn't." [1]

president harry s truman
october 15, 1948

I never was bright enough to read "Atlas Shrugged" as a teenager and I am quite sure if I had been my **ADHD** addled brain could have never concentrated on that behemoth. Finishing that novel would have been just like passing a literary kidney stone. And to be honest, I find that my perception of it now hasn't changed any at all.

But back then I did read and I read a great deal. My reading was eclectic, at least in the sense that it was cross genres.

I read almost everything Louis L'Amour wrote. He was a very successful writer of westerns, if you didn't know. I loved Doc Savage stories, which were reprints of pulp magazines from the Depression era. Tarzan books were fun and of course, I devoured Sir Arthur Conan Doyle's Sherlock Holmes stories and novels.

Sherlock Holmes was really cool, once you worked through the Victorian era language and references. I am sure everyone has at least heard of Sherlock Holmes and Dr. Watson. Sherlock Holmes solved case after case by using his superior powers of observation and applying precise deductive reasoning to find solutions to mysteries that no one else could seem to solve.

The only story in which Sherlock Holmes was outsmarted was "A Scandal in Bohemia". Even more surprising was the fact that it was a woman that outsmarted Sherlock Holmes. This woman, named Irene Adler, occupied a place in Holmes' mind forever, according to his sidekick, Doctor John Watson. Watson's first two lines in this story sum it up:

> To Sherlock Holmes she is always THE woman. I have seldom heard him mention her under any other name. In his eyes she eclipses and predominates the whole of her sex.[2]

Holmes viewed her as the perfect idea of a woman and with good reason as she had outsmarted him. Before you say anything, yes I do realize it was fiction, but if the Rand cultists can speak of John Galt as a real person, I will take the same liberties with Sherlock Holmes.

The plot of the story is pretty simple. A mysterious man comes to Holmes' home at 227B Baker Street one day. He's wearing a mask and he identifies himself as Count Von Kramm. The Count claims to be representing a king, but Holmes sees right through that foolishness and recognizes the count.

Holmes calls him on it and even addresses the Count by his full name: Wilhelm Gottsreich Sigismond von Ormstein, Grand Duke of Cassel-Felstein, the hereditary King of Bohemia. For the sake of this exercise, let's just call him "King Wilhelm."

The King is about to be wed and he's worried that a compromising photo of him and an actress, the lovely Miss Irene Adler, might surface. Even one with a prestigious position such as Wilhelm has to be conscious of social standing. His in-laws would not approve if they knew of his past with such a scandalous woman, an American at that. The King did not know how lucky he was to live in a world that had not become wide enough for the World Wide Web.

But he approaches Sherlock Holmes in order to enlist his services in finding the photo and retrieving it. The King advises Holmes that the photo is too big and bulky to carry on her person and he has had his royal goons ransack her place before; but to no avail as she is too clever. He must have that photo!

Holmes accepts the case and boastfully tells Watson that he will simply have Miss Adler tell him where it is. As per usual, Watson is dumbfounded at such a claim.

Holmes' plan worked like this: Holmes would dress as a doting old clergyman and fake an injury so Miss Adler would take him to her room to recover. The room was upstairs in an inn where Miss Adler was staying. This was not only before the internet but also before the days of television evangelists, so she really had no reason to fear for her chastity. Holmes had instructed Watson to wait for his signal. Watson would then drop a lit flare into the main part of the inn and then yell "FIRE!" You could get away with that kind of thing in Victorian England but I wouldn't recommend this tactic today.

Holmes waits for the right moment and then goes to the window under the guise of wanting fresh air and signals Watson. The flare is lit and dropped; the alarm sounded by Watson and as predicted the panic ensues. Sherlock Holmes evacuates and meets back up with Watson, where he smugly tells Watson he now knows where the photograph is. He had watched her take it out of a hidden safe right in front of him.

Once again, Watson is stunned, dazed and confused by Holmes. "How?" he asks Holmes. Holmes with his air of superiority replies that it was quite elementary, it was the fire alarm that made her tip her hand.

> "*It was all-important. When a woman thinks that her house is on fire, her instinct is at once to rush to the thing that she values most. It is a perfectly overpowering impulse and I have more than once taken advantage of it.*"[3]

Holmes had outsmarted the very clever American floozy, or did he? When Holmes returned to confront her, he found her gone and the landlady gave him a letter that Miss Adler had written for him. She told him that she knew that she had been duped when the fire turned out to be a false alarm and she then deduced that the simple country parson was in reality the world's greatest detective. She high-tailed it out of there, after writing this letter of course. She went on to say that she is now married and happy, but will hold onto the photo forever as protection and furthermore, if the King ever stepped out of line, she would publicize it.

So, Irene Adler escapes, Sherlock Holmes is defeated and the King realizes he needs to stay discreet lest his crown jewels get trampled by hot to trot woman.

There's a truth in this story, more than the obvious one about high-ranking government officials and indiscretions. Holmes reveals the truth as he recounted his method for discovering the hiding place of the photograph. Sherlock Holmes establishes a truth about all people, not just Irene Adler. When the fire alarm sounds we all will grab our most important possession to salvage as we hastily exit.

I use this truth to illustrate the claim put forth in this chapter. A claim I am sure that will be passionately denied by those whom I accuse. I say to all of you conservative Christians who are justifiably outraged by what you have read thus far on Ayn Rand, and who claim that you would never be an Objectivist or supporter of hers: you are just as guilty as she is and her followers are and you prove this to me by, to use this metaphor, what you consistently grab from the safe as the fire alarm sounds.

I'm sure some of you are all shouting "BULL CRAP!" out of disbelief (and also because you will refuse to use a more common mono-syllabic four letter word because of the perceived sin factor) And for some of you, that would be correct, as there are sincere, loving Christians out there who do not hate the poor and do not worship wealth, Ayn Rand style. But I'm not seeing those types in the Republican leadership. In fact I see quite the opposite. And I see almost all of the decent true followers of Christ following the wolves who seek to devour them; lockstep as they repeat the wolves' language, agenda, and phrases.

All the while they posture themselves as men and women of God. Don't try to make your case to me as to how unlike the phonies you are, that's between you and God. If the shoe fits, you can stick it somewhere, because if it does fit you deserve to wear it inside of an orifice, not outside on an appendage.

Let me also be clear that one need not wear the label in order to promote the brand. During the Cold War, particularly during the times in this country when anti-Communist hysteria was at a peak, a label was used to describe those who were sympathetic to the Communists by actions, in spite of them not technically being Communists.

The term used was "fellow traveler" as in someone who wishes to go to the same place, traveling alongside, but not necessarily in the specific traveling party.[4]

Without a doubt, I would not care what you call yourself, if you worked hard to accomplish my goals. Your motives would not even matter in this case.

Objectivists believe themselves to have a lock on truth, and to be driven by pure reason. So they would view any fellow traveler as someone who reached the right conclusion with the wrong or incomplete logic.

I should add, that in addition to fellow travelers there was a subset of enablers that were called by the communists "useful idiots." I am accusing the Religious Right of being fellow travelers to be nice.

This is not to say that guilt by association exists, where everything associated with a person or group is evil. For example, Hitler invented the autobahn, which was the forerunner of our interstate highway system. It really should not have to require courage to praise the autobahn even though it was indeed an Adolph Hitler production.

Care must be taken to examine each position on its own merits; to determine whether or not it violates or supports ones ethics or morals. Ayn Rand's choice of Coke versus Pepsi shouldn't really matter much, but her view that charity is evil should at least send up a red flag to anyone who even merely gives lip service to the idea of holding an opposite morality.

That being said, Ayn Rand has not only co-opted the entire Republican Party, but she has seduced the conservative religious establishment. The so-called Religious Right has embraced the goals of Ayn Rand, even without claiming her by name.

The Religious Right is now full of fellow travelers within its ranks, and its leaders are not even that innocent. They are full-fledged Randites with their own policies and agendas. The Religious Right has completely bought into the notion of class warfare, where the poor are demonized and the wealthy worshipped.

I see it almost everyday. Whenever I discuss the need for a stronger safety net for the poor, particularly in these hard times, I hear this argument, or some variation of it:

"I will not pay extra taxes while someone sits on their ass and refuses to work! I should not pay for someone to have babies just to increase their welfare check! People on food stamps eat better than we do, they eat steaks and we have to eat sandwiches, that isn't right"

This argument isn't right, and by not right I mean both not moral and not correct. Those are falsehoods-demonstrably so. Call any state Department of Human Resources; ask to speak to a caseworker, particularly if you are in a conservative state. I called a friend of mine who has worked for over 22 years with the state of Alabama. She confirmed that the biggest misconception is that people are living the life of luxury off the public dole (Defense contractors are the exception as they are indeed very well compensated, but that's another story). For instance lets look at the food stamp myth, where the recipients eat steak and lobster while the rest of us working stiffs eat Hamburger Helper. The National Center for Children in Poverty, which is part of the Mailman School of Public Health at Columbia University, has a website with a 50-state policy wizard.[5]

With this tool, you can see what is required and disbursed with respect to all of these programs. In Alabama, there is a threshold for a person with a family of three, for instance let's look at a hypothetical case of single mother, abandoned by a husband with two kids. This isn't a far-fetched scenario. This income threshold is $21,588/year, for this or any other family of three. This works out to be approximately $10.79 per hour. If the family makes more than that, then no more food stamps. If the woman is lucky enough to get child support, that's considered part of income. Also, since that is an income threshold, there is no incentive to work overtime, as making extra kills the benefits. What is the payoff for being poor enough for the good Christian voters of Alabama to acknowledge you and your needs? A whopping $408 per month. Have you purchased groceries lately? How many steak dinners will that buy for a family of three, four or five, particularly if there are teenagers?

But, the myth persists that the poor are living it up at our expense. I've yet to hear any indignant conservative complain about the theft of hundreds of millions by CEO's. The average conservative will rail on the bailout of the automakers, as it rewarded those "no good, lazy, union thugs". But where is the outrage for CEO Rick Waggoner of General Motors, who received $14 million as his reward for bankrupting the auto giant?

Let us not forget the one of the most recent and outlandish class warfare statements that conservatives make. The recent financial meltdown that destroyed the world economy? Yep, it was all the fault of the poor. Especially the darker shades of poor. The Community Reinvestment Act forced all of those oppressed bankers into lending money to unworthy minorities, and look what we have to show for it. Never mind the greed and avarice of completely immoral Wall Street wizards. Never mind the statement issued by the Federal Reserve that said, and I quote:

> The Federal Reserve Board has found no connection between CRA and the subprime mortgage problems. In fact, the Board's analysis found that nearly 60 percent of higher-priced loans went to middle- or higher-income borrowers or neighborhoods, which are not the focus of CRA activity.[6]

Conservatives, just as characters in Sherlock Holmes stories, will always grab what is most important to them when the alarm goes off. And it will invariably be that the poor people are to blame. Which is exactly what Ayn Rand would do. Many conservative Christians are just Objectivists that take time to say grace over meals now and then.

Don't hear what I am not saying. I am not saying that you, me or anyone else should enable laziness, or suffer to provide comfort for those unwilling to pursue it themselves.

One concept that the conservatives get right that liberals will struggle with is the concept of moral hazard.

One of the greatest movies of all time, possibly the greatest movie you have never seen, is a classic from 1941 titled "Sullivan's Travels." This film is so highly thought of, that in 1990 the National Film Registry of the Library of Congress included it in their list of films considered "culturally, historically, or esthetically important".[7]

This movie was also the inspiration for the Coen brothers' modern classic, "O Brother Where Art Thou?" "Sullivan's Travels", written and directed by Preston Sturges, revolved around the adventures of an idealistic movie director named John L. Sullivan.

Sullivan was wildly successful and incredibly wealthy from his movies. But he was disillusioned because his movies were considered escapist fluff. His directorial style was the mindless musical comedy, instead of a deep, dark drama that showed the truth of man's misery.

Sullivan wanted to break typecast and direct a movie based on a novel (a fictional book, merely a plot device) called "O Brother Where Art Thou?" This was to be a "Grapes of Wrath" type serious drama, exposing the underbelly of humanity.

His bosses at the studio challenged him, pointing out that he had no experience being poor. A fit of guilt overtook him, and he decided that he need to experience poverty first hand, to better tell the tale of the common man. So, he concocts a scheme where he goes around the country as a hobo observing and experiencing life while eating out of trashcans.

One memorable scene, of many, was of his butler as he was preparing to leave. His butler cannot understand why a wealthy man would want to study poverty up close when he did not have to do so. He remarked very pointedly to his boss:

> "You see, sir, rich people and theorists - who are usually rich people - think of poverty in the negative, as the lack of riches - as disease might be called the lack of health. But it isn't, sir. Poverty is not the lack of anything, but a positive plague, virulent in itself, contagious as cholera, with filth, criminality, vice and despair as only a few of its symptoms. It is to be stayed away from, even for purposes of study. It is to be shunned."[8]

The butler is correct in one big way. Poverty isn't the lack of money. You cannot fix social conditions by pouring a bucket of money on someone. Some liberals do not get this but conservatives understand this on an intuitive level.

The problem is that many conservative Christians take the butler's whole statement as truth, and enthusiastically endorse his suggestion that poverty "is to be shunned."

That has become the attitude of the Republican Christian movement towards the poor. Let them eat cake, as long as I don't have to pay for it.

For some in the Tea Party, it would probably be best if the poor would die, based on the applause from the crowd at the prestigious CNN/Tea Party Republican debate in September. Enthusiasm rang out for the idea of a hypothetical uninsured man being left to die.[9] What a pity being uninsured isn't a capital offense, with the sick in Texas, so the applause could have lasted twice as long.[10]

The statement that rings the most insincere from those who profess to be Christians is the phrase "I've been blessed." Sure they give all appearances of saying it with conviction, but only because they realize that society expects them to do so.

One definition of blessed is "divinely or supremely favored". But another definition exists, that of "worthy of being worshiped", which the use of the latter definition would negate my claim of the words usage being insincere. I can certainly see plenty of earnest expressions of gratitude for the latter.

The former definition is one that attributes all success and accomplishment to God, the latter to oneself.

If one were truly grateful for the blessings, then he or she would acknowledge them as a gift from God. But more times than not I hear the same person turning it around and saying "I work hard for what I have and I do not want to give anything to anyone who will not work". This is merely a self-righteous justification to hate and reject those who need. The self admitted blessed person has no material need and he feels imposed upon by anyone with the audacity to need food, clothing, healthcare, or even compassion.

The only moral requirement that a Republican Christian adheres to is to oppose abortion. That love for the fetus' right to life is unconditional, provided it doesn't grow into a child, teenager, or adult that needs healthcare. We just can't afford to pay for that.

Sure, the unwed teenager needs to suck it up and bear the consequence of the pregnancy because it is moral, but don't expect us to help you pay for its health and wellbeing, God understands our needs and He certainly understands our need for low taxes.

The smug "I am blessed but I deserve this" attitude from Republican Christians is in no way different from the words of any Ayn Rand cultist.

On November 25, 2009, Debi Ghate, the Vice President of Academic Affairs at the prestigious Ayn Rand Institute published an editorial in all places, "The Christian Science Monitor."

Her topic was the holiday at hand: Thanksgiving. Her catchy title was "Celebrate Thanksgiving the Ayn Rand way: Thank yourself."

At face value it would be offensive, as she asked rhetorically why we thank God on this day when we deserve the credit, but philosophically her attitude is much more honest than many who give superficial credit to their Creator for blessings.

Anyone who works hard for what they have can certainly endorse Ms. Ghate's plea to embrace materialism and reject the true meaning of Thanksgiving.

> *From a young age, we are bombarded with messages designed to undermine our confident pursuit of values: "Be humble," "You can't know what's good for yourself," "It's better to give than to receive," and, above all, "Don't be selfish!" We are scolded not to take more than "our share" - whether it is of electricity, profits, or pie. We are taught that altruism - not mere benevolence or generosity, but selfless sacrifice for others - is the moral ideal. We are taught to sacrifice for strangers, who inexplicably have a claim to our hard-earned wealth. We are asked to bail out failing banks and uninsured patients. We are asked to serve rather than lead.* **We are taught to kneel rather than reach for the sky.** *[emphasis mine]...We should take pride in being rationally selfish.*
>
> *Thanksgiving is the perfect time to appreciate and celebrate the fruits of our labor: our wealth, health, relationships, and property - all the values we most selfishly cherish. We should thank authors whose books made us rethink our lives, engineers who gave us the BlackBerry and iPhone, and financiers whose capital has helped build entire industries. We should thank ourselves and those individuals whose production makes our lives more comfortable and enjoyable - those who help us live the much-coveted American dream.*
>
> *As you sit down to your sumptuous Thanksgiving dinner, think of all the talented individuals whose innovation and inventiveness made possible the products you are enjoying, even if the spread is a little smaller this year. As you celebrate with your chosen loved ones, thank yourself for everything you have done to make this moment possible. It's a time to selfishly and proudly say: "I earned this."*[11]

So I am saying these things, and saying them as clearly as I can: If you use the expression "blessed" or acknowledge God's will in your life, i.e. if you claim to be a Christian, but you are one that has earned what he has, you are a follower of Ayn Rand just as much as any whiney Objectivist billionaire who complains about his unfair tax burden. If you sincerely claim to be a Christian, then it is your duty to want food, shelter, health care, or any basic substance for the poor. You have no option. Christ commands it.

The lamest excuse I get from Republican Christians is that even though the specific commandment of Christ is to take care of the least of these, they see no civic mandate from Christ for the taking care of the poor.

Odd that they use that loophole to get out of the duty to the poor, while at the same time they insist on a civic mandate against abortion, gay marriage, birth control, gambling, liquor on Sundays, or any other morality fad that appeals to their spiritual vanity.

According to the Republican Party, as the official representative for God, we are to privatize all charity to inoculate it from tax dollars, as we demand "In God We Trust" be tattooed upon our currency. It's more important to brag about being God's favorite than it is to actually do the things He asked us to do.

I was raised as a fundamentalist Christian, and although I do not embrace many of the fundamentalist beliefs today, I certainly have enough experience with fundamentalist Christianity to speak with some authority on the subject.

What I see now in the fundamentalist community is a ghettoization of Christianity, where the fundamentalists wish to extract themselves from the "world", or the secular portion of the world that they inhabit.

The conservative Christians pull away to home schools or private schools if they can afford it, and constantly retreat into cocoons of like-minded people all in the name of maintaining an elevated level of holiness.

Then after recharging with like-minded zealots, the Christians look to interject their presence back at the societal level, as they wish to establish a moral code upon the secular society they shun in all other ways. There is an attempt to have it both ways, to form a separatist community on social matters that affect them, but to force the rest of society to adhere to their Pharisee style code of conduct.

The conservative Christian mindset is that the world is at war with them, waging this war by taking away their right to pray over loudspeakers at a football game, or by refusing to say Merry Christmas, as the secular left forces them to hear Happy Holidays instead. There is no compromise with this group, as they feel they are the only moral side in this debate and the world is sinful. The conservative Christians revel in the hate they receive from those unsaved masses, as they cheer for the destruction of their enemies, all the while pretending to hurt in their hearts for the lost condition of the lost.

I will concede one point. Evangelical Christians are generally hated, not because they follow Christ, but because they loudly claim to follow him, and live in the most anti Christ way possible. There is more materialism, selfishness, hate, bigotry and anger from so-called Christians than there is from a battalion of atheists.

Granted, there have been atheists that have behaved badly, to be sure, but there is a special contempt that society holds, rightly so, for the pious hypocrite that proclaims Christianity without living its tenets.

If a Christian devoted their energy to actually following the words of Christ, rather than trying to speak for Him, then no one would hate them. Who would criticize anyone for wanting compassion for the poor, or loving their neighbor?

Well, I did forget that the most virulent criticism of helping the sick and poor comes from those who proclaim to be Jesus' flock on earth. Look no further than this alert put out by one of the loudest components of the GOP's God Squad, the Family Research Council:

> "This week Congress is debating President Obama's plan to seize control of your personal health care. It will produce a moral disaster that puts you and your family under the thumb of politicians and federal bureaucrats.
>
> But with your help today, Family Research Council (FRC) will battle back against this massive, unprecedented attack on faith, family, and freedom." [12]

Ha, unprecedented attacks on faith, family, and freedom. Universal coverage for healthcare is a much bigger attack on the freedom of Christians than the lions dens were for the first century bunch. Those folks in Saudi Arabia have nothing on the Religious Right. They only THINK they know persecution. Life for the believer is tough under Obama.

No need for any defenses of any Christian to me for his or her life. I realize there are many that are true in their beliefs, and practice love, and to those sincere people, I thank you for your earnestness and good works. But make no mistake, I am attacking those on the right wing who proudly proclaim their humility and usher in Ayn Rand in the name of Christ the capitalist. So as the saying goes, if the shoe fits, wear it.

For those who are of this bunch, you need to realize that you help the cause of Ayn Rand in ways you refuse to recognize. What on earth do you offer the unbeliever that would entice him to your world? A ticket to heaven? Who would want to spend eternity with you?

You offer materialism and a feeling of smug satisfaction? Sure, you do, but Ayn Rand's cult does it better, without all of the ridiculously stringent moral legalism you demand. At least their selfishness is uncoated by hypocrisy and they do not impose their anti-scientific worldview upon others by doing things such as demanding no birth control, no stem cell research or even refusing to give the HPV vaccine as it is better to risk cervical cancer than to let some teenager think it safe to have sex.

Your world is foolish, and it is quite frankly a Hell on earth. You offer no enticement for an afterlife if you are representative of the sample that populates the streets of gold.

Why do I think this way? I look at your agenda, and your leaders. Your cause is corrupt from the top down. I can only believe that you are just as corrupt as your leaders, until you prove otherwise. And your de facto embracing of Ayn Rand isn't really convincing me that you are all that holy.

There is no better example of the corruption of the Religious Right than the case of Ralph Reed, former director of the Christian Coalition.

In order to fully examine his duplicity, we need to examine the devils triangle of Reed, Grover Norquist, and Jack Abramoff.

Abramoff is the disgraced former lobbyist who spent time in the federal penitentiary system for several counts of corruption.

In short, his crimes included a very sophisticated bribery scheme for many members of Congress, including the former Republican House of Representatives Majority Leader Tom DeLay, who has been convicted of money laundering in relation to campaign contributions and is on parole pending his appeal. [13]

Be careful not to draw the wrong conclusion from this sordid story I am about to relay; that is that all politicians are corrupt and subject to corruption through graft and bribery, indeed they are. But this particular case exhibits the widespread nature of the corruption within the Religious Right, the evangelical movement that ostensibly promotes God's work through politics. Bear with me please as I attempt to untangle this complex tale.

Jack Abramoff was one of the top lobbyists in Washington, and he sold his services based on his access to members of Congress. He was also a very passionate right wing ideologue. He believed in the conservative movement. He was the president of the College Republicans during the eighties, as he came of age during the Reagan years.

Jack Abramoff was born in Atlantic City, New Jersey, but moved to Beverly Hills when he was ten years old. He graduated high school in Beverly Hills, where he was an accomplished athlete, as he was both a championship weightlifter and an all conference football player. He was very involved in politics during high school, which grew to participating in Republican Party politics while in college. He was elected as national president of the College Republicans. In that capacity, he formed a tight alliance with Grover Norquist, who is now president of Americans for Tax Reform, Ralph Reed, who later founded the Christian Coalition with Pat Robertson.

Abramoff made a name for himself with his aggressive promotion of the Republican agenda. He also began skirting the legal system with dubious financial transactions. He formed and led the USA Foundation, a group with tax-exempt status because it purported to be nonpartisan. However, the rallies organized by Abramoff always seemed to be pro Reagan rallies, and they coincidentally happened in election year. [14]

Abramoff was very successful in this capacity, as he raised lots of money and more importantly, the profile of the College Republicans. He also established a habit of burning through cash faster than it came through the front door, a reckless habit that proved to be his undoing.

After a brief stint as a movie producer during the eighties, Jack Abramoff returned to his true love, politics and became a lobbyist. Newt Gingrich had stunned the political world and brought the Republicans to a majority party position in Congress for the first time in four decades. During this time, Abramoff met and quickly became friends with Representative Tom Delay of Texas, who would become the Republican Majority Leader under Speaker of the House Newt Gingrich.

Abramoff made a name for himself and quickly got his employers attention. His employer at this time was Preston Gates, a prestigious lobbying firm, with Bill Gates, Sr. as a partner. (This was one of many employers, as Abramoff wore out his welcome at several firms, not coincidentally because of ethical concerns and legal liability of the partners.) But Abramoff was able to impress because he brought Tom Delay into the firm so quickly.

Abramoff rapidly became known as a rainmaker, as he had success with the Mississippi Tribe of Choctaw Indians, as a lobbyist for their tax concerns. Republican Congressman Bill Archer of Texas was chairman of the powerful House Ways and Means Committee (the committee where all taxation bills must originate per the Constitution.)

Archer had proposed taxing the proceeds from the Indian casinos, and the tribe had hired Abramoff to fight this. Abramoff framed this as a conservative concern, as conservatives were the champions of low, or no taxes. He was able to enlist his old college buddy Grover Norquist, who by this time had founded Americans for Tax Reform, and they were able to persuade Tom Delay into exercising his clout in killing this measure. This would be the first of many similar collaborations, all in the name of conservative principles. [15]

Abramoff, Delay and Norquist all had the same vision: a permanent Republican majority. They not only wanted to defeat the left at the ballot box, they wanted to rule Washington with an iron fist and run all liberals out of town. They devised a strategy to defund the left, where money would have to flow to conservatives, not just Republicans, but true conservatives dedicated to destroying the government, Ayn Rand style.

Deval Patrick, the Democrat governor of Massachusetts, recounts a conversation with Grover Norquist, who actually was a college classmate of his. Norquist told him of his scheme decades ago in college, where the Republicans would maintain a permanent majority, and how he and others would make it impossible for a "Democrat to govern as a Democrat."[16] Be careful what you wish for, you just might get it. It isn't what it is cracked up to be.

And the Republicans got it, due in no small part to the foursome of Tom Delay, Jack Abramoff, Grover Norquist, and Ralph Reed, who brought almost all conservative Christians into the GOP.

The Center for Public Integrity, a watchdog group that concerns itself with lobbying and campaign contributions, conducted a study and found that in the early 1990's, political donations from 19 major industries - including pharmaceuticals, defense, commercial banking and accounting - were split about evenly between the two parties, but by 2003 had overwhelmingly favored Republicans, as they received at a 2-1 advantage.[17]

Tom Delay declared that the GOP was open for business, and that the business of the GOP was business. He lamented that there was too little money in politics, as he felt democracy could not be served unless the underrepresented business interests made their voices known by way of contributions. Delay also told corporations that if they expected an audience with the Republican leadership, they had better hire Republican lobbyists. This led to a purging of any lobbyists who weren't ideologically aligned with the Republicans.[18]

Then the money started rolling in for all concerned. The process was repeated over and over, and perfected. With respect to money laundering and campaign finance, it was lather, rinse, repeat.

It worked like this: a wealthy client, some Indian tribe, a sweatshop owner, or Russian oil interests would hire Abramoff. They would want their political interests (i.e. financial interests) represented. Abramoff would take a huge fee, and then contact Delay, who would consider the issue and move on it if he deemed it worthy. Delay would often deem those projects worthy that donated to his favorite "charities".

The money was funneled from the special interest into a third party, like Grover Norquist's Americans for Tax Reform, or Ralph Reed's Christian lobbying group, Century Strategies, and into the campaign coffers of the politician and/or charity. This is where the greed really got out of hand, and not coincidentally, the Religious Right got involved. Most of what follows, with respect to the Indian matters, is documented in a U.S. Senate Committee on Indian Affairs hearing conducted in 2005.

I use the term most, because the Senate committee, chaired by John McCain, purposely excluded some damning facts from testimony or its records. There was plenty that damned Abramoff and his partner in crime Michael Scanlon, to be sure, but the testimony that damned almost all of Congress was deemed to be not in the scope of the investigation.

Therefore, any testimony that implicated most of Congress never saw the light of day in committee. Ralph Reed and Grover Norquist were never even subpoenaed, even though the evidence suggested possible federal crimes involving money laundering and bribery. It would have been nice to have them under oath to clear their names and put to rest all of these questions.

The report by the Senate Committee on Indian Affairs, (linked here [19] establishes a narrative, and a case by case documentation of how the shakedown occurred. The general narrative worked thusly: an Indian tribe was concerned about government policy, at first it was strictly tax issues, later it evolved to a fear of competition from other tribes who wished to enter into the lucrative gaming business.

For taxation purposes, Abramoff would take a large retainer, and then arrange for the funding of some trip, or the contribution to a favorite charity of Tom Delay, or even a campaign contribution, after it had been funneled through an appropriate charity or lobbying group, as not to appear that the devout evangelical Tom Delay was on the take for gambling interests.

Delay's initial reaction to criticism when details of this scam were first brought to light was to say that he was under attack because of his beliefs as an evangelical Christian, and that this was part of a broader attack on Christianity. [20]

What better man to defend a fellow conservative Christian than Ralph Reed, the "right hand of God?" as described by a fawning Time magazine cover story.[15] Reed at 33 had been instrumental in the rise of the Republicans, as his Christian Coalition had brought in evangelical Christians to the Republican fold. Now, a decade later, Reed had spun off his own consulting firm, Century Strategies, which brought an expertise in Christianity based lobbying.

Ralph Reed was old friends with Jack Abramoff throughout his college days, and had worked closely with each other throughout their political careers. While the Lord works in mysterious ways, Reed carried the Lord's work further, working in covert, fraudulent, yet profitable ways. The U.S. Senate's Committee on Indian Affairs documents all the details and evidence.

Abramoff had developed a close working friendship with Michael Scanlon. Scanlon was an independent political consultant. He got his start as the media spokesman for Tom Delay, where in this capacity he met and formed a friendship with Jack Abramoff.

In 2000, he quit to go in business for himself as a consultant. He had all the traits needed for super success, charm, a strong work ethic, and dishonesty. He started his consulting lobbying career still in debt with his student loans, in four years however he had received $82 million in fees from Indian tribes between 2000 and 2004. [21]

Abramoff was successful, no doubt, but he wasn't making enough money for his efforts. Michael Scanlon approached him about a brilliant idea to enrich both of them, where Abramoff would recommend to his clients that they should hire Scanlon, as Abramoff would endorse him as one of the best in the business. The tribe would hire Scanlon, he would demand outrageous fees, but promised results that no one else could deliver. Unbeknownst to the tribes, Scanlon would kick back half of the fee to Abramoff. This was not disclosed of course, and some would call it fraud. Not Scanlon and Abramoff, they called it "gimme five." "Gimme five" became the codeword they used among each other, and in emails. Boy howdy did they discuss this in emails. The Senate committee had thousands of emails to use to hang around Abramoff's neck. The emails did not paint a pretty picture of Abramoff, Scanlon, as you might have guessed, or of Ralph Reed and Grover Norquist.

In 1999, Ralph Reed had sent an email to Abramoff saying,

> *"Hey, now that I'm done with electoral politics, I need to start humping in corporate accounts! I'm counting on you to help me with some contacts."* [22]

Of course his lust for money didn't begin there, and this email does not explain why he was through with electoral politics. He had resigned from the Christian Coalition one step in front of an investigation. [23]

But now Ralph Reed was free to chase the dollar, and Abramoff gave him a contract to help the Mississippi Choctaws, who were afraid that gambling was about to be legalized in Alabama, which would cause great suppressing effect on the wages of sin, at least with the Choctaw's cut. Ralph lobbied to prevent gambling in my home state. Later, when confronted with the fact that he defeated gambling using gambling money, Ralph Reed told this big ole whopper:

*"I was approached in 1999 by a friend that I met in
the College Republicans," says Reed. "He said, 'There's an
effort to bring five new casino-style operations to Alabama.
Would you be willing to help us stop them?' And I said, 'Yes,
I would. I'm opposed to casino gambling expansion, but I can
only do it if I won't be paid with revenues from other
casinos.'... "If I had known then what I know now, I would
have turned that work down. But I will tell you that the work
that I did either prevented from opening, or closed, eight
gambling casinos, and we will never know how many
marriages and lives were saved by the work that I did."[24]*

A closer look at Senate testimony shows that the
"Right Hand of God" must have had his left hand behind
his back, with his fingers crossed:

Quoting from the Senate's Committee on Indian
Affairs report:

*Abramoff saw an opportunity: he suggested a
grassroots effort and recommended the Choctaw hire Reed to
orchestrate an anti- gaming effort.*

*The Tribe agreed to hire Reed to mobilize
grassroots opposition to various legislative proposals
throughout the Gulf Coast that would have increased gaming,
thereby diminishing the Choctaw casino's market share.*

*No one from the Choctaw had any direct contact
with Reed; rather, Abramoff served as the liaison with Reed
and his firm, which eventually became a subcontractor to
Preston Gates.[25]*

To summarize this point: Ralph Reed went to
work for Abramoff's firm, Preston Gates, therefore all pay
was through them. But, there's more.

Continuing from the report, citing a letter of
agreement that Reed and Abramoff made:

*According to a draft engagement letter from Reed
to Abramoff, Reed was hired to defeat a bill that had passed
the Alabama House of Representatives "authorizing dog
tracks in the state to install video poker and other casino-style
games on their sites."*

*Reed promised to "build a strong grassroots
network across the state against the extension of video poker
and [REDACTION]."*

> He claimed that no firm had better relationships
> than his with the grassroots conservatives in Alabama,
> including the Alabama Christian Coalition, the Alabama
> Family Alliance, the Alabama Eagle Forum, the Christian
> Family Association, and "leading evangelical pastors such as
> Frank Barker of Briarwood Presbyterian Church in
> Birmingham."
>
> Reed boasted that "Century Strategies has on file
> over 3,000 pastors and 90,000 religious conservative
> households in Alabama that can be accessed in this effort."[26]

Ralph Reed could not have possibly doubted whom his financial masters were when he received an email from Abramoff with the subject line "Disbursements from Choctaw Indians", which contained explicit accounts of the payments and how they were to be laundered through Preston Gates. Ralph even responded with pride that he was bringing in one of the biggest names in God's work, Dr. James Dobson.:

> Reed also claimed that he was leveraging his
> contacts within the Christian community for the Choctaw's
> benefit. Reed reported to Abramoff that there would be "a
> saturation statewide radio buy with a new ad by Jim Dobson
> that he will record tomorrow."
>
> Reed assured Abramoff, "We are opening the
> bomb bay doors and holding nothing back. If victory is
> possible, we will achieve it," and, one day later, again
> promised, "All systems are go on our end and nothing is
> being held back."[27]

Somewhere along this time, the prestigious firm of Preston Gates got skittish about participating in money laundering. Grover Norquist, had no second thoughts about it, provided of course that he was reimbursed for his trouble.

Grover Norquist's Americans for Tax Reform was used as a money-laundering vehicle, from the Choctaw Indians, to Americans for Tax Reform, to Ralph Reed's Century Strategies, minus Grover's handling fee.

It should be obvious that a political operative such as Grover Norquist who devotes his life to promoting selfishness at the expense of his country would not do anything without a fee attached, even if it were doing the Lord's work, like Ralph Reed was doing. Ayn Rand would have been proud, she would have been prouder still to know that Grover Norquist now controls the entire Republican Party, but that is for later.

Back to Ralph Reed, the Right Hand of God. Quoting the Senate report:

> The question arises why the Choctaw paid money to Reed through various conduits, such as Preston Gates and ATR, rather than directly. [Director of the Choctaw's financial affairs Nell] Rogers told Committee staff, "I always assumed it's because Ralph was more comfortable with that."
>
> Rogers understood from Abramoff that "Ralph Reed did not want to be paid directly by a tribe with gaming interests. It was our understanding that the structure was recommended by Jack Abramoff to accommodate Mr. Reed's political concerns."
>
> Nevertheless, the work Reed and his company Century Strategies performed and for which they were paid through Preston Gates and ATR was on the Tribe's behalf and for its benefit. The Tribe has no complaints about the quality of work Reed undertook on its behalf.[28]

Ralph Reed claimed to have not known about being on the dole of gambling (incidentally he was running for office when he made that claim) but the Choctaw's surely knew who he was, and went through a lot of trouble to get the money to him.

Grover Norquist could not stomach this for too long. He quit laundering money for Ralph Reed after he contemplated the possibility of his good name being sullied with anti gambling interests. Grover Norquist has principles, and those principles direct him to seek money from all that would wish to avoid taxation, and if it were known he were part of a moral crusade to crush gambling, then gambling interests would not pour money his way. Grover Norquist then took a stand and washed his hands of the whole sorry mess, and let Ralph Reed and Abramoff worry about money laundering on their own.[29]

This template was used several times, with money paid to Reed through neutral organizations, so that gambling interests would not be tied to him, and he could portray himself as a moral crusader. Ralph Reed never had a problem disclosing his work for Enron, in fact he recommended that they hire Abramoff due to his close relationship with Tom Delay. [30] But taint from casinos would be too much for Ralph's pristine reputation. But the taint did nothing to prohibit Ralph Reed receiving over 5 million in fees from them.

Michael Scanlon through all of this accumulation of wealth never forgot his roots, that is, his lifeguard roots. He continued to work part time as a lifeguard, working out to maintain his David Hasselhoff physique and lifestyle, even as he was raking in millions of dollars.

Scanlon's pals were all lifeguards and were astonished at how their buddy had become so successful, and they couldn't help but notice, as he always bragged about his mansion, formerly owned by the Dupont family, on the Delaware shore, an estate in St. Bart's and an in-town apartment at the Ritz-Carlton in the District. Michael Scanlon felt he was so stretched out that he had to charter a helicopter to take him back and forth to work. [31]

Scanlon went just a little too far when he created a dummy organization, and staffed it with dummies.

He got one of his lifeguard buddies on board to become a president of a think tank. He created the prestigious American International Center, or the AIC. This was alleged to be a respected international think tank. Which was true, except for the parts about it being respected, the international designation, or the classification as a think tank. It actually wasn't anything more than a title, an address, and a means to funnel money.

To head the prestigious AIC, Michael Scanlon recruited a lifeguard buddy named David Grosh whose professional experience consisted of tanning, surfing, and saving the occasional distressed swimmer. David Grosh conceded he thought it odd to be asked, but what-the-hey? Party on, dude!

Quoting the Senate's report:

192

> *In his interview with Committee staff, he readily concedecd that his professional and educational background were completely unrelated to the purported mission of AIC of "enhancing the methods of empowerment for territories, commonwealths and sovereign nations in the possession of and within the United States."*
>
> *He also conceded that his background did not qualify him to serve on the board of "an international think tank."*
>
> *Throughout the time that Grosh served as a director of AIC, he thought that "this was some silly game that Scanlon was playing."[32]*

For his hard work as director of this organization, David Grosh received 3000 dollars, and a promise to go surfing in St. Bart's, which he never had to opportunity to exercise that compensation perk.

The various Indian tribes paid AIC tens of millions of dollars in fees, and Ralph Reed personally received over 4 million for his services.[33] I am assuming that he had no idea that the institute that gave him 4 million dollars was in fact a beach house with a couple of computers, given his shock at being duped by gambling interests before. He really should research his clients better, or at the least make it a policy to know who is writing any million-dollar check he might receive.

The most egregious case of this duplicity came with regards to the Tigua Tribe in Texas. Abramoff and company, including Ralph Reed, were lobbying hard to close down the casinos in Texas, as it posed a threat to one of their clients.

Ralph Reed used his connections in the network of churches in Texas, including the Second Baptist Church of Houston, Texas, with over 12,000 members. Thanks in part to Reed's efforts, Texas shut down the casino.

Meanwhile, Abramoff was working to get the Tigua's business. He offered his expertise in getting the casino reopened; even though unbeknownst to them he accelerated it closing. He admitted he knew Ralph Reed, but he said Reed was "crazy, like other folks in the Christian Coalition."[34]

GEORGE KELLEY

Abramoff offered to represent them for free, and recommended they hire Michael Scanlon, with no disclosure of his partnership. Scanlon was hired, and jacked up his price, and received 4.2 million in three months, which he promptly split with Abramoff. Abramoff and Scanlon would exchange mocking emails about the tribe, and then approach them the next day with crocodile tears about their plight. Abramoff had the tribe pay several hundred in donations to a Congressman's campaign, Republican Congressman Robert Wey of Ohio, so he would then attach a rider to a bill with language authorizing the casino.

At the end of the day, it fell apart, with the Tigua's getting no relief on the casino, but Abramoff and company millions richer, and Congressman Wey compensated for his trouble.[35]

Abramoff saw that his greed was bleeding the tribe, which distressed him greatly, as it would have no more money to pay him. He then devised a win/win solution for everyone! He was to arrange for life insurance policies for every member of the tribe over 75, and the death payouts would go towards his fee. He called this the "Tigua Elder Legacy Project", which was a nice way of saying it was a dead Indian Fund."[36]

Abramoff never got the opportunity to pull the trigger on that one, as the tribe said, in their words, "it felt uncomfortable." Notwithstanding the Tigua's wimpiness in the refusal to sell the corpses of their elders, Abramoff he did have a brainstorm as to how it could be bigger and more lucrative project. He sent his old buddy Ralph Reed an email on June 22, 2003, wanting to discuss his expanded vision. The subject line was "*Black Churches insurance program.*" Since the family of God crosses racial lines, Ralph had a great deal of credibility in black churches, and discussed the insurance policies on the elders in the black churches. Abramoff wrote

"Per our previous discussion. Let me know how we can move forward to chat with folks who can set this up with African American elders. It can be huge. Thanks."[37]

Ralph Reed was always quick to follow his moral compass, which was always pointed towards money, so he replied,

> *"Yes, it looks interesting. I assume you'll set up a meeting in DC as a next step, or whatever we should do next, let me know."*

Ralph Reed's spokesperson dismisses this as just another unsolicited offer to make money. She said that Ralph never took that seriously.[38]

But perhaps one could justify Ralph Reed's excursion into gambling lobbying by believing it was for a good cause, as he used their money to stop the spread of gambling. And maybe, just maybe he wanted the insurance policies for the benefit of the black church elders. One might think Abramoff was just projecting when he told his buddy Scanlon in an email that Ralph Reed was "a bad version of us!"[39] These things could possibly be rationalized, but it would take an active imagination for anyone to explain his defense of slavery, rape, and forced abortion all in the name of Jesus Christ.

The Commonwealth of the Northern Mariana Islands is a tropical paradise, if you are a tourist. If you happen to work there, it hasn't always been a paradise. Not because of the oppression from the government that all good Republicans feel when their opportunity to crush the working class is hindered in any way. But because of the fact that there were no government protections in place for workers for the longest time, in a territory that is part of the United States of America no less.

The United States inherited the Mariana Islands during World War II. It became a territory under our jurisdiction then, and subsequently enjoyed all of the benefits that come with the protection of the United States and its military. It did not enjoy our immigration and labor laws. It was promoted as a place where businesses could flourish without any government regulation.

Tom Delay proudly called it a "Petri dish of capitalism." What that actually meant is that sweatshops could open for business in Saipan, located in the Mariana Islands, with no minimum wage, no environmental standards, and no troublesome OSHA requirements.

All of these perks for businessmen and they even got to put "Made in the USA" on the tags of the blouses and shirts produced, and never even had to consider tariffs, as the clothes were indeed made in the USA's territory.

Well, wouldn't you know it, those union types really wanted to rain on the parade of prosperity. They saw the "Made in the USA" label, with no tariff, as unfair to American workers who had to pay a livable wage. Who could compete with labor that worked for $2.50 per hour? Not only that, the worker drones would not only work for near nothing, they'd do most anything else for peanuts, and often they were forced to.

The workers were almost all immigrants, and many from China. In fact, the communist Chinese government owned the sweatshops in a large part. They would bring immigrants in to the Mariana's and then slap a huge price tag on the transport, and confiscate their passport until it was paid off. You can probably do the math and decide that it would take many hours at two bucks per hour to pay off these human herders. To add to the indignity, the workers were forced to live in shacks behind barbed wire fence. The factories boasted of free housing, but it turned out to be the type of housing that chain gang members get over here. Women immigrants would be raped, sodomized, and beaten by the factory management. Some were chained to their sewing machines; the doors to the factories were locked so that the workers didn't sneak out.

The worst was the forced sexual slavery. Young women were forced into prostitution, or working in strip clubs by their capitalist overlords. If they got pregnant they were advised to either abort or to face deportation back to China. [40]

All of this is documented in a Department of Interior report from 1995, several reports from human rights groups and testimony given to Congress here, and Democratic Representative George Miller of California, when he visited the island.

I note that Representative Miller heard the testimony first hand on the island, but I do not mean to imply that he was the only one that visited. Over 40 members of Congress, almost all Republicans with a few pro-business Democrats (not all of us are socialists) visited the island on a fact-finding mission sponsored by Jack Abramoff. Abramoff had been hired by the sleazy sweatshop owners to fight any type of federal regulations, and through his buddy Tom Delay he was able to shoot down all of the efforts to regulate the sexual slave trade out of existence. [41]

One Republican who visited was Representative Bob Schaffer, Republican-Colorado. He had ventured to Saipan with his wife, to investigate fully these horrible charges. He said, *"'I plan to walk right into those factories and living quarters to see for myself what conditions exist."* As far as he could tell, none of those conditions existed. Of course most of the time he and his wife were sightseeing, snorkeling, playing golf, and staying at the luxury hotel provided by the group that sponsored his trip. The group was an organization with very pious sounding name, the Traditional Values Coalition. Apparently the traditional values promoted were old school traditions; the values of slavery, exploitation, and power of the wealthy over the feudal class. Quoting a Denver Post article on Congressman Schaffer:

> Schaffer's $13,000 trip was paid for by the Orange County, Calif.-based Traditional Values Coalition, which Schaffer described as a religious group "concerned with human rights."
>
> "Whatever involvement (Abramoff) had with Traditional Values Coalition wasn't known at the time," Wadhams said.
>
> Later investigations have shown that in many instances, TVC – which claims to represent 43,000 churches – acted virtually as a political arm of Abramoff's lobbying operation. [42]

God bless them all for doing the Lord's work!

It should be noted that none of the Republican members who visited took the time to speak to workers without management present. Representative George Miller did, and had one immigrant beg him to buy one of his kidneys so that he could pay off his masters on the island and return back to China. [43] Tom Delay met with the factory owners, in between rounds of golf and sunbathing, and told them:

> *"You are up against the forces of big labor and the radical left. Dick Armey and I made a promise to defend the island's present system. Stand firm. Resist evil. Remember that all truth and blessings emanate from our Creator."* [44]

That is truly standing up for what is right! Just like in the Book of Judges, when the Israelites were smiting Philistine union thugs and calling down God's wrath upon those who would enslave them with the minimum wage. The Children of Israel left Egypt for precisely that reason, refusing to take union benefits like paid vacations and sick leave when they were building the Pharaoh's pyramids. God's will be done, on earth as it is in Heaven, with no complaining allowed from those who toil.

But even with Tom Delay's moral crusade to protect the owners from the feds, Abramoff had to enlist the Right Hand of God, Ralph Reed. Ralph received a nice chunk of change to lobby members of Congress, including Congressman Bob Riley of Alabama, who would later become Alabama's governor. Ralph sent out mailings to thousands of Alabama voters that said

> *"The radical left, the Big Labor Union Bosses, and Bill Clinton want to pass a law preventing Chinese from coming to work on the Mariana Islands,"* the mailer from Reed's firm said. The Chinese workers, it added, *"are exposed to the teachings of Jesus Christ"* while on the islands, and many *"are converted to the Christian faith and return to China with Bibles in hand."* [45]

Ralph Reed when confronted with this in 2006, as he was running for the Lt. Governor of Georgia, expressed shock that any thing like this was going on, just as the Congressmen who visited the island were shocked. Even though he received millions from the Mariana Islands, Ralph simply had no idea these things were going on. [46] Besides, prostitution and slavery beat union life every day of the week.

Why would you take Ralph Reed's moral guidance, or for that matter, his word on any matter? Ralph Reed instructed his Christian Coalition troops that unions were against God's will and were sinful. The verse he justified this worldview with had to do with slaves respecting their masters. Of course this is the view of "The Fellowship", a cult like group of evangelicals who sponsor the National Prayer Breakfast. Conservative Christians angrily condemned President Obama for not attending one year. I don't see why anyone would be compelled to go to this Holy Roller dog and pony show. This group was founded on the principle that too much attention was given to the poor in Christianity, and not enough to the wealthy. Doug Coe, the highly influential leader of this group asks that new recruits study Hitler, to see what a few motivated men can do. [47] Why does they feel the need to embrace Hitler's method of spreading his message, did the Apostle Paul not inspire them enough? Of course, the same question can be asked of any one who uses Ayn Rand to promote capitalism, rather than Adam Smith.

Ralph Reed should have known about all of these things. But he cashed the checks and claimed ignorance, and currently has a new organization, the Faith and Freedom Coalition. [48]

On this site you can see Ralph with all of the major Republican candidates, all of them: Michelle Bachman, Mitt Romney, Herman Cain, Rick Santorum and every other candidate.

They are all there pictured with Reed, aligned with him to kiss his ring. On the site, you can find menu links to donate, and to join prayer groups, appropriately in that order. You can also find Ralph Reed's Twitter feed linked, and at the very moment I am typing this, his latest Tweet reads:

"@ralphreed: News Corp stock continues to rebound. http://on.wsj.com/nBNBi0"[49]

That's just like Ralph Reed, never too far away from financial news; particularly the financial fortunes of the right wing propaganda machine, News Corp, which owns Fox News and the Wall Street Journal. Ralph had to be wrapped up in hours of fervent prayer for News Corp given the scandals that have been brought to light about Rupert Murdoch.

So why in the world would Christians link themselves to politicians? What are the causes that would justify the cheapening of the brand name, Christian? Tax cuts and corporate abuses? Indian gambling? Sexual slavery and forced abortions? Are these the crusades that are worthy enough to pick up under the Christian banner?

Americans have had a shameful relationship with religion and politics. The Civil War saw both sides claiming God on their side. The Southern Baptist Convention became the SOUTHERN Baptist Convention because they were convinced that God wanted the darkies to be slaves, never mind the commandment to love thy neighbor as thyself. That was for Yankees.

Of course the Southern Baptist Convention was noble enough to admit it was wrong, in 1995. As a two for one, they threw in an apology for their stance on segregation.[50]

So I ask, why the change in policy? Are God's commandments for us not eternal? If it were a sin to free slaves then, would it not be the same today? What about the ministers that burned Elvis Presley records during the 1950's claiming they were of the devil? Has God changed his mind now that Elvis overdosed on prescription pills and peanut butter/banana sandwiches?

Why the passion for fads? Would it not lead you to think that perhaps not every cause attributed to God is actually of God? Perhaps sometimes evil and cynical people use God to motivate very emotional and gullible people to do their bidding, and in the process allow them to have warm fuzzies about how special they are? Maybe the term "useful idiots" applies more than "fellow travelers?"

But will conservatives protest these abuses? Don't bet on it. Will they demand the removal of Ayn Rand's books? I doubt it. The last time I recall evangelicals getting up in arms about books (other than text books that teach evolution or that FDR was a good president) was with the Harry Potter books. Harry Potter is of Satan, those books promote witchcraft, and all of the good evangelicals tell us to avoid them. Imagine my surprise when I found this opinion piece, written by the mother of all witchcraft, J.K. Rowling, from the "London Sunday Times." Just in case you aren't aware, J.K. Rowling is quite wealthy from her Harry Potter tales. She's a billionaire, and one of the top (non royalty) people in England in terms of wealth. She would be a Christian Republican's dream girl in most situations.

This editorial was written in advance of the Parliamentary election in 2010. David Cameron and the Tories (the conservatives who favor low tax, less welfare) were on the verge of defeating the Labour Party (the liberals who wish to support social programs through taxes).

Her editorial was entitled "*The single mother's manifesto*" with the subheading "*David Cameron says the 'nasty party' that castigated people like me has changed. I'm not buying it.*"

Rowling goes on to explain within this editorial how difficult life was before she wrote Harry Potter. She was a single mother, abandoned by her husband. She was on welfare, and didn't have much more than what the government gave her.

201

The Tories had a great idea to encourage family values by offering a bonus to welfare moms who get married. Rowling recounts having her flat broken into, and not even having money to call a locksmith to fix the lock. She states in response to this policy of encouraging marriage through financial rewards:

> "Nobody who has ever experienced the reality of poverty could say "it's not the money, it's the message". When your flat has been broken into, and you cannot afford a locksmith, it is the money. When you are two pence short of a tin of baked beans, and your child is hungry, it is the money. When you find yourself contemplating shoplifting to get nappies, it is the money. If Mr Cameron's only practical advice to women living in poverty, the sole careers of their children, is "get married, and we'll give you £150", he reveals himself to be completely ignorant of their true situation."
>
> "How many prospective husbands did I ever meet, when I was the single mother of a baby, unable to work, stuck inside my flat, night after night, with barely enough money for life's necessities? Should I have proposed to the youth who broke in through my kitchen window at 3am? Half a billion pounds, to send a message – would it not be more cost-effective, more personal, to send all the lower-income married people flowers?"[51]

It would seem that British conservatives have the same knee jerk reaction and demonize the poor, although they haven't been as successful at rolling back the safety net.

Rowling then tells the reader that she is indeed wealthy, and she made a conscious choice not to move away from England, in spite of their ridiculously high taxes. She did not want to be a tax dodger. I'll let her explain her motives:

> "I chose to remain a domiciled taxpayer for a couple of reasons. The main one was that I wanted my children to grow up where I grew up, to have proper roots in a culture as old and magnificent as Britain's; to be citizens, with everything that implies, of a real country, not free-floating ex-pats, living in the limbo of some tax haven and associating only with the children of similarly greedy tax exiles.

> *A second reason, however, was that I am indebted to the British welfare state; the very one that Mr. Cameron would like to replace with charity handouts. When my life hit rock bottom, that safety net, threadbare though it had become under John Major's Government, was there to break the fall. I cannot help feeling, therefore, that it would have been contemptible to scarper for the West Indies at the first sniff of a seven-figure royalty cheque. This, if you like, is my notion of patriotism".* [52]

My goodness. What am I to think? I am told by evangelicals that this woman has pushed evil on our children, yet in her attitude I see more patriotism for her country and more of Christ's compassion than I do in millions of our own Tea Party Prayer Warrior Patriots. In fact, the Tea Party Prayer Warriors are constantly pushing a book that is a whole lot less entertaining than "Harry Potter" on us, and a great deal more nefarious, in "Atlas Shrugged." What should I think?

So what does the duty of the Christian entail? I don't profess to have the answers; I just can share my convictions. It isn't my place to condemn Jews, atheists, homosexuals, or Democrats to Hell. I will leave that task to God, and if He has delegated it to the Republicans, then we are all in trouble. I don't understand most of the Bible, and I find some stories like Noah's Ark difficult to accept on a factual basis.

But as I have said, facts aren't necessarily truth. I do see a lot of truth in the Bible, and I do understand those truths loud and clear. I understand the part about helping the least of these, and like J.K. Rowling, I recall in the most painful manner being one of those myself.

C.S. Lewis, in his classic work "Mere Christianity," makes a case that the worse sin of mankind is pride. Pride got Adam and Eve expelled, if one believes the Garden of Eden. Pride got Lucifer cast out of Heaven. Pride will damn your eternal soul as you think you do not need God, if one were to believe the Gospels. The antithesis of pride is humility, which was the essence of Christ.

There is no pride with God incarnate as man, dying for those who did not deserve it. The meek shall inherit the earth. The Messiah did not come to be served; but to serve. Lewis adds this passage in the section on pride:

> "That raises a terrible question. How is it that people who are quite obviously eaten up with Pride can say they believe in God and appear to themselves very religious?
>
> I am afraid it means they are worshipping an imaginary God. They theoretically admit themselves to be nothing in the presence of this phantom god, but are really all the time imagining how He approves of them and thinks them far better than ordinary people: that is, they pay a pennyworth of imaginary humility to Him and get out of it a pound's worth of Pride towards their fellow men. I suppose it was of those people Christ was thinking of when He said that some would preach about Him and cast out devils in His name, only to be told at the end of the world that He had never known them.[53]

I'll be the first to admit that I struggle with pride, as all men do. But it isn't me with Ayn Rand in my midst. You who thump the Bible the loudest need to check your premises, as Ayn would say.

Going back to "Sullivan's Travels," there are two profound scenes that represent false Christianity versus real Christianity.

As I noted, the plot is about wealthy director John L. Sullivan, who is on a search to witness suffering. During this journey, he meets an actress that becomes his sidekick. After roughing it for a short while in homeless shelters, he returns full of pride, as if he now knows what it is like to go without. He wants to thank the little guys for showing him the truth. He goes amongst the homeless with a thousand bucks in cash, giving a five spot to everyone he sees. One tramp, who had stolen Sullivan's shoes coincidentally, follows him to knock him on the head and shoves his body into a freight car. A train kills the tramp as he dropped his cash on the tracks, and Sullivan wakes up disoriented and without his memory down south, and ends up assaulting a railroad thug in self-defense.

Sullivan at this time is groggy because of the head injury. He goes to trial and cannot remember his name. The judge treats him with the same justice that comes to all poor vagrants with no money and influence; he sentences him to hard labor on a chain gang. Sullivan is transferred to the farm, and realizes now what true suffering is. One night as a treat, all of the convicts are taken to a poor black church, where they had a Mickey Mouse cartoon for entertainment. He realizes the importance of a simple laugh, and comes to see how essential his escapist movies were.

He escapes the prison by confessing to his own murder, as the national press had thought him dead. He gets out, decides that the true value in films comes from taking peoples minds off of their troubles, and tosses "O Brother Where Art Thou?" aside.

The Christian allegory here is not explicitly stated, but it is there. Two scenes demonstrate this.

One has Sullivan and his sidekick in a crowded homeless mission. This portion of the film has no dialogue; it just has music playing as if it were a silent film.

In the shelter, you see a wild-eyed preacher waving his arms, pounding his Bible. You don't know what he is saying, but you sense it is passionate.

The camera pans and shows the homeless: bored, tired and just trying to get along while waiting for food and shelter. No one there is listening to the preacher, except maybe the preacher.

Fast forward to later in the movie when Sullivan is on the chain gang. In this remarkable scene the gang shuffles into the poor black church, as guests of the church's members. Given the state of blacks socially in 1941, particularly in the south, this scene stands out.

The minister tells his flock that they have special guests coming, and to clear the first two rows. He warns them sternly, *"Do not by any word or action make them feel uncomfortable. We are all sinners and you do not judge them."*

Here the film shows the lowest of all social stratum, the poor black citizen, showing love, respect, and mercy to the one group that was actually lower; the shackled convict. They come in and watch Mickey Mouse and Pluto, and laugh loudly as they escape from their misery.

That's the Gospel; sharing love, making someone laugh, and helping him or her by lightening their load. It isn't in preaching doctrine; it this case, it was a cartoon, and in my case it was a hot dog.

I was in basic training for the army at Ft. Sill, Oklahoma in 1984. On July the 1st, many of us were taken off base to visit the First Baptist Church of Lawton, Oklahoma, as it was a Sunday and the church had a special Fourth of July service.

I sat through the service and couldn't tell you what it was about, or if I agreed with it. I am quite sure it had some theological or doctrinal lesson for us. But afterwards, they fed us, and honored us for being in the military.

A nice woman gave me a hotdog, and she hugged my neck and said "Thank you for your service." I remember that very well. It was the first act of kindness I had received since arriving in basic training. I was overwhelmed.

I have never given the sermon a second thought, except to remember I was there and I actually stayed awake to be polite, just as the hobos did in the movie "Sullivan's Travels." But I have never forgotten the hotdog. The hotdog was more of the Gospel than the preaching, in my opinion. It had love attached to it, no other strings, no proselytizing, or lecturing.

Forget about social programs or food stamps, I ask you Republicans: O brother, where art thou, when the poor need love?

One more note, and I'll close this chapter. Christian fundamentalists worry about God's wrath and His destroying the U.S. because we have strayed. I hear that abortion may finally do us in, or it might be that we now allow gays to marry. We are told that Sodom and Gomorrah should be lessons for us to heed. Let me quote from the Bible, Ezekiel 16:49

> "Now this was the sin of your sister Sodom: She and her daughters were arrogant, overfed and unconcerned; they did not help the poor and needy."

GEORGE KELLEY

SOURCES CONSULTED FOR CHAPTER 4

[1] Truman, H., *Campaign Speech Indianapolis, Indiana October 15, 1948*, 1948. Available from <u>Campaign speech, Indianapolis, Indiana, October 15, 1948. President's Secretary's Files, Truman Papers.</u>
[2] **Doyle, Arthur Conan** "A Scandal In Bohemia": The Strand Magazine ,London; July to December 1891 Vol. 2 Available from: <u>Electronic Text Center, University of Virginia Library</u>
[3] Ibid.
[4] Radosh, R., *"Commies: A Journey Through the Old Left, The New Left, and the Leftover Left"*. Independent Women's Forum, 2001 Available from: http://www.iwf.org/news/show/18760.html
[5] <u>National Center For Children In Poverty-50 State Policy Wizard</u>
[6] Board of Governors Federal Reserve System. *"Did the Community Reinvestment Act (CRA) contribute to foreclosures and the financial crisis? And, is the CRA being reformed?"*. Current FAQs Informing the public about the Federal Reserve; Available from:<u>FAQ's for Board of Governors Federal Reserve Bank</u>
[7] *National Film Registry*. National Film Preservation Board ; Available from: http://www.loc.gov/film/registry_titles.php
[8] IMDB. *Quotes from "Sullivan's Travels"*.; Available from: http://www.imdb.com/title/tt0034240/quotes
[9] Stoller, Paul. "Tea Party America" The Huffington Post, September 14, 2011.Available from http://www.huffingtonpost.com/paul-stoller/tea-party-america_b_962093.html
[10] Howard, Rev. Anne. "Christians Clapping for Death?" The Huffington Post Available from http://www.huffingtonpost.com/anne-howard/christianity-view-of-death-penalty_b_955952.html
[11] Ghate, D. "Celebrate Thanksgiving the Ayn Rand way: Thank yourself" Christian Science Monitor November 25, 2009 Available from: <u>http://www.csmonitor.com/Commentary/Opinion/2009/1125/p09s01-coop.html</u>
[12] *"To Hell with Health Care Reform: Religious Right Leaders Attack Obama, Spout GOP Dogma about "Socialism" While Fanning Flames on Abortion"*. Right Wing Watch Date; Available from: <u>http://aara.pfaw.org/rww-in-focus/to-hell-with-health-care-reform-religious-right-leaders-attack-obama-spout-gop-dogma-about-so</u>
[13] Author Unknown "Ex-House leader Tom DeLay convicted of money-laundering" Wed Nov 24, 2010 [cited July 15, 2011]Available from: <u>http://www.reuters.com/article/2010/11/24/us-usa-politics-delay-idUSTRE6AN6O520101124</u>.
[14] Gibney, A., *"Casino Jack and the United States of Money"*, 2010, Magnolia Pictures United States.
[15] Stone, P.H., *Heist: Superlobbyist Jack Abramoff, his Republican allies, and the buying of Washington*2006: Farrar Straus & Giroux. P. 35
[16] Patrick, D. "How Grover Norquist hypnotized the GOP" Washington Post June 30, 2011 Available from: <u>http://www.washingtonpost.com/how-grover-norquist-hypnotized-the-gop/2011/06/30/AGYOUIsH_story.html</u>
[17] Purdum, T.S., *Go Ahead, Try to Stop K Street*. The New York Times January 8, 2006 Available from http://www.nytimes.com/2006/01/08/weekinreview/08purdum.html
[18] Stone, P.H., *Heist: Superlobbyist Jack Abramoff, his Republican allies, and the buying of Washington*2006: Farrar Straus & Giroux. P. 38

[19] ""GIMME FIVE"— INVESTIGATION OF TRIBAL LOBBYING MATTERS, in FINAL REPORT BEFORE THE COMMITTEE ON INDIAN AFFAIRS, ONE HUNDRED AND NINTH CONGRESS. Available from http://indian.senate.gov/public/_files/Report.pdf

[20] Matthews, C., "Is Christianity under attack? Tom DeLay says there is a "war on Christianity" in America ", in Hardball March 30,2006. Available from http://www.msnbc.msn.com/id/12079836/ns/msnbc_tv-hardball_with_chris_matthews/t/christianity-under-attack/

[21] Grimaldi, S.S.a.J. "Witness May Have Pivotal Role in Probe of Alleged Corruption" Washington Post Novemeber 20, 2005 Available from: http://www.washingtonpost.com/wp-dyn/content/article/2005/11/19/AR2005111900937.html

[22] Ibid

[23] Kilgore, E. Deviously Ineffective: Ralph Reed has a long history of corruption-and of losing WASHINGTON MONTHLY Available from: http://www.washingtonmonthly.com/features/2006/0604.kilgore.html

[24] Moser, B. RALPH REED: THE DEVIL INSIDE NATION-NEW YORK-Available from: http://www.thenation.com/article/devil-inside

[25] "GIMME FIVE"— Available from http://indian.senate.gov/public/_files/Report.pdf

[26] Ibid

[27] Ibid

[28] Ibid

[29] Ibid

[30] Steffy, L. "Birds of a Feather..." February 6, 2006 Chron.com February 6, 2006 [cited July 20, 2011]; Available from: http://blog.chron.com/lorensteffy/2006/02/birds-of-a-feather/

[31] Grimaldi, S.S.a.J.V. "The Fast Rise and Steep Fall of Jack Abramoff How a Well-Connected Lobbyist Became the Center of a Far-Reaching Corruption Scandal" Washington Post December 29, 2005 Available from: http://www.washingtonpost.com/wp-dyn/content/article/2005/12/28/AR2005122801588_pf.html

[32] "GIMME FIVE"— Available from http://indian.senate.gov/public/_files/Report.pdf

[33] Ibid

[34] Ibid

[35] Burnett, J., "Tigua Indians Learn Tough Lesson From Abramoff", in All Things Considered February 16,2006, NPR. Available from: http://www.npr.org/templates/story/story.php?storyId=5220081

[36] Flynn, S. "The Sins of Ralph Reed" GQ August, 2006 Available from: http://www.gq.com/news-politics/newsmakers/200607/ralph-reed-gop-lobbyist-jack-abramoff?printable=true

[37] Ibid

[38] Ibid

[39] "GIMME FIVE"— Available from http://indian.senate.gov/public/_files/Report.pdf

[40] Flynn, S. "The Sins of Ralph Reed" GQ August, 2006 [cited July 21, 2011]Available from: http://www.gq.com/news-politics/newsmakers/200607/ralph-reed-gop-lobbyist-jack-abramoff?printable=true.

[41] Moser, B. RALPH REED: THE DEVIL INSIDE NATION-NEW YORK-Available from: http://www.thenation.com/article/devil-inside

[42] Riley, M. "Abramoff ties cloud Schaffer's 99 fact-finding trip" The Denver Post April 10, 2008 Available from: http://www.denverpost.com/ci_8872607.

[43] Gibney, A., "Casino Jack and the United States of Money", 2010, Magnolia Pictures United States.

[44] Moyers, B., *"Capitol Crimes"*, in *Moyers on America July* 2008, PBS. Available from: http://www.pbs.org/moyers/moyersonamerica/capitol/

[45] Edsall, T.B. "Another Stumble for Ralph Reed's Beleaguered Campaign" Washington Post May 29, 2006 Available from: http://www.washingtonpost.com/wp-dyn/content/article/2006/05/28/AR2006052800964.html.

[46] Edsall, T.B. "Another Stumble for Ralph Reed's Beleaguered Campaign" Washington Post May 29, 2006 Available from: http://www.washingtonpost.com/wp-dyn/content/article/2006/05/28/AR2006052800964.html.

[47] Sharlet, J., *The Family: the secret fundamentalism at the heart of American power* 2009: Harper Perennial.

[48] http://ffcoalition.com/

[49] @ralphreed, Twitter

[50] NPR, *"Southern Baptists Apologize For Slavery Stance"*, in *Faith Matters*, NPR, August 29, 2009. Available from http://www.npr.org/templates/story/story.php?storyId=112329862

[51] Rowling, J.K. "The single mothers manifesto" The Sunday Times April 14, 2010 Available from: http://www.timesonline.co.uk/tol/comment/columnists/guest_contributors/article7096786.ece

[52] Ibid

[53] Lewis, C., *Mere Christianity. 1952.* New York.

CHAPTER 5: THE G.O.P.: GROVER'S OWN PARTY

*The members of this board were very
sage, deep, philosophical men; and when they
came to turn their attention to the workhouse,
they found out at once, what ordinary folks would
never have discovered- the poor people liked it! It
was a regular place of public entertainment for the
poorer classes; a tavern where there was nothing
to pay; a public breakfast, dinner, tea, and supper
all the year round; a brick and mortar Elysium,
where it was all play and no work. "Oho!" said the
board, looking very knowing; "we are the fellows to
set this to rights; we'll stop it all, in no time." So,
they established the rule, that all poor people
should have the alternative (for they would compel
nobody, not they), of being starved by a gradual
process in the house, or by a quick one out of it.* [1]

charles dickens
"oliver twist", 1838

One way to look at today's Congress is through
the lens of history, particularly with respect to the Cold
War. For those not old enough to recall this era, the name
had to do with our relationship with the Soviet Union, post
World War II, up until around 1989, which is when the
Berlin Wall came down. There is no consensus on the
actual end date, as some consider the end as not
happening until the Soviet Union disbanded in 1991.

This war was described as cold, due to the fact we
weren't in a full-fledged hot war; it was not a shooting war
with battlefields and fronts, as we had in World War I and
World War II: the sequel to the first world war, with a cast
of millions more and a nuclear finale.

It was everything short of a shooting war, with espionage, propaganda, and wars conducted by third parties. Both sides wished to destroy the other; both the west-the United States and its orbit of capitalism loving nations, and the eastern bloc-the Union of Soviet Socialist Republics, or the puppets of Russia and the Kremlin.

Both sides recognized that they were mutually exclusive entities, with a capitalistic system requiring new territories for markets and resources and a Marxist system requiring the elimination of markets as socialism spread. Therefore distrust and paranoia existed in great quantities on both sides; with much overreacting all around. Tensions reached almost catastrophic levels as nuclear arms were accumulated. How did we go from being allies in the great war, to adversaries in the most fragile peace?

It started with the Yalta agreement. At the end of the war the Allies had mostly the same goals: to ensure peace going forward. Britain and France weren't in a position to maintain peace, the United States did not want to commit to forces stationed in Europe throughout eternity (which essentially happened with the Cold War and NATO). Russia wanted peace, but only through protecting its borders. It wanted a wide enough belt around it to prevent another invasion. So, with those goals in mind, all four of the above mentioned victors decided to keep Germany from rearming, and each country would maintain influence in the portion of Europe it occupied at the end of the war. This of course led to the Soviet Union having control of countries like Poland, and the eastern part of Germany, with the other Allies having control of "west" Germany. [2]

Some people on the United States foreign policy team, particularly in the administration of Harry S Truman, were overly idealistic and believed that the cooperation during the war would continue afterwards; that is that the Soviets could be trusted to act in the best interest of all players. [3]

This all changed after a United States diplomat to Russia sent a telegram to his superiors in Washington. The diplomat was named George Kennan. He sent his observations in an extremely long telegram, appropriately referred to since then as the "Long Telegram". [4] Later he would publish his observations anonymously for the public at large in Foreign Affairs, an influential foreign policy journal. He signed this as "X", and it became known as the "X Article", although its formal title was "The Sources of Soviet Conduct." [5]

Kennan was a serious scholar and an authority on Russia's history, culture and politics. He combined his academic background with his own observations from living in Moscow and laid to rest any notion of Soviet cooperation. Kennan documented multiple historical precedents to reinforce his own observations and concluded that communism and capitalism could not coexist, and the Soviets were a threat to expand beyond their borders, from the Persian Gulf, to Turkey, and Greece. Based on these observations the United States developed a policy known as "containment", where all efforts would be made to contain the Soviet Union, to figuratively put a fence around them and not let them expand.

This became the United States' Cold War policy for the most part for the next fifty years, as the United States and its allies met Soviet aggression with alliances, foreign aid and proxy wars in places such as Korea, Vietnam and Afghanistan.

Containment was costly in lives, money and in the careers of politicians. Lyndon Johnson, for example, declined to seek a second term due to the public's dissatisfaction with the Vietnam War.

Also, legitimate questions remain to this day as to whether or not American involvement in Korea and Vietnam were crucial to containment, and there certainly have been unintended consequences in places such as Afghanistan, as we learned on September 11, 2001.

But nevertheless, the Soviet Union finally capitulated; the Berlin Wall came down and the Cold War was over, with the United States as victors.

213

Despite the success of containment, there were critics of the policy. Not with any objections to our challenging the Soviet Union, but for our not being aggressive enough as we did so. These critics favored a strategy known as "rollback", where we forced the Soviet Union to roll back and give up territory it had gained, to the point of wiping communism off the planet. This disagreement on strategy was certainly on display when General Douglas MacArthur publicly undermined his commander in chief, Harry Truman during the Korean Conflict. MacArthur threatened China in the media with the not so veiled threat that the United States would invade; a move that very possibly would have instigated World War III. President Truman was not one to mince words, and he immediately fired MacArthur as commander of the U.S. troops in Korea.

Truman's political enemies, the Republicans, exploded with rage. Truman's approval rating dropped to 26 percent, as many Americans thought he was too soft on the communists. In his enemy's minds and expressed through public statements, war with China was what we needed to better roll back the red carpet that had covered countries from Moscow to Asia. [6]

The next president, Dwight Eisenhower resisted rollback. As a retired 5-star general, he knew the costs of war and was satisfied with containment and worked towards avoiding another catastrophic war for America and the world. For his efforts, he was called a communist sympathizer by the John Birch Society. [7]

As an aside for those not old enough to remember, the John Birch Society was a group of fanatical anti communist zealots who saw communism and conspiracies behind any action, statement, or directive that fell short of nuking the Russians.

The society didn't stop at outing the president as a communist, it brought public attention to communist plots in government anytime the government tried to move towards a totalitarian system. One of the most passionate causes the John Birch Society had in its fight against communist takeover was its opposition of fluoride in drinking water. The average citizen may have believed it was to fight tooth decay, but that's what THEY, the government, wanted the sheep to believe. The John Birch Society loudly screamed to whoever would listen that fluoride was the first step towards a government takeover of all aspects of life. [8]

I'll leave it to the reader to decide whether or not this was a valid national security concern, or a significant threat to our liberties. However, I must identify one of the chief founders of the John Birch Society as Fred Koch, an unbelievably wealthy oilman. The John Birch Society still exists, and is still passionate about fighting communism. Never mind the fact that both the Soviet Union and Fred Koch have died; the John Birch magazine, The New American, lavishes praise upon Fred Koch, who died in 1967, for his leadership in fighting the communists who dared to try to infiltrate our schools, churches, town halls, and dentist offices.

It[9] should also be pointed out that Fred left his sizable estate to his sons, Charles and David. Koch Enterprises has become the largest privately held corporation in the world, which gives the brothers a combined fortune of 35 billion dollars. Only Bill Gates and Warren Buffet have more wealth. The Koch boys (pronounced like the soft drink, Coke) have spent over 100 million dollars on conservative political organizations, in order to rollback communism everywhere it doesn't exist. They founded a group as their father did, but this one has more respectability. It is called the Tea Party. [10] But more on the Koch brothers later, let's return to the Cold War, when communism was actually a threat.

The call for rollback intensified during the Vietnam war, as conservative critics accused those who wished to limit the scope of the war, in other words by practicing containment, of fighting not to win. Barry Goldwater wrote and released a very blunt and straightforward book in 1962 titled "Why Not Victory?". [11] This book promoted rolling back the Russians with nukes if necessary. Surprisingly, the American voters soundly rejected Goldwater and the aggressive pursuit of nuclear war in the election of 1964.

To the point, for the most part we exclusively practiced containment during the Cold War, and to good effect. Some argue that Ronald Reagan brought in a policy of rollback, with his speaking of the Soviet Union as an evil empire and consigning them to the "ash heap of history. [12]"

Their claim is to better fight communism; Reagan financed rebels in Afghanistan, El Salvador, and Nicaragua, with the last listed adventure almost resulting in his impeachment. It is debatable whether or not Reagan actually did practice rollback; if he did, it was only in Latin America and done without the commitment of any U.S. troops, save the brief excursion in Grenada. Reagan made no effort to rollback the Soviet Union in Europe in the Eastern bloc, notwithstanding his rhetoric. Reagan's policy with the Soviets was containment through arms buildup, implying massive retaliation if the Soviets got out of their box.

Can anyone say with a straight face that we should have practiced rollback at any stage with the Soviet Union? It's easy to shoot off one's mouth over beers, and talk about invasions and kicking ass, but in terms of cost benefit analysis, is it worth it? Does anyone actually believe that after World War II ended, the United States should have turned its guns upon the Soviet Union and finished what the Nazi army could not do? Would picking a fight with the army that destroyed our common enemy, the Nazis, been prudent or even good strategy immediately after the bloodiest war in world history?

In more recent history, the answer should be even more obvious. With the Soviet Union armed to the teeth with nuclear weapons plus a massive number conventional ground and sea forces. It would have been mutually assured destruction to engage them. It should be perfectly clear that rollback would have been dangerous, foolhardy, and costly. Containment was the only prudent way to deal with the Soviet Union.

I use this foreign policy example to better illustrate where the Republican Party is today; that is rollback mode, as compared to the responsible days of conservative politics, containment.

And with respect to Ayn Rand, the rollback mentality has metastasized in the culture. Ayn Rand gives intellectual cover to those who have bought into class warfare, and harbor resentment whether or not the resentment is actually based on facts. What we have today is a culture that blames the poor for any social ill, and accuses those who wish to see the wealthiest pay a bit more rent for being a citizen of punishing success. This plays into the hands of an opportunistic Republican Party, which is being driven by a fanatical band of rabble, calling itself the Tea Party. The Tea Party is of a unique pedigree; founded, fueled and financed by billionaires in order to feed off a fear of government and not coincidentally, a black president. The Tea Party and its flying monkeys were oh so calm in the days that George W. Bush spent multitasking wrecking the economy, stretching the military too thin, spending the Social Security surplus by pandering to the wealthy and putting it all on the nation's credit card.

Instead of cutting Bush off, they stood silently as he gave away billions to corporations in tax loopholes or direct giveaways. The waste that Tea Party Republicans fear in welfare, food stamps, or school lunches pales in comparison to the waste in the Department of Defense that sucks billions out of the budget with no questions asked. Ironically, or perhaps hypocritically, or more likely intentionally, this debt that was brought on by the lethal cocktail of recession, tax cuts, unfunded wars and corporate giveaways and this is giving the Republicans the fig leaf needed to cover their blatant contempt for Social Security and Medicare with the appearance of good stewardship. Their well-coordinated refrain is: We just can't afford entitlements anymore. We have to end them. Also, while we are at it, lets cut taxes. God bless America.

Back before George W. Bush, before Newt Gingrich, before Ronald Reagan, and even before Barry Goldwater, the Republican position was to accept Social Security and it accepted it as part of the necessary social safety net. Franklin Roosevelt had completely redefined the nature of government, and instituted one of the most popular government programs of all time in Social Security. Harry Truman tried to expand it with universal healthcare, but was rebutted, even losing Congress to the Republican Party.

The Republicans won the White House in 1952, as Dwight Eisenhower took office and stayed for the next 8 years. It should be noted that Ayn Rand absolutely loathed Eisenhower. Biographer Jennifer Burns notes that Ayn felt that he damaged the country more than any Democrat could do. Why you may ask? Ike "destroyed the possibility of an opposition" to the Democrats and ended "any semi-plausible or semi-consistent opposition to the welfare state." Ayn's disgust with Eisenhower ran so deeply that she at that point she declared herself no longer a conservative, and realized that the conservatives and her were not really on the same side. [13]

To be more precise, Eisenhower had no intention of rolling back either the Soviet Union or the New Deal. Yet today, the Republican Party, as defined by the base, is committed more to the ideology of Ayn Rand, and not Eisenhower. Or put it this way, if you buy into all of the stuff conservatives spew today, you would have called the five star general Republican president who won World War II a socialist along with most of the conservative movement.

Of course that special type of knuckle dragging let-the-poor-read-by-candlelight-in-their-outhouses conservative had been out of vogue for about twenty something years, as their system of governance and laissez-faire regulations had left something to be desired. Ayn, the cranky Russian immigrant had all these really cool theories about unregulated markets, but the bulk of Americans at that time had lived through the spectacular rise and fall of the true conservative Republican Party, which made them less likely to embrace the total liberating effects of poverty.

Conservatives seemed to lose more ground in the sixties. After the assassination of John F. Kennedy, President Lyndon Johnson brought us his war on poverty with aid for the poor in food stamps, welfare, and especially Medicare, a single payer health insurance plan for the elderly. Both Social Security and Medicare have been assessed as the "third rail of politics" [14] in the sense that if you touch them, you die due to their tremendous popularity with voters.

As popular as Ronald Reagan was, he dared not attack Social Security or Medicare. In fact, he saved them both, with ironically Ayn's faithful henchman, Alan Greenspan heading a special committee to save it.

Let's not praise Greenspan too much, his solution was to dramatically raise taxes on the poor and middle class while leaving the rich alone with any bothersome Social Security contributions. [15] Ayn would have appreciated the effort.

Democrats have had much success running "Mediscare" ads, where they accuse Republican candidates of stealthily trying to destroy Medicare. And these ads worked, as they scared Republicans to the point of denying any ill intentions towards it.

In the past, moderate Republicans such as Bob Dole have refuted this claim with some success, although it did damage Dole against Bill Clinton in 1996. But in the past Republicans could defend themselves from this charge with a straight face, because there were many who sincerely believed that we as a nation needed the safety net of Social Security and Medicare. Not so today as things are different and the Republican Party is under new management and under no such pretense.

In the spirit of Ayn Rand, the Republican Party is fully ready and determined to destroy both Social Security and Medicare, along with most other social safety net programs.

The Republicans have morphed from the party of containment, from the party of Eisenhower, and even Ronald Reagan, where they prudently kept the government from growing too much, while keeping needed policies in place; to now playing the part of rollback, where they have the stated goal of completely destroying whole programs that are needed by the elderly and poor, lest we trouble Daddy Warbucks by asking him to pony up.

There have always been those in the Republican Party who wanted the safety net gone, and always will be. The difference is that in the past, the Republican Party has had great leaders who had concerned about the common man and woman. Today? If they are there, they conduct a conspiracy of silence rather than anger the billionaire funded rent a mobs that wear colonial garb and tote misspelled signs.

What changed and how did the Republican Party develop this newfound courage to touch the so-called third rail? It has been through a systematic and deliberate approach for the past thirty years where a crisis has been intentionally created to force the American people to willingly give up two successes of government that are both sorely needed by the elderly and poor.

The strategy is simple: Republicans have deliberately run up deficits to dangerous levels, and created a crisis and now they demand drastic cuts in programs that would have never be considered to be on the chopping block in normal times.

You may recall this hand being played with the debt-ceiling debacle recently. It was the execution of a strategy that has been in place for three decades. Sound too conspiratorial? Let us examine the record.

I'll start by introducing you to Bruce Bartlett. Bruce Bartlett has a conservative pedigree that any right-winger would love. He began in politics as a staffer for Congressman Ron Paul, the darling of all small government worshippers everywhere. While working with Congressman Paul, Bartlett became familiar with economic issues, particularly federal regulations and tax policies. Bartlett still speaks fondly of his old boss, even today.[16]

After leaving Ron Paul's employ, Bartlett joined the staff of Jack Kemp. You[17] may remember Kemp as the former quarterback of the Buffalo Bills, or you may remember him as Bob Dole's running mate when Dole challenged Bill Clinton for the presidency in 1996. What you should remember about Jack Kemp for the sake of this discussion is that he was one of the biggest cheerleaders, if not the biggest, of "supply-side economics", as it was called during the Reagan years. Kemp was co-sponsor of the Kemp-Roth Tax Bill, which was signed into law and became the basis for the Reagan tax cuts, which lowered the rates for all Americans, particularly the wealthiest.

After working for Jack Kemp, Bartlett joined
Ronald Reagan's administration as an economic adviser.
He later served in the first President Bush's administration
as a Deputy Secretary of the Treasury. His credentials as a
conservative shouldn't be questioned, and his experience
in the economics of tax policy; particularly with respect to
tax cuts, should be acknowledged. You may remember
Bartlett from his two books published during the Reagan
administration that heavily promoted supply-side
economics, "Reaganomics: Supply Side Economics in
Action" in 1982, [18] and "The Supply Side Solution" in
1983. [19] Or, perhaps you don't.

I mention the term supply-side. Allow me to
explain. If you think of the actors in the marketplace, the
buyers and sellers, you should think of supply and
demand. In an economy, the supply side is the side of the
producers, the manufactures and industrialists, the
financiers and capitalists; who are most likely the wealthy.
The demand side is the side that purchases, the demand
of the economy. This side consists of consumers, from all
sources who purchase.

The standard view of economics for most of the
twentieth century has been what is called Keynesian,
named after Sir John Maynard Keynes.

Keynes believed that in good times, governments
should raise taxes and run surpluses, while when things
slow down, it should lower taxes and run deficits so it can
build the infrastructure of the country along with boosting
its GDP.

This was the basis of the New Deal, and what
Franklin Roosevelt did. Not everything was as successful
as it was wished to be in the New Deal, but the economy
did pick up.

Pay no attention to the naysayers, who have an
axe to grind against FDR; as the GDP rose every year of
the 1930's, as soon as the spending began.

Actually to be truthful, it fell in 1937 and a
recession ensued, after Roosevelt gave into conservatives
and tried to cut back government spending. Makes you
wonder what we can expect next year after the massive cuts
brought on by the Tea Totalitarians, huh?

Besides, if the revisionist historians are correct, and it took WWII to get us out of the depression, what was WWII but massive government spending financed by debt?

The supply-siders are all about the tax cuts. They don't want to cut them as Keynes wished, where the little guy has a little extra bling in his pocket and goes to the picture show with his lady, boosting the economy with consumption. No, that's not enough to make supply-side work. You have to massively cut taxes for the big dogs, so they can howl unrestrained at the moon of economic growth. Cut them enough, the theory goes, and droplets of money will tinkle down upon us, as tycoons create jobs by hiring some working stiff to stable and feed his polo pony.

Back to Bartlett, Kemp and the supply-side revolution of Ronald Reagan. The supply-siders of the seventies and eighties not only promised stimulus effects from tax cuts, they promised more revenues.

Its editorial page editor Robert Bartley promoted this collection of tax- cutting- revenue -enhancing conservatives on the editorial pages of The Wall Street Journal. Bartley used his platform to spread the gospel of lower taxes, and promised economic expansion as the payoff; enough expansion to more than cover the revenues lost from tax cuts.

Bartley wrote a book about this philosophy called "The Seven Fat Years", in which he praises all of the pioneers and advocates of the supply-side revolution (including his own contributions of course).

This book lays out the theory plainly, if you cut taxes on the wealthy, they will invest more, and therefore more tax revenues will come as a result. In other words, higher taxes meant less revenue, lower taxes mean more. [20]

If it sounds a bit far fetched, it should. Yes, there can be incentive-killing effects of too high of a tax rate, for example, who would work at a one hundred percent or a ninety-eight percent tax rate? But it is important to note that many of the supply –side zealots who pushed this idea were not trained economists; passionate advocates such as Bartley, Kemp and Bartlett. This lack of training is relevant in examining the numbers. This claim was constantly repeated by George W. Bush and Dick Cheney, in spite of all evidence to the contrary; to wit, the exploding deficits under Reagan and Bush after such tax cuts. George W. Bush's own staff of trained economists disputed that notion. Time magazine reported in 2007, in an article titled "Tax Cuts Don't Boost Revenues":

> *"If there's one thing that economists agree on, it's that these claims are false. We're not talking just ivory-tower lefties. Virtually every economics Ph.D. who has worked in a prominent role in the Bush Administration acknowledges that the tax cuts enacted during the past six years have not paid for themselves--and were never intended to. Harvard professor Greg Mankiw, chairman of Bush's Council of Economic Advisers from 2003 to 2005, even devotes a section of his best-selling economics textbook to debunking the claim that tax cuts increase revenues.* [21] *"*

But the point isn't that Republicans have said this, the point is that they do not believe the lower taxes more revenue myth, save for the true believers such as Robert Bartley and Jack Kemp, both of whom have passed away. Bruce Bartlett is currently in the land of the living and he has lived long enough to recognize reality. He no longer believes the rhetoric, and for his apostasy he no longer finds himself in good favor with the conservative establishment.

Bartlett fell out of sorts with fellow Republicans by calling for the dismissal of Vice President Dick Cheney, for his criticisms of the so called "flat tax" idea, and especially for his book "Impostor: Why George W. Bush Bankrupted America and Betrayed the Reagan Legacy." [22]

For the last bit of heresy, he was fired from a conservative policy think tank, the National Center for Policy Analysis, a Dallas based research group. Bartlett says he was dismissed because wealthy Republicans refused to donate money to an organization that would vocally criticize conservative policy. [23]

As a rule, turning on the Bush administration by a former rabid conservative is always admirable and to be commended; I did it myself. But what is of note, and what should be more of interest to you is his research and publications on the subject of "starving the beast".

In an article published in 2007 for the Independent Institute, a scholarly think tank, Bartlett outlined the history and strategy of starving the beast. Economists and policy makers never really bought into the idea that tax cuts produced more revenue, in fact they knew that they would diminish them. The highest income tax rates in the 1950's was 90%, but the Republicans of all people refused to lower them, as they believed in balanced budgets. President Eisenhower, a Republican threatened to veto any tax cut lest the deficit get out of hand. Incidentally, the deficit then was higher than it is now, as a percent of the nation's GDP, with the war debts still existing.

John F. Kennedy ran on a platform of tax cuts, and wished to lower the top rate down from 90% to 70%, which would be termed today by the Tea Partiers as transitioning from communist to socialist.

After Kennedy's assassination, President Johnson was able to get the cut passed, but he did it without Republican support, as Bartlett quotes the Congressional record as recording 126 out of 155 House of Representative Republicans voting against the tax cuts in 1963. The fear of deficits was just too great. [24]

Obviously, this fear of deficits didn't last, as the Republicans mustered up their courage and grew to love them. A prediction was made at the time that the Republicans would do just this; embrace tax cutting, not as a means to boost the economy, but as a way to stop the government. John Kenneth Galbraith was an economist in the Kennedy administration, and one of the most widely read economists in the world. He testified to Congress in 1965 that he felt that tax cuts that just passed were dangerous, and would be used later by conservatives to cut spending. In his testimony he said:

> "I was never as enthusiastic as many of my fellow economists over the tax reduction of last year. The case for it as an isolated action was undoubtedly good. But there was danger that conservatives, once introduced to the delights of tax reduction, would like it too much. Tax reduction would then become a substitute for increased outlays on urgent social needs. We would have a new and reactionary form of Keynesianism with which to contend" [25]

If you have even halfway paid attention the last twenty years, you will realize that Galbraith was absolutely correct. Once conservative lawmakers took a hit on the tax cut bong, they were hooked; at first loving the taste, and longing for more, then becoming so dependent upon it that it became the sole purpose of their existence.

It took Ronald Reagan to bring it to full addiction status, as he soothed deficit fears with his "government is the problem" rhetoric. What if we ran up deficits? Heck, it didn't matter, most of the government was bureaucratic waste anyway, and we'd be better off without it. Hit me again!

Yet no effort was made by Reagan to cut government, even as he made a name for himself as Mr. Small Government. The supply-siders got their deficits, their tax cuts, but none of the shrinking of government.

The conservatives were forced to go cold turkey with their tax cut habit in 1993, as Bill Clinton raised taxes in the name of deficit reduction, with most of the higher taxes on the wealthy.

He claimed it would balance the budget, the Republicans claimed it would destroy the economy. Clinton proved to be correct, as the federal budget was balanced, and a surplus appeared.[26]

The Republicans were beside themselves. They were jonesing really bad for some tax cut action, and all Bill Clinton wanted to do was tax, spend, and retain revenues. They wanted out of this fiscal rehab, and quick. So when Clinton's term ended, George W. Bush came on the scene to act as their supplier, feeding them the drug of tax cuts that they craved so desperately for the eight years of Clinton. Like any street dealer, he didn't care about the consequences, not that dealers who are strung out on their own poison are all that effective in helping other junkies come clean.

One would think that during the Clinton administration, all would be right with the world, but in reality, the balanced budget caused much consternation among Republicans.

As his administration began, they were terrified that a Democratic president would run up a debt and we would all be punished, and of course, kill jobs, the ultimate evil in the conservative world. But shockingly it didn't and it turned out that a balanced budget was the absolute WORST thing that could happen.

There is a fundamental problem here, which is by balancing the budget, and even running a surplus, the Clinton administration showed that an effective government could pay for itself, and not run up deficits.

Nowhere was this disgust more evident than in the writings of Stephen Moore. Mr. Moore is a very influential person in the right wing. He is president of a lobbying group called Club for Growth. Club for Growth advocates, well, growth. But not necessarily for all of us, but for the wealthy. Most anytime you see Club for Growth in the news, you can bet your bottom dollar that they are advocating the United States getting down to its bottom dollar with tax cuts. They stress that growth only comes from freeing up capital for the capitalists.

Stephen Moore enhances his influence by frequently writing for both Rupert Murdoch's Wall Street Journal, and the Reverend Sun Myung Moon's - leader of the financially successful, if not theologically challenged group, the Moonies- Washington Times.[27] The alliance of the conservative movement and religion continues unabated here. What better way for the conservative Christian to discern God's will politically than to get it from the source: the very man chosen by Jesus in a vision to carry on His mission as the new messiah? This new and improved messiah is a staunch anti tax warrior, unlike the small business owner carpenter of two thousand years before.[28]

Now would be a good time to explain to you what you may have already guessed: notwithstanding the sacred nature of his employer Reverend Moon, Stephen Moore is a devout follower of Ayn Rand. He published an editorial in the Wall Street Journal titled *"Atlas Shrugged: From Fiction to Fact in 52 Years"*. In this he frets about how we are almost teetering on the edge of communism, and we are in danger of losing all of our blessed CEO's and hedge fund managers to Galt's Gulch if we don't pay them more respect (and give them their tax money back to boot). As per his normal style, he offers advice for Barrack Obama's administration, just as he did for Bill Clinton. His opening paragraph:

> *"Some years ago when I worked at the libertarian Cato Institute, we used to label any new hire who had not yet read "Atlas Shrugged" a "virgin." Being conversant in Ayn Rand's classic novel about the economic carnage caused by big government run amok was practically a job requirement. If only "Atlas" were required reading for every member of Congress and political appointee in the Obama administration. I'm confident that we'd get out of the current financial mess a lot faster"*[29]

I hope I am not spoiling the ending of this editorial when I tell you that he suggests that the Obama administration abolishes all income taxes.

A pertinent detail should be brought to light: this unsolicited advice on how to fix the Obama administration was published exactly three weeks before President Obama was sworn in. Before President Obama had any cabinet in place. Before President Obama had submitted any proposals to Congress. Before President Obama placed his hand on the infidel Bible (in the manner that an Indonesian Muslim would be expected to do), Stephen Moore had the confidence that Obama would fail, because he did not propose tax cuts as a solution.

He does not reconcile the fact that the mess that he recognizes the United States to be in came as a result of deregulation of the wealthiest, yet most irresponsible members of society, and under the watchful eye of the most pro tax cutting president in history, George W. Bush.

But for now, back to the pages of the Washington Times.

Moore's transformation from one who feared for the country's future because of deficits to one who became disgusted with a surplus is evident in the pages of the Washington Times.

In June of 1994, he describes the deficit as leading us to the brink of bankruptcy. So the only solution was term limits, as he noted that once Congressmen learned their jobs, they realized that the government needs money and they might ask the silver spoon fed trust fund babies to chip in for the good of the US of A. [30]

By 1997 Moore realized term limits weren't going to happen and they wouldn't solve the budget problem, so he devoted his energy to the new cause: the balanced budget amendment. If the Congress can't balance the budget on its own, at least it would be prohibited by the Supreme Court from running deficits.

Yet, the wild-eyed liberals wouldn't go for it; neither would moderates and most state legislatures for that matter. [31]

229

In spite of all of Mr. Moore's pleading for the Clinton administration to do the right thing, with the right thing in Mr. Moore's eyes being tax cuts for the wealthy along with a balanced budget amendment; the administration proceeded with its own plan and refused to cut Social Security or Medicare.

Moore was furious, and gave the budget of 1998 an F, three of them as a matter of fact. In his cleverly titled editorial called "Fiscal Fraud and Fantasy", Moore lambastes Clinton for not giving his homies enough tax cuts and then accuses him of lying about the budget surplus he predicts. In no uncertain terms he states:

> *"If it seems that this can't possibly add up to a balanced budget, it's because it doesn't."*[32]

But it did.

The budget was balanced in 1998, in 1999, and 2000, the last three years of Clinton's second term.[33]

But Moore wasn't easily convinced. As the budget was signed into law, he express skepticism at the notion of a balanced budget, as he claimed that because there were no tax cuts in the future, there could be no balanced budget. His logic is that if you fund the government at only 98% of its budget, you prevent it from growing.[34]

Reality can only be ignored so long, and the budget surplus appeared in 1998; documented by an official Congressional Budget Office estimate.

Stephen Moore acknowledged this, but had one major complaint. It seems that the CBO had greatly underestimated the budget surplus that Stephen Moore predicted would never come. His editorial title said it all, *"CBO's fractured crystal ball"*.

He faulted the CBO for taking a too conservative (it is not often when something is too conservative for Stephen Moore) approach in forecasting upcoming budget. He then, as always, graciously offered his policy solutions.

He said that they should work into the numbers a higher growth rate for the economy, and therefore this would project higher revenues, and so the budget surpluses will be even higher. Oh, by the way, he also said because of all of the surplus bucks on paper, we would need to give a whopping capital gains tax cut, which overwhelmingly favors the wealthy. [35]

Around this time, the perpetual right wing mouthpiece Washington Times revealed their true feelings towards the deficit. It wasn't or isn't the deficit that matters, it is the size of the government. In 1997, editor Jeff Jacoby wrote:

> Surely, then, the near-evaporation of the deficit is a major piece of good news, right?
>
> Wrong. It is a very minor piece of good news. It means simply the federal government will pay its bills this year without (too much) borrowing.
>
> But those bills - the budget of the U.S. government - are bigger than they have ever been before. Though the deficit has been slashed, spending continues to skyrocket. [36]

In 2000, as the Clinton administration was coming to a close, Moore had yet another editorial about the surplus- that- he- said- would -never happen- but-was-always-underestimated-by-the-CBO. He said that the worst thing that could happen would to be to keep the surplus and pay down the deficit. Quoting Moore:

> Republicans must start to refer to the "surpluses" as "taxover payments." Language matters in politics. Tax overpayments should be returned to the people who overpaid. End of argument. [37]

Actually, it isn't the end of the argument, and not even on his own terms. His policy suggestion (which was ultimately adopted by the Bush administration) did a great disservice to the actual people that overpaid, and it gave their overpayment to people who didn't pay in at all.

The surplus that Clinton had was with regard to debt to the public. Every year when the U.S. needs more debt (even in balanced budget times, this is true because tax inflows don't come at the same times outflows happen) the U.S. will issue Treasury Bills/Bonds.

These Treasurys are the way that the government borrows. They are sold on the open market to any investor, and that is why China holds more of them than anyone else. The Chinese have a bunch of dollars from our always buying their cheaply made stuff at Wal-Mart, so they park their billions of dollars in Treasurys.

When Clinton had the budget balanced, he had it in the sense that no outside debt was issued; there was no reason to get money in the market place from the Chinese or anyone else. But, internal debt was still there. Where did this debt come from?

Social Security. [38] Social Security has taken in more in taxes than it has paid out, since the liberal Ronald Reagan saved it in 1984. [39] The trust fund has purchased U.S. Treasurys as a safe place to park the money since then. When Clinton ran the surpluses, the actual surplus number was positive only because the surplus of Social Security paid in. It was plainly the money paid in by taxpayers; not only taxpayers, but all lower and middle class tax payers as no one pays into Social Security for income over $106,800. [40]

So when Mr. Moore called for the overpayment that the government held in the form of a surplus, he was referring to the Social Security trust fund. Mr. Moore was disingenuous, perhaps even dishonest, to suggest that the wealthiest paid that surplus. It was "given back" in the form of massive tax cuts for the wealthiest, draining the Social Security surplus, and also increasing the need for more outside debt and increasing the total deficit. The wealthy came in and looted our retirement. Now we are in a pickle, and their flunkies in Congress tell us, we just can't afford it.

Government is absolutely necessary, and it serves an essential function. It regulates industry, which would rather not be regulated or constrained in any way so it might make more profit. Government builds infrastructure, and from this economic growth truly happens, and that benefits all of us.

And lastly, government is the only outlet that can provide a social safety net, which protects the weakest members of society; which conservative Christians who are complicit in the destruction of the safety net refuse to acknowledge that but for the grace of God, goes them. Ayn Rand, and her protégés in the conservative world preach that the least of these are the least important; nay, the unimportant.

Is there room for reform in government? Absolutely. But to admit that is to embrace containment, not rollback. There are no calls from conservatives to reform and make government more efficient and responsive, unless you call nihilism and the complete destruction of the government reform. The debate should be how to make the regulatory state and safety net better, not how to make it non-existent.

The debate is constantly poison by outlets such as talk radio and Fox News; with neither of these being objective. The big corporations have willing mouthpieces to build up public support for tearing down the wall of government. This was not accidental. Republicans have hated Social Security since its founding, yet the voters have loved it, and it has been instrumental in helping seniors live above the poverty line. The Republicans hated even more Medicare and Medicaid, and all of the Great Society programs of Lyndon Johnson. Medicare, just like Social Security, is extremely popular with the common folk. It is so popular; that many ill informed and easily manipulated anti-healthcare reform protestors would shout at Democratic Congressmen during the debate to "keep the government's hands out of my Medicare!" [41]

With past frontal attacks on Social Security and Medicare always resulting in a complete failure; the Republicans have opted for a more covert and sinister strategy. This strategy would be the aforementioned starving the beast, referenced in the publication by Bruce Bartlett cited earlier.

With this strategy, Republicans could work on reducing government by reducing the amount of revenue for it. They did not have the popular mandate to do this honestly, so it became imperative to create a crisis and force cuts upon the American people.

This was on display with the debt ceiling controversy leading up to August of 2011. The radical Tea Party Republicans used their position to force a hostage situation with the nation's credit rating. Never mind that the debt ceiling had been raised 18 times by Ronald Reagan, and 8 by George W. Bush. [42] But the Tea Party wing of the Republican Party suddenly found the practice abhorrent, and they refused to raise the ceiling, which was only authorization to borrow for spending already incurred. There would be no money for any bills, payrolls, or interest on our debt to a world of investors unless a spending dollar for debt ceiling dollar cut in the budget was made.

A degree in economics is not necessary to imagine the damage that would be done, not just to our economy but also to the world's economy, if we were to default on our debt.

Brinkmanship is the appropriate word. It was used in the Cold War, to describe the fun times had by all when both sides almost bombed the world back to the time of our original founding fathers; the ones that lived in caves. Merriam-Webster defines brinkmanship as "the art or practice of pushing a dangerous situation or confrontation to the limit of safety especially to force a desired outcome." [43]

A more commonly used word also works: hostage. The Republicans took the world economy hostage, threatening to blow it up unless granny had her benefits cut.

The summer of 2011 was the moment to strike for the Republicans. The debt had reached a point to where it was startling enough to put the fear of God and default in every citizen, and it was scary enough to finally make it on the priority list.

The GOP was all on the same page; they were claiming that this spending was unsustainable, entitlements had to be reformed, and that we were spending too much money. [44]

Overspending was the claim when we had a deficit back in the days of after George H.W. Bush, it was the claim when we had a surplus, and it is now the claim today, after the days of George W. Bush, as the deficit is reaching near historical highs.

If you examine history, the Republicans statements and actions, and current intent, there is can only be one conclusion. The government is overspending in all matters but defense and barest functions for commerce. All programs for education, the health and welfare of the elderly, mentally retarded, tornado, flood and hurricane victims, should be left to the states. Good luck with that for the poor folks of Alabama, which is one of the most revenue starved states of all states, which wishes the government to be full of Christian showboating with respect to erecting Ten Commandment rocks, but not so with Christian love with respect to care for the poor. Alabama has the lowest tax rate in all 50 states, which incidentally would inspire a supply side skeptic to ask why it doesn't have the highest revenues? [45]

According to the GOP, the states corporations themselves should do almost all regulations. Say goodbye to any clean water or air provisions brought to us by regulations of the EPA.

The current republican talking point is to do away with this agency. Mitt Romney, Rick Perry and others blast the EPA for stifling job growth, though no data is given as to how many, and to what cost to the water and air we all depend upon.

Michelle Bachman, the hero of Tea Partiers, makes no bones about her ambitions:

> *"I guarantee you the E.P.A. will have doors locked and lights turned off, and they will only be about conservation. It will be a new day and a new sheriff in Washington, D.C."*[46]

It is relevant to the discussion that the Republican candidates mentioned here are all major recipients of campaign funds from "the petroleum industry, utilities, coal companies, heavy manufacturers and the U.S. Chamber of Commerce",[47] all with a vested interest in reducing regulations, not so much to create jobs, but to create more value for the shareholder.

The playbook for big business Republicans has not changed in over 100 years. They are always the first to cry foul when confronted with regulation and higher taxes, as they cost jobs. But no jobs would be forthcoming, as the lower taxes padded the profits of the corporations. No time is a good time for taxes, or regulations. No regulation is fully embraced by businesses, if left to their own devices. The regulations that were opposed back then seem to be no-brainers today; regulations to which no reasonable person would object.

In spite of all Ayn Rand's self importance about being such an original thinker, the position of letting the super wealthy have their fun with no chaperones isn't one that she invented.

It was the way of the world for many years as the United States became more urban and industrialized. Robber Barons and Republicans were hating on poor folks long before Ayn Rand and Fox News started doing it, and thumbing their nose at the public will just to prove that they could. Currently, their nose thumbing is often aimed at doing away at regulations we all used to view as essential.

Fat chance getting those regulations enforced or any new ones passed, we can barely fund the ones we have, and in many industries we cannot cover the industry adequately because of being short handed. A government-funded agency cannot compete with a battery of highly paid corporate lawyers. We can't hire new people or good people, because of the deficit and budget constraints.

We can't raise revenues to fight this deficit. That's out of the question, based on the decrees of the most powerful man in the United States Congress. The most powerful man in the United States Congress is unelected, and not even particularly likable, so it is doubtful that he would get many votes if he tried to get elected. But he doesn't have to run for office, he effectively controls Congress by extortion; as he threatens to use a foolishly signed anti-tax pledge against anyone who dares to act in the best interest of the country instead of pandering to the wealthy.

Grover Norquist is this man, and he is Ayn Rand's dream man. He is the man behind the curtain; like the Wizard of Oz. Except the actual Wizard was a likable person with a good heart.

Grover was born with the proverbial silver spoon in his mouth, in an affluent family that was able to send him to Harvard. He witnessed first hand growing up the horrors inflicted upon the wealthy, and obviously vowed to protect them from oppression at an early age. Grover proudly tells the story of his father raising him correctly, where dad would buy the kids ice cream after church, and then take it back, bite by bite and say "Oops, income tax. Oops, sales tax."[48]

From that point on, it was full speed ahead for Republican causes, as he came up through the College Republicans.

As recounted in the previous chapter, Grover Norquist served as a money launderer for Jack Abramoff, as he gave a cover to Ralph Reed by laundering money from the Choctaws to Reed's group, just so Reed might claim that he didn't know gambling interests were paying him millions.

Grover didn't do it out of love of his sleazy friends Abramoff and Reed, he did it for his true love, money, and demanded and received a cut of the action for these under the table transactions.[49]

Back in the day of Grover's hero, Ronald Reagan, Abramoff and his geek posse of Ralph Reed and Grover Norquist weren't really embraced by Republicans; quite the opposite. Rich Bond, the deputy director of the Republican National Committee recalled to the Washington Post that he banished them from the party's headquarters in 1982 and told them "You can't be trusted." [50]

Newt Gingrich and his band of Republicans learned to trust Grover Norquist, Ralph Reed and Jack Abramoff. Abramoff brought lots of money to Republicans; albeit much of it was of questionable legality. Ralph Reed delivered evangelical Christian voters, and Grover wrote the famous Contract With America for Newt.

Grover fondly displays on his Americans For Tax Reform website, in the section About Grover, Newt's warm praise for him. Newt tells us that Grover is...

> *"The person who I regard as the most innovative, creative, courageous and entrepreneurial leader of the anti-tax efforts and of conservative grassroots activism in America . . . He has truly made a difference and truly changed American history."* [51]

Grover impressed even more of the GOP establishment. He was the driving force behind Bush's deficit inducing tax cuts; the architect of this latest beast starvation round.

He now owns essentially all of the GOP in Congress, with I-will-not-raise-taxes,-ever pledges from 236 out of 240 Republicans. [52] Two Democrats have signed this deal with the devil also.

Grover, who has a history of being conspiratorial, and described as "strange" by people who knew him in college, [53] keeps every pledge locked into a vault. If any Congressman should break the pledge, it will get pulled out in a primary fight, presumably to replace the revenue raiser with an easier manipulated Tea Partier. [54]

Here is where the sane conservatives are deceived. They claim that they only want waste eliminated, and want incentive killing regulations, taxes and programs curtailed or shut down. That's a legitimate debating point. But Norquist wants it all gone. The federal government for all intents and purposes, eliminated.

Grover heads up a conference call every Wednesday morning, and it is the most influential in Washington. In these calls, he lays out the agenda. His meetings are by invitation only, and he emphasizes the agenda.

Many conservatives come to him, much like the meek Sicilians did in The Godfather, asking for a favor with respect to getting some policy passed. Grover's coalition includes religious conservatives, libertarians, the NRA, homeschoolers, and of course big business. By his own admission, he wants to destroy, not defeat at the polls, but destroy the minimum wage, unions, public education and of course the Democratic Party. His vision of the perfect American is:

> *"My ideal citizen is the self-employed, homeschooling, IRA-owning guy with a concealed-carry permit," says Norquist. "Because that person doesn't need the goddamn government for anything."*[55]

That's a pretty honorable goal for a man who was born on third base into wealth, and who was given the opportunities that a Harvard education can bring.

His self-reliance and bootstraps are certainly inspirational, but many of us didn't have enough foresight to pick wealthy parents to sire us. Praise be to Grover for working hard to force all Americans to be more self-reliant than he had to be.

Grover isn't subtle with these ambitions, he is blunt and crude with his strategies; he's the equivalent of a coach who decides to run it every play and dares you to stop him. He will never compromise. His quote *"Bipartisanship is another name for date rape,"* speaks loads. He's patient.

"We plan to pick up another five seats in the Senate and hold the House through redistricting through 2012," he says. "And rather than negotiate with the teachers' unions and the trial lawyers and the various leftist interest groups, we intend to break them."[56]

The election in 2012 is shaping up to be a battle, with major differences on both sides. Grover's Ayn Rand world, with a federal government "small enough to drown in a bathtub" and all authority delegated to the states or the private sector.[57]

For those under the delusion of the supremacy of states rights, and who are inclined to believe that the Tenth Amendment provides the solution to combat unelected dictators of public policy such as Grover Norquist, I say to you, not hardly.

In my opinion, there exists ample evidence for the need to restrain corporations. Corporations were not forced into treating its employees as subhuman at the turn of the last century, nor was it just a historical anomaly. They did it deliberately and were motivated by greed. They weren't forced to pollute drinking water with waste, and they weren't force to sell contaminated food. They did these things because preventing such actions would cut into the most important function, profit and shareholder value. Only the hand of the federal government was big enough to change these things.

I say it must be the federal government, because state and local governments do not have the resources or will to restrain industry and the wealthy. The conservative counter is that federalism is our system, the rights of states are sacred and must be protected. With this club, big business has been able to beat down almost all attempts at restraint. The theory of federalism is that local governments are best for democracy as it is closer to the citizen, and therefore more responsive. The conservative majority on the Supreme Court has quoted this reasoning in upholding states rights. In Gregory v. Ashcroft 1991, Justice Sandra Day O'Conner writes for the majority:

240

> *This federalist structure of joint sovereigns preserves to the people numerous advantages. It assures a decentralized government that will be more sensitive to the diverse needs of a heterogeneous society; it increases opportunity for citizen involvement in democratic processes; it allows for more innovation and experimentation in government; and it makes government more responsive by putting the States in competition for a mobile citizenry*[58]

To paraphrase Justice O'Connor, we need to put the states in control so that the diverse interests of society can be addressed, and that the average citizen can participate. Plus, the states can experiment with what works and what doesn't; and all states will be competing for citizens in the marketplace, as citizens can vote with their feet and move if they don't like it.

That's the theory. It may be the primary reason that many poor and middle class align themselves with the very forces that work hard against their interest, big business and the super-wealthy. States rights are a sacred tenet of conservatism, and they are a most effective tool for the powerful to force their will upon the masses.

Does anyone believe that the Supreme Court's reasoning holds today? The average citizen is becoming less able to have his voice heard, at the state and federal level. Corporations and money interest control state governments.

State governments do not have the funding to adequately regulate any major corporation, nor do they want to do so. Regulations cost money through enforcement and inspections. State budgets are pressed in times like this recession, as tax revenues go down. States can't raise revenue through income tax increases on the wealthy, because they, and they alone, have the power to invoke the "*competition for a mobile citizenry*[59]" quoted by Justice O'Connor.

The wealthy can pack up and leave, so that leaves revenue generation to fall upon the middle class and poor with regressive taxes such as sales taxes. As to the mobility of the poor, let's just say they have a lot less flexibility. They are stuck in place, and dependent upon the good graces of government and their employers.

So just how effective are states with regulation? Not very. To begin with, Grover owns 10 governors and over 1,200 state legislators. [60] That in and of itself isn't damning, although it should make you apprehensive to see so much power concentrated into one person's hands, particularly one that is not elected, and who looks to destroy a not insignificant portion of society that stands in his way. But Grover is aided and abetted by ALEC, or the American Legislative Exchange Council.

ALEC sounds innocuous at face value, as they pledge for all the things that conservatives, even containment conservatives, claim: a commitment to free markets, less regulation, and smaller government. ALEC has over 2000 state legislators in its organization (in addition to the 85 members of Congress), and is sponsored by over 300 corporations.

The corporate sponsors actually drive the agenda from the top down. They issue cookie cutter pieces of legislation to their members and have them introduce them into their respective state legislatures. They have legislators in all fifty states, and their bills are constantly introduced for consideration as law, with many of them making it through to be signed by ALEC governors. [61]

What issues are covered in these corporate written thousands of bills? Nothing of importance to us average citizens, just laws that have to do with food safety, air and water quality, damages received for wrongful death, and the constant lowering of taxes on corporations.

Their hot ticket item is the establishment of Councils on Efficient Government, which tries to privatize functions of governments.

This idea seduces conservatives, as they believe that the private sector is much more superior in all organizations than the government, because the private sector makes a buck and is efficient.

Some of the private sector transformation involves prisons, where corporations are now running prisons, which I hope most would agree to be a legitimate function of government. However, the love of money is the root of all evil, even with the money involves locking up evildoers; or those who are labeled as evildoers.

Conservatives drool when they hear that a judge is tough on criminals, and they love one that has a reputation as a "hanging judge." Mark Ciavarella is a double hero to the right wing. He was a tough on crime judge, showing no mercy to the punks he faced down in court, and he developed into quite the wealthy entrepreneur.

Mark Ciavarella was a juvenile court judge in Pennsylvania, and he made a name for himself along with another judge, and couple of state officials. Judge Ciavarella became known as a dependable judge to send children for lockup, no matter what crime they committed, or no matter if they had no criminal record.

Judge Ciavarella sent one kid to prison for two years, just for borrowing his parents' car for a joyride, with no priors. One kid that got sent to prison became so despondent he committed suicide. Not much of a way to apologize for that one.

His honor, in acting without honor, took over a million dollars from the owner of the private kids prison, to drum up more business. The for profit institution got so much per head from the state to house the delinquents, and it was good for all concerns. Well, except for the kids, they didn't really count. Consider it a lesson in American civics, where they learned that the profit motive is the highest calling. [62]

The judge received 28 years for his entrepreneurship. [63] It is not known whether or not he will go to a prison owned by the public, or a private one.

Pennsylvania was heavily lobbied by ALEC's Councils on Effective Government to privatize prisons in Pennsylvania, among other states. There are many more opportunities to make a buck with states. ALEC has left a big footprint in this:

> In the past few years, with at least three additions
> this session alone, legislation establishing a state Council on
> Efficient Government has been introduced in Virginia,
> Maryland, Arizona, Kansas, Oregon, Illinois and South
> Carolina. In each case, the concepts in the bill mirror the
> ALEC proposal. In some cases—South Carolina, Arizona and
> Illinois—the state bills read as copies of ALEC's model
> legislation. Virginia's, Oregon's, Maryland's and Kansas' bills,
> to varying degrees, contain language directly from ALEC's
> model.[64]

Speaking of prisoners, ALEC is pushing hard for prison labor. Which is another excitement inducing prospect for conservatives. Why should prisoners get air-conditioned cells and get free gym equipment while we work? Make them do labor.

There is a problem with this, besides the moral one of it being slave labor, but I won't use that one as conservatives fought a war to defend that particular states right.

It is troublesome because it gives free labor to corporations to make their products, providing an unfair advantage against those who either have the moral aversion to slavery, or were too cheap to bribe their legislator.

In Florida, there are 41 industries done by prison labor, including the printing industry where prisoner labor dominates, forcing small businesses out of the market. California has 60 such industries. These prisoners are not paid, but given early time off, if they please the warden and the corporate boss.[65] It's Cool Hand Luke without the egg-eating contest.

I realize the average conservative hates unions, but c'mon, I would think you'd have to admit that the unions are right on this one? Why let decent hard working guys be penalized by ruthless corporations who wish to use free labor?

Whose interest is being served when we as citizens shirk our responsibility for government? Not the citizens, but those who use the force of law and government to extort money from the government. It's downright baffling that conservatives were terrified of the so called Public Option in President Obama's health care reform as being destructive to competition, yet seem to embrace this endgame in every other industry. Too much federal government scares the Tea Party into the Pee Party, yet they usher in the greatest threat to liberty this country has seen, the royal corporate class, one not based on democracy unless you vote with millions of dollars.

In the above-mentioned Supreme Court case, Gregory v. Ashcroft 1991, Justice Sandra Day O'Conner cites The Federalist Paper, number 45 as justification for preserving the sacred notion of states rights. James Madison, the author of the constitution, wrote this particular one. She willfully neglects this portion of that writing, in which Madison says that states rights are the means to an end, not the end; with the end being the happiness of the people.

> It is too early for politicians to presume on our forgetting that the public good, the real welfare of the great body of the people, is the supreme object to be pursued; and that no form of government whatever has any other value than as it may be fitted for the attainment of this object.
>
> Were the plan of the convention adverse to the public happiness, my voice would be, Reject the plan. Were the Union itself inconsistent with the public happiness, it would be, Abolish the Union.
>
> In like manner, as far as the sovereignty of the States cannot be reconciled to the happiness of the people, the voice of every good citizen must be, Let the former be sacrificed to the latter. [66]

Where are we today? With the public good usurped by corporations, unelected lobbyists, and greed. We need the federal government that we used to have.

GEORGE KELLEY

SOURCES CONSULTED FOR CHAPTER 5

1 Dickens, C., Oliver Twist. 1838. Paris, Baudry, 1839.
2 Kissinger, H., Diplomacy1994, New York: Simon & Schuster. P. 462
3 Politics and Polices of the Truman Administration, ed. B.J. Bernstein1972, Chicago: Quadrangle Books. P. 16
4 Kennan, G., The Long Telegram, D.o. State, Editor 1946: Moscow. Available from: http://www.gwu.edu/~nsarchiv/coldwar/documents/episode-1/kennan.htm
5 X, "The Sources of Soviet Conduct". Foreign Affairs, 1947. 25(4). Available from: http://www.foreignaffairs.com/articles/23331/x/the-sources-of-soviet-conduct
6 McCullough, D., Truman1992, New York: Simon & Schuster.
7 Davidson, L. "FBI files shed light on Ezra Taft Benson, Ike and the John Birch Society" The Salt Lake Tribune November 13, 2010 Available from: http://www.sltrib.com/sltrib/news/50349153-78/benson-hoover-fbi-society.html.csp
8 Anton, M. "For Some, fluoridated water still hard to swallow" Los Angeles Times December 22, 2007 Available from: http://articles.latimes.com/2007/dec/22/local/me-fluoride22.
9 Scaliger, C. Fred Koch: Oil Man Against Communism The New American June 10, 2011 Available from: http://www.thenewamerican.com/history/american/7771-fred-koch-oil-man-against-communism
10 Mayer, J. "Covert Operations" New Yorker August 30, 2010 Available from: http://www.newyorker.com/reporting/2010/08/30/100830fa_fact_mayer
11 Goldwater, B., "Why not victory?: A fresh look at American foreign policy" 1962: Greenwood Press.
12 Pipes, R. "Ash Heap of History: President Reagan's Westminster Address 20 Years Later - Remarks by Dr. Richard Pipes". Date; Available from: http://www.reagansheritage.org/html/reagan_panel_meese.shtml
13 Burns, J., Goddess of the market: Ayn Rand and the American right P. 146
14 Chadwick, P. "Social Security - Still the Third Rail of Politics".; Available from: http://www.cnbc.com/id/41411671/Chadwick_Social_Security_Still_the_Third_Rail_of_Politics
15 Bartlett, B., "Starve the Beast" Origins and Development of a Budgetary Metaphor. The Independent Review, 2007. XII(1) Available from: www.independent.org/pdf/tir/tir_12_01_01_bartlett.pdf
16 Bartlett, B. "Not Your Average Republican Presidential Candidate" January 23, 2007 The Right Stuff January 23, 2007; Available from: http://bartlett.blogs.nytimes.com/2007/01/23/not-your-average-republican-presidential-candidate/#more-25
17 Bruce Bartlett Biographical Information The Fiscal Times; Available from: http://www.thefiscaltimes.com/Authors/B/Bruce-Bartlett.aspx
18 Bartlett, B.R., Reaganomics: Supply-side economics in action 1982: Quill.
19 Bartlett, B.R. and T.P. Roth, The supply-side solution 1983: Chatham House Pub.
20 Bartley, R., The Seven Fat Years and How to Do It Again. New York, 1992.

21 Fox, J. "Tax Cuts Don't Boost Revenues" Time December 06, 2007 Available from: http://www.time.com/time/magazine/article/0,9171,1692027,00.html

22 Bartlett, B.R., Impostor: how George W. Bush bankrupted America and betrayed the Reagan legacy 2006: Random House of Canada.

23 Bumiller, E. "An Outspoken Conservative Loses His Place at the Table" New York Times February 13, 2006 Available from: http://www.nytimes.com/2006/02/13/politics/13letter.html?ex=11404980 00&en=36f1df68daa92365&ei=5070&emc=eta1

24 Bartlett, B., "Starve the Beast" Origins and Development of a Budgetary Metaphor. Available from: www.independent.org/pdf/tir/tir_12_01_01_bartlett.pdf

25 Ibid

26 The Budget and Deficit Under Clinton. FactCheck.org Date; Available from: http://www.factcheck.org/2008/02/the-budget-and-deficit-under-clinton/

27 Duin, J. Rev. Sun Myung Moon passes the torch Washington Times October 14, 2009 Available from: http://www.washingtontimes.com/news/2009/oct/14/rev-sun-myung-moon-passes-the-torch/

28 Rev Sun Myung Moon, His Teachings. Date; Available from: http://reverendsunmyungmoon.org/rev_moon_teaching.html

29 Moore, S. "Atlas Shrugged" From Fiction to Fact in 52 Years" Wall Street Journal January 9, 2009 Available from: http://online.wsj.com/article/SB123146363567166677.html

30 Moore, S. "A sure cure for fiscal gridlock?" Washington Times June 14, 1994.

31 Moore, S. "Balanced Budget Test Case: The States" Washington Times February 4, 1997.

32 Moore, S. "Fiscal Fraud and Fantasy" Washington Times February 18, 1997.

33 The Budget and Deficit Under Clinton. FactCheck.org Date; Available from: http://www.factcheck.org/2008/02/the-budget-and-deficit-under-clinton/.

34 Penny, T,S.Moore.. "Mismatch of hoops and hoopla?" Washington Times May 13, 1997.

35 Moore, S. "CBO's fractured crystal ball" Washington Times June 9, 1998.

36 Jacoby, J. "Smaller deficit, bigger government" Washington Times November 3, 1997.

37 Moore, S. "How to win at surplus politics" Washington Times July 11, 2000.

38 The Budget and Deficit Under Clinton. FactCheck.org Date; Available from: http://www.factcheck.org/2008/02/the-budget-and-deficit-under-clinton/

39 Water, P.N.V.d., "Understanding the Social Security Trust Funds", in Social Security2010, Center on Budget and Policy Priorities. Available from: http://www.cbpp.org/files/10-5-10socsec.pdf

40 Contribution and Benefit Base. Date; Available from: http://www.ssa.gov/oact/cola/cbb.html

41 Heuvel, K.v. "Keep Your Hands Off My Medicare!". Date May 5, 2011; Available from: http://sanders.senate.gov/newsroom/news/?id=e45c4ce4-e9f7-416b-8884-9c93042ec080

42 Farley, R. PolitiFact: Obama says Reagan raised debt ceiling 18 times; George W. Bush seven times St. Petersburg Times July 28, 2011 Available from: http://www.tampabay.com/incoming/politifact-obama-says-reagan-raised-debt-ceiling-18-times-george-w-bush/1182782

43 Definition of brinkmanship, in Merriam-Webster. Available from: http://www.merriam-webster.com/dictionary/brinkmanship

44 Lambro, D. "Daring GOP stab at reining in overspending: Paul Ryan grips politics' 'third rail' with both hands" Washington Times April 5, 2011 Available from: http://www.washingtontimes.com/news/2011/apr/5/daring-gop-stab-at-reining-in-overspending/

45 Beyerle, D., "Alabama taxes still lowest in the nation", 2010, Alabama Policy Institute. Available from: http://www.alabamapolicy.org/press_media/print.php?updateID=147

46 Broder, J.M. "Bashing EPA is New Theme in GOP Race" New York Times August 17, 2011 Available from: http://www.nytimes.com/2011/08/18/us/politics/18epa.html

47 Ibid

48 Scherer, M. Grover Norquist: The Soul of the New Machine Mother Jones January/February 2004 Available from: http://motherjones.com/politics/2004/01/grover-norquist-soul-new-machine

49 Finney, K. Norquist History 101 The Hill July 25, 2011 Available from: http://thehill.com/opinion/columnists/karen-finney/173399-norquist-history-101

50 Grimaldi, S.S.a.J.V. "The Rise and Fall of Jack Abramoff" Washington Post December 29 2005 Available from: http://www.pulitzer.org/archives/7035

51 About Grover.; Available from: http://www.atr.org/about-grover#ixzz1Vmq7e7PF

52 Yakabuski, K. Grover Norquist: The man behind the pledge to never, ever raise taxes The Globe and Mail August 11, 2011 Available from: http://www.theglobeandmail.com/news/world/konrad-yakabuski/grover-norquist-the-man-behind-the-pledge-to-never-ever-raise-taxes/article2127203/

53 Gibney, A., "Casino Jack and the United States of Money", 2010, Magnolia Pictures United States. 118 minutes.

54 Yakabuski, K. Grover Norquist: The man behind the pledge to never, ever raise taxes The Globe and Mail August 11, 2011 Available from: http://www.theglobeandmail.com/news/world/konrad-yakabuski/grover-norquist-the-man-behind-the-pledge-to-never-ever-raise-taxes/article2127203/

55 Scherer, M. Grover Norquist: The Soul of the New Machine Mother Jones January/February 2004 Available from: http://motherjones.com/politics/2004/01/grover-norquist-soul-new-machine

56 Ibid;

57 Lynch, D.J. Who's Afraid of Grover Norquist? Business Week July 28, 2011 Available from: http://www.businessweek.com/magazine/whos-afraid-of-grover-norquist-07282011.html

58 Gregory v. Ashcroft, in US 1991, Supreme Court. p. 452. Available from: http://www.law.cornell.edu/supct/html/90-50.ZO.html

59 Ibid;

60 Scherer, M. Grover Norquist: The Soul of the New Machine Mother Jones January/February 2004 Available from: http://motherjones.com/politics/2004/01/grover-norquist-soul-new-machine

61 Banerjee, T.H.a.N." State legislative bills raise conservative group's profile" Los Angeles Times July 13, 2011 Available from:http://www.latimes.com/news/nationworld/nation/la-na-epa-states-20110714,0,5030269.story

62 Bates, D. Cash for kids judge took $1million kickback from private jail builders to lock children up UK Daily Mail Available from: http://www.dailymail.co.uk/news/article-1359154/Cash-kids-judge-took-1m-kickback-private-jail-builder-lock-children-up.html

63 McCoy, C.R. U.S. judge gets 28-year sentence in 'cash for kids' case Montreal Gazette August 11, 2011 Available from: http://www.montrealgazette.com/news/judge+gets+year+sentence+cash+kids+case/5242189/story.html

64 Dresser, J.R.a.L. ALEC Exposed: Business Domination Inc. The Nation August 1, 2011 Available from: http://www.thenation.com/article/161977/business-domination-inc

65 Sloan, M.E.a.B. The Hidden History of ALEC and Prison Labor The Nation Available from: http://www.thenation.com/article/162478/hidden-history-alec-and-prison-labor

66 Hamilton, A., et al., The Federalist Papers . No. 45; Available from: http://avalon.law.yale.edu/18th_century/fed45.asp

GEORGE KELLEY

CHAPTER 6: BACK TO THE FUTURE - 1905

> *Mayor Hewitt, of New York, is complimented by the newspapers for brave words spoken on the labor question. They are all in criticism of the Labor men.*
>
> *Some obvious blunders of the leaders and mistakes in methods are easily pointed out. But there is no bravery in it, and I suspect not much wisdom. The real difficulty is with the vast wealth and power in the hands of the few and the unscrupulous who represent or control capital. Hundreds of laws of Congress and the state legislatures are in the interest of these men and against the interests of the workingmen. These need to be exposed and repealed.*
>
> *All laws on corporations, on taxation, on trusts, wills, descent, and the like, need examination and extensive change. This is a government of the people, by the people, and for the people no longer. It is a government of corporations, by corporations, and for corporations. -- How is this?*

president rutherford b. hayes
diary entry march 11, 1888

The following is a true story.

Once upon a time, a rabbi named Rabbi Loew lived in Prague during the reign of Rudolf II in the sixteenth century. Rabbi Loew was concerned about the plight of the Jews in Prague as vile accusations were made about them from those who hated the Jewish people. These accusations involved outlandish claims that Jews took blood from Gentile children and used it to cook into their wafers. The claims would inflame the passions of the anti-Semitic mobs, which would become incited to commit violence upon the whole Jewish community.

Rabbi Loew created a being out of dust, called "Golem" in order to protect the Jewish people from harm. The Golem was made of clay from the banks of the Vltava River and came to life after a ritual. The Golem was incredibly strong and took orders literally from Rabbi Loew.

Rabbi Loew was sure to deactivate the Golem on every Sabbath by changing the word on the Golem's forehead. Rabbi Loew had inscribed the Hebrew word "emet" on the forehead of the Golem, which meant "truth". To deactivate the Golem, he would erase the first letter, leaving "met", which means "death" in Hebrew.

But the Golem became more and more menacing, destroying trees, and attacking people. Instead of the protector he was designed to be, he became a monster who destroyed for his own sake. With his unworldly strength, no man could stand against him, and many were crushed while trying to flee. Rabbi Loew was disturbed and knew something had to be done. Rabbi Loew was approached with a plea to strike down the Golem, so that the Rabbi's people would no longer be persecuted. He agreed and removed the "e" and the Golem returned to dust. [1]

This story is certainly true, but not in the factual sense where it actually happened; although there seems to have been a Rabbi Loew, and there is actually a statue of the Golem in Prague to this day. [2] The truth lies in the application of the story not merely in the facts, just as I've discussed truths in novels and art previously. The truth on display here is that sometimes artificial beings created for good and protection will morph into something completely unintended; malevolent monsters with powers far superior to average humans or even their creators. The monsters that I speak of with this truth are among us today and are programmed to rule the world according to Ayn Rand's vision i.e. corporations

Corporations were initially created to protect the proprietors of business from total liability; be it financial or legal. However, the case can now be made that they protect their owners from moral liability as well.

The standard perception of corporations is of neutral morality with its motivation only being the best interest of the shareholder. However, "the best interest of the shareholder" is subject to interpretation and the definition of who the shareholder actually is. Gone are the days when shareholders were predominately families that held stock in corporations over generations, passing down wealth and control. These still exist, of course, but the standard shareholder model is the institutional shareholder such as pension funds, mutual funds, and other investment vehicles.

What this means for corporations is that they are more susceptible to wild swings in their stock prices, as institutional investors are less likely to hold stocks long term, and fund managers will only be as loyal to the corporations as the most recent earnings report will allow.

Therefore, the loyalty to the shareholder isn't directed to the old family fortunes, but rather to the new family mutual funds; and this demands more immediate gratification for the market.

So ask yourself, what will a CEO do to meet analyst's expectations in order to satisfy shareholders? Almost anything. And many have done almost everything, which should surprise no one given the astronomical amounts of money that these "Atlas'" make.

This leads to all sorts of mischief, some of it illegal, some of it fraudulent, some of it exploitative, and some of it downright evil. But the shareholders are only happy if the firm makes money and they do not punish corporations for immoral behavior; they only punish for losing stock value.

The shareholders are a faceless, amoral mass of individuals who only want results. Therefore, anything goes in the pursuit of shareholder happiness. The Golem becomes the master of the creator, with no capacity or even desire to heed his words.

These days whenever people want to score purity points, they invoke the words "Founding Fathers". By doing this they show the world that they know what the owner's manual for America has in it, and they know the proper use of government. Invocation of the Founding Fathers is overdone, and for the most part, irrelevant. Why would we care what John Adams thought of the internet, even if he could have imagined it?

Ironically, one thing the Founding Fathers despised were corporations. This hatred drove them to conduct the famous Boston Tea Party. So it is doubly ironic when you consider the fact that today's Tea Party movement are would be imitators that are heavily funded by corporations.

The original Tea Party was a reaction to a monopoly installed by the British crown. The monopoly was the infamous and powerful East India Tea Company. The East India Tea Company had gotten itself into trouble by overproducing tea and crashing the market in Europe - not unlike the over supply of everything through out history from railroads to housing - and the only solution was to dump the tea on the American colonies because it was unlikely that they could smuggle it back to England.

To facilitate this dumping, the Crown lowered the export tariff for the company but kept the import tariff in place for the colonies.

Not only that, but the East India Tea Company was to only authorize certain stores the right to sell tea. All other tea was to be blockaded, as it came from smuggling.

This pissed off the chief smuggler in Boston, John Hancock, and he was able to rally the rank and file Boston merchant class to his cause, based on the logic that if the East India Tea Company were allowed to exclusively control the distribution of tea, they could also do it with any other product they wished.

It's plain to see that the East India Company was the Wal-Mart of its day. The fabled Founding Fathers had very little trust in corporations. In fact there were only six corporations in existence at the time of the Constitutional Convention, other than bank corporations. One was for organizing a fishery in New York, another for conducting trade in Pennsylvania, one for trade in Connecticut, one for fire insurance in Pennsylvania, one for operating a wharf in Connecticut and one for running a pier in Boston.

In his book, "Gangs of America: The Rise of Corporate Power and the Disabling of Democracy", Ted Nace documents how the intent of corporations was for the public good, to better facilitate the development of trade and infrastructure. It was imperative to the Founding Fathers that corporations are kept on a short leash. Nace quotes Ben Franklin as advising steamboat inventor Robert Fulton to distinguish himself from the East "*India or Guinea Company...who blindly* [enslave] *one half of the human race to enrich the other*". [3]

James Madison proposed on two different occasions putting the federal government in charge of corporations for *"cases where the public good may require them and the authority of a single state may be incompetent*". [4]

Just in case you aren't familiar with the views of these specific Founding Fathers, Madison was on the side of Jefferson; he hated a strong national government. Apparently he hated the idea of a strong corporation more.

Corporations stayed on a short leash until the railroad boom in the 19th century.

At that point, they used money and influence - both of these things were plentiful amongst the railroad tycoons - to change the laws through buying legislators and judges.

A brief history of the 19th century is in order, if that is even possible. The period between 1800 and 1900 was one of enormous change, both in the world and America, and does not lend itself to simplification. With that in mind, I'll try to simplify

255

The United States changed as the 19th century progressed but none of the changes were as dramatic as the Civil War, obviously. Nowadays people intuitively know slavery was a core issue involved (contrary to what neo Confederates say today - many of them southern Republicans - slavery was THE issue). Slavery was the wedge that split the nation, not in the sense of federal government moving to eradicate it in the conservative southern states but rather it was a fight about the potential expansion to the new territories of the rapidly westward expanding United States.

Two events happened on January 1, 1863 that were of massive importance in American history. One of them is widely known - if not the date of enactment or the scope of the directive - the Emancipation Proclamation. This was signed by President Lincoln and emancipated all slaves in the states currently in rebellion, the confederate states. It did not liberate the slave-holding states that stayed in the union, to wit: Maryland, Missouri, West Virginia, Kentucky and Delaware. It did not completely end slavery, but it was a major starting point.

Another blow for freedom for the common man, this one being for mostly poor whites, was the Homestead Act. It became the law of the land on the same day that the Emancipation Proclamation came to be, after being passed in May 1862. [5]

This is just as significant, maybe even more so than the Emancipation Proclamation, as a blow to equality for the common man. It wasn't perfect, but it may have given the United States the "safety valve" it needed to escape a revolution of the poor against the rich. Conditions in the southern United States for blacks were terrible, no doubt, but they were hardly a walk in the park for the laborers in the factories up north.

There is a mythology that Americans like to embrace about America being a perfect land of opportunity where a common man can go from rags to riches. There were examples of this happening, but it was hardly wide spread. John D. Rockefeller started dirt poor as did Andrew Carnegie. Both became insanely wealthy with Rockefeller most likely becoming the wealthiest American of all time even when factoring in adjustments to today's dollars. But they were the exception and not the rule.

A survey was taken of 300 unskilled laborers in Newburyport, Massachusetts that examined the thirty-year period between 1850 and 1880. Not one person was found to have advanced even as high as shop foreman. The best you could hope for was advancing within the ranks of the working class. You couldn't advance from blue collar to white collar. A survey of 194 executives in the 1870's showed that only sixteen actually spent any time as a former laborer. [6]

The industrial revolution here and in Europe brought discontent and class war to the western world. As the rich got richer off of new technology, the poor suffered. In Europe it was worse. Read Charles Dickens for an idea of how great life was for the poor during the mid 1800's. Dickens' father was sent to debtor's prison for his debts and Charles Dickens himself was forced into near slavery in a factory at 12 years old to work to pay off the debts. [7]

Karl Marx was certainly paying attention. He based his life's work and the concept of the perfect Communist utopia upon the notion of the lower classes rising up and over throwing the oppressive capitalists that exploited them.

He and his partner in crime, Friedrich Engels, wrote an essay in 1851 on the Revolution in 1848 in Germany titled, quite appropriately, "Revolution and Counter-revolution: or, Germany in 1848 ". In this they noted quite optimistically for their worldview, which was that terrible social conditions would incite the lower classes into violence in spite of their traditional disinterest in politics before.

257

> *These three latter classes of the agricultural
> population, the small freeholders, the feudal tenants, and the
> agricultural laborers, never troubled their heads much about
> politics before the Revolution, but it is evident that this event
> must have opened to them a new career, full of brilliant
> prospects.* [8]

But Germany did not fall to Communist
revolution in the 19th century, why? In no small part due
to the efforts of Prime Minister Otto Von Bismarck, who
was far from being a bleeding heart, but nevertheless
instituted the first welfare state in the west in the 1860's,
due to this social unrest. His theory was that the
underclass would be pacified against revolution and also
support his party if basic pension benefits were provided
for the old, sick and infirm [9]. Bismarck's strategy worked.
That's something to consider when screaming for
entitlement cuts and elimination these days.

Also, you need to consider that the pure Marxists
hated the welfare state more than Tea Partiers do today.
Consider the "X Memorandum" mentioned in Chapter
Five as the founding document of the Cold War.

George Kennan who wrote this, was one of the
foremost experts in United States history on the Soviet
Union. In his original source for this memo, his "Long
Telegram", he notes that Lenin despised more than any
rabid capitalist the liberals with their welfare state.

> *Among negative elements of bourgeois-capitalist
> society, most dangerous of all are those whom Lenin called
> false friends of the people, namely moderate-socialist or
> social-democratic leaders (in other words, non-Communist
> left-wing). These are more dangerous than out-and-out
> reactionaries, for latter at least march under their true colors,
> whereas moderate left-wing leaders confuse people by
> employing devices of socialism to seine interests of
> reactionary capital.* [10]

In plain English, Lenin saw those who offered
welfare and benefits to the poor as enemies of his cause,
and worse than the hard-core capitalists.

The Soviets viewed the capitalistic system as doomed to fail, and absolutely loved the idea of laissez-faire capitalism. It would create such class inequality and suffering, revolution would take place. But the moderate socialists were "false friends of the people", according to Lenin, because they used the bare minimum of the government to help the working stiff, therefore keeping revolution from happening. Isn't it odd that Vladimir Lenin and the Tea Party both despise the social safety net? One side despises it because it thwarts Communism, and the other side accuses it of being Communism. Which side do you think has given it more serious thought and reflection? Hint: it's not the side with the misspelled placards and polyester red, white and blue windbreakers.

So what does all of this have to do with the Homestead Act? I offer those facts to establish that conditions were terrible for workers worldwide. But the United States did not face the serious revolutionary threat that Europe did. The most famous historian of the 19th century, Fredrick Jackson Turner opined in 1844 on the reason why:

> "In Europe labor said, raise wages or we fight. In the United States labor said, raise wages or we will go West."[11]

The Homestead Act was the outlet to relieve stress on the capitalistic system. There wasn't any real chance of advancing through business. The wealthy had that monopolized with their children, who had the luxury of education at 12 years old and above instead of the factories and coalmines that educated the poor children. As noted, a few - very few - rose up out of the shackles of poverty into wealth. But for the most part they were privileged, extraordinary talented, lucky, or completely ruthless and immoral in their climb to the top. Many cases had elements of all of these components on the path to success of the wealthy.

But make no mistake; the Homestead Act was a government giveaway to the poor, and redistribution of wealth at that. And it did not have universal support amongst the party of big business. In 1877 a Congressman from Pennsylvania, Hendrick Wright, filed a bill as a response to 20,000 of his constituents who were suffering from unemployment brought on by a severe depression. Quoting Congressman Wright:

> *"The working men of this land are better entitled to the bounty of Government than aggregated wealth...It is a wonder to me that they..still comply with the laws of this country."*[12]

Wright had received a letter from a non-working workingman who had said

> *"It would seem as though this Republic was drifting from its foundations. This is no idle twadel [sic]. But there may come a time when patience ceases to be a virtue and farewell thou wreck of an American Republic."*[13]

Congressman Wright took this threat seriously enough to propose the radical welfare of a $500 loan to homesteaders, to better facilitate the little guy's chances at the American Dream.

This socialistic nonsense was shot down by Congress (on a vote of 274-35 in the House of Representatives) on the principle that the poor needed to work for what they had, and not expect the government to give them any help.[14]

But then, as now, not all welfare is created equal. The Congress had unanimously passed a resolution giving 100 million acres to the railroads, along with $100 million in loans from 1868 to 1872. However, this shouldn't be mentioned in polite company. It was considered class warfare by the power players.[15] Representative Wright complained nonetheless:

> *"Congress can grant railroads money and land, but if it talks of relieving the poor and oppressed, the cry comes, 'We cannot reward idleness.'"*[16]

Representative Wright was voted out the next election after being labeled "the Pennsylvania Communist".[17] It appears that President Obama was not the first Communist in our government's history. I would not have been surprised if Hendrick Wright had been a closeted Muslim from Kenya also, maybe even black. The Communists will stop at no deceit to overthrow our freedom.

So while the Homestead Act wasn't repealed, it was drained of funding. That's a tactic that can be used to great effect by conservatives and still is to this day. It works just as well these days as it did then. The wealthy that pull the strings aren't the type to give up once a policy comes into effect. If they hate it or it runs counter to their interest, they will exercise their power to defund it and let it die on the vine. It's often a win-win, as it is neutered by lack of funds and it serves as an example of government that does not work. Meanwhile, the dogmatic insistence that the free market *always* works is shouted from Republican rooftops.

As the rich got richer in the Gilded Age, they learned to use their power more effectively and more often. The power of the wealthy in America increased even more with the fabrication of a bogus constitutional status: corporations as people.

One of the biggest myths constantly being pushed by the right wing noise machine is one of an out of control Supreme Court that legislates from the bench, not the constitution. If you were to believe Fox News, Rush Limbaugh, and any other right wing cheerleader, you'd think that the constitution was followed strictly until liberals created the "right to privacy" out of thin air. This game started long before the liberals got involved and conservative Court members, mostly Republican appointees, did it.

After the Civil War, the Railroad tycoons worked hard to get control of the Supreme Court. Why was this necessary? After all, they had Congress bought and paid for and they could put a President into office if they wished. And they did so with President James Garfield.

James Garfield was running for president for the term beginning in 1880. He was in a very closely contested election. He needed to spend $100,000 in the last week of the campaign to turn Indiana around. Luckily for him, railroad developer Jay Gould was nice enough to write him a check for $150,000. [18]

Jay Gould is almost forgotten now, but he shouldn't be. He should always be held up as an example of the corrupting nature of wealth. Mark Twain had such strong opinions of Jay Gould, and others like him, that he requested that his autobiography not be released until 100 years after his death. This quote on Jay Gould from Mark Twain's autobiography, released in 2010, tells you what you need to know:

> *Jay Gould had just then reversed the commercial morals of the United States. He had put a blight upon them from which they have never recovered, and from which they will not recover as much as a century to come. Jay Gould was the mightiest disaster which has ever befallen this country. The people had desired money before his day, but he taught them to fall down and worship it. They had respected men of means before his day, but along with this respect was joined the respect due to the character and industry which had accumulated it.*
>
> *But Jay Gould taught the entire nation to make a god of the money and the man, no matter how the money might have been acquired. In my youth there was nothing resembling a worship of money or of its possessor, in our region. And in our region no well-to-do man was ever charged with having acquired his money by shady methods.*
>
> *The gospel left behind by Jay Gould is doing giant work in our days. Its message is "Get money. Get it quickly. Get it in abundance. Get it in prodigious abundance. Get it dishonestly if you can, honestly if you must."* [19]

Good thing those days are behind us.

Jay Gould willfully parted with his money, which was normally quite dear to him, in order to secure a promise from James Garfield to appoint pro railroad judges to the Supreme Court.

Garfield agreed and the transaction was final. James Garfield never had the opportunity to live out his post presidency years as a toadie to the Robber Barons, as he had no post presidency years. He was shot dead by an assassin only 200 days into his presidency.

But the question remains, why did the railroads interest themselves in Supreme Court justices when they could buy even the president? Because of states rights. The states were hindering their acquisition of wealth.

In the book "Gangs of America: The Rise of Corporate Power and the Disabling of Democracy", Ted Nace documents this issue.

> Bribery by railroad lobbyists was rampant among senators and Congressmen. For example, between 1875 and 1885 the Central Pacific spent $500,000 yearly on graft; in a single year, the LaCrosse and Milwaukee Railroad spent $872,000 for influence, including $50,000 for a governor, $10,000 for a state controller, $125,000 for thirteen legislators, and so on.
>
> Among the fruits of these expenditures by railroad interests were immense land grants. Ultimately, they acquired to hundred million acres of land-a tenth of the area of the entire country.
>
> But at the state level the railroad barons did need help from a Supreme Court -one willing to throw thunderbolts from Washington invalidating state legislation on constitutionality grounds. Such help was not required in every state...But in the Midwest and the West, railroad corporations repeatedly found themselves ambushed and outgunned by agricultural and labor movements that seemed to come out of nowhere. Such movements often succeeded in enacting regulatory legislation and taxes aimed directly at the railroads.[20]

Therefore, it was important to have the Supreme Court legislate from the bench and strip the states of their sovereignty. These charges are currently leveled at liberal judges by right wing noisemakers, but it was originally introduced by the corrupt influence of millionaires in the 19th century. They created many bogus rights and established precedents to which we are still subjected.

No judge was ever more of an ass-kisser to the railroads than Justice Stephen Field. Field was on the Supreme Court for over 30 years and was not beloved by too many beyond big business.

Prior to the Supreme Court he served as Chief Justice of the California Supreme Court and had a special jacket made that could hide two pistols. There was always the threat of someone shooting him down since he had accumulated plenty of enemies.

Field was no friend of blacks, the poor, immigrants, or the environment - even by 19th century standards where almost any pollution was tolerated. He wrote a famous dissent in what was known as the "Slaughterhouse" case criticizing the Court for upholding a state chartered monopoly, because it interfered with a God given right to work at one's trade. He even quoted philosopher Adam Smith in his dissent, saying that a man's work was his own property and the government couldn't deny him of that property without due process of law.[21]

This right to practice one's trade in this case had to do with slaughtering animals and dumping their remains into drinking water next to a city. His logic held that this was so sacred the state couldn't regulate it. He used Section One of the Fourteenth Amendment as justification and he effectively invented the legal reasoning that was used roughly 100 years later to justify Roe v. Wade called "Substantive Due Process".

Section One of the Fourteenth Amendment reads as follows:

> "Section 1. All persons born or naturalized in the United States, and subject to the jurisdiction thereof, are citizens of the United States and of the State wherein they reside. No State shall make or enforce any law which shall abridge the privileges or immunities of citizens of the United States; nor shall any State deprive any person of life, liberty, or property, without due process of law; nor deny to any person within its jurisdiction the equal protection of the laws."

Now, the original intent of the amendment was to protect newly freed slaves from oppressive laws called "Black Codes" which southerners enacted in order to effectively keep them in slavery.

Justice Field dismissed that intent and said that the Fourteenth Amendment actually protected rights that were apparent in nature, like the right to conduct one's business. And the Supreme Court had the obligation to find any violations of this natural right and strike them down.

Later in another case decided in 1886 titled Santa Clara County v. Southern Pacific Railroad, he persuaded all of his peers on the ruling and wrote the majority opinion. The ruling he wrote wasn't very influential but the case was. From this the idea of a "person", as the Fourteenth Amendment viewed it, was decided to include corporations. The text of the case never said such, but it was in the summary written by the court reporter, called a 'headnote'. And that is how we grew into the corporate personhood we have today. The Golem has full constitutional rights.

The author Ted Nace notes that it was inevitable that corporate personhood would come to be recognized since the fanatical laissez-faire judges that derived it from the headnote would have surely fabricated it later. But he said it would probably have been more easily amended or overturned had it come by way of legal reasoning within an opinion, rather than a casual aside:

> "Instead, the muddled and confusing circumstances behind the Santa Clara decision, combined with the lack of any stated rationale for it, served the interests of those seeking the broadest possible interpretation of the decision as a basis for corporate empowerment." [22]

Justice Field had enormous influence as the second longest serving justice in history, and the second most frequent author of opinions for the court.

His doctrine was the basis of manufactured rights, not written in the constitution in any shape or form, but "implied".

Conservatives never complained about these rights for one hundred years. Only when the implied "right to privacy" emerged in the 1960's and by extension, the right to abortion, did they begin to panic and feel that our very constitution and freedom were threatened.

The Stephen Field groupies were numerous and dominated the court up until the New Deal, where Franklin Roosevelt explicitly rejected the doctrine of "Substantive Due Process" as it applied to commerce.

One of the true believers in Field's worldview was his nephew, David Brewer, who also served on the Supreme Court. Brewer told an audience in 1891 his views on private property, which were not coincidentally similar to his uncle's, Ayn Rand's, John Galt's, and the current Republican Party.

> "When, among the affirmatives of the Declaration of Independence, it is asserted that the pursuit of happiness is one of the unalienable rights, it is meant that the acquisition, possession and enjoyment of property are matters which human government cannot forbid and which it cannot destroy."[23]

Justice Brewer not only bound us to the words of the Declaration of Independence - which has zero legal authority - but also to a perverse interpretation of it, where the ambiguous right to "the pursuit of happiness" only applies to the wealthy who want a yacht, and not to the working man who wants weekends off with his family.

From this springboard, hosts of state and local laws were overturned. In the case "In re Jacobs in 1885", the State of New York had a statute overturned that prohibited manufacturing of cigars in tenement dwellings because it violated the "right to contract" of the immigrants. It was the God-given right for every person to negotiate his own wages and conditions, not that of some meddlesome state legislature.

The California Supreme Court, on the same grounds, found a city ordinance requiring eight-hour days for employees violated the employees' rights. Coal mines had eight hour day restrictions for children overturned because they violated the rights of children. The little fellers should be allowed to bargain for the right to work seventy hours if they wished.[24]

The right to negotiate in the marketplace sounds fair at face value, but the right to contract and negotiate was always only one way.

The theory was that everyone has the right to march up to his boss and say, "I demand this, take it or leave it" and the boss would decide if that was hunky-dory.

Chances are that most times the boss won on that one. But if the workers collectively got together, and said we as a group of employees want this; that too was a violation. That's what unions do and they are against the natural law of God.

They were against the laws of man also, they were "criminal conspiracies in restraint of trade."[25]

So the only recourse for bad labor conditions is to talk it over with your boss, man to man, and see if you can get some relief. It should be obvious that a 9-year-old child would never have consented to working in a coal mine unless they felt they got a good deal. Just like the women who chose to go into prostitution and abortions in the Marinara Islands. That was the right to contract personified. Tom Delay was correct in opposing any intervention from union thugs who would take that sacred freedom away.

And it was sacred, it was based on God's plan for all of us. Almost every justice on the Supreme Court and every judge under the jurisdiction of the court told us that. Stephen J. Field wrote in a court opinion once:

> "Indeed, there is nothing which is lawful to be done to feed and clothe our people, to beautify and adorn their dwellings, to relieve the sick, to help the needy, and to enrich and ennoble humanity, which is not to a great extent done through the instrumentalities of corporations."[26]

Who could argue with that? Corporations are a force for good, chosen by God to bring food, clothing and the Gospel to the masses. Most of the activist judges who pushed this were extremely devout and viewed this as God's will. The extremely wealthy owner of a coal mine, George Baer, told a correspondent for the New York Times in 1905

> "The rights and interests of the laboring man will be protected and cared for-not by the labor agitators, but by the Christian men to whom God in His infinite wisdom has given the control of the property interests of the country, and upon the successful management of which so much depends."[27]

For God so loved the world, that He gave it capitalism, coal mines, and rich pompous assholes to take care of it. That's not really a verse in the Bible, I need to clarify.

But it has been constantly presented as a truth both in this country and through the history of the world as a whole. It was manifested first as the "Divine Right of Kings" where kings were kings only because God chose them to be so. If He happened to choose you to be a peasant, so be it. It kept the masses in line. A bunch of upstart colonists disputed this theory in 1776 and they broke from God's chosen leader to start their own club.

Then, a little over one hundred years later, the super wealthy were lecturing us, along with their puppets on the courts and in Congress that it was God's will that we subordinate to the wealthy. God loves Job-Creators more than the rest of us. One hundred plus years after that, our current day, we find some political leaders such as Tom Delay and Ralph Reed telling us that God loves capitalism and unions are sinful, because they encourage the lower class to rebel against the God ordained leadership. The verse used to beat the drones into submission can be found in 1 Peter 2:18-19:

> *Slaves, submit yourselves to your masters with all respect, not only to those who are good and considerate, but also to those who are harsh. For it is commendable if a man bears up under the pain of unjust suffering because he is conscious of God.*

You see, we are slaves, that's the way God intended it to be. The Christian Capitalists really don't have that big of a gulf with Ayn Rand after all. Once you get past the silliness of praying and giving thanks, all the rest is the same. The slaves are here for the masters, and better damn well shut their mouths.

David Barton is a scholar of dubious talents, but he has quite the audience amongst a group of Christians who call themselves Dominionists.

David Barton writes many books and advises textbook committees in states on textbooks. The subject he is most interested in is God and His place in America. God was on the minds of the Founding Fathers, and also corporations. Apparently God is getting very angry at the United States these days, what with its sinful talk of higher taxes.

> *Two days after the November 2010 elections, Barton, Newt Gingrich, and Jim Garlow (who runs Gingrich's Renewing American Leadership group), held a conference call with pastors to celebrate conservative political gains. On the call, Garlow and Barton asserted a biblical underpinning for far-right economic policies: Taxation and deficit spending, they said, amount to theft, a violation of the Ten Commandments. The estate tax, Barton said, is "absolutely condemned" by the Bible as the "most immoral" of taxes. Jesus, he said, had "teachings" condemning the capital gains tax and minimum wage.*
>
> *Barton also enlists Jesus in the war against unions and collective bargaining. Two years ago Barton devoted his Wallbuilders Live radio show to celebrating a Supreme Court decision that upheld an Idaho law ending state withholding of public employee union political funds. Barton's co-host Rick Green called for activists to "spark a fire" and encourage other states to take up the effort to disrupt unions' political activities. Barton called the Supreme Court's decision "the right historical position and the right biblical position," and went on to explain why the Bible is anti-union.*[28]

It's the Divine Right of Kings. It's been updated to the Divine Right of Capitalism. Money is the new throne but all the rules remain the same.

Mark Twain found himself skeptical of this notion of divine right and skewered it in "A Connecticut Yankee in King Arthur's Court"

> *Before the day of the Church's supremacy in the world, men were men, and held their heads up, and had a man's pride and spirit and independence; and what of greatness and position a person got, he got mainly by achievement, not by birth.*

> *But then the Church came to the front, with an axe to grind; and she was wise, subtle, and knew more than one way to skin a cat -- or a nation; she invented "divine right of kings," and propped it all around, brick by brick, with the Beatitudes -- wrenching them from their good purpose to make them fortify an evil one; she preached (to the commoner) humility, obedience to superiors, the beauty of self-sacrifice; she preached (to the commoner) meekness under insult; preached (still to the commoner, always to the commoner) patience, meanness of spirit, non-resistance under oppression; and she introduced heritable ranks and aristocracies, and taught all the Christian populations of the earth to bow down to them and worship them.*[29]

But Americans, little by little, had bucked the will of the wealthy posed as "the will of God". And while the meek did not quite inherit the earth, they had better conditions in which to endure it. Progressive reforms slowly took hold: the 40-hour week, 8 hour days, time and a half overtime, elimination of child labor, safety standards for workers, and the outlawing of the employers right to chain you inside a factory to keep you from leaving during a fire.[30]

So things weren't all lost for the little guy. Theodore Roosevelt enraged the corporations with new workers' rights. The corporation retreated even more after the Great Depression, or more precisely, **FDR**. Unions were more common, and working conditions became safer, better, and the strange phenomenon known as the middle class developed through the good wages. The corporations were beaten back into their hole, free to profit, but not at the expense of life and not at outrageous margins. The corporations and labor existed side by side for almost fifty years in a mutually beneficial arrangement.

For many years, decades actually, the people deemed the corporations a threat to the people and the people used the government to protect them from oppression.

But today, the American people don't think of corporations as the oppressors, they visualize them as the oppressed. All corporations want to do is make money, and to make money they need workers. Ergo, they create jobs. The Job-Creator is a Golem of sorts, a powerful creature worthy of favor from the government and worship from the masses.

Job-Creators are a funny bunch. They are the most efficient, imaginative, creative force in the world - we know this because they tell us. They drive the economy, they are bound and determined to raise the GDP and lift all boats, if only the government would get out of their way and let them do their thing. They have almost supernatural powers and are fearless. Well, almost fearless. There are two things, which are like Kryptonite to these super-beings. Taxes and regulations.

Taxes and regulations are severe inhibitors to the Job-Creator. Even the threat of higher income taxes will scare these heroes away from the marketplace, their natural habitat where they roam free and wealthy. The mere mention of more government oversight and revenues enhancement will ripple through the herd like a thunderclap on a cattle drive. The resulting stampede will not be pretty and the little man who needs a job will be the one trampled.

Job-Creators have driven this point home and to challenge it is to incite class warfare. Class warfare only occurs when the bottom attacks the top. The top never participates in class warfare. They are merely speaking truth to the masses and it just sounds like class warfare to the untrained ear.

What of these high taxes that Job-Creators pay? High is a relative term. Certainly they are higher than the poor or middle class pay, but not higher than their historical peers have paid.

For instance, consider the plight of Job-Creator John Fleming, who is a Republican Congressman from Louisiana. In a television interview he quickly smacked downed the impertinent interviewer who questioned his aversion to higher taxes.

The interviewer, MSNBC's Chris Jansing, asked him about his revenues of $6.3 million last year from his string of Subway sandwich shops and UPS franchises. He quickly disabused her of the notion that he was successful as he demonstrated quite effectively that he was struggling just like the rest of us little guys:

> *"If you have to pay more in taxes, you would get rid of some of those employees?" Fleming responded by saying that while his businesses made $6.3 million last year, after you "pay 500 employees, you pay rent, you pay equipment, and food," his profits "a mere fraction of that" — "by the time I feed my family, I have maybe $400,000 left over."*
>
> *Jansing pointed out that whining about tax increases while making $400,000 annually is "not exactly a sympathetic position." Fleming could only respond by saying that "class warfare has never created a job" and that his success is a "virtue.* [31]

Sheesh, what does it take to get through the liberal media's head? Representative Fleming ONLY has about $400,000 left per year after he takes his $200,000 per year salary and feeds his family. This excludes, of course, his paycheck as a public servant of the corporations as a Congressman. He gets an additional $174,000 per year for that. But the larger point stands; he only has $400,000 per year left with which to create new jobs. Higher taxes for this struggling Job-Creator would only hurt those who need jobs.

One has to wonder about the detrimental effect of denying the world of more sandwich technicians. Will it really hurt us as a society to have less $8 per hour jobs with no benefits? Notwithstanding, let's examine his source of income.

Both Subway and UPS Stores are franchises. Representative Fleming pays a fee for exclusive rights in an area to operate them. What does he get in return? The already established name and reputation along with proven best practices and standards.

As most Job-Creators stumble and fall within their first years because of the fierce market, it can be very beneficial to hang up a shingle with a nationally or internationally recognized name on it. Subway, for instance, has suppliers lined up for their franchisees. The corporate office handles almost all advertising and they can accurately forecast costs and expenses based on decades of experience.

Running a restaurant is hard work, no doubt, but it is considerably easier doing so under the banner of an established multi-billion dollar entity with all of its support and infrastructure. Subway boasts of this on their website, as they note that it is the largest restaurant chain in the world, and they offer to the franchisee training, product development, a purchasing cooperative to buy with the economy of scale, field support and much more. [32]

Representative Fleming is subject to the top income tax rate of 35%, both personal and corporate. He tells us he cannot expand and create more jobs if the rate were raised.

Fred DeLuca established the original Subway sandwich shop in 1965. He struggled for his first summer, but by the end of the first year he had his second store and made a $7,000 profit. Not bad for a $1,000 initial investment.

By 1974, he had 16 franchises [33]. The top tax rate for individuals when Mr. DeLuca formed his company was 70%, [34] twice what our most successful Job-Creators pay today. The top corporate rate was 48%, compared to the maximum 35% that corporations pay today. [35]

In 1974, after a decade of strong growth, the tax rates were the same, 70% and 48% respectively.

In 1998, Subway had opened it's 10,000th store. [36] The top personal income tax rate in 1998 was 39.6%, higher than today's. [37] Corporate taxes were the same rate, 35%, although the effective rate -which is what the corporations actually pay after deductions and write offs- was considerably higher, 41%. The effective rate today is 32% for Representative Fleming, as he has more tax credits and discounts to use than businesses did in 1998. [38]

I'm a bit confused. I wonder how Fred DeLuca could brave much higher tax rates and raise the corporation from a pup to the largest restaurant in the world while Representative Fleming cannot expand even by one unit if taxes are raised to the level that Subway's founder endured? Perhaps the spirit of the Job-Creator is not as strong in Representative Fleming as it was in the chest of the super Job-Creators such as Fred DeLuca? One could almost surmise Representative Fleming's complaints as a sign of weakness. Real Job-Creators are fearless and blaze trails against all sorts of government oppression.

Somewhere, Jared Fogle is mocking Representative John Fleming and sneeringly urging him to man up, quit whining and fight through the adversity of a few percentage point increase of his tax rates.

But let's not jump to conclusions about Representative John Fleming of Louisiana. I do realize that his arguments are straight out of Ayn Rand but he isn't on her side, regardless of how much his whine sounds like pure greed and materialism. He's on the side of good.

His website proudly lists his service as a Deacon, Sunday School teacher, and School Department Director at First Baptist of Minden,, LA. [39] I'm sure his Sunday School classes explain away the class warfare of Christ with His "no man serving God and mammon" [40] nonsense. If you take in all four gospels, Matthew-Mark-Luke-John Galt, there is no contradiction.

But it isn't about Representative Fleming although I am sure he would appreciate the spotlight diverting from his meager income and struggles to get by. It's about the question "Will low taxes create jobs?"

If you bear with me a bit, I'd like to explain an economic concept that is measured and followed as a barometer of the state of the economy.

It's called Capacity Utilization. Think of the concept this way, if an auto factory can produce 100 cars a day, but only by employing every means possible; every machine, employee, and resource, then the maximum capacity for output is 100 cars. Simple enough. Say the economy slows down, then production drops to 80. The plant is now at a Capacity Utilization of 80%.

Only in the theoretical world is utilization 100%, as there are always sick employees, new employees, broken down machines and other factors that will inhibit production.

The average Capacity Utilization for the U.S. Economy from 1972-2010 averaged 80.4. That was the average of good times and bad. In the 1980's, the high was in 1988 at 85.2.

That dropped to a low of 76.8 during the 1991 recession, which killed the first President Bush's reelection chances. In 1994-1995, it peaked again at 85.1, which ensured President Clinton's reelection. The absolute low during this period was in 2009, where it dropped to 67.3.

It's up now, to 77.4, according to the very latest data from the U.S. Federal Reserve released in September 2011.

I don't blame you if you doubt this because these are statistical facts and everyone knows that facts have a liberal bias. But, if you are gullible enough to believe the economists and statisticians at the Federal Reserve - hmmph, what do they know?-then you can access the data I just quoted here from the Federal Reserve Board's online database, located here at this link. [41]

Pay attention to the numbers. They are intuitive but there is more to it than a sliding scale. It is obvious that in good times the capacity used by businesses is higher (1988 and 1995), and in bad times it is lower (1991 and whoa!..2009). This results from reduced demand in the economy and will usually follow with layoffs as not as many people are needed.

But think of the silver bullet always proposed by Republicans to protect Job-Creators: lower taxes. The theory is that with fewer taxes and more take home pay for Representative Fleming and others like him then more investment in the business can take place and it will put more people to work.

But what smart businessman will invest in more machinery or new plants if capacity utilization is so low? In booming times Capacity Utilization is at roughly 85%. If it is 77% then the Job-Creator can produce more without one dime of investment in new equipment.

Think of how bad things were in 2009, when Stephen Moore chided President Obama for not eliminating taxes. What would the lowering of taxes do? Put more money in the pockets of the big dogs but that's about it. Brokers would see commissions rise as they had more money to play with on behalf of their clients. But working guys would not benefit.

Republicans are a lot of things, but stupid isn't one of them. They know this. Yet they tell us that they care about the little man and that tax cuts are for job creation only. If billionaires happen to get richer because of them, so what? Everybody wins.

Except when everybody loses except the very top. Which is how we got in our current mess to begin with. Republicans aren't stupid, but they are liars, at least those who wish to cut taxes to appease the godlike Job-Creators.

Job-Creators are truly mythical beasts because they don't really exist as single entities. Sure ideas bloom and businesses thrive, with jobs all around for everyone. But it is more honest to say the Job-Creator isn't the owner or entrepreneur. He is the facilitator. The real Job-Creator is demand. It is the demand of the consumer - whether he/she wants an iPad, a new truck, a TV, or a Subway sandwich - that creates the job and the need for more.

No businessman will hire for the sake of hiring, and I daresay that most don't care about creating jobs as much as they do creating profits for themselves.

Heck, they wouldn't whine nearly so much about a few percentage points marginal tax increase if they weren't concerned with maximizing their wealth. Their concern for more jobs is only to the extent that they need more people in position to serve the customers who buy from them.

Our problem today is not with suppliers and businesses not having enough capital to expand and create jobs; it is with the customer base of the businesses not wishing to purchase as much from them. Create demand, you create jobs.

So, when did the empire strike back? When did the tide turn in favor of the corporation? You can't just find one trail of tracks away from the scene of the crime.

There were lots of factors that all worked together to strengthen the strong and make the middle class shrink. Ronald Reagan wasn't really a friend of the middle class, contrary to the mythology taught today. He financed his government with the largest deficits in history up to that time. He cut taxes for the rich and spent massively, which created those deficits. And he raised taxes on the poor and middle class via Social Security and promptly started the process of giving the surplus away.

One of the worst things he did, of which most aren't even aware, is to refuse to enforce anti-trust legislation.

What this meant in practical terms is that corporations became super-corporations. They began to gobble up the smaller ones, consolidating and using raw power to grow even more. When two companies merge, there are redundancies and duplications. So jobs are eliminated, most of them good jobs for the middle class.

Free trade hurt the cause of the workingman and that was accelerated more from the Clinton Administration than from Reagan and Bush the First. Of course, deregulation has been systematically put into practice since Reagan and continues unabated. If elected, every single one of the Republican candidates for president will continue to deregulate, that's a promise they've made and I trust them to keep it if given the opportunity.

But the real spark that started this Ayn Rand fire to burn came in 1971 in a memo that is not well known today and would not be known at all if not for an investigative reporter named Jack Anderson. Those who know this memo know it as the Powell Memo;[42] is so named after its author, Lewis Powell. Powell wrote this memo on August 23, 1971. He was a corporate attorney and served on the board of 11 corporations. He was very much like Justice Stephen J. Field, he saw corporations as the source of all the good in the world.

Lewis Powell was very disturbed about the state of the world in 1971, specifically the state of the capitalistic system. The Powell Memo was devoted to the expression of his fear and his call for action. He sent it to his friend Eugene Sydnor, Jr., the Director of the U.S. Chamber of Commerce. Powell was disturbed because only 15% of the American public trusted corporations to do the right thing opposed to just seeking profits. It had been 70% ten years before.[43]

In the memo Powell outlined the attacks he saw on the beloved free enterprise system. He noted the popular sentiment against the pure profit motive was growing and the threat to our economic existence given to by our beloved profit motive was frighteningly real. He saw a clear and present danger posed by government regulations and hostility against American business on college campuses, in churches, in the media, in the arts and sciences, and in government. His solution was a new assertiveness by corporations, "surveillance" of textbooks and television, and a purge of left-wing elements.[44]

Powell's title for his memo was "Attack of American Free Enterprise System" which was quite catchy as it reminds one of a horror movie. Surprisingly, it wasn't that popular as it failed to inspire a sequel until forty years later, after the election of Barack Obama. However, it was popular enough initially and the Chamber of Commerce took his suggestions to heart. The Chamber used its vast financial resources to implement his plan.

What were his observations and recommendations?

For one, the real threat to America didn't come from the card carrying Communists. No, he categorized the threat as "*the perfectly respectable elements of society*"[45].

He identified these as the college campus, the pulpit, the intellectual and literary journals, the arts, and from politicians. He complained about them being the most articulate, vocal and most prolific in their writing, and how they were able to turn heads with all of their fancy talking and writing.

The worst offender was Ralph Nader. He was a single-handed threat to the corporation. Powell quoted this offensive passage about Nader in the memo:

> *"The passion that rules in him -- and he is a passionate man-- is aimed at smashing utterly the target of his hatred, which is corporate power.*
>
> *He thinks, and says quite bluntly, that a great many corporate executives belong in prison -- for defrauding the consumer with shoddy merchandise, poisoning the food supply with chemical additives, and willfully manufacturing unsafe products that will maim or kill the buyer. He emphasizes that he is not talking just about 'fly-by-night hucksters' but the top management of blue chip business."*

Had I known this, I might have campaigned for Nader in 2000. Another missed opportunity for me I suppose.

What did Nader do to piss off Powell so much? He advocated for seat belts to be installed in cars plus more engineering for safety reasons. He wrote a book "Unsafe At Any Speed" about the industry and accused the car making Job-Creators of neglecting safety for the pursuit of profits. GM responded with dignity, and hired a private investigator to smear Nader, [46] even to the extent of hiring prostitutes to entrap him. It came to light and they had to pay him almost $300,000 after admitting guilt.[47] Yet Powell saw Nader as the threat to the country.

Powell gave a call for action; he said that corporations should enlist **PR** guys to give their side of the story. Also every function of society must be taken over by corporate influence, and to do so the campus needed to be attacked as the hotbed of liberalism that it was.

He had a caveat though:

> *"Few things are more sanctified in American life than academic freedom. It would be fatal to attack this as a principle"*

Therefore, the tact was to develop a stable of intellectuals for the right wing, to finance them with money, cultivate them in think tanks, and to offer them up as speakers and a counter weight to respectable academics. Also it was important to try to control textbook content, to make sure anti-business statements were excluded.

Powell noted as the controllers of purse strings to universities, the corporations should insist upon right wing professors.

He suggested, how about financing graduate schools of businesses, to teach about the free enterprise system?

That was for schools, the public was another matter. Television was a threat because it had *"so-called education programs (Such as "Selling of the Pentagon")* [48] [all emphasis in the original] where big business was portrayed as so hungry for profits that they would corrupt government officials. Powell stated that business should demand equal time on all television shows to give their point of view, which in itself is fascinating, given the right wings' terror at the thought of the so-called "Fairness Doctrine" applying to Rush Limbaugh.

But the most ominous suggestion was labeled "Neglected Opportunity in the Courts." Powell saw business threatened by the assertion of rights of individuals over corporations.

> *"Under our constitutional system, especially with an activist minded Supreme Court, the judiciary may be the most important instrument for social, economic and political change"* [49]

That Powell saw the court as a major battleground for the interests of big business shouldn't surprise anyone. It shouldn't surprise anyone that he wished for a strategy to influence the Supreme Court. What may surprise the reader is that Richard Nixon nominated Lewis Powell two months after writing this memo to the United States Supreme Court. He was confirmed and served from January 7, 1972 until June 26, 1987, when he retired.

Powell was instrumental in pushing the courts towards even more rights for corporations. He authored an opinion on a stunningly brazen gift to corporations; he gave them "negative free speech" rights. In a case involving a utility giant, PG&E (Pacific Gas & Electric),

> "In Pacific Gas & Electric (1986) the Court established a novel new corporate right, that of "negative free speech." In this case, the management of an electrical utility company had a newsletter expressing one set of political views on energy policy, but the state regulatory body, wishing to increase the diversity of opinions, passed a rule requiring the utility company to enclose the newsletter of a consumer group four times each year in its billing envelopes."

Justice Powell argued in his opinion that the message from a ratepayer's group, the customers of the utility, violated the free speech of the company. The company has a right not to be associated with speech it disagreed with. It would violate the company's conscience to be forced to provide equal time.

Justice William Rehnquist, who was later named Chief Justice over one of the most conservative courts in history, dissented.

> "Extension of the individual's freedom of conscience decisions to business corporation strains the rationale of those cases beyond the breaking point. To ascribe to such artificial entities an "intellect" or "mind" for freedom of conscience purposes is to confuse metaphor with reality."

No matter, it became yet another of the many rights corporations came to possess at the expense of real humans.

The Powell Memo itself was influential. Because of it, industry mobilized and financed the creation of advocacy groups and think tanks.

> Soon thereafter, the Chamber's board of directors formed a task force of 40 business executives (from U.S. Steel, GE, ABC, GM, CBS, 3M, Phillips Petroleum, Amway and numerous other companies) to review Powell's memo and draft a list of specific proposals to "improve understanding of business and the private enterprise system," which the board adopted on November 8, 1973.
>
> Historian Kim Phillips-Fein describes how "many who read the memo cited it afterward as inspiration for their political choices." In fact, Powell's Memo is widely credited for having helped catalyze a new business activist movement, with numerous conservative family and corporate foundations (e.g. Coors, Olin, Bradley, Scaife, Koch and others) thereafter creating and sustaining powerful new voices to help push the corporate agenda, including the Business Roundtable (1972), the American Legislative Exchange Council (ALEC - 1973), Heritage Foundation (1973), the Cato Institute (1977), the Manhattan Institute (1978), Citizens for a Sound Economy (1984 - now Americans for Prosperity), Accuracy in Academe (1985), and others.[50]

Extremely wealthy men who had fanatical viewpoints had existed and been vocal since the days of FDR. They were particularly vocal during the Eisenhower Administration due to the fact that they felt deep disappointment at Ike's refusal to overturn the New Deal.

Ike's domestic policy of 'containment' (mentioned in Chapter Five) infuriated the true believers and the most fanatical - which included the wealthiest - believers branded Five Star General Dwight Eisenhower a Communist. Eisenhower told a business leader in a letter that economic inequality was the greatest danger facing America.[51] Because of that kind of thinking, the man who saved the world from the Nazi's was deemed to be desirous of destroying freedom.

Ike had dismissed these people as lunatics, including a Texas oilman by the name of H.L. Hunt. Hunt was a founding member of the John Birch Society along with Fred Koch, another oilman.

In a letter President Eisenhower wrote to his brother, a far right-winger who condemned Ike as a sellout to the Communists Ike blasted the type of discourse, which has become the norm in today's Tea Party/Fox News/Rush Limbaugh America.

To quote from Ike's letter:

> Now it is true that I believe this country is following a dangerous trend when it permits too great a degree of centralization of governmental functions. I oppose this--in some instances the fight is a rather desperate one.
>
> But to attain any success it is quite clear that the Federal government cannot avoid or escape responsibilities which the mass of the people firmly believe should be undertaken by it. The political processes of our country are such that if a rule of reason is not applied in this effort, we will lose everything--even to a possible and drastic change in the Constitution. This is what I mean by my constant insistence upon "moderation" in government. Should any political party attempt to abolish social security, unemployment insurance, and eliminate labor laws and farm programs, you would not hear of that party again in our political history. There is a tiny splinter group, of course, that believes you can do these things. Among them are H. L. Hunt (you possibly know his background), a few other Texas oil millionaires, and an occasional politician or businessman from other areas. Their number is negligible and they are stupid.[52]

To reiterate: millionaires and billionaires can be stupid too, and those who try to destroy Social Security, unemployment and the social safety net were stupid in Eisenhower's eyes.

Which brings us to the Koch Brothers, Charles and David. They are two sons of Fred Koch, co-founder of the John Birch Society. Fred was of the "negligible number who were stupid" bunch to which Ike referred in his letter. Eisenhower's negligible number of nincompoops felt everything was a Communist plot; not just Social Security, but also fluoride in drinking water.[53]

They were negligible in President Eisenhower's day, but the Powell Memo gave them motivation to gather, and now they are the Republican Party. Fred Koch had some outlandish ideas, but they really don't differ much from those of his sons' sponsored Tea Party:

> In 1958, Fred Koch became one of the original members of the John Birch Society, the arch-conservative group known, in part, for a highly skeptical view of governance and for spreading fears of a Communist takeover.
>
> Members considered President Dwight D. Eisenhower to be a Communist agent. In a self-published broadside, Koch claimed that "the Communists have infiltrated both the Democrat and Republican Parties." He wrote admiringly of Benito Mussolini's suppression of Communists in Italy, and disparagingly of the American civil-rights movement. "The colored man looms large in the Communist plan to take over America," he warned. Welfare was a secret plot to attract rural blacks to cities, where they would foment "a vicious race war." In a 1963 speech that prefigures the Tea Party's talk of a secret socialist plot, Koch predicted that Communists would "infiltrate the highest offices of government in the U.S. until the President is a Communist, unknown to the rest of us.

The old man, Fred, died in 1967 and left his estate to his four sons. Charles and David had a falling out with the other two brothers, bought them out, and established dominance over Koch Industries. Charles is the control freak and runs the company; David acts as his right hand man. Together, they both are worth around $40 billion. Their company is privately held and has revenue over $100 billion a year. And chances are you have never heard of it, or them.

They own Georgia Pacific. They own Dixie Cups. They own Stainmaster Carpets. They also own a staggering amount of oil and gas interests; from refineries to oilfields. The Brawny paper towel guy? He works for the Kochs; chances are he hates his job, even though he's just a cartoon guy with a thick mustache on a plastic wrap. I bet his plaid flannel shirt is covered with some cancer causing chemical discharge from one of their factories.

Here's where I have to be careful as the Koch's are some of the wealthiest people in the country, most likely the world. They create jobs, including jobs for lawyers that would shut me down for the wrong accusation or implication.

The Koch brothers have their critics and I am one of them. They are very diligent in responding to their critics. Go to Koch Industries website, www.kochind.com. The site is less about their business ventures and more a propaganda platform. You can find op-eds written by Charles Koch and you can find attacks on critics of the Kochs, by Koch Industries and sycophantic blogs and journalists. It reminds me of the Ayn Rand Institute's website, in message and in style. It's a celebration of freedom; their freedom, not yours.

Charles Koch currently has a few editorials posted and praises freedom and the free market. He waxes poetical about the free market and how it was the basis of the Constitution. He clearly buys into the "corporations as people" theory and believes the Bill of Rights to be for corporations. God help us all if Koch Industries uses its Second Amendment right to bear arms to its full capacity.

Charles Koch and his Koch-heads make noble claims about wanting all government out of his way, even the government that gives him breaks. As quoted on his website:

> Koch's consistent opposition to subsidies reflects our commitment to free-market principles. As Charles Koch, chairman and CEO of Koch Industries, Inc. said in an op-ed to the Wichita Eagle, "Unfair programs that favor certain companies – such as the current well-intentioned but misguided suggestion that the natural-gas industry should receive enormous new subsidies – don't just happen. They are promoted, in large part, by those seeking to profit politically, rather than by competing in a market where consumers vote with their wallets."

> Commenting on the NAT GAS Act (H.R. 1380) currently being debated in Congress and promoted by T. Boone Pickens, Dr. Richard Fink echoes this, saying: "Koch has consistently opposed subsidies that distort markets. We maintain that the marketplace, while not perfect, is the best mechanism for allocating resources to consumers."

> " People deciding what fuels to purchase, instead of the government, is best for consumers and our country.

285

> *Likewise, if natural gas vehicles are truly*
> *advantageous and economically efficient, then consumers will*
> *demand that they be developed without political mandates*
> *that exhaust more taxpayer dollars."*
>
> *"...However, we believe history has demonstrated*
> *over and over that these subsidies end up undermining the*
> *long term prosperity of the country. For these principled*
> *reasons, we oppose this bill to give tax incentives to buyers*
> *and makers of natural gas-powered vehicles and related*
> *infrastructure. We also consistently oppose subsidies for all*
> *other fuels whether or not we benefit from them.* [54]

To be clear, subsidies for T. Boone Pickens'
project are an insult to us all, but the Koch's have
benefitted from oil subsidies and government contracts,
according to a study by Media Matters reported in the
New Yorker, to the tune of $100 million. [55]   In case you
weren't familiar with T. Boone Pickens, he is proposing
investing in wind powered electricity, as he believes it is a
more responsible direction for our country than oil
dependency. The Koch's just happen to be by pure
coincidence, major players in the oil industry. That of
course has nothing to do with their opposition to these
subsidies. It's principle driven, or is it spelled principal?
With interest accumulating.

The Koch's have been heavily involved in political
activism much of their adult life. David ran as the vice
president candidate for the Libertarian Party against
Ronald Reagan in 1980. Reagan was a bit too leftist for
David Koch. His platform called for

> *"The abolition of the F.B.I. and the C.I.A., as well*
> *as of federal regulatory agencies, such as the Securities and*
> *Exchange Commission and the Department of Energy.*
>
> *The Party wanted to end Social Security,*
> *minimum-wage laws, gun control, and all personal and*
> *corporate income taxes; it proposed the legalization of*
> *prostitution, recreational drugs, and suicide. Government*
> *should be reduced to only one function: the protection of*
> *individual rights."* [56]

Of course that isn't extremist. It's all about
freedom and the individual's right to collect yachts and
million dollar homes.

The Koch's founded American's for Prosperity, without explaining that the prosperity that they are for is theirs. The Tea Party has latched on to them for guidance as American's for Prosperity provides them with "hit lists" of Congressmen that the Tea Party wishes to be defeated.

The Koch's call the shots here, they give money conditionally. If their will not be done, thy bill not be paid. David Koch has said:

'If we're going to give a lot of money, we'll make darn sure they spend it in a way that goes along with our intent," he told Doherty. "And if they make a wrong turn and start doing things we don't agree with, we withdraw funding."

The Koch's apply this to all of their ventures. For instance, they donated money to Florida State University and the strings attached to this money provides the Kochs with veto power over faculty assignments. [57] So much for academic integrity. The Job-Creators are diversifying into the Thought-Creator role.

The Kochs pour money into politicians, think tanks, and activist organizations. Ever wonder how it is that some scientists are convinced climate change is real and man-made from burning carbon-based fuels such as oil, yet some say it is bunk? Typically, those who say climate change is real publish in peer-reviewed journals while the deniers are on the payroll of the Kochs.

Greenpeace did an interesting report on the Climate Change denial machine [58] that is financed by the Koch's. They've spent more than Exxon on this, almost three times as much. Of course it is about freedom, job creation, and not about preserving their source of wealth, oil. The only dishonest motives out there are those that liberals have.

They've spent more than Exxon on this, almost three times as much. Of course it is about freedom and job creation and not about preserving their source of wealth - oil. After all, the only dishonest motives out there are those that liberals have.

The New Yorker did a very long and informative piece on them last year, which I have linked in my footnotes. It was titled "Covert Operations." The Kochs responded to it, as they do with any criticisms made against, them, on their website in a convenient section they provide for us called Koch Facts.

According to the Kochs, the entire world is lying and all they are trying to do is protect freedom. And jobs. And profits too, if they happen to make any. They aggressively respond to any piece against them and often use the word "liberal" to discredit their detractors. The word "liberal" works with conservatives because; quite frankly they don't think as much as they react. That word will induce a reaction of distrust and questioning of motives. Not of the one who invokes it, but the one that is the object of the word.

Go back to President Eisenhower's letter to his right wing brother. In it he blasts his non-thinking critics. In this example it is with respect to foreign policy, but the same truth applies today in all policy matters. Especially with regards to current day individuals' version of "freedom" and the idea of regulations. President Eisenhower wrote:

> "As a matter of fact, if you will press any individual who brings to you all these strictures and comments, I venture that your experience will be the same as mine. That experience is that these individuals have no idea of what the "foreign policy" of the previous Administration was and what the present one is. They have heard certain slogans, such as "give away programs." They have no slightest idea as to what has been the effect of these programs in sustaining American security and prosperity. Moreover, they have no idea whatsoever as to comparative size of them now as compared to even two or three years ago." [59]

Allow me to paraphrase. There are many dumb-asses out there who are so manipulated by the unscrupulous that catch phrases suffice for debate. Ignorance is bliss for the sheep, as they will easily panic and accuse any alternate thinking as being evil. It's how Joseph McCarthy made his living.

The American people are panicked into believing that their liberty is taken away because of regulations, when it fact it is their liberty that is being protected. The liberty taken is from those who oppress.

Franklin Roosevelt in 1936 quoted the greatest Republican president, or more accurately the greatest president of all time, Abraham Lincoln on this matter:

> *The shepherd drives the wolf from the sheep's throat, for which the sheep thanks the shepherd as his liberator, while the wolf denounces him for the same act, as the destroyer of liberty...Plainly the sheep and the wolf are not agreed upon a definition of the word liberty; and precisely the same difference prevails today among us human creatures...and all professing to love liberty. Hence we behold the process by which thousands are daily passing from under the yoke of bondage hailed by some as the advance of liberty, and bewailed by others as the destruction of all liberty." And, in closing, Lincoln said this:*
>
> *"Recently, as it seems, the people...have been doing something to define liberty, and thanks to them that , in what they have done, the wolf's dictionary has been repudiated.*[60] *"*

We need jobs, for sure. But we need jobs where we can be safe from harm in the workplace or in the environment we live. Where we have the assurance of dignity, and the promise of a livable wage. We also need jobs from people who don't want so much freedom that they can build feudal empires.

Today's Job-Creators don't want to give us any of these things. In fact they wish to throw off the authority of the shepherd that keeps them from our throats. Today's Job-Creators are too often wolves in Job-Creator's clothing.

It's time to repudiate the Kochs and their ilk, and throw away their wolf's dictionary, before they devour us all.

Freedom for the wolf has to be curtailed sometimes, and it is done through regulation. Republicans will balk at the idea of ANY regulations, because regulations destroy jobs and the wolves are capable of regulating themselves. This script has played out for over one hundred years.

Consider the following example:

The stock market has had some major crashes, we all know that. Maybe you also know of the widespread corruption that has taken place under laissez-faire Republican rule - where Ponzi schemes were used to snooker investors of their life savings, insiders profited at the expense of the average investor, and rampant speculation drove the market to unheard of highs before hitting rock bottom.

Enter Congress in order to try to regulate the stock market in order to bring integrity to the process. Congress called Richard Whitney, the President of the New York Stock Exchange, to testify and to offer reasons why there shouldn't be more oversight. From his testimony:

> "Whitney admitted to no serious fault in the past operations of the Exchange or even to the possibility of error. He supplied the information that was requested, but he was not unduly helpful to senators who sought to penetrate the mysteries of short selling, sales against the box, options, pools, and syndicates.
>
> He seemed to feel that these things were beyond the senators' intelligence.
>
> Alternatively he implied that they were things that every intelligent schoolboy understood and it was painful for him to have to go over the obvious...
>
> The government, not Wall Street, was responsible for the current bad times, Whitney averred, and the government, he believed, could make its greatest contribution to recovery by balancing the budget and thus restoring confidence.
>
> To balance the budget he recommended cutting... pensions and benefits...and also all government salaries.
>
> When asked about cutting his own pay, he said no-it was "very little."...
>
> His attention was drawn by the committee members to the fact that this was six times what a senator received, but Whitney remained adamantly in favor of cutting the public pay, including that of senators." [61]

That was just to Congress. To the public, through the media, he was even more certain of doom if the government did not back out. He had predicted the takeover of the stock market by the government! Even worse for the rest of us, it would...gasp...destroy jobs.

> [Whitney] *characterized the powers proposed for the the stock market regulatory agency as "so great that many of the functions of management are, in effect, transferred to an administrative department in the government."*
>
> *... Whitney forecast: "There is no important aspect of the economic life of this country, whether it be agriculture, industry, banking or commerce, which will not be adversely affected by this bill. This bill, if passed by Congress, will not only destroy our security markets but will as a necessary consequence interrupt the flow of credit and capital into business."* [62]

A couple of points need to be brought to light. Whitney was president of the New York Stock Exchange from 1930 to 1935. It should also be disclosed that he was arrested in 1938, for embezzlement. He had stolen about $6 million from various funds, including a widows and orphan's fund for brokers and from his father-in-law. The $6 million would be worth about $90 million these days. [63]One can understand why he felt no regulation was necessary. Warren Buffet is famous for saying "You never know who is swimming naked until the tide goes out. [64]" Richard Whitney had been skinny-dipping for a while, and laissez-faire gave him all the cover he needed.

Doesn't Wall Street seem silly from all of their idiotic cries of socialism, government take over, and destruction of jobs? I'm not talking about the 1930's, which should be obvious. I'm talking about today.

After the collapse of Enron, Tyco, World-com and other companies because of fraud driven by greed, Congress passed the Sarbanes-Oxley Act. This law requires CEO to sign off on their financial statements, verifying them as true. Wall Street, Republicans, and the Chamber of Commerce howled. It would bring lawsuits to every corporation in America; it was a trial lawyer's dream. The president of the U.S. Chamber of Commerce Thomas Donohue said the bill would "*hand American corporations back to the trial lawyers for summary execution.* [65] "

I wish. In the ten years since the passage, class action lawsuits resulting from the Sarbanes-Oxley decreased. Perhaps the ineffectiveness of the law prompted Donohue to change his mind. He remarked in 2010 that the law was "Fair enough. A lot of it was well worth doing.[66]"

You'd think that Donohue would have learned from the Chicken Little sky-is-falling mantra he chanted in the past. But no, his reflex was to fight regulation aimed at protecting the consumer from predatory lenders, pay day loan operators, and check cashing companies; all of which are nothing more than loan shark operations located in strip malls rather than street corners. Donohue brought 'experts' to testify that job creation, the only purpose of mankind in this life, would shrink by 4% because *"entrepreneurs would not be able to get the credit they need.[67] "*This from regulation of payday lenders. I have no data to back this up, but I doubt "You keep the corporation, we keep the title" is a popular way of starting up companies.

The Tea Party, not to be outdone, came up with even more hysterical predictions:

> *"Main Street non financial businesses would be hit with taxation, regulation, and possible nationalization by the Federal Reserve."*
> *Proposals to give shareholders a greater say in corporate governance would empower union pension funds and other progressives by forcing companies to fund their Saul Alinsky-style campaigns for a company's board of directors." The coalition imagined that the directors would seek to make peace with the shareholders by, among other things, 'kicking conservative media personalities off the air.'*[68]

I hope this sounds as outlandishly buffoonish to the reader as it does to me, the writer. How on earth can a Communist totalitarian society emerge from a bill that regulates payday lending? But to the viewers of Fox News and the firearm collecting hordes of paranoid lunatic conservatives, it all makes perfect sense. The real menace of financial regulations is the threat to Rush Limbaugh.

The wolves, er..Republicans, tell us Job-Creators are the only true endangered species and therefore they must not be exposed to the most toxic of viruses: regulations. Regulations kill jobs dead, to paraphrase the old Raid commercial. That is the favorite song of the Republicans as long as they have been dancing with big business. Currently they are pushing a bill for consideration that involves the state of Alabama.

The Republicans solution to our current job crisis is to deregulate and they are starting with the cement industry. Their solution is the Cement Sector Regulatory Relief Act, which uses an Alabama firm, the National Cement Company, as its poster child.

The president of National Cement Company, located in Ragland, Alabama, sat with Speaker Boehner during the president's last address to Congress. Spencer Weitman is the president of National Cement and he is one of the majestic Job-Creators. Well, he would be if we would just get out of his way.

He is aching to spend $320 million on new operations in Alabama, which will create many construction jobs...but the implementation of new EPA standards is just too burdensome. Sorry Ragland, there will be no Christmas this year, thanks to the Grinches at the EPA. [69]

Republican voters are all too willing to sign on to the notion that regulation kills jobs, therefore it must be done away with. John Boehner and his Ayn Rand foot soldiers are more than happy to oblige. We will look closer at the Cement Sector Regulatory Relief Act in a few minutes, but a brief background on regulations is in order.

Ask yourself, are all regulations of business bad? How about the regulation of Wall Street, which was non-existent with respect to derivatives for instance? Do you believe that the government should inspect food? The laws ensuring the safety of food and drugs took decades to pass, even when it became obvious that something needed to be done.

293

This issue can be used as an example of everything that is wrong when big business controls Congress and, by extension, America. In it you see the same problems caused by ruthless materialism, you see the power of lobbyists to thwart reform, and you see the public's health and welfare taking a back seat to the powers of big business. And you see this all in the name of protecting the consumer and little guy. Most of all, you see the same script being played out by the defenders of greed, for well over a century, almost word for word. You can see it in history, and it doesn't take much imagination to see it today.

Back at the turn of the 20th century, corporations were unregulated. The public mood was for states rights, and a free hand for businesses.

It ought not to shock anyone when I say that the wealthy always favor local government as a regulator. Because the wealthy can control the local yokels a whole lot more effectively than they can the U.S. Congress, although I must say that they do a wonderful job these days of keeping their servants in Congress from becoming actual public servants.

But these were the good old days that Ayn Rand and her cult longed for. Things were absolutely golden for the big money guys, but conditions were steadily worsening for first the workers, and then the consumers. Food quality was one of the first areas that cried for government regulation. By the time of the Spanish American War, things had gotten so bad that hundreds of Theodore Roosevelt's Rough Riders took ill from eating spoiled meat sold to the army. In fact, there were more deaths from eating spoiled meat in the Spanish American War than there were from battle. [70]

In an illuminating academic journal article published in 1933, the scholar C.C. Reiger, then of the University of West Virginia noted that opposition to food safety legislation came from three factions which still exist today in the same form.

They are: 1) conservative southerners who hate the idea of an expanded federal government, 2) those who were uninformed on the severity of the issue and manipulated by the corporate lobbyists, and 3) those who stood to make a butt-load of money in an unregulated industry.[71] Ok, he didn't say butt-load, but he did express the sentiment.

So back to the Cement Sector Regulatory Relief Act. The act concerns itself with overturning EPA regulations of mercury emissions from kilns at these plants. No one argues that the plants emit mercury. It's basic science. No one argues that mercury poisons the water supply and poisons fish. No one argues that the poison fish, water and air present a terrible health risk.

The cement industry has never been regulated on this matter, until last August. The EPA proposed upgrading the oldest and most inefficient kilns in the industry, in order to reduce mercury emissions.

> The rule, according to Clean Air Watch will eliminate more than 8 tons of mercury air pollution, and will also significantly reduce soot (a.k.a. particulates); hydrocarbons; sulfur dioxide, nitrogen oxides and other acid gases; and toxic gases. Soot, hydrocarbons and sulfur dioxide contribute to smog, and sulfur dioxide also causes acid rain. Each of these pollutants will be reduced 78-97% under the new rule (with the exception of nitrogen oxides, which is slated for just a 5% reduction).[72]

Compare this with food safety. Who could argue with the need for safe and uncontaminated food? The corporations that produced it, that's who. Professor Reiger notes that the first law was passed to protect and ensure the purity of food on January 20, 1879. President Theodore Roosevelt signed into law the Pure Food and Drug Act of 1906, which became the genesis of the FDA, the Food and Drug Administration. Between these two laws, 190 bills were introduced, and only 8 were passed, inclusive of the two mentioned. The first law in 1879 was not even that restrictive of a law.

In spite of multiple petitions, which were concerned with the overall safety of food, the first law Congress passed regulated the quality of IMPORTED foods, and not really food, but *"adulterated and spurious teas"*.[73] With the tainted tea menace subdued, Congress went back to the business of Congress, which was ignoring the public welfare for the benefit of business. It took over twenty-five years to get a comprehensive law inspecting the safety of food.

In the 1933 study, Professor Reiger documents that almost all instances of the food regulations failure in Congress were the result of an agreement between the house and senate, with each house taking turns in defeating the legislation.

Note his wording of the reasons the bills were shot down, and see if you notice any similarity of strategies between the safety of food over a hundred years ago, and the passage of health care reform, financial services reform, or any other action that might be considered hostile to big business today.

From 1933:

Among the most common were more pressing legislation, agreement in principle but opposition to construction, the desirability of letting the states handle their own problems in their own way, and the prevention of hasty legislation[74]

Let's examine these four perpetual excuses that Professor Reiger found way back in 1933, used to block food safety laws over 125 years ago, and see if they apply today to the currently debated Cement Sector Regulatory Relief Act:

"More Pressing legislation" Jobs. The need for jobs trumps these regulations, never mind the clear and present danger of poison in our water and air.

"The desirability of letting the states handle their own problems in their own way" Republican Congressman Steve Chabot of Ohio announced a proposal for turning over the enforcement of mercury emissions to the states on September 22, 2011.[75]

"Agreement in principle but opposition to construction" *"There are reasonable regulations that protect our children and help keep our environment clean,"* [the Republicans] *wrote in a letter to the president. "But there are also excessive regulations that unnecessarily increase costs for consumers and small businesses, and make it harder for our economy to create jobs. The rules addressed by the bills the House will consider this week are examples of such harmful government excess."*[76]

"The Prevention of Hasty Legislation" Quoting from the actual bill proposed by the Republicans: *"A legislative stay for a sufficient period of time, moreover, is essential to ensure EPA has adequate time to resolve difficult technical issues and develop more workable rules for the sector"*[77]

See how easy this is? Also refer back to Professor Reiger's three groups that constantly blocked food safety laws:

1) Conservative southerners that did not want expansion of the federal government. Sadly, these obstructionists have spread like a virus, and the Tea Party carries this barrier to progress all over the United States like rats carry infected fleas.

2) Those who are uniformed about the severity of the issue. I'd have to give opponents a benefit of the doubt that I don't wish to do, as I think they do understand, but just don't care. But let's be charitable. Can anyone actively seek to have mercury emissions go unregulated after knowing the dangers for citizens?

3) Those who stood to make money by keeping it deregulated. These quotes from an article in Roll Call shed light upon this issue in a not so complimentary way for the Republicans:

> *After years of persistent lobbying, cement's political moment has apparently arrived.*
>
> *The small industry facing new environmental standards has spent millions of dollars to make itself the poster child for Republican deregulatory fervor...*

>*...though the cement industry only employs about 15,000 Americans, such concerns have caught the attention of Republican leaders looking to highlight ways that regulations are stifling the economy...*
>
>>*...In the first six months of this year, the relatively small industry with just*
>>
>>>*$6.5 billion in annual revenue spent $1.2 million on lobbying, according to disclosure records.*[78]

Does this not make you the least bit suspicious? The usual suspects are doing what they do best, obstructing and obfuscating for the interest of corporations. Even if you still wanted to give the Republicans the benefit of the doubt, wouldn't you think you owe it to the rest of us to check and see just how potentially dangerous the overturning of these regulations could be? Besides, if the Republicans truly cared about the plight of the cement industry, they'd pass a massive infrastructure project; say for example the one proposed by President Obama. It would put many more people to work without damaging the air and water, and I suspect move enough cement to pay for these upgrades. But that would require doing the right thing, which is not something the right has been doing lately.

The Republican Party has one goal and only one goal in mind, and it is to achieve Ayn Rand's vision for America. Which is simply an unregulated and unencumbered business sector.

Consider this: does anyone seriously believe that any Republican presidential candidate, Congressman or woman would propose anything to help the common man? If costs of employees are too high, what is the solution? Get rid of the employees. It happens, even to the point where people are being fired as the close in on retirement date, lest they burden the company with expensive pensions.[79]

Herman Cain charms the Fox News Nation as a perfect man for the Oval Office, because he was a CEO of a pizza chain. He was also the head of a lobbying agency fighting against health care rights for employees, aligning himself with the tobacco industry to fight local regulations to ban smoking - bans which have been overwhelmingly successful and popular with no hardship on the service industry noted- and he worked hard against the strengthening of DUI laws, as he feared the loss of liquor sales.[80] Who's side is Herman on anyway?

The Koch Brothers, that's who. Herman has been da-man for the Koch empire, speaking at their events for a couple of years as an affirmative action hire for the reactionaries. There are strong suspicions that he has been well compensated for his efforts. Much like the movie "Trading Places", the two pompous old white geezers find a black man to execute their nefarious selfish ambitions. Herman Cain isn't as vulgar as Billy Ray Valentine was and seems less naive. In fact, he seems downright complicit in the brothers' scheme to amass even more wealth with his billionaire boosting 9-9-9 tax scheme.[81] It's better in the long term than cornering the orange juice market.

The Koch's, as serial polluters and Cain as a shill for billionaires - a "shillionaire" if you will - will claim that the nearly non existent leash around big business is strangling them, all the while they tighten the noose around our necks.

So how long of a leash do we keep corporations? Or more accurately, how long of a leash should we ask them to keep us on? The mantra from the right, from all of the Koch financed organizations, right wing talk radio and of course Fox News is that we need to back off and let them do their thing. Create jobs, make money, and let the crumbs fall from the table so we can all feast.

It is pure Ayn Rand. Atlas deserves a break, he works so hard for us under him. But shouldn't the playing field be a little bit more balanced? What if an employee of Wal-Mart used their name, corporate logo, or any trademark to enrich himself in so much as a lemonade stand? What do you think would happen? Lawyers would descend upon the little guy, and gobble up any type of financial benefit he made sponging off of Wal-Mart. Wal-Mart states this clearly on its website:

> Unless otherwise noted, all materials, including images, text, illustrations, designs, icons, photographs, programs, video clips and written and other materials that are part of this Site (collectively, the "Contents") are copyrights, trademarks, trade dress and/or other intellectual property owned, controlled or licensed by walmartstores.com, one of its affiliates or by third parties who have licensed their materials to walmartstores.com and are protected by U.S. and international copyright laws. The compilation (meaning the collection, arrangement, and assembly) of all content on this site is the exclusive property of walmartstores.com and is also protected by U.S. and international copyright laws. [82]

How about the lovable mouse, Mickey and his magical employer, Disney? The mouse and his posse will light your ass up with flaming cease and desist orders at the first sign of copyright infringement. They are notorious for a zero tolerance position with respect to their intellectual property. A family in Florida bought two bootleg costumes of Eyeore and Tigger off eBay to wear at kids' birthday parties. Disney sued them for a cool million, plus their court costs. [83] Homey don't play that.

The average American is reasonable and sympathetic towards rights of corporations to protect their brand and image; but is the average American so calloused where they can allow the wealthiest corporations in the world to exploit the very lives of their lowest paid employees for profit?

When I use the phrase "exploit the lives of their lowest paid employees", I am not speaking in a radical, Marxist sense. That's a rhetorical trick, and the other side can explain their behavior as not being exploitive, but part of the process of job creation. I'm speaking literally of shenanigans that are used by the biggest and wealthiest corporations to enhance profit, including the two mentioned above, Disney and Wal-Mart.

What type of shenanigans am I speaking of? Take for instance dead peasant insurance. The technical name for this is called "corporate owned life insurance" or "COLI". This shouldn't be mistaken for life insurance policies for the employee, paid for by the company and given as an employee benefit. This isn't a benefit, at least not for the employee. It's a payoff for your boss if you die; he's put money down on your demise like most of us do a football or NCAA March Madness pool.

The original intent of this device was to insure against the sudden loss of a key person in a corporation, for example a Steve Jobs with Apple. But ingenious corporate leaders found a way to insure against losses further down the line-way down the line. Corporations started taking out policies on all of their employees, including the janitors. The employees had no idea that they were in a corporate dead pool. Their surviving families were often shocked and infuriated when they found out that the corporations received a couple of hundred grand payout when the breadwinner kicked the bucket. The insurance payoff was tax-free, it was reported as income and the dead peasant is none the wiser.

The term dead peasant comes from an official company document from Winn Dixie, your neighborhood grocer. Winn Dixie found itself in a lawsuit and a memo surfaced from one of its insurance consultants. This consultant was collecting data and requested it from the company.

The attorney Mike Myers (no relation to Austin Powers or the psychotic killer from "Halloween") has been successful in retrieving insurance payouts from corporations and bringing some relief to the actual family members. On his blog, he recounts the Winn Dixie episode:

> In 1993, Winn Dixie Stores bought COLI policies on approximately 36,000 of its employees, without their knowledge or consent. The Coventry Group, a large insurance brokerage firm well-versed in COLI transactions, helped place the policies, which were underwritten by AIG Life Insurance Company. On October 30, 1996, Lawrence J. Kramer, the Coventry Group's vice president and general counsel, distributed a memo stating, "Here is a very rough beginning of the booklet we are preparing for Winn-Dixie. A section on Dead Peasants remains to be written, and Peggy is preparing sample journal entries for various scenarios." The "dead peasants" referenced in the memo were deceased Winn-Dixie employees whose deaths resulted in policy benefits to the company. A similar memo states "I want a summary sheet that has Surrender in one column, the Exit Strategy 1A in the second column and the Dead Peasants in the third column."
>
> These memos were part of the court's record in a lawsuit in which the United States Court of Appeals for the Eleventh Circuit held that Winn-Dixie's COLI policies were a sham transaction for federal income tax purposes. The memos were later used by reporters such as Ellen Schultz and Theo Francis of the Wall Street Journal and L.M. Sixel of the Houston Chronicle and incorporated into articles about corporate owned life insurance. Thus, the phrase "dead peasant insurance" is not a creation of the media. It is a term used within the insurance industry to describe employees whose lives are insured by policies of corporate owned life insurance for an employer's benefit.[84]

It appears that the "Beef People" in Winn Dixie's slogan referred to the slabs of meat they employed.

The Wall Street Journal did a whole series of articles on the widespread nature of this practice.

In one article, the Journal recounted the story of Mrs. Margaret Reynolds of Union-town, Ohio. This particular peasant worked for Camelot Music and she suffered from Amyotrophic Lateral Sclerosis, or as we commonly know it, Lou Gehrig's disease. If you have any familiarity with the disease, you know it is always fatal and it is completely debilitating. In her last years, Mrs. Reynolds had to be cared for by her five children.

Mrs. Reynolds made $21,000 per year as an administrative assistant, but she was more valuable than her salary suggested. Camelot viewed her as so indispensable they took out a $180,000 life insurance policy on her - with the payoff for the corporation, not the employee.

Mrs. Reynolds' family was indignant when they found out about this policy. Particularly since they had begged the company's Human Resource department during her final days for $5,000 out of her health plan to cover a specialized wheelchair so she could go to church. The company denied this selfish request. Providing jobs for peasants is costly, so it is essential that dead peasants be the gift that keep on giving to corporations. [85]

Camelot ran numbers projecting income from insurance payoffs, and calculated that young (apparently) healthy employees could pay about $400,000 to $500,000 in death benefits, but older corpses were still profitable at $120,000. [86]

Which begs the question: to what was this revenue applied? Job creation? More benefits? Raises? Not exactly. Records show that Camelot used $165,875 of the death benefit of 29-year-old Felipe Tillman to pay executive bonuses. Atlas didn't shrug, but he did bend over to pick up spare change from the bodies of dead peasants. Mr. Tillman's death also benefitted the nephew of Camelot Music's founder, who received $280 from the payout to pay child support payments. [87]

303

The practice was not just applied to a few companies. A lawsuit in 2002 revealed that companies were using benefits from deceased worker drones to smooth over earnings; that is to say, buffer up the numbers to appear more profitable. [88] This is very effective in satisfying Wall Street, and it pleases the shareholders, who include multimillionaire CEO's and mutual fund managers. What's the harm in paving the streets with rotting corpses, as long as it reduces the bumps in the road for the producers as they drive to the Hampton's? Its not like the low-lives were using their bodies at that point anyway.

Why don't regulators do anything about this? Uh, because they can't. They can't even tell you how much corporations are doing it. The General Accounting Office (GAO) did an investigation of the phenomenon of Corporate Owned Life Insurance back in 2002, and found out that they didn't really know jack about it. The report is available on the internet and is essentially a 65 page summary of why the government doesn't have tangible facts on this. To summarize the summary, it's because businesses do not wish to disclose this. The title and these selected headings in this report demonstrate the toothless bite of regulators:

BUSINESS-OWNED LIFE INSURANCE
More Data Could Be Useful in Making Tax Policy Decisions

Available Information on the Prevalence and Use of Business Owned Life Insurance Is Limited

Federal Bank Regulators Have Collected the Most Data on the Prevalence of the Policies, but Not All Banks and Thrifts Provided Information

*SEC Has Not Specifically Required
Reporting on the Policies, but Some Insurers
Have Reported Sales*

*IRS Has Not Collected Information on
the Policies, but Federal Revenue Estimators
Have Estimated the Forgone Tax Revenues*

*State Insurance Regulators Have Not
Collected Data on the Prevalence of the Policies*

*Businesses May Purchase Business-
Owned Life Insurance for Various Purposes but
Generally Are Not Required to Use Policy
Proceeds for Those Purposes*[89]

My personal favorite is the last heading here, acknowledging that businesses can purchase the insurance for some specific (presumably noble) purpose, but really don't have to use the proceeds for that purpose. The payoff might have been earmarked as helping with employee health care costs, but could at the last minute be diverted into the "CEO Hooker Employment Fund".

Oh regulators, where is thy sting? Oh government, where is thy victory? They aren't to be found against the insurance industry. The federal government has very little power over the insurance industry. Way back in the day when corporations were growing up in front of the country and becoming full fledged humans, poor little insurance companies were designated as less than human; not even businesses, at least not in their own eyes.

The insurance industry had not even been considered a business until the 1940's. Congress deemed them "non-commerce", mostly because if they were found to be involved in commerce, then they could be regulated by the feds and anti-trust laws could apply. But since they weren't commerce, they could pool resources and collude, run monopolies in each state, and fix prices. They were behaving so badly, the federal government took the industry in Georgia to the Supreme Court and won, and lo and behold, the Supreme Court ruled that insurance was actually a business in 1945. The feds did have the authority to regulate it. Congress reacted quickly by passing a law titled "McCarron-Ferguson Act" which took away Congress's right to regulate the insurance industry, and stipulated that it was the job of states.[90] So much for that idea.

Now, the only control on the insurance companies is from state government. And the Republican solution for everything of course is to let the states regulate. Therefore we end up with denial of life saving medical treatments in the name of profit from insurance companies, the denial of payouts for hurricane victims who had paid insurance premiums over the years- including former Senate Majority Leader Trent Lott- and the profiting from policies wagering on the lives of peasants and janitors.

This is regulation that kills jobs? Where are these stringent regulations that so dangerously strangle our economy, according to the right wing?

Is the financial sector too regulated? Unless you have just returned from a coma, your answer ought to be "no" based on the events of the last ten years, when the financial industry was *deregulated* and new regulation was blocked.

What about the oil industry? BP surely didn't suffer much under the federal boot before and after the near destruction of the Gulf of Mexico. The official commission report for the President on the matter has this telling quote:

> *"Federal oversight followed the philosophy of 'minimum regulation, maximum' cooperation"*[91]

Who can blame the government for its light hand? BP is a job creator. Of course the jobs it created then were jobs for sea gull bathers and oil skimmers, never mind the thousands of jobs it nearly destroyed.

Taking it closer to home for me, I picked up the local Nashville paper on June 4, 2011 and noted the top headline *"Feds call for Gallatin plant's overhaul but don't have power to enforce it"*[92]

The story was about terrible workplace accidents in Gallatin, TN, a small town just out of Nashville, which killed four workers in the preceding four months. The U. S. Chemical Safety board cited numerous hazardous conditions for workers, which ultimately resulted in deaths, but also noted that they had absolutely no power to sanction, levy fines, or even shut them down. That's the way the pro Job-Creators in Congress want it, we don't want the federal governments to have too much power. One month later, the Tennessean headline read *"As OSHA debates, more die: Decades old danger of explosive dust, linked to Gallatin blasts, is unregulated"*[93]

Despite the almost universal agreement on the life threatening dangers of combustible dust in the air, there are no regulations in place to protect people. You know governments, they are big bureaucracies and they move slowly. What you may not know is that they are designed to move slowly, almost to the point of standing still, by those who would destroy government for the benefits of Job-Creators.

"Under federal law, such a review involves 39 steps, years of study and a requirement that the safety agency consider not only the risks to workers' lives, but also the cost of doing business that new rules might place on industries.[94]

Republicans feel our pain, they don't like for people to die, but that kind of things happens. You have to look at the big picture, how much money do we save for the corporations that don't have to spend money to make the factories safer? In the long run, it balances out, particularly if you weigh money at a higher rate than human life.

But this is small time stuff compared to the worship of the false god Job-Creator that came to fruition in West Virginia in the Upper Big Branch mine disaster.

The mine was owned by Massey Energy and Massey's CEO was Don Blankenship. Don Blankenship is a Triple Crown winner as he is a poster boy for Ayn Rand, the Tea Party and Satan. The association with Satan is merely speculative on my part as it is entirely possible Satan would be feel slandered by an association with Blankenship.

Ayn would have loved Blankenship because he represents wealth and power achieved purely through ruthless selfishness. The Tea Party, and by extension the current conservative movement, loves him because his methods are their goals for the rest of America: the destruction of unions, the subjection of courts to business interests, the flaunting of government oversight, and the manipulation of elections with the perversion of purchased free speech.

Everything that is disgusting about Don Blankenship is everything Republicans worship: true freedom.

Republicans piously preach to us the virtue of freedom, praising wealth as choosing correctly and poverty as choosing incorrectly. The Republican's favorite examples for bad choices are always a single mother, an alcoholic, or someone with a lazy disposition.

There are no examples of bad choices made from the world of the wealthy; Republicans would have us to believe. To you conservatives, I offer you Don Blankenship.

Don Blankenship is a local West Virginia boy who found financial success as the most powerful CEO in the coal industry. West Virginia is dependent upon coal as a livelihood. A "good job" to a local boy is getting a job in the mines. Don Blankenship made a name for himself as a manager by destroying unions. When he took over a mine, he would shut it down until the contract expired, then re-open it as non-union. The former union members were blackballed for life.

In 1978 120,000 West Virginians were union members. There are less than 15,000 today. That is in large part because of Don Blankenship.

Don believes in freedom, for him, so he can destroy competition. He lost a $50 million lawsuit in 2002 that established that he illegally destroyed a rival's corporation. Don appealed it, but didn't stop there. He targeted a member of the state's Supreme Court that had a history of ruling against coal companies. He hand picked a hack lawyer to run for the seat, which happened to be the chief justice seat. Don Blankenship spent an unbelievable $3 million to elect his guy, and it worked. Not surprisingly, the state's Supreme Court threw out the $50 million verdict by a vote of 3-2, with Don's man as the deciding vote.

But later, photographs emerged of the Chief Justice and Don Blankenship vacationing together - on the French Riviera. The date stamp was when Don was actually in front of the Court.

The case ended up before the U.S. Supreme Court, where even Chief Justice John Roberts' "pro-business" court was offended. They threw out the verdict, essentially saying "Come 'on Don, try not to be so obvious"

It went back through the West Virginia court system, and was defeated twice more on technicalities. [95]

But the most recent disaster in the Upper Big Branch mine, a massive explosion occurred, and 30 miners were trapped inside. One was severely injured for life, the other 29 died horribly. Don Blankenship's reaction was to blame the federal regulators for the explosion in the mine.[96] Don Blankenship would tell this one over and over, until the governor's official report on the disaster was released. In it, facts such as these were documented:

> "[F]rom 2000 to 2010, no United States coal company had a worse fatality record than Massey Energy. Fifty-four workers were killed in Massey Mines during that time...
>
> During the 10-year time period examined, the reporters found that Massey had been cited for 62,923 violations, including 25,612 considered 'significant and substantial." During that time MSHA proposed $49.9 million in fines against Massey, $15 million more than any other company."[97]

So what exactly were the regulations that kill jobs in this case? It looks to be the case where the lack of regulations killed those who worked the jobs, but sadly not at the CEO level, only at the lower end of the totem pole.

It is dishonest to speak of freedom without the acknowledgment that freedom carries choices, and the wrong choices can be made with perfect freedom. These wrong choices are all on display in these corporate abuses, particularly Don Blankenship. So where are the consequences? How do we prevent them?

Republicans, and you who vote Republican, you are to blame. Everything you ask for you received with Don Blankenship. You hate unions? He destroyed them. Yet unions could have called a strike to prevent entry into such dangerous conditions. Unions can shut down a bad company faster than regulations can, as evidenced in these previous examples. Perhaps that is why Job-Creators hate them so much?

What about relief from the courts? You Republicans hate trial lawyers; you want "tort reforms" which are nothing more than laws that lower fines and settlements for the Don Blankenships of the world, where he and others can write a check with no consequence, as one would pay for a speeding ticket.

It doesn't matter if you win in the courts anyway, he can buy judges through massive spending in campaigns. And you conservatives will vote for the man who is the most conservative and protects the Job-Creators every time; no matter what protections they strip from those who work.

Don't get me started on another favorite conservative reform: "loser pays". The right wing would have it where if you sued a noble beast such as Blankenship, you damn well better win. If you lost, you would be on the hook for all of his expenses. Who do you reckon would run out of money first?

What of the regulatory state helping? Ha..fat chance! Conservatives have destroyed funding, and then proceed to whine about the regulations that cannot and will not be enforced against them. And those with polyester red, white, and blue clothing will cheer all day long, while praying for the safety of the unborn as they ignore the plight of the living. Don Blankenship is no doubt anti-abortion, as it reduces the labor pool of those willing to work for peanuts in dangerous mines.

Let's not forget the most important enabling by the right wing. Every conservative voter in America feels that Don Blankenship takes home too little of his paycheck. He struggled to get by as CEO making $18 million a year, and those who celebrate freedom while pretending to mourn the deaths of workers insist that he keep more of it. Why, pray tell? He took the risk! He is a Job-Creator, he put his money on the line.

Someone needs to tell conservatives that the money can always be replaced. Lives can't. The Job-Creator has 30 openings in the Upper Big Branch Mines.

These jobholders didn't risk any money in creating those mines like Don Blankenship and his Republican friends, I concede that. But no one can't say that they didn't take risks, and they lost as the worst-case scenario played out. Too bad in this society, the fear of losing money is a greater one than the fear of losing lives.

After World War II, thousands of Nazi's escaped and avoided war crimes trials. One of the most notorious was Adolf Eichmann, the man rightly referred to as the architect of the Holocaust.[98] Eichmann was only a Lieutenant Colonel, but in his position he arranged the logistics of the transporting of the Jewish people across Europe to the death camps.

He lived across Europe immediately after the war, under five assumed names. Finally in 1950, he entered into Argentina under the assumed name of Ricardo Klement, where he expected to live the rest of his life in anonymity.[99]

The State of Israel had other intentions, as he had been classified as one of the highest priority fugitives and much effort had gone into the search for Eichmann. In 1960 he was discovered, kidnapped by Israeli Mossad agents in a dramatic fashion, and brought back to Israel to face trial for crimes against the Jewish people.

A well known political philosopher and intellectual named Hannah Arendt, who was Jewish, flew to Israel and covered Eichmann's trial for the New Yorker magazine. Arendt expanded her article into a book and the subtitle coined a new phrase. Her book "The Eichmann Trial: A Report on The Banality of Evil", published in 1963, created a controversy with the idea behind the subtitle.

What the "Banality of Evil" suggested was that true evil isn't always traced back to the fanatics, the sociopaths, or psychotic. Normal everyday people can participate in the process, just because that's the way things are done.

Arendt didn't see much anti-Semitism in Eichmann, if any. What she saw was an intellectually dim, cliché-spouting company man. It was merely a cruel twist of fate that the company that Eichmann promoted with such vigor was Nazi Germany.

Arendt portrayed Eichmann in the most buffoonish way, as a company man who knew nothing but clichés and catch phrases; one could almost picture Dwight Schrute from the television show "The Office", except with a more sinister role to play in a more sinister organization. Arendt surmised:

> *"Despite all the efforts of the prosecution, everybody could see that this man was not a "monster," but it was difficult indeed not to suspect that he was a clown."* [100] ...
>
> ..."*[Eichmann] apologized, saying, 'Officialese is my only language." But the point here is that Officialese became his language because he was genuinely incapable of uttering a single sentence that was not a cliché. ..To be sure, the judges were right when they finally told the accused that all he had said was "empty talk"-except when they thought the emptiness was feigned, and that the accused wished to cover up other thoughts which, though hideous, were not empty. This supposition seems refuted by the striking consistency with which Eichmann, despite his rather bad memory, repeated word for word the same stock phrases and self-invented clichés (when he did succeed in constructing a sentence of his own, he repeated it until it became a cliché) each time he referred to an incident or event of importance to him.".*
>
> ..."*The longer one listened to him, the more obvious it became that his inability to speak was closely connected with an inability to think, namely to think from the standpoint of somebody else."* [101]

If you have spent time in a corporate or bureaucratic environment, you know these people exist. Company men-by the book men-who quote chapter and verse regulations and standards; that have immersed themselves into the standard operating procedure as their compass for life.

The larger point of Arendt's book was "how much should we hold the foot soldier accountable for the orders given from above?" Hence the expression, banality of evil, as evil becomes nothing more than a banal exercise of routine, tradition, regulations or laws.

Corporations epitomize the notion of the banality of evil. Before you recoil in outrage over a comparison you may view as over the top, consider the case of **I.G. Farben.**

I.G. Farben was a German super-corporation that manufactured all sorts of chemicals. When the S.S. found the perfect site for a "quarantine camp" at Auschwitz, **I.G.** Farben, the job creators, found a perfect site for a factory, coincidentally at Auschwitz. Labor costs were remarkably low, in fact non existent, as they used slaved labor from the death camps to manufacture their synthetic coal-oil. [102]

I.G. Farben went even further in the interest of shareholders; they invented, patented and sold to the government Zyklon-B crystals, a poison that was effective at killing mass quantities of prisoners. Bills of lading for delivery turned up at the Nuremberg trials.

William Shirer discussed the evidence in "The Rise and Fall of the Third Reich":

> *"But the records of the courts leave no doubt of the complicity of a number of German businessman, not only the Krupp's and the directors of the I.G. Farben chemical trust but smaller entrepreneurs who outwardly must have seemed to be the most prosaic and decent of men, pillars-like good businessmen everywhere-of their communities."*[103]

The worst nightmare for these Job-Creators happened after the war as many were convicted of war crimes and sent to prison. The Job-Creators prefer to roam free and unobstructed by international borders or neighborhoods; migrating internationally and traveling with the herd to luxurious vacation spots. Now the threat of confinement was upon them. Job-Creators do not adapt to captivity very well, even though many of them seem better suited for it.

Nothing describes the evils associated with corporations better than Hannah Arendt's "Banality of Evil". It involves just shrugging your shoulders and saying "It's my job", regardless of the damage it does. Standing up for what is right in the business place is given a lot of lip service, but it really isn't valued.

Don Blankenship didn't do what he did by himself. He had an army of well-compensated executives who willingly destroyed the jobs, the environment, and the lives of innocent working people for profits. Not one of them has been prosecuted for the arrogant flaunting of the law. Not one of them has lost a dime in fines paid to the overly oppressive government. I doubt seriously that any of them have lost sleep over it.

Jobs are important, but not at the expense of our values and certainly not at the expense of our lives. The government exists for a reason. It provides services and protection. Both are being destroyed by the wealthiest and most privileged in our society, and those who are hurt the most are cheering them on as heroes. Something isn't right with this picture.

SOURCES CONSULTED FOR CHAPTER 6

[1] The legend of the Golem, located many places on the net, available here   at http://www.myczechrepublic.com/prague/history/prague_legends.html
[2] Image   available   from http://www.flickr.com/photos/dylanramos/3783430758/
[3] Ibid;
[4] Ibid;
[5] Beatty, J., "Age of Betrayal: The Triumph of Money In America, 1865-1900". !st ed 2007, New York: Vintage Books. P. 72.
[6] Ibid; p. 83.
[7] "The Life of Charles Dickens: Beloved Bully" The Economist October 1, 2011 Available from: http://www.economist.com/node/21530937
[8] Karl Marx, F.E., "Revolution and counter-revolution: or, Germany in 1848" 1851: Charles H. Kerr & Company.
available   from   Google   Books   at http://books.google.com/books?id=VTkbAAAAMAAJ&dq=karl%20marx%20and%20the%20revolutions%20of%201848&pg=PA16#v=onepage&q&f=false
[9] White, D., Social Policy and Solidarity, Orphans of the New Model of Social Cohesion. The Canadian Journal of Sociology, 2003. 28(No. 1) Available   from: http://www.jstor.org.proxy.library.vanderbilt.edu/stable/3341875
[10] Kennan, G., The Long Telegram, Dept.o. State, Editor 1946: Moscow. Available   from http://www.gwu.edu/~nsarchiv/coldwar/documents/episode-1/kennan.htm
[11] Beatty, J., "Age of Betrayal: The Triumph of Money In America, 1865-1900". P. 88.
[12] Beatty, J., "Age of Betrayal: The Triumph of Money In America, 1865-1900". P. 94
[13] Ibid;
[14] Beatty, J., "Age of Betrayal: The Triumph of Money In America, 1865-1900". Pgs. 94-95
[15] Beatty, J., "Age of Betrayal: The Triumph of Money In America, 1865-1900". P. 95.
[16] Ibid;
[17] Ibid;
[18] Nace, T. "Gangs of America: The Rise of Corporate Power and the Disabling of Democracy" 2003 Berrett-Koshler Publishers, Inc. Location 1154 out of 3771
[19] Twain, M. Autobiography of Mark Twain 2010 Editors of the Mark Twain Project University of California Press. P. 364
[20] Nace, T. "Gangs of America: The Rise of Corporate Power and the Disabling of Democracy" 2003 Berrett-Koshler Publishers, Inc. Location 1175 out of 3771
[21] Beatty, J., "Age of Betrayal: The Triumph of Money In America, 1865-1900". !st ed 2007, New York: Vintage Books. P. 158
[22] Nace, T. "Gangs of America: The Rise of Corporate Power and the Disabling of Democracy" 2003 Berrett-Koshler Publishers, Inc. Location 1364 out of 3771
[23] Beatty, J., "Age of Betrayal: The Triumph of Money In America, 1865-1900". !st ed 2007, New York: Vintage Books. P. 159
[24] Ibid; Pages 160-161.

[25] Allen, A.M., "Criminal Conspiracies in Restraint of Trade". Harvard Law Review, 1910. 23 (7).

[26] Nace, T. "Gangs of America: The Rise of Corporate Power and the Disabling of Democracy" 2003 Berrett-Koshler Publishers, Inc. Location 1095 out of 3771

[27] Morris, E. "Theodore Rex" 2002 Modern Library Paperback. P. 137

[28] Montgomery, P. "Jesus Hates Taxes: Biblical Capitalism Created Fertile Anti-Union Soil". Date; Available from: http://www.religiondispatches.org/archive/politics/4366/jesus_hates_tax es:_biblical_capitalism_created_fertile_anti-union_soil/

[29] Twain, M. "A Connecticut Yankee In King Arthur's Court" Available from http://www.pagebypagebooks.com/Mark_Twain/A_Connecticut_Yankee _In_King_Arthurs_Court/The_Boss_p2.html

[30] "Don't Mourn-Organize: Lessons Learned From the Triangle Shirtwaist Factory Fire" available from http://www.osha.gov/oas/NYCOSH_Triangle_Jounal.pdf

[31] Seitz-Wald, A. "Multi-Millionaire Rep. Says He Can't Afford A Tax Hike Because He Only Has $400K A Year After Feeding Family". Date September 19, 2011; Available from: http://thinkprogress.org/economy/2011/09/19/322405/gop-rep-whines-400k/

[32] Subway franchising information available from http://www.subway.com/subwayroot/own_a_franchise/whychoosesubwa y.aspx

[33] Subway history available from http://www.businessesforsale.com/franchises/F36/subway-franchise/articles/Subway-franchise-the-history

[34] Historical Individual Tax Rates available from http://www.taxpolicycenter.org/taxfacts/displayafact.cfm?DocID=543&To pic2id=30&Topic3id=38

[35] Historical Corporate Tax Rates available from http://www.taxpolicycenter.org/taxfacts/displayafact.cfm?DocId=65&Topl c2id=70

[36] Subway history available from http://www.businessesforsale.com/franchises/F36/subway-franchise/articles/Subway-franchise-the-history

[37] Historical Individual Tax Rates available from http://www.taxpolicycenter.org/taxfacts/displayafact.cfm?DocID=543&To pic2id=30&Topic3id=38

[38] Effective Corporate Tax Rates available from http://www.taxpolicycenter.org/taxfacts/displayafact.cfm?Docid=323&To pic2id=70

[39] Congressman John Fleming biography available from http://fleming.house.gov/Biography/

[40] Matthew 6:24: "No one can serve two masters. Either he will hate the one and love the other, or he will be devoted to the one and despise the other. You cannot serve both God and Money."

[41] U.S. Federal Reserve Capacity Utilization Data Release for September 2011 available from http://www.federalreserve.gov/releases/g17/Current/g17.pdf

[42] A copy of the original Powell Memo found here at http://research.greenpeaceusa.org/?a=download&d=5971

A more readable copy is found here at http://reclaimdemocracy.org/corporate_accountability/powell_memo_le wis.html

[43] Nace, T. "Gangs of America: The Rise of Corporate Power and the Disabling of Democracy" 2003 Berrett-Koshler Publishers, Inc. Location 1711 of 3771.

[44] *Biographies of the Robes"*. Date; Available from: http://www.pbs.org/wnet/supremecourt/rights/robes_powell.html

[45] Ibid:

[46] Unsafe at Any Speed summary available from http://www.bizjournalismhistory.org/1960_1965.htm

[47] "The Law: Nader v. G.M." Time Magazine August 24, 2011 Available from: http://www.time.com/time/magazine/article/0,9171,902654,00.html

[48] Powell Memo

[49] Ibid;

[50] The Lewis Powell Memo: Corporate Blueprint to Dominate Democracy August 25, 2011 PRWatch August 25, 2011; Available from: http://www.prwatch.org/news/2011/08/10984/lewis-powell-memo-corporate-blueprint-dominate-democracy

[51] Phillips-Fein, K., *"Invisible Hands" The Making of the Conservative Movement from the New Deal to Reagan"* 2009: W.W. Norton. P. 57.

[52] Eisenhower, Dwight D. Personal and confidential To Edgar Newton Eisenhower, 8 November 1954. In *The Papers of Dwight David Eisenhower*, ed. L. Galambos and D. van Ee, doc. 1147. World Wide Web facsimile by The Dwight D. Eisenhower Memorial Commission of the print edition; Baltimore, MD: The Johns Hopkins University Press, 1996, http://www.eisenhowermemorial.org/presidential-papers/first-term/documents/1147.cfm

[53] Anton, M. "For Some, fluoridated water still hard to swallow" Los Angeles Times December 22, 2007 Available from: http://articles.latimes.com/2007/dec/22/local/me-fluoride22.

[54] http://www.kochind.com/Viewpoint/

[55] Mayer, J. "Covert Operations" The New Yorker August 30, 2010 Available from: http://www.newyorker.com/reporting/2010/08/30/100830fa_fact_mayer?currentPage=all.

[56] Ibid;

[57] Hundley, K. Billionaire's role in hiring decisions at Florida State University raises questions St. Petersburg Times May 10, 2011 Available from: http://www.tampabay.com/news/business/billionaires-role-in-hiring-decisions-at-florida-state-university-raises/1168680

[58] http://www.greenpeace.org/usa/en/media-center/reports/executive-summary-koch-indus/

[59] Eisenhower, Dwight D. Personal and confidential To Edgar Newton Eisenhower, 8 November 1954. In *The Papers of Dwight David Eisenhower*, ed. L. Galambos and D. van Ee, doc. 1147. World Wide Web facsimile by The Dwight D. Eisenhower Memorial Commission of the print edition; Baltimore, MD: The Johns Hopkins University Press, 1996, http://www.eisenhowermemorial.org/presidential-papers/first-term/documents/1147.cfm

[60] Franklin Roosevelt 207 Address at Wilmington, Del. October 29, 1936. Available from the Complete Messages and Papers of Franklin D. Roosevelt.

[61] Galbraith, J.K., *The Great Crash 1929* 1954 Boston: Houghton Mifflin. P. 157

[62] Lincoln, T., *"Industry Repeats Itself"*, 2011, Public Citizen. Available from http://www.citizen.org/documents/Industry-Repeats-Itself.pdf

[63] Con Artist Hall of Fame available from http://www.thehallofinfamy.org/inductees.php?action=detail&artist=richard_whitney

[64] Warren Buffet quote available from http://www.goodreads.com/quotes/show/109034
[65] Lincoln, T., "Industry Repeats Itself", 2011, Public Citizen. Available from http://www.citizen.org/documents/Industry-Repeats-Itself.pdf
[66] Ibid;
[67] Ibid;
[68] Ibid;
[69] "Speaker Boehner to Host Private-Sector Job Creators in House Gallery for President Obama's Address ". Available from: http://www.speaker.gov/News/DocumentSingle.aspx?DocumentID=258776
[70] Hutt, P.B., "Harvey Wiley, Theodore Roosevelt, and the Federal Regulation of Food and Drugs", 2004, Harvard Law School.
[71] Regier, C.C., "The Struggle for Federal Food and Drugs Legislation". Law and Contemporary Problems, 1933. 1(1) Available from: www.jstor.org/stable/1189447.
[72] Shapley, D. "The 23 Most Highly Polluting U.S. Cement Plants" The Daily Green; Available from http://www.thedailygreen.com/environmental-news/latest/mercury-cement-47012002#ixzz1aRO2tjDB
[73] Bailey, T.A., "Congressional Opposition to Pure Food Legislation, 1879-1906". American Journal of Sociology, 1930. 36(1): p. 52-64 Available from: http://www.jstor.org/stable/2767223
[74] Regier, C.C., "The Struggle for Federal Food and Drugs Legislation". Law and Contemporary Problems, 1933. 1(1) Available from: www.jstor.org/stable/1189447.
[75] Sink, J. "GOP Lawmakers Ask Obama to Delay Mercury Regulations" The Hill's Blog Briefing Room; Available from: http://thehill.com/blogs/blog-briefing-room/news/183277-gop-lawmakers-ask-obama-to-delay-mercury-regulations
[76] Kollipara, P. "Republicans take aim at EPA's cement pollution regulations" October 3, 2011 FuelFix October 3, 2011; Available from: http://fuelfix.com/blog/2011/10/03/republicans-take-aim-at-epas-cement-pollution-regulations/
[77] Cement Sector Regulatory Relief Act available from http://www.gpo.gov/fdsys/pkg/CRPT-112hrpt227/pdf/CRPT-112hrpt227.pdf
[78] Ali, A. "GOP Deregulation Push Makes Cement a Star" Roll Call September 14, 2011 Available from: http://www.rollcall.com/issues/57_28/Cement_Suddenly_a_Sexy_Issue-208690-1.html
[79] Examples see IBM here http://www.recordonline.com/apps/pbcs.dll/article?AID=/20090427/BIZ/904270317/-1/BIZ2101
[80] Stolberg, S.G. "Cain, Now Running as Outsider, Came to Washington as Lobbyist" New York Times October 23, 2011. Available from http://www.nytimes.com/2011/10/23/us/politics/herman-cain-running-as-outsider-came-to-washington-as-lobbyist.html
[81] Mayer, J. "Herman Cain and the Kochs" The New Yorker October 20, 2011. Available from http://www.newyorker.com/online/blogs/newsdesk/2011/10/cain-and-the-kochs.html
[82] Terms and conditions of Walmart available from http://walmartstores.com/7736.aspx
[83] Wallace, D. "Disney Sues Small Family Business: Whose Side Are You On?". Date; Available from: http://www.disneyorama.com/2008/07/disney-sues-family-business/

[84] Myers, M. "How 'Dead Peasant' Insurance Got Its Name" August 13, 2008 Contingent Fee Business Litigation August 13, 2008; Available from: http://www.contingentfeeblog.com/2008/08/articles/corporate-owned-life-insurance/how-dead-peasant-insurance-got-its-name/

[85] Francis, E.E.S.a.T. "Valued Employees: Worker Dies, Firm Profits--Why?--Many Companies Insure Staff, Yielding Benefits on Taxes, Bottom Line--Where to Put Dead Peasants?" The Wall Street Journal April 19.2002.

[86] Ibid:

[87] Ibid;

[88] Francis, E.E.S.a.T. "Case Shows How 'Janitors Insurance' Works to Boost Employers' Earnings" The Wall Street Journal April 25, 2002.

[89] GAO Report:
BUSINESS-OWNED LIFE INSURANCE
More Data Could Be Useful in Making Tax Policy Decisions available from http://www.gao.gov/new.items/d04303.pdf

[90] Macey, G.P.M.a.J.R., "The McCarren-Ferguson Act of 1945: Reconceiving the Federal Role in Insurance Regualation". Yale Law School Legal Scholarship Repository, 1993 Available from: The McCarran-Ferguson Act of 1945: Reconceiving the Federal ...

[91] Drilling, N.C.o.t.B.D.H.O.S.a.O., "Deep Water: The Gulf Oil Disaster and the Future of Offshore Drilling", 2011. available from http://www.gpoaccess.gov/deepwater/index.html

[92] III, G.C.W. "Feds call for Gallatin plant's overhaul but don't have power to enforce it" The Tennessean June 4, 2011. Page 1A

[93] G. Chambers Williams, I. "As OSHA debates, more die" The Tennessean July 3, 2011. 1A

[94] Ibid, 6A.

[95] Goodell, J. "The Dark Lord of Coal Country" Rolling Stone November 29, 2010 Available from: http://www.rollingstone.com/politics/news/the-dark-lord-of-coal-country-20101129

[96] Ibid;

[97] McAteer Upper Big Branch Report, 2011, Report to the Governor. Available from http://www.nttc.edu/programs&projects/minesafety/disasterinvestigations/upperbigbranch/toc.asp

[98] Sanders, E. "50 Years Later, Eichmann Trial Seen as Israel Turning Point" Los Angeles Times April 22, 2011 Available from: http://articles.latimes.com/2011/apr/22/world/la-fg-israel-eichmann-qa-20110422

[99] 1. Bascomb, N., Hunting Eichmann 2009, Boston: Houghton Mifflin Harcourt. P. 74.

[100] Arendt, H., "Eichmann in Jerusalem: A Report on the Banality of Evil". Kindle Edition ed 2006: Penguin Books. Location 1209

[101] Ibid; Location 1104-1124.

[102] Shirer, "Rise and Fall of the Third Reich", p. 664.

[103] Ibid; P. 973.

PART THREE: THE GHOST OF AYN RAND YET TO COME

"Ghost of the Future!" he exclaimed, "I fear you more than any spectre I have seen. But as I know your purpose is to do me good, and as I hope to live to be another man from what I was, I am prepared to bear you company, and do it with a thankful heart. Will you not speak to me?"

It gave him no reply. The hand was pointed straight before them.

"Lead on!" said Scrooge. "Lead on! The night is waning fast, and it is precious time to me, I know. Lead on, Spirit!"

ebenezer scrooge
& the ghost of christmas yet to come
"a christmas carol", 1843

GEORGE KELLEY

CHAPTER 7: WHO IS GEORGE KELLEY?

There is a time for everything,
And a season for every activity under the heavens;
A time to be born and a time to die,
A time to plant and a time to uproot,
A time to kill and a time to heal,
A time to tear down and a time to build,
A time to weep and a time to laugh,
A time to mourn and a time to dance,
A time to scatter stones and a time to gather them,
A time to embrace and a time to refrain from
embracing,
A time to search and a time to give up,
A time to keep and a time to throw away,
A time to tear and a time to mend,
A time to be silent and a time to speak,
A time to love and a time to hate,
A time for war and a time for peace.
ecclesiastes 3:1-8

Does anything last forever? Does man create anything permanent or perfect? If you are a Christian, the answer should be obvious. If you are an agnostic/atheist/skeptical scientist, the answer should be the same. The Second Law of Thermodynamics' notion of entropy should suggest that decay and imperfection are the way of the universe.

What then are political and economic ideas but finite and imperfect creations of man? Why do so many cling to the notion of a free, unrestrained market as a perfect solution?

There is efficiency to be sure, but there is an efficiency to be had in nature as the herd abandons the eldest and weakest and animals surrender to more dominant younger beasts.

Are humans such beasts that we design our society based on this idea? It is beyond ironic that millions of people who dispute Darwin and reject textbooks that give his theory credence embrace Social Darwinism; where his ideas are applied across society and the species that adapt or perish are classes of human beings.

But we as humans do not change in our nature, nor we do not want to change without extreme outside pressure and circumstances changing. The status quo of blacks being "non-human" and certainly non-citizens had to be changed after the bloodiest American war in history. Aid for the elderly and unemployed had to be introduced for the first time in American history after the complete collapse of the economic system.

The nature of progressive reforms is that it is always reactive; that is it has to be in response to calamity or extreme conditions. This is because the vast majority of people are always resistant to change. If you have ever been in management and have been tasked with turning around a troubled business unit you will find this. I have experienced this in former management capacities. "We have always done it this way" is the most common refrain the would-be reformer encounters.

But change does happen and sometimes at a degree much greater than the original reformers wish to happen. There is a time for everything, and now is the time for change.

Ayn Rand is "winning", but she won't win. And it could be very well that when she is defeated, we will all lose. Not because we need to live in her world of selfishness, but because this has played out in history time and again and overreactions have taken place every time self-regulation was rejected.

Contrary to the whines of the wealthy, we are living in an Ayn Rand-topia. Disparity of wealth is at an all time high. The top 1% owns approximately 50% of all wealth in the United States. Add to it the next 9%, making it the top 10% and you have 88% of all wealth. The bottom 90% of all Americans owns 12%. [1]

So what? Big deal you say?

Consider Iran under the infamous Shah. Why would anyone prefer the tyranny of Iran's Islamic Revolution over the "very friendly to America" Shah of Iran? For one thing, the economy really stunk there. In the mid seventies, just a few years before his downfall, a study showed that 44% of the population was considered undernourished. With the Iranian people starving, the Shah would celebrate his wealth and prestige by throwing a week long party commemorating the history of the monarchy for hundreds of foreign dignitaries, and spending tens of millions, perhaps hundreds of millions, on excesses such as flying in food daily from Maxim of Paris to feed the masses-the masses that were on the guest list, not the masses who were actually citizens. [2]

By 1978, one fifth of all Iranian households depended upon the state for their living. So when the Shah decided to impose frugality in government they suffered the most. [3] In 1961, over 36% of high school graduates entered college, but in 1978 only 12% had a shot at a better life through education. The university system was substandard anyway, as the government didn't spend any money on it to speak of. [4]

The United States thought highly of the Shah, so much so that the Eisenhower administration overthrew the duly elected president of Iran to install him. The Shah became our puppet and rewarded not only America, but also Americans. Many Americans took jobs in Iran and got rich while the locals didn't do so well. One Iranian wrote "Almost all of them (Americans) seemed to have more money than they were judged to deserve." [5]

So with all of this display of wealth with a very undernourished and over-agitated local population, the Ayatollah Khomeini found a willing supply of revolutionaries.

Similarly, the people of Russia starved under the Tsar. This is well documented. Vladimir Lenin riled up the workers with statements like "Bread, Peace, and Land", three things that the little guy didn't have. They trusted the Communists to bring all three to them. [6] They did not choose wisely.

China[7] suffered economic calamity through hyperinflation, where prices rose so rapidly that money lost all value. The starving masses sided with Mao, as they perceived the government to be in the hands of the wealthy elites.

Germany also suffered incredible hyperinflation in the 1920's, as it struggled to pay its war debts. The German solution to war debts was to print money; in fact they printed money twenty-four hours per day. Madness ensued.

The price increases began to be dizzying. Menus in cafes could not be revised quickly enough. A student at Freiburg University ordered a cup of coffee at a cafe. The price on the menu was 5,000 Marks. He had two cups. When the bill came, it was for 14,000 Marks. "If you want to save money," he was told, "and you want two cups of coffee, you should order them both at the same time."

...A factory worker described payday, which was every day at 11:00 a.m.: "At 11:00 in the morning a siren sounded, and everybody gathered in the factory forecourt, where a five-ton lorry was drawn up loaded brimful with paper money. The chief cashier and his assistants climbed up on top. They read out names and just threw out bundles of notes. As soon as you had caught one you made a dash for the nearest shop and bought just anything that was going." Teachers, paid at 10:00 a.m., brought their money to the playground, where relatives took the bundles and hurried off with them. Banks closed at 11:00 a.m.; the harried clerks went on strike.

The flight from currency that had begun with the buying of diamonds, gold, country houses, and antiques now extended to minor and almost useless items -- bric-a-brac, soap, hairpins. The law-abiding country crumbled into petty thievery. Copper pipes and brass armatures weren't safe. Gasoline was siphoned from cars. People bought things they didn't need and used them to barter – a pair of shoes for a shirt, some crockery for coffee. Berlin had a "witches' Sabbath" atmosphere. Prostitutes of both sexes roamed the streets. Cocaine was the fashionable drug. In the cabarets the newly rich and their foreign friends could dance and spend money.[8]

In the next election, the previously discredited Nazi Party picked up 23 seats. The German Nationalist Party, which later allied with Hitler and enabled him to achieve dictatorial powers, picked up over 100 seats as a result of the economic calamity.[9]

Of course it is never fair to make Hitler and Nazi comparisons. It's plain to see that things were unique in Germany leading up to Hitler's ascent. The only reason Germany got in such economic trouble was because of an unbalanced budget. They foolishly gave in to the wishes of the wealthiest Germans and industries and refused to tax them. Quoting William L. Shirer from his massive 1200 page history, "The Rise and Fall of the Third Reich" (which was drawn from literally tons of German internal documents. Shirer, who spent almost two decades as a foreign correspondent in Germany, witnessed first hand the rise of Hitler and World War II):

> *German currency had become utterly worthless. Purchasing power of salaries and wages was reduced to zero. The life savings of the middle classes and the working classes were wiped out. But something even more important was destroyed: the faith of the people in the economic structure of German society. What good were the standards and practices of such a society, which encouraged savings and investment and solemnly promised a safe return from them and then defaulted? Was this not a fraud upon the people?*
>
> *And was not the democratic Republic, which had surrendered to the enemy and accepted the burden of reparations, to blame for the disaster?*
>
> *Unfortunately for its survival, the Republic did bear a responsibility. The inflation could have been halted by merely balancing the budget-a difficult but not impossible feat. Adequate taxation might have achieved this, but the new government did not dare to tax adequately. After all the cost of the war-164 billion marks-had been met not even in part by direct taxation but 93 billions of it by war loans, 29 billions out of Treasury bills and the rest by increasing the issue of paper money. Instead of drastically raising taxes on those who could pay, the republican government actually reduced them in 1921.*

...The masses of the people, however, did not realize how much the industrial tycoons, the Army and the State were benefitting from the ruin of the currency. All they knew was that a large bank account could not buy a straggly bunch of carrots, a half-peck of potatoes, a few ounces of sugar, a pound of flour. They knew that as individuals they were bankrupt. And they knew hunger when it gnawed at them, as it did daily. In their misery and hopelessness they made the Republic the scapegoat for all that had happened. Such times were heaven-sent for Adolf Hitler"[10]

We look back in disbelief at a country that would start expensive wars and refuse to tax its citizens to pay for them just to benefit the wealthy. It's hard to imagine that citizens can be so unpatriotic as to refuse to pay any extra for foreign wars. Of course, we have too many people who proudly wear flag lapel pins and say the Pledge of Allegiance for this to ever happen here

Let's take a look at what did happen here. In the last part of the 19th century the railroads had bankrupted themselves. Cutthroat competition driven by greed had driven almost all railroads into receivership. Pure laissez-faire capitalism. The railroads responded by cutting wages of the common folk, and strikes and riots resulted. Hundreds of people were killed by national guards and militias, which were directed by the wealthy.

Conditions were terrible for workers for the next 25 years, particularly the immigrants. Strikes were organized or even spontaneously happened. The wealthy had all the political power and constantly used violence from the police and National Guard to beat down dissent.

A working class family of five (with most families having more than three children due to the lack of birth control and high infant mortality) needed an annual income of $500 to survive, which the highly skilled received. However the poorest received much less. A cigar maker was asked how he and his family made it on $5 per week, to which he replied "I don't live. I am literally starving. We get meat once a week, and the rest of the week we have dry bread and black coffee."[11]

Things went from bad to worse. Furniture makers' wages dropped approximately 60% in four years between 1873 to 1877. Textile workers lost almost 50%. About 70% of New York lived in slums.

But the rich got richer. Jay Gould's net worth was approximately $77 million. He was one of the most obnoxious-and criminal-of the Robber Barons. He once boasted "I can hire one half of the work class to kill the other half" [12]

Leon Czolgosz (pronounced Chol-goesh) was an immigrant to America and he worked many of these terrible jobs. He found himself laid off and losing income. However, he was bright enough to see this wasn't just his problem. He saw massive inequalities across society. He was a radical, more radical than most socialists and Marxists, and he believed the root of the problem was the government that gave so much favoritism to the wealthy while oppressing the workers.

He took out his frustrations on September 6, 1901 when he stalked and shot the president of the United States, William McKinley. McKinley died on September 14, 1901. Czolgosz calmly said as bystanders took him down "I done my duty." [13]

Leon Czolgosz confessed and demanded his statement be taken down for history's sake:

> *"I know what will happen to me,-if the President dies I will be hung. I want to say to be published-'I killed President McKinley because I done my duty. I don't believe in one man having so much service, and another man should have none."* [14]

History has shown us that the real threat to society isn't from the top down, where pampered billionaires take to the streets. It comes from the bottom up, where the lowest of the low lose hope. What obligation to society does a man have who has watched his loved ones sacrificed to make a wealthy man wealthier?

There are no trickle down revolutions when inequality reigns. Atlas may shrug, but only after taking a slug in his shoulder from an angry peasant's gun.

That was then, this is now. Mitt Romney opened up his presidential campaign by saying, "We are only inches away from ceasing to be a free market economy." [15] Clearly Romney is scared Mittless.

He should be OK, as he is worth around $250 million. He's a wealthy man. He shows us in this statement what the wealthy think of the world we live in, but what do the advisers of the wealthy think about the current state of the world?

On September 29, 2006 Citigroup analysts Ajaj Kapur and Niall Macleod coauthored an analyst report entitled "The Plutonomy Symposium-Rising Tides Lifting Yachts." This memo was not intended for the proletariat, but it does concern them. It was leaked to Michael Moore, which he exposed in his movie "Capitalism, A Love Story"

Regardless of what you think of Michael Moore, I would urge you to watch this one. He has some objectionable views, and a bit of a caustic personality, but that should not dissuade you from listening to what he has to say. You do not have to agree with his conclusions, I do not; but, you cannot dispute his research on such matters, including this revealing memo.

The memo is 64 pages long. A copy is on display here. [16] The analysts use the term "Plutonomy", which is one that they have coined.

It is a play on words derived from the world "plutocracy", which Merriam-Webster defines as "government by the wealthy." [17]

Contrary to Mitt's opinion, the Citigroup analysts think things are just fine for the wealthiest.

The title is also a play on words from John Kennedy's famous saying, "A rising tide lifts all boats." President Kennedy used it to push the notion that lowering taxes would lift the economy, therefore benefiting everyone, not just the wealthy. These highly compensated analysts for one of the largest financial institutions in the world believe otherwise. Their title suggests, and the subsequent memo plainly states, that the only boats that are floating now are the yachts.

On page 8 of their report they begin with an explanation of the title and update the reader that they have just returned from a Plutonomy Symposium in London, where many "luxury goods companies, or companies servicing the ultra-high net worth community" met and discussed the state of the world.

Quoting the analysts from page 8:

> *"Over the last 20 years or so, in certain countries, the rich have been getting substantially richer. As Figure 1 shows, the share of the top 1% of the population of income has grown substantially in countries such as the US, UK and Canada. The countries, which apparently tolerate income inequality, are what we call plutonomy countries— economies powered by a relatively small number of rich people"*[18]

I disagree. We do more than tolerate, we downright encourage it. Not all of the news is good. They show in Figure 2 of their report that not every country has been as good to their wealthy. The levels of income in Switzerland, France, Japan, and Netherlands have stayed the same since the mid 1970's. That is, the poor and middle class have steadily increased along with the wealthy, and the gap has not grown.

Kapur and Macleod proceed with more data and offer conclusions, one of the main ones being that there is not really an "average" consumer. He is a mythological beast, much like Bigfoot. Their data shows that the bottom 50 percent of America does not even register economically. They don't have enough or spend enough to even show up on radar. The top twenty percent account for about 60% of all consumption. [19]

In this report Kapur and Macleod produced an index of stocks which serve the ultra rich and note that the prices of these stocks have risen to twice the rate of inflation. [20] The analysts met with consultants for the very rich who informed them of the four reasons the wealthy give as to why they purchase high end merchandise:

1. I want to show off (I think its safe to say this is the least shocking revelation)

2. I want to explore

3. I work hard and deserve this. (Ayn Rand is somewhere, most likely looking up, and smiling)

4. I want others to ask me about this. [21]

The analysts would be remiss if they did not warn of possible threats. These were: war; financial collapse (this memo was before the actual collapse); the end of the technology wave where more flowed down to the little guy and 4. the threat of political action, this was the most serious!

They note that the gains in wealth for the richest have come at the expense of workers' wages. Immigration and free trade have kept those wages low, resulting in bigger paychecks for the big-dogs. The boys at Citigroup warn that this will not last forever. [22]

They conclude however, that the threat doesn't appear to be as great as it could be. Quoting Mr. Kapur and Mr. Macleod:

> So, is plutonomy under threat politically? We are keeping an eye on this one. At the moment, it is too early to make this call. Calls for protectionism and an end to immigration grow louder by the day, but they are difficult to measure. But a substantial percentage of Americans are in favor of repealing the estate tax (though only 2% roughly, will ever pay it), which does not resonate as a population determined to destroy wealth inequality.
>
> The political process is the greatest threat to plutonomy. We don't see it as a threat today in most countries. But we are alert to changes here. "[23]

Thanks guys! Keep us updated. You can almost hear them snickering at the idea of the bottom 98% fighting like Hell to repeal the estate tax, even though they will never pay it. The view is great for us under the boot of the plutocrats, why would we move to change it?

Mitt Romney is Ayn Rand's dreamboat. Rich, handsome, arrogant and completely indifferent to the plight of the poor. Rich man Mitt told a group of unemployed guys he understood their pain, as he had been unemployed for two years. [24] He didn't grasp the fact that it is easier to be unemployed when you are worth a quarter of a billion dollars.

He likes to brand himself as the most successful businessman in the current Republican race - hoping to achieve mythical job-creator status. But Mitt was more of a wealth creator than job-creator - not that the job-creators that roam our land are much different from that these days. How did Mitt Romney make his money? The wealth Mitt Romney created was for himself and his partners at Bain Capital.

Bain Capital is an investment bank and took the path to wealth via leveraged buyouts. This means Bain borrowed millions of dollars to buy companies, and paid them back by sawing off huge chunks of the business and firing tens of thousands of workers.

Romney had the reputation of being a detailed oriented yet dispassionate analyst when it came to companies under his scrutiny. From the Boston Globe:

> When Bain partners discussed shutting down failing businesses in which they invested, Romney never suggested they had to do something to save workers' jobs. "It was very clinical," the former employee said. "Like a doctor. When the patient is dead, you just move on to the next patient."[25]

Romney now has a personal fortune around $250 million for his trouble.[26] He touts to anyone who will listen that his qualification for the US presidency is his business experience. His solution for our ills is to take home more of his money, and for all those in his financial situation to take home more of theirs.

What will Romney do for America? Cut taxes, cut regulations, and cut out any opportunity of wage increases for the average Joe. Mitt Romney's published plan for his presidency is straight out of Ayn Rand's diary - excluding references to child murderers of course.

Mitt has a first day wish list if he were to become President. To wit: five bills proposed for day one and also five executive orders for day one.[27] The first day in Congress he will propose:

1) The American Competitiveness Act which reduces the corporate income tax rate to 25% - as corporations aren't rich enough these days;

2) The Open Market Act - implementing more free trade agreements expanding to Columbia, Panama, and South Korea to give outsourced businesses more variety in selection;

3) The Domestic Energy Act - opening up all available public lands to oil exploration- think of this as **BP Oil Spill, The Sequel**- Our National Parks,

4) The Retraining Reform Act- reforming federal job trainings by pushing them down to the underfunded states- Reform by extinction; and

5) The Down Payment on Fiscal Sanity Act - immediately cuts non security spending by 5 percent - also known as the "Let Them Eat Cake Act of 2012".

To facilitate this, he will sign the following executive orders:

1) An Order to Pave the Way to End Obamacare - nothing motivates workers like crushing healthcare debt for their kids. Absenteeism is lowered as workers show up for every shift - volunteering in order to pay off chemo treatments.

2) An Order to Cut Red Tape -"Designed to immediately initiate the elimination of Obama era regulations that unduly burden the economy or job creation"- in case you have difficulty distinguishing which regulations these are, they all do.

3) An Order to Boost Domestic Energy Production- Big Oil wants a piece of the pie too, you know.

4) An Order to Sanction China for Unfair Trade Practices- Mitt will personally send a nasty email to the Chinese Ambassador once a year. Other than that, business as usual with China will continue.

5) An Order to Empower American Businesses and Workers- "Reverses the executive orders issued by President Obama that tilt the playing field in favor of organized labor"- Workers will soon have the freedom to vote themselves no overtime pay, no vacations, no forty hour weeks and no workman's comp.

With one day's work, Mitt Romney can open up the borders so jobs can leave to go all the way to South Korea, bring back pollution to small towns, take away any and every right of the working stiff, ensure oil spills and accidents all over the United States and at the same time keep us sucking on the Saudi pipeline, cut the budget, cut taxes, increase the deficit and the need to cut budgets some more. That's pretty ambitious.

But I think it is very doable, and it would be done. But not just by Mitt Romney. I don't see any Republican candidate who would do anything radically different. Sure, some would push more aggressive anti-gay, anti-immigrant or anti-abortion measures, and some would go after NPR and colleges, but the backbone of the Republican plan would be very much like Mitt's vision, which not coincidentally, is very much like Ayn Rand's.

To be clear, you get Ayn Rand with the Republican Party. No Republican voter should delude himself into thinking that there are moderate checks and balances on the most extreme fanatics. The situation that the country is in at the moment is unique. What makes the Republican Party such a dangerous presence is Grover Norquist. He holds the keys to all legislation pertaining to budgets, and the budgets are getting tighter and tighter, like a noose around the neck of the country.

Neither Republicans, nor Americans at large, can trust the Republican Party to moderate the voice and power of Grover Norquist. He is working to destroy all government, or drown it in the bathtub as the case may be. We have a current state in which one extremist runs the party and the false assumption persists that he won't be able to do everything he wishes. Like almost all current events, there are historical precedents that illustrate the danger.

One such precedent is a man by the name of Wayne Wheeler. Wayne Wheeler is most likely a name that really doesn't register with you. He was never president, nor ever a member of Congress - in fact he was never elected to public office. But you need to know him and his influence and judge for yourself if it was a good thing for all Americans.

335

One man, unknown to most Americans a hundred years after his influence, almost single handedly pushed upon America one of the most disastrous public policies we have ever adopted.

He was so powerful, he had the United States Constitution amended with an amendment that was so foolish and destructive it became the only constitutional amendment ever repealed.

Wayne Wheeler was the one man most responsible for the idiocy of prohibition. And as such, he is responsible for the waste of hundreds and maybe thousands of lives lost in raids and enforcement or imprisoned through overzealous prosecution. He is responsible for the loss of public revenue through the criminalization of liquor, which had been the number one revenue generator for the federal government for decades. And loss of revenues due to the fact that prosecuting this zealot cost astronomical amounts of money.

Wayne Wheeler could be remembered as a successful job-creator though. His policy brought organized crime to America and enriched the criminals who gave the country what it wanted, liquor. Millions of immigrants and native-born citizens had lucrative job opportunities in organized crime as a result of Wayne Wheeler.

Wayne Wheeler came into the temperance movement as a true believer. He was to the casual observer a mousy little man, only about 5-foot-6 or 7, wearing glasses and having a receding hairline. He was described as looking like an insurance clerk, but also described by the newspapers of the day as a man who "made great men his puppets." [28]

When Wheeler joined the anti-alcohol movement it wasn't effective on a national level, even though it had been a force for over seventy years. The leadership was localized and weak. Also, the movement would dilute its own message by embracing a host of other issues ranging from government ownership of utilities to vegetarianism. [29]

He was 24 when he joined the Anti-Saloon League in Ohio and he quickly made a name for himself in that state. Wheeler invented a term that applied to his group and most certainly to groups of today, such as those headed by Ralph Reed, Jesse Jackson, and Grover Norquist. His term: "political pressure groups". [30]

Wheeler learned how to exert pressure with a minority, albeit a vocal minority. He would focus his efforts on anyone that stood against his principles and target them in elections. He was almost always successful. The man who inspired Wheeler and ultimately hired him at the Anti-Saloon League was Rev. Howard Hyde Russell. His vision, adopted and executed by Wayne Wheeler, was to make the Anti-Saloon League utilized "for the purpose of administering political retribution." [31]

Wayne Wheeler spread his gospel of going dry to as many venues as he could reach, traveling the state and working tirelessly. One by one he coerced elected officials in Ohio to sign his no liquor pledge. He had led opposition to 70 sitting legislators of both parties (which was approximately half the legislature) and he had defeated every one of them with his politicians. With this powerful bloc, he pushed to make the town of Cincinnati completely dry. [32]

The Republican governor Myron T. Herrick thought the bill was too extreme and posed too much of a drastic move so he had it amended to a less harsh law. Wayne Wheeler preferred his liquor bills straight up and was furious at the watering down of his legislation. He therefore funneled his energy into defeating Governor Herrick in the next election in 1905.

Governor Myron Herrick was very popular. He had been elected in 1903 by the largest plurality in Ohio history. He was staunchly entrenched in the Republican machine. He had a close personal friendship with Senator Mark Hanna of Ohio, one of the most powerful Republicans of all time. [33]

Another historical parallel needs to be noted here, the Mark Hanna connection. Mark Hanna was the man responsible for William McKinley's presidency. Hanna was a very wealthy man and powerful within the Republican Party. He was the "kingmaker".

Karl Rove has said on numerous occasions that his greatest historical inspiration came from Mark Hanna and the McKinley campaign. Karl Rove's role model has always been Hanna and Rove's America bears no small resemblance to Hanna's America.

Both are Gilded Ages where the distribution of the wealth was/is heavily skewed towards the top 1% and working class conditions worsened. [34]

It's funny how people can see the same thing and come away with different conclusions. Most historians, and readers of history for that matter, come away with the idea that the Gilded Age was a bad time for most Americans. Karl Rove wished to repeat it. But that's the theme of this book, isn't it? Back to Wayne Wheeler.

So, in spite of the strong Republican base in Ohio (Republicans had only lost one governor's race in the previous twenty years), in spite of the powerful influence of Republican kingmaker Mark Hanna, and in spite of having massive amounts of campaign funds, Myron Herrick was defeated in 1905. [35]

Wheeler attacked Herrick unmercifully. He sponsored over 300 anti-Herrick rallies throughout the state and mobilized supporters in churches by telling church members Herrick was the pawn of the liquor industry. The Brewer's Association sent out a confidential memo to its members urging them to support Herrick with money but keep it on the down low. Wheeler got a copy of the letter, photographed it, and then sent it to thousands of churches in the state. Turnout for the election was the highest in history at that time. When it was over, every Republican on the statewide ticket was elected, except one - Governor Myron Herrick. [36]

Wheeler took this success modestly. He said *"Never again will any political party ignore the protests of the church and the moral forces of the state."* [37]

Wheeler took his act on the road, going state by state with success. He then developed a strong contingency in Congress.

In 1913 a bill passed both houses of Congress called the Webb-Kenyon Act, which outlawed importing booze into a dry state. President William Howard Taft vetoed it. However, due to Wayne Wheeler's influence, Congress overturned his veto, 246 to 95. [38]

The national papers recognized the power of Wheeler, even if the average voter didn't even recognize his name. The New York Evening World proclaimed him "the legislative bully before whom the Senate of the United States sits up and begs." [39]

How did he do it? Three ways: First, he kept his focus on the one issue that mattered to him, prohibition.

Secondly, he built coalitions based upon this.

One such coalitions was with the evangelist Billy Sunday - a forerunner of today's modern televangelist. Sunday was eloquent, popular and wealthy. Billy Sunday was also described in a 1918 newspaper article as materialistic and as only in it for the money:

> The Billy Sunday Corporation is guilty of the most brazen-faced commercialization of religion the world has ever known, but his defiant rejoinder is, "It is nobody's business what I do with my money." [40]

Billy Sunday had an unlikely ally in Jane Addams. She was a pioneer in social work, very sympathetic to the Socialists and their goals. [41] She aligned herself with Billy Sunday because of Wayne Wheeler. The Ku Klux Klan aligned itself with the Industrial Workers of the World (IWW) on the prohibition issue due to the coalition building of Wayne Wheeler. [42]

And third, Wheeler knew how to leverage minorities as a voting bloc. He confided in a reporter his method:

> "I do it the way the bosses do it, with minorities. We'll vote against all the men in office who won't support our bills. We'll vote for candidate who will promise to."
>
> "We are teaching these crooks that breaking their promises to us is surer of punishment than going back on their bosses, and some day they will learn that all over the United States- and we'll have national prohibition." [43]

If you'll refer back to Chapter Five in this book note that Grover Norquist has the single minded goal of reducing revenue until the beast is starved to death; in other words, the death of a functional government and regulatory state. Note his coalition consisting of religious conservatives, libertarians, the NRA, home-schoolers, and big business. The very last component mentioned is probably the most passionate about the cause, the most coldhearted, and the wealthiest. Their resources are at Grover's disposal. Lastly, note Wheeler's ruthless vindictiveness with elected officials, threatening their seats and offices. Sound like anyone we know?

Grover's vision will come to fruition, just as Wayne Wheeler's did, and it will damage our country more than Wayne Wheeler's wagon that he placed the country upon. Not one Republican can or will stand up to him. The Republicans are not the solution. They will be the mechanism used to destroy the government.

The most frequent response I get from fellow citizens when I speak of the dangerous state of the Republican Party is a shrug and "everybody is corrupt". Yes and no. Corruption exists in many forms and it is not confined to one political party, for sure. But the Republicans of today are corrupt in a historical sense. Not since the late nineteenth century, the time of Robber Barons and railroad millionaires, has a party been owned by big money in such a way.

One of the problems in conveying this truth is that most Americans are uninterested and uninformed even if they are interested.

It doesn't help matters at all that outlets such as Fox News distort the news for propaganda purposes while maintaining the largest market share of any news network.

Add to the problem that the legislative process is complex and just plain boring. Who wants to spend their time watching CSPAN when "Dancing With The Stars" is on the tube?

But allow me to make my case to you that the "both sides are bad" retort is dangerously uninformed. Mike Lofgren wrote a very lengthy rant on the internet on September 3, 2011. It's title is "Goodbye to All That: Reflections of a GOP Operative Who Left the Cult".

Mike Lofgren isn't well known. A senior editor of the Atlantic Magazine, James Fallows, gives a bit of background as to who Mike Lofgren is:

> Lofgren's name is barely known to the general public, but among people who have covered or worked in the national-security field, he is a familiar and highly esteemed figure. He spent 28 years as a Congressional staffer, mainly on budget matters, mainly in the defense-and-security realm, and mainly for Republican legislators. "

Lofgren let it all hang out in an editorial online on Truth-out.org. His title says it all. He feels he has left the cult after serving almost 30 years as a high-ranking staffer. He knows Washington, he knows his party, and he knows the direction that it has taken. He even mentions in this op-ed piece how he is perplexed the Republican voters embrace Ayn Rand so readily.

He begins his piece with a quote from a famous motion picture from 1944 titled "Double Indemnity". The movie's plot involves a wife (Barbara Stanwyck) seducing an insurance agent (Fred McMurray) to help her kill her husband for the insurance payoff. (Barbara should have incorporated and hired her husband, then it would have been legal and tax free to boot, but I digress.)

At a critical point, Barbara Stanwyck tells Fred McMurray "We are both rotten" To which he replies "Only you are a little more rotten". [45]

Lofgren quickly disabuses the reader of the notion that both sides are equally to blame. This from a lifelong Republican who worked 28 years in Congress.

> But both parties are not rotten in quite the same way. The Democrats have their share of machine politicians, careerists, corporate bagmen, egomaniacs and kooks. Nothing, however, quite matches the modern GOP.

341

To those millions of Americans who have finally begun paying attention to politics and watched with exasperation the tragicomedy of the debt ceiling extension, it may have come as a shock that the Republican Party is so full of lunatics. To be sure, the party, like any political party on earth, has always had its share of crackpots, like Robert K. Dornan or William E. Dannemeyer. But the crackpot outliers of two decades ago have become the vital center today: Steve King, Michele Bachman (now a leading presidential candidate as well), Paul Broun, Patrick McHenry, Virginia Foxx, Louie Gohmert, Allen West. The Congressional directory now reads like a casebook of lunacy.

It was this cast of characters and the pernicious ideas they represent that impelled me to end a nearly 30-year career as a professional staff member on Capitol Hill. A couple of months ago, I retired; but I could see as early as last November that the Republican Party would use the debt limit vote, an otherwise routine legislative procedure that has been used 87 times since the end of World War II, in order to concoct an entirely artificial fiscal crisis. Then, they would use that fiscal crisis to get what they wanted, by literally holding the US and global economies as hostages. [46]

Lunatics? His words, not mine. I've tried to be nice in describing the Republican Party. Well, OK, maybe I haven't always tried that hard.

Lofgren gives example after example. The Republicans, responding from the pressure of the "lunatics" shut down the Federal Aviation Administration (FAA). It's not like that agency is important anyway. Air traffic safety is so overrated.

The GOP laid off 4,000 FAA employees, 70,000 private construction employees, and forced the necessary personnel that remained to work without pay, and even forced them to pay for their own travel.

What was the issue that drove this? The inclusion of union busting regulations. [47]

The Democrats cave on a regular basis, but they finally grew a backbone and refused to back down on this issue. The Republicans finally allowed FAA officials to go back to work. It could have been done faster if someone had promised the Republicans more pollution in return, which seems to be the highest priority in job creation.

Lofgren acknowledges that both sides have always had crackpots, but today the crackpots have become the mainstream in his party: The uniformed citizen will observe the complete halt of government as a failure of government itself. Which, according to Republicans in Congress who with Lofgren has spoken, that's exactly what they want you to think.

These accusations of intentional nihilism aren't new. What makes this example so unique is that they come from someone who was entrenched in the center of power at the highest levels of Republican policy. A brief aside is in order so as to provide context.

Sam Tanenhaus, a former editor of the New York Times Book Review and noted biographer, wrote a very educational book entitled "The Death of Conservatism" where he describes the Republican Party's conservative movement from its origins to the full bloom state of how it is today.

Tanenhaus' thesis is not that conservatism is dead, where conservatives will no longer be electable. He uses the word "conservatism" in more of a classical way, based on the definition by philosopher Russell Kirk in his classic book "The Conservative Mind" published in the 1950's.

To explain Kirk's definition in a terribly oversimplified way: conservatism is a respect for tradition and a reluctance to rush into radical change. Today's conservatives, according to Tanenhaus, are no longer conservatives but radicals willing to radically change the world to fit their worldview.

The Russell Kirk conservative could be characterized as a "containment" conservative rather than a "rollback" conservative, as explained in Chapter 5.

But with Barry Goldwater, whom Ayn Rand adored, rollback became the goal. There was no such thing as good government, unless it was dead government.

Tanenhaus quotes Barry Goldwater as saying:

343

> *"I have little interest in streamlining government or in making it more efficient, for I mean to reduce its size. I do not undertake to promote welfare, for I propose to extend freedom. My aim is not to pass laws, but to repeal them. It is not to inaugurate new programs, but to cancel old ones that do violence to the Constitution, or that have failed in their purpose, or that impose on the people an unwarranted financial burden"*[48]

That statement is a Rorschach Test, people will read into it what they wish. Most conservatives will cheer, either out of blind ideology or ignorance to the true nature of the words. The statement is filled with emotionally charged words that aren't interpreted universally. "Freedom" means the freedom to discriminate against people for race - Goldwater opposed the Civil Rights Act. "An unwarranted financial burden" means no penalties at all for corporations. No regulations, no fines, no penalty but what the marketplace can enforce. And the invocation of the "Constitution" means simply the narrowest minded and strict interpretation of it. But at the same time embracing the creative interpretation of the laissez-faire judges who saw a "right to contract" in the document.

Tanenhaus asks a rhetorical question which every voter should ask: "Should the party that calls the government evil, inefficient, wasteful and a burden be trusted to run it?"

Would you consult a surgeon to operate on you that didn't believe in surgery? Why would you trust a pharmacist that thought medicine was a fraud, and even poisonous? That's exactly what Americans do when they elect conservatives.

Nobel Prize winning economist Paul Krugman puts it even more succinctly. His explanation kills the "they are all rotten" argument. He says that conservatives and liberals are not mirror images of each other. Conservatives want to cut government for the sake of cutting-small is better. And Conservatives assume liberals want to grow government for the sake of growing government - the conservatives believe liberals want big government for its own sake. Quoting Krugman:.

> [T]he willingness of right-wingers to believe this
> particular myth has a lot to do with projection. On the right,
> people are for smaller government as a matter of principle —
> smaller government for its own sake. And so they naturally
> imagine that their opponents must be their mirror image,
> wanting bigger government as a goal in itself.
>
> But it's not true. I don't know any progressives who
> gloat over increases in the federal payroll or the government
> share of GDP. Progressives have things they want the
> government to do — like guaranteeing health care. Size per se
> doesn't matter. But people on the right apparently can't get
> that.⁹

Back to Mike Lofgren, and the intentional
destruction by Republicans of the democratic process.
Quoting Mr. Lofgren on the intention of the Republicans
during shutdown and gridlock moments:

> As Hannah Arendt observed, a disciplined
> minority of totalitarians can use the instruments of democratic
> government to undermine democracy itself.
>
> John P. Judis sums up the modern GOP this way:
> "Over the last four decades, the Republican Party
> has transformed from a loyal opposition into an
> insurrectionary party that flouts the law when it is in the
> majority and threatens disorder when it is the minority. It is
> the party of Watergate and Iran-Contra, but also of the
> government shutdown in 1995 and the impeachment trial of
> 1999. If there is an earlier American precedent for today's
> Republican Party, it is the antebellum Southern Democrats of
> John Calhoun who threatened to nullify, or disregard, federal
> legislation they objected to and who later led the fight to
> secede from the union over slavery."
>
> A couple of years ago, a Republican committee
> staff director told me candidly (and proudly) what the method
> was to all this obstruction and disruption. Should Republicans
> succeed in obstructing the Senate from doing its job, it would
> further lower Congress's generic favorability rating among the
> American people. By sabotaging the reputation of an
> institution of government, the party that is programmatically
> against government would come out the relative winner.

*A deeply cynical tactic, to be sure, but a
psychologically insightful one that plays on the weaknesses
both of the voting public and the news media. There are tens
of millions of low-information voters who hardly know which
party controls which branch of government, let alone which
party is pursuing a particular legislative tactic. These voters'
confusion over who did what allows them to form the
conclusion that "they are all crooks," and that "government is
no good," further leading them to think, "a plague on both
your houses" and "the parties are like two kids in a school
yard." This ill-informed public cynicism, in its turn, further
intensifies the long-term decline in public trust in government
that has been taking place since the early 1960s - a distrust
that has been stoked by Republican rhetoric at every turn
("Government is the problem," declared Ronald Reagan in
1980).[50]*

Take a minute to soak that in. This revelation
from a high ranking **GOP** staffer of almost 30 years should
provide the justification for the thesis of this book; which is
that the forces of **Ayn Rand** wish to overthrow the
government by destroying it and to turn the keys to the
kingdom over to the wealthiest.

If there is gridlock, and the process does not
work, who wins? The party that preaches the gospel of
government not working. It becomes a self-fulfilling
prophecy. Does anyone believe that the rabid conservative
will approach the duties of government in good faith?
Does anyone believe in the integrity of those who wish to
dismantle government with respect to making the
necessary functions work?

Americans have been conditioned to believe
government is evil. They have been conditioned to believe
all regulations kill jobs.

And they convince themselves that they only want
wise stewardship of the government and that moderate
forces will restrain the radicals who wish to destroy it.
However, there are no moderate forces on the right. And
nothing can restrain the radicals except the ballot box -
which means the removal of the radical element from
office.

This book asks you, over and over, chapter-by-chapter what are your values? What are the values you wish to see in your government? Lofgren, who is certainly in a position to know, gives us the Republicans values:

> As for what they really believe, the Republican Party of 2011 believes in three principal tenets I have laid out below. The rest of their platform one may safely dismiss as window dressing:
>
> 1. The GOP cares solely and exclusively about its rich contributors. The party has built a whole catechism on the protection and further enrichment of America's plutocracy. Their caterwauling about deficit and debt is so much eyewash to con the public.
>
> Whatever else President Obama has accomplished (and many of his purported accomplishments are highly suspect), his $4-trillion deficit reduction package did perform the useful service of smoking out Republican hypocrisy. The GOP refused, because it could not abide so much as a one-tenth of one percent increase on the tax rates of the Walton family or the Koch brothers, much less a repeal of the carried interest rule that permits billionaire hedge fund managers to pay income tax at a lower effective rate than cops or nurses.
>
> Republicans finally settled on a deal that had far less deficit reduction - and even less spending reduction! - than Obama's offer, because of their iron resolution to protect at all costs our society's overclass....
>
> 2. They worship at the altar of Mars. While the me-too Democrats have set a horrible example of keeping up with the Joneses with respect to waging wars, they can never match GOP stalwarts such as John McCain or Lindsey Graham in their sheer, libidinous enthusiasm for invading other countries. McCain wanted to mix it up with Russia - a nuclear-armed state - during the latter's conflict with Georgia in 2008 (remember? - "we are all Georgians now," a slogan that did not, fortunately, catch on), while Graham has been persistently agitating for attacks on Iran and intervention in Syria. And these are not fringe elements of the party; they are the leading "defense experts," who always get tapped for the Sunday talk shows. About a month before Republicans began holding a gun to the head of the credit markets to get trillions of dollars of cuts, these same Republicans passed a defense appropriations bill that increased spending by $17 billion over the prior year's defense appropriation. To borrow Chris Hedges' formulation, war is the force that gives meaning to their lives....

3. Give me that old time religion. Pandering to fundamentalism is a full-time vocation in the GOP. Beginning in the 1970s, religious cranks ceased simply to be a minor public nuisance in this country and grew into the major element of the Republican rank and file. Pat Robertson's strong showing in the 1988 Iowa Caucus signaled the gradual merger of politics and religion in the party. ...

The Constitution to the contrary notwithstanding, there is now a de facto religious test for the presidency: major candidates are encouraged (or coerced) to "share their feelings" about their "faith" in a revelatory speech; or, some televangelist like Rick Warren dragoons the candidates (as he did with Obama and McCain in 2008) to debate the finer points of Christology, with Warren himself, of course, as the arbiter. Politicized religion is also the sheet anchor of the culture wars. But how did the whole toxic stew of GOP beliefs - economic royalism, militarism and culture wars cum fundamentalism - come completely to displace an erstwhile civilized Eisenhower Republicanism?[51]

Lofgren sums up the intentions of the party of Ayn Rand:

If you think Paul Ryan and his Ayn Rand-worshipping colleagues aren't after your Social Security and Medicare, I am here to disabuse you of your naïveté.

They will move heaven and earth to force through tax cuts that will so starve the government of revenue that they will be "forced" to make "hard choices" - and that doesn't mean repealing those very same tax cuts, it means cutting the benefits for which you worked......

The GOP cult of Ayn Rand is both revealing and mystifying. On the one hand, Rand's tough guy, every-man-for-himself posturing is a natural fit because it puts a philosophical gloss on the latent sociopathy so prevalent among the hard right. On the other, Rand exclaimed at every opportunity that she was a militant atheist who felt nothing but contempt for Christianity. Apparently, the ignorance of most fundamentalist "values voters" means that GOP candidates who enthuse over Rand at the same time they thump their Bibles never have to explain this stark contradiction. And I imagine a Democratic officeholder would have a harder time explaining why he named his offspring "Marx" than a GOP incumbent would in rationalizing naming his kid "Rand."[52]

America, you've been warned. I've been screaming it throughout this whole book. I started researching and writing this book in April 2011. The above column from Mike Lofgren appeared in September 2011 when I was well into the writing process with the whole book outlined and most sources documented. I had never heard the name Mike Lofgren until his column came out. I doubt he knows me. Yet here he is saying the same thing I have said for approximately 300 pages. My thoughts came from observation and research, from outside the halls of power. His came from experience, deep within the workings of government, and within the inner circle of the very party he is condemning now.

He lays out the Republican platform for today, regardless of the candidate: No taxes on the wealthy, destroy as much government as possible, enrich the defense industry (the only good government spending to the Republicans) and invoke the name of God while you do it.

Ayn Rand is everywhere in government. She is nowhere more evident than she is in Ron Paul. Ron Paul has been the most consistent in his rhetoric out of all of the "government is evil" types. His son, Rand Paul, is following suit. But what does that mean? Do we want purity in this or any other ideology?

Here is the end result of this consistency and it becomes the lever with which the conservatives rule the masses. The conservative purist preaches the abstract - the noble idea of absolute property rights and freedom. So much so that reality - the oppression, exploitation, and tyranny over those without property - doesn't even matter any more.

Purity in ideology in Ron Paul's "Mini-Me"-Senator Rand Paul- meant disavowing the Civil Rights Act of 1964. The sacred right of property, along with the sacred right of states, stands more important than the protections of minorities.

> *"If you decide that restaurants are publicly owned and not privately owned, then do you say that you should have the right to bring your gun into a restaurant even though the owner of the restaurant says, 'Well no, we don't want to have guns in here,' the bar says, 'We don't want to have guns in here because people might drink and start fighting and shoot each-other.' Does the owner of the restaurant own his restaurant? Or does the government own his restaurant?"*[53]

I will go out on a limb here and challenge Senator Paul's logic, in spite of his being a medical doctor and myself only being married to one.

I don't have a footnote for this, but anecdotal evidence suggests that gun owners were not born with guns in hand. The guns appeared there after conscious decisions. Therefore decisions, as they always have consequences, will sometimes result in discrimination.

However, there seems to be a trend among black people in which they all seem to be born that way. I have yet to find a black man, woman, or child who elected to become black.

Therefore, discrimination against them would carry a different moral weight than discrimination against gun owners. But I defer to Senator Dr. Paul and if he produces scientific research showing the genetic nature of gun ownership, I shall reconsider my position.

But the larger point remains. Paul is offended by the notion of discrimination, but more sacred principles overrule reality. Ayn Rand fan Clarence Thomas, who worships freedom at the highest level, feels the same about the personal freedom of individuals in their own homes.

In the case of Lawrence v Texas, (2003) the laws of Texas with respect to private conduct were challenged. Here are the facts of the case as recorded by the U.S. Supreme Court:

> *Responding to a reported weapons disturbance in a private residence, Houston police entered John Lawrence's apartment and saw him and another adult man, Tyron Garner, engaging in a private, consensual sexual act. Lawrence and Garner were arrested and convicted of deviate sexual intercourse in violation of a Texas statute forbidding two persons of the same sex to engage in certain intimate sexual conduct*[54]

To expound: two men were arrested in their own home for engaging in homosexual activity. They weren't breaking any laws save for the sodomy law in Texas that outlawed such acts.

The cop had entered on a false report - the crime reported had not happened. He coincidentally found these men in their own apartment by accident and arrested them on the spot. The issue involved is whether the state of Texas, or any other state, has the right to barge into your home and arrest you for consensual acts between adults.

The Supreme Court said no and threw out all sodomy laws across the land. It wasn't unanimous. Justice Scalia- a passionate Catholic opposed to birth control and abortion and therefore with an agenda to deny the right to privacy – dissented as did Justice Clarence Thomas.

In his dissenting opinion Justice Thomas wrote:

> *I join Justice Scalia's dissenting opinion. I write separately to note that the law before the Court today "is ... uncommonly silly." Griswold v. Connecticut, 381 U.S. 479, 527 (1965) (Stewart, J., dissenting). If I were a member of the Texas Legislature, I would vote to repeal it. Punishing someone for expressing his sexual preference through noncommercial consensual conduct with another adult does not appear to be a worthy way to expend valuable law enforcement resources.* [55]

Clarence wants us to understand he thinks this law is just plain dumb. It's so dumb that he would vote against it if he were in the Texas legislature. But read closely, it isn't dumb because of the sacred notion of a man's home being his castle, or even a free will argument that people should be allowed to make their own lifestyle decisions.

No, the argument that Clarence Thomas supports is the sacred rights of the states to do what they wish to do by brute force regardless of what minority factions in the state feel or would suffer.

To him, reality is nothing compared to the higher idea of "freedom" for the state, but not for the people the state oppresses. His opinion is printed above in its entirety and it plainly states that he agrees with Scalia's points but wanted to add to it that the law is dumb and a waste of money. That's it. Clarence certainly understands your outrage and it is a damn shame taxpayer money goes towards oppression, but there is nothing he can do. He'd vote against it if he were in the Texas legislature. But it should be self evident that he isn't nor will he be. It's empty rhetoric. Tough cookies for those who live under this law. The little guys need to know they are being sacrificed for freedom's sake; it's just not for their freedom.

The purists will always say that personally they are appalled at oppression.

Personally they are appalled at the idea of gold flakes on $175 hamburgers as wasteful excess.

Personally they are appalled at the notion of people dying because of lack of healthcare coverage.

But their consistency demands that they never consider the other solution, or even a compromise, whatever the reality may be and no matter how many real people are victimized by this reality. We feel your pain, but there is nothing we can do about it because there are high ideas that mean more than people. In his speech in Peoria in 1854, Abraham Lincoln addressed this very issue:

> Near eighty years ago we began by declaring that all men are created equal; but now from that beginning we have run down to the other declaration, that for SOME men to enslave OTHERS is a ``sacred right of self-government." These principles cannot stand together. They are as opposite as God and mammon; and whoever holds to the one, must despise the other. [56]

Or to put it more scornfully, Ralph Waldo Emerson is famous for saying

> A foolish consistency is the hobgoblin of little minds, adored by little statesmen and philosophers and divines. [57]

We are governed by little minds - those who cannot adjust to realities and a changing world. We are enslaved by traditions and the out of context words of ghosts from over two hundred years ago. The little minds have grasped the shiny trinket of some man-made philosophy and clutched it like Gollum in the "Lord of the Rings" to the point where their own destruction and the destruction of their world becomes inconsequential compared to the preservation of the precious ideology.

As noted before, Ron Paul is consistent. But let's examine what this means. On September 12, 2011 Republican candidates for president participated in a debate co-sponsored by CNN and the Tea Party. Wolf Blitzer asked Ron Paul a hypothetical question about the fate of a young man who forgoes insurance because of cost, yet dies and runs up a huge tab. Quoting an ABC News blog::

> *"What he should do is whatever he wants to do and assume responsibility for himself," Paul responded, adding, "That's what freedom is all about, taking your own risk. This whole idea that you have to compare and take care of everybody..."*
>
> *The audience erupted into cheers, cutting off the Congressman's sentence.*
>
> *After a pause, Blitzer followed up by asking, "Congressman, are you saying that society should just let him die?" to which a small number of audience members shouted "Yeah!"*
>
> *Paul, a doctor trained in obstetrics and gynecology, said when he got out of medical school in the 1960s "the churches took care of them."*
>
> *"We never turned anybody away from the hospital," he said. "We've given up on this whole concept that we might take care of ourselves or assume responsibility for ourselves. Our neighbors, our friends, our churches would do it. That's the reason the cost is so high."*[58]

The purists in the crowd loved it - some even loved the thought of the freeloaders dying, as noted by this account and by countless YouTube clips that exist of this exchange. But it wasn't really hypothetical.

Ron Paul's campaign manager, Kent Snyder, had died of complications from leukemia in 2008 and had been without insurance. According to Ron Paul, he was the man responsible for Ron Paul's national recognition:

> "It was Kent more than anyone else who encouraged and pushed Ron to run for president," said Jesse Benton, a spokesman for Mr. Paul. "Ron would not have run for the presidency if it had not been for Kent. Ron was really hesitant, but Kent drove him forward."[59]

Kent was an important part of Ron Paul's political career and a major believer. He approached it on a cost benefit analysis. He made the wrong choice in not getting insurance, because he died penniless and stuck his family with a $400,000 hospital bill. Before we shake our head at his foolishness, take note that he chose not to get insurance because of the astronomical costs associated with pre-existing conditions.

> He was uninsured, his sister Michelle Caskey said, because a pre-existing condition made the premiums too expensive.
>
> "I don't think he would ever have realized he'd be in the hospital this long," she said. "It's very nice (that people are trying to help)."[60]

Ron Paul mentioned the good old days where churches chipped in and helped everyone out in the community. Where was Ron Paul's church in this matter? How did it get to the point where his campaign manager's mother got stuck with a $400,000 tab?

A couple of points bear highlighting here. First, Paul's campaign manager made the decision, in no small part, due to the astronomical rates charged on preexisting conditions. They will be outlawed with full implementation of Obama's Affordable Health Care Act, which Ron Paul wishes to repeal. There are no Republicans on record who propose any legislation to outlaw this practice. Every Republican candidate for President promises to overturn this law.

Second, Ron Paul becomes passionately furious when he speaks out against the estate tax, which he calls the "death tax". This is a tax on estates over a baseline amount designed to prevent family dynasties from taking hold.

Ron Paul rails against this as immoral as the government does not have the right to steal a family's lifetime accumulation. Yet he endorses the right of medical industries to steal a family's lifetime accumulation through astronomical medical bills. To keep a family member alive, you must make a choice: every one of your assets, or your loved one's life.

You should know that the estate tax is waived for this year, 2011, but in 2012 it comes back. All assets over $5 million are taxed at a 35% rate. [61] Ron is morally angered at the thought of millionaires stripped down to $5 million tax free, but is stoic and philosophical about the complete destruction of the middle class from health care costs. His comments at the time of Kent Snyder's death tell us everything we need to know.

> "Like so many in our movement, Kent sacrificed much for the cause of liberty," Mr. Paul wrote last Sunday on his Web site for his Campaign for Liberty. The recently launched political committee is working to elect more Republicans in the Paul mold. "Kent poured every ounce of his being into our fight for freedom. He will always hold a place in my heart and in the hearts of my family." [62]

For Ron, Kent Snyder died in the cause of liberty. What liberty? The liberty to make a buck at the expense of desperate, dying people. It's about the liberty of the rich to remain rich no matter what befalls them. It's not the liberty of the common man to fight for a child's, spouses, or his own life with every available possibility.

It has to be a terrible choice. Throw away your lifetime's earnings, both past and yet to come, or watch your loved ones die painfully with no care. Somewhere Tea Partiers are standing up and applauding at this notion - much like they did when Ron Paul refused to speak up for the right to life for non-fetuses.

Dying for liberty is what gave us our freedom. But something noble should be the cause. Dying on the fields of Gettysburg has a higher meaning when the context of freedom from slavery is the higher idea. Farm boys dying on the shores of Normandy seems worth it when we think of the higher notion of Nazism being destroyed.

But how noble is the idea of liberty when it means the liberty to bankrupt your family? That's the liberty expressed by the extreme purists. The liberty to go without seat belts, the liberty to not wear a motorcycle helmet, and the liberty to go without health insurance. The reality of the financial catastrophe means nothing to the purist like Paul, the idealistic notion means everything. It is all worth it if we maintain the right to be selfish.

Ron Paul believes in the liberty to pass hundreds of millions of dollars down untaxed, but not the liberty to live free of financial ruin from sickness. His son Rand Paul believes in the liberty of businessmen to throw out blacks, gays, Hispanics, or anyone else they choose merely because they own the property. But he doesn't believe in the liberty of the affected minority to live without harassment.

Clarence Thomas believes in the liberty of states controlled by powerful special interests and wealth and to take away the most private dignity of a person's home, but doesn't believe in the fundamental liberty of the individual to make decisions about his or her own body in his or her own home.

In protecting all liberties, the state must be involved. In each case mentioned, the state and the power of police force is used to enforce these specialized liberties at the expense of individuals. Police would remove offending blacks from lunch counters all within the confines and requirements of the law. The courts would enforce foreclosure of homes to pay off creditors resulting from healthcare costs. The police would have authority to arrest anyone in their own home for crimes that even constitutional enablers like Clarence Thomas call "silly".

The power of the state is always used to enforce freedom. The choices made by the purists, the Ayn Rand worshippers, puts the power of the state in sole hands of the wealthy.

It is never used to curtail them. It is always used to oppress those without the voice, the money, or influence. It is the tyranny of the majority and it is sold as a mantra of freedom. But no one asks, freedom for whom?

To me, one of the most baffling things about Ayn Rand's cult of followers is their stubborn insistence that her work was prophetic or even reflective of reality. I find more truth, along with entertainment value, in Harry Potter novels. Ayn Rand promoted a mythology that never existed, doesn't exist today, and isn't even real enough to be consistently pursued by Ayn's fans, Ayn's disciples, nor Ayn herself.

To begin with, if one were fashioning a new morality, would Ayn have been the best role model? William F. Buckley beamed with *schadenfreude* at the Ayn Rand/Branden rift and rightly so. For Ayn to declare herself the prophetess of a new religion based on reason and dispassionate objectivity and then explode with petty jealousy and the fury of a woman's scorn would be high comedy in any movie. Yet to her band of merry men she shows the way to a perfect life.

Also, Ayn's premise of the disincentive effect of regulation and taxes were overstated to say the least and she was consistently wrong in predictions of doom from the statist and collectivists she so despised and feared.

Ronald Reagan had a story he told over and over to anyone that would listen about how and why he became a believer in tax cuts. I give President Reagan full benefit of the doubt and I believe he believed it, and that he believed his conclusions.

Reagan would recount the epiphany he had when he would refuse to make movies in the 1950's. He was in the top income bracket; he wouldn't gain much with each additional movie as additional income was taxed at over 90%.

So Reagan would relax and play golf. One day he saw a guy he knew from the studio, an average working guy who built sets. He said he was out of work and Reagan was puzzled why. He told Reagan that because Ronald Reagan refused to make more movies, there was less demand for set builders, therefore the disincentive of high income taxes had killed his job. [63]

To Reagan it made perfect sense, even though it really didn't have the facts backing it. One big hole in this theory is the assumption that because Ronald Reagan didn't make movies, movies didn't get made. That's false. The studios were free to hire lesser known, lower paid actors and actresses, and they did. And the number of jobs should have stayed the same, all things considered.

But the number of the peripheral jobs that little guys do - like building sets, photography, costumes, electricians, and plain old hired hands paid to move stuff - should have increased, as they did. Why? Television. TV became the next big thing and there was a demand for content - almost all of it coming out of Hollywood. So, someone who built sets for Reagan's classic "Bedtime for Bonzo" would find work building sets for "Gunsmoke." A quick trip to the Internet Movie Data Base bears this out.

The 90% top tax rates were in effect for the 1950's. Therefore there should have been decreasing opportunities in Hollywood, according to Ronald Reagan. According to the **IMDB** for these years:

    1950 4,160 titles were produced. [64]
    1951 4,907 titles were produced. [65]
    1952 5,865 titles were produced. [66]
    1953 6,474 titles were produced. [67]
    1954 6,889 titles were produced. [68]
    1955 7,705 titles were produced. [69]
    1956 8,078 titles were produced. [70]
    1957 8,088 titles were produced. [71]
    1958 8,924 titles were produced. [72]
    1959 9,576 titles were produced. [73]
    1960 10,549 titles were produced. [74]

Hollywood survived the Ronald Reagan movie boycott just fine. The number of titles produced from Hollywood increased every year. The precise reason that Reagan's set maker was unemployed is not known, but one can make the case that "I Love Lucy" was hiring, even if Ronald Reagan was not.

Another core belief of the Randians is the belief of the superiority of the producer. Those who produce owe nothing to society, nor should they as they have created, while the rest of us have merely freeloaded. We should feel lucky that they allow us to gaze upon them as they drive by - provided we take care not to make eye contact.

But how much has the individual genius done individually? There are very few industrial and technological innovations throughout history. Most are just improvements upon existing technology, creators borrowing from others before them.

Kirby Ferguson, a New York-based filmmaker, has an excellent series of films titled "Everything is a Remix", which are available online. He provides astonishing facts that destroy the mythology of genius working in a vacuum. He lists three elements of creation: copy, transform, and combine.

> *"James Watt created a major improvement to the steam engine because he was assigned to repair a Thomas Newcome steam engine. He then spent twelve years developing his version.*
>
> *Christopher Latham Sholes' modeled his typewriter keyboard on a piano. This design slowly evolved over five years into the QWERTY layout we still use today.*
>
> *And Thomas Edison didn't invent the light bulb — his first patent was "Improvement in Electric Lamps" — but he did produce the first commercially viable bulb... after trying 6,000 different materials for the filament.*
>
> *These are all major advances, but they're not original ideas so much as tipping points in a continuous line of invention by many different people.*
>
> *But the most dramatic results can happen when ideas are combined. By connecting ideas together creative leaps can be made, producing some of history's biggest breakthroughs.*

Johannes Gutenberg's printing press was invented around 1440, but almost all its components had been around for centuries.

Henry Ford and The Ford Motor Company didn't invent the assembly line, interchangeable parts or even the automobile itself. But they combined all these elements in 1908 to produce the first mass market car, the Model T.[75]

He gives many more examples using computers. Xerox started the ball rolling with its personal computer. A long line of imitators perfected the personal computer up to Apple. All advances in technology through the marketplace launch off the platform built by previous innovators, who did the same.

Ferguson also documents how many ideas develop simultaneously along different paths, including his own idea.

And actually, this — the video you're watching — was written just before the New Yorker published a Malcolm Gladwell story about Apple, Xerox and the nature of innovation. We're all building with the same materials. And sometimes by coincidence we get similar results, but sometimes innovations just seem inevitable.[76]

During the credits, a quote from Henry Ford drives the point home. Henry Ford was just the type of creator that Ayn Rand worshiped, one that deserved worship because of his genius. Henry Ford did not see himself that way. In his closing credits, Mr. Ferguson displays this quote:

"I invented nothing new. I simply assembled the discoveries of other men behind whom were centuries of work. Had I worked fifty or ten or even five years before, I would have failed. So it is with every new thing. Progress happens when all the factors that make for it are ready and then it is inevitable. To teach that a comparatively few men are responsible for the greatest forward steps of mankind is the worst sort of nonsense." -- Henry Ford[77]

Will that change the mind of the true believer? I'm guessing, no. Mostly because they can excuse the inconsistencies and the lies of their leaders because it fulfills a need to do so.

The Republicans, the Ayn Rand fans, the CEO's and super wealthy - which in many cases are the same - need Ayn Rand to justify their greed. They need her to justify their existence, which brings no value to anyone on this earth except themselves and their heirs. Ayn Rand makes it OK to hate your neighbor, to feast while others starve.

And it makes no difference to those who need Ayn Rand's inverted morality to justify to them the fact that Ayn Rand's life choices are impossible to follow. Or it just may be that it is inconvenient to follow when you have an opportunity to benefit from not following.

Take for instance Friedrich Hayek. He is Ayn Rand-lite. They had a mutual admiration society, Ayn positively swooned when Hayek praised her, and referred to her as a man to boot! Hayek wrote the famous book "Road to Serfdom" where he explained to all of us who would be tempted to ask the government for relief that we were on the way to slavery to said government. Not much difference between him and Ayn. He probably had more friends, but that is about it.

Charles Koch tried hard to get Hayek over here; he was living in England, to spread the gospel of "little government". Hayek was apprehensive about coming over here, as he was in poor health. In a recently discovered correspondence, Koch sold Hayek on the benefits of socialism:

> *"You may be interested in the information that we uncovered on the insurance and other benefits that would be available to you in this country. Since you have paid into the United States Social Security Program for a full forty quarters, you are entitled to Social Security payments while living anywhere in the Free World. Also, at any time you are in the United States, you are automatically entitled to hospital coverage."*
>
> *Then, taking on the unlikely role of Social Security Administration customer service rep, Koch adds, "In order to be eligible for medical coverage you must apply during the registration period which is anytime from January 1 to March 31. For your further information, I am enclosing a pamphlet on Social Security."*[78]

Hayek had warned us about the evils of Social Security. He devoted a whole chapter to it in his book, and declared it a "fundamental absurdity" to pay for pensions with tax dollars. Ironically, he had no objections when he was offered it however. The Nation, which broke this story, summarizes the situation perfectly:

> But the exchange between Koch and Hayek exposes the bad-faith nature of their public arguments. In private, Koch expresses confidence in Social Security's ability to care for a clearly worried Hayek. He and his fellow IHS libertarians repeatedly assure Hayek that his government-funded coverage in the United States would be adequate for his medical needs. None of them—not Koch, Hayek or the other libertarians at the IHS—express anything remotely resembling shame or unease at such a betrayal of their public ideals and writings. Nowhere do they worry that by opting into and taking advantage of Social Security programs they might be hastening a socialist takeover of America. It's simply a given that Social Security and Medicare work, and therefore should be used.[79]

The megabank BB&T has donated millions to spread Ayn's gospel in some of the most prestigious colleges in the country. John Allison the CEO has proudly proclaimed Ayn Rand as truth. Yet his bank took $3.1 billion from the federal government in the form of a bailout. This hypocrisy was not lost on some people:

> Or in the case of BB&T's hypocritical acceptance of taxpayer dollars, who is John Allison?
>
> Despite the millions of philanthropic dollars it has invested in helping college students see Ayn Rand's vision of the threat government poses to free minds and markets, BB&T is taking $3.1 billion of precious taxpayer funds that could be better invested in tackling urgent social problems.
>
> At this precarious moment in U.S. history, BB&T should remember in the marketplace the lessons it wants college students to learn in the classroom.[80]

Paul Ryan would have no room to criticize, as he attended college on Social Security benefits. U.S. News and World Report informs us that

> Ryan's father died when Paul was only 16. Using the Social Security survivors benefits he received until his 18th birthday, he paid for his education at Miami University in Ohio, where he completed a bachelor's degree in economics and political science in 1992.[81]

But for the rest of us, Social Security is a collectivist scheme. It offends Paul Ryan now and he wishes it gone so that the rich, who really don't pay into Social Security anyway, can live in more freedom.

What on earth would Ayn Rand think of her partners in purity all dipping from the collectivist well? She would have probably ignored it. You see, Ayn Rand was the biggest hypocrite of all. She spent her life promoting freedom, and the right to succeed and the right to fail. The wealthy had the moral responsibility to be selfish. Except when their selfishness hurts Ayn Rand.

The Ayn Rand Institute published yet another book on Ayn Rand in 2010, this one called "100 Voices: An Oral History of Ayn Rand" [82]. As the title suggests, one hundred people who knew Ayn were interviewed. One of the interviewees was Evva Joan Pryor, who had been a social worker in New York in the 1970s. Ayn's attorneys hired Ms. Pryor after Ayn took ill with lung cancer.

The attorneys were worried about Ayn's fortune after she became ill. The gospel of greed was ok for her, but it was a threat to her livelihood when the greed was of the medical industry. They recruited Ms. Pryor, and Ayn, in order to facilitate assistance and save her life savings, assigned her power of attorney. Quoting Ms. Pryor:

> "She was coming to a point in her life where she was going to receive the very thing she didn't like, which was Medicare and Social Security.
>
> I remember telling her that this was going to be difficult. For me to do my job, she had to recognize that there were exceptions to her theory...
>
> ..She had to see that there was such a thing as greed in this world. Doctors could cost an awful lot more money than books earn, and she could be totally wiped out by medical bills if she didn't watch it. Since she had worked her entire life and had paid into Social Security, she had a right to it. She didn't feel that an individual should take help.
>
> After several meetings and arguments, she gave me her power of attorney to deal with all matters having to do with health and Social Security. Whether she agreed or not is not the issue, she saw the necessity for both her and Frank."

Ayn came around, of course. It made it easier to violate her core beliefs because it was her fortune that was saved. No one could expect someone to watch his or her savings waste away for some political philosophy. Only some brainwashed freak like Ron Paul would hang on to the point of watching someone die and life savings vanish. Thank goodness there aren't too many like him. Or maybe there are. Based on the direction we have been going, there are too many Americans like him. Fanatical drones that hang on some silly philosophy even to the point of death and bankruptcy.

These people aren't even clear headed enough to see the hypocrisy from the top down, and they rule this country. They are killing our government one budget cut and tax cut at a time. To make it go down easier, they spread what ever lie or myth that comes to mind.

The biggest lie is the one told the loudest: that government does not work. It does work, it has worked, and it will work as long as we keep those who wish to destroy it out.

Electricity came to the rural parts of the United States because of the government. Electricity took off as an industry in the 1880's but the moneymaking possibilities were not in the rural areas, particularly the south.

Herbert Hoover, as an engineer, saw this but pushed for the states to pick up the mantle, but states failed miserably, as they always do on projects of this scale. When the depression hit, the incentive for the states, along with the funds, disappeared. President Roosevelt created a federal agency to accomplish this.

Presidential Executive Order 7037 created the Rural Electrification Administration, or R.E.A., on May 11, 1935. With passage of the Norris-Rayburn Act the following year, Congress authorized $410 million in appropriations for a ten-year program to electrify American farms. ...

Cooperatives were not-for-profit consumer-owned firms organized to provide electric service to member-customers. Each cooperative was typically governed by a board of directors elected from the ranks of its residential customers. The board established rates and policies for the cooperative, and hired a general manager to conduct the ordinary business of providing electricity to customers within the service region. Only two restrictions were placed on the formation of cooperatives: they could not compete directly with utility companies, and coop members could not live in areas served by utilities or within a municipality with a population of 1500 or more.[83]

The end result? A resounding success.

Five decades after urban municipal electrical distribution system first appeared in the United States, the process of introducing rural areas to the twentieth-century economy began with the creation of the Rural Electrification Administration. The R.E.A. overcame the unwillingness of private utilities to bring power to households, farms and businesses in sparsely populated regions where profits were too low. The failure of the market, which left rural areas literally and figuratively in the dark, required an aggressive federal initiative to insure that residents of sparsely populated areas were no longer comparatively disadvantaged in the twentieth-century American economy.

The R.E.A. is considered one of the most immediate and profound successes in the history of federal policy-making for the national economy. By the end of 1938, just two years after its inception, 350 cooperative projects in 45 states were delivering electricity to 1.5 million farms. The success of the R.E.A. over the next two decades was even more impressive, especially as a self-sustained financing agency. By the mid-1950s nearly all American farms had electrical service that was provided through the R.E.A. or by other means. Monies lent through the R.E.A. were also largely repaid, as the default rate was less than one percent.

> *Moreover, as with any significant surge in investment, the accompanying new demands for household electrical appliances spurred growth in home appliance manufacturing, and spawned the electrical and plumbing trades in rural communities. Electrical service also brought revolutionary new mediums of communication to rural farms, firms and households. Radio was followed by television, and the new streams of information narrowed the cultural, educational and commercial divide between urban and rural America. Rural electrification contributed to the rapid growth of suburbs, and helped create a more integrated national market.* [84]

Take note at the relevant points: the market failed to provide investment, the program paid for itself for the most part, and it stimulated growth, as farmers all of a sudden had reasons to buy toasters, electric clocks, electric fans and ovens.

Who could complain? The Ayn Rand purists-the Republican Party. No billionaires were created, wages rose as opportunities were created, and no one had the chutzpah to claim exemption from taxes because of some special status as a Job-Creator. The government created jobs through infrastructure development. Private enterprise was enhanced, not suppressed. And we all benefited, particularly the poor.

The Interstate Highway System is the largest government project in the history of the world. Larger than anything the Soviet Union, China, or socialized Europe have attempted. It's socialism. But it also boosted our economy and sparked tremendous growth.

It has cost us in the trillions, all told. What are the undisputed benefits?

- Lower production costs for consumers
- Increased productivity for businesses
- Economic growth for rural areas in jobs created. [85]

Straight from the government to your hand. Sure, it was a hand out. But it works and who needs to complain about this?

The cost cutting mania pushed by the low tax Randians at the state and federal level are slowly starving the system. Our infrastructure is crumbling. We are falling behind countries like China as it spends twice what we spend relative to GDP. We also lag behind Russia and Western Europe.[86] Government does this right, but can only do this right if we fund it.

One of the greatest boosts to our productivity as a nation came from the government in the form of redistribution of wealth. The G.I. Bill was a stunning success as it increased the number of college graduates - mostly from a pool that would not have had the opportunity to go to college.[87]

This will shock you, but I offer full sources and you may judge for yourself. The best medical treatment in the United States recently was the much-maligned Veterans Administration (VA) Hospital system. Don't believe it? Consider this:

The New England Journal of Medicine in 2003 rated VA hospitals against fee for service Medicare in eleven metrics. VA won all.

The Annals of Internal Medicine in 2004 published a study that compared veterans' health facilities with commercial managed care systems in their treatment of diabetes. In seven out of seven metrics, the VA won.

In 2006 a study comparing the life expectancy of elderly patients in the VA system versus the Medicare Advantage Program showed the mortality rates were "significantly higher" for the Medicare Advantage. Medicare Advantage is the more expensive, private insurance version of Medicare, in case you didn't know.

In 2009 the Journal of Surgical Research published a study of outcomes of coronary surgery at VA hospitals versus other hospitals. Even though the VA patients were considerably sicker on average, suffering nearly twice the rate of myocardial infarction, their mortality rate was barely half of those outside thee system.[88]

There is more. It's well documented in the book, "Best Care Anywhere: Why VA Health Care is Better Than Yours". When you read it, it makes sense. The VA uses outcome-based medicine, where a best practice system is utilized. This controls costs and increases outcomes. The VA was one of the first agencies to put in a digital documentation system. They kept digital medical records and therefore had fewer errors in administering the wrong medicine, operating on the wrong patient, and monitoring what worked and what didn't. And they used open source software for the system, developed by their in-house computer people. If you ever bought software for a system, you know how expensive this can be.

This was part of the Clinton-Gore Reinventing Government Initiative. It took the basic position that government can work if you make serious efforts to let it do so. Bill Clinton and Al Gore took the worst veterans care system in the U.S. and turned it into one of the best in the world.

But, not enough wealth was created so the Bush Administration took control of the software development and purchased proprietary software. Millions in cost were accrued, but it went to the private sector, so that was OK.

The software has a "black box" which no user can modify and it elevates costs for the user, with the end user being we - the American tax payers.[89]

Conservatives will dispute all this since they refuse to consider anything that challenges their worldview. This worldview comes from a loud minority, which is in collusion with the forces of big business. They tell us that government will fail, and then work with evangelical fervor to destroy government when they assume power. Why would we take their assessment on how effective government can and will be? If the universal goal of the conservative is to destroy government, reduce it down to only the bare necessities, what functions will be deemed worthy enough to be the necessities?

One is the defense industry. For some reason it works as far as the conservatives are concerned. Maybe because the wealthy feel that a strong defense will stomp out the threat of communism again and their squeezing of the middle class can continue unabated?

Here's something that is amusing - well maybe not - but I find ironic when exposing the raw hypocrisy of conservatives. For example, they tell us it is nothing personal against Obama (and it's certainly not because he is black!) but they just can't stand the idea of government waste.

The voting in a Republican Congress backs this up. They wish for Paul Ryan's budget, lower taxes, cuts in social programs, and increases in defense.

Pay attention to the last item of this list. According to conservatives, we need to increase defense even though there is no Soviet Union, no Nazi Germany, and Osama Bin Laden is dead, thanks to the president that conservatives hate.

But no one cares about the waste from defense. Did you know that over $6.6 billion was stolen? In cash? Of course you didn't. Because it wasn't on any Tea Party protest signs nor was it on Fox News. But the Pentagon has admitted that over $6 billion in shrink wrapped hard American currency was stolen.

> Pentagon officials determined that one giant C-130 Hercules cargo plane could carry $2.4 billion in shrink-wrapped bricks of $100 bills. They sent an initial full planeload of cash, followed by 20 other flights to Iraq by May 2004 in a $12-billion haul that U.S. officials believe to be the biggest international cash airlift of all time.
>
> This month, the Pentagon and the Iraqi government are finally closing the books on the program that handled all those Benjamins. But despite years of audits and investigations, U.S. Defense officials still cannot say what happened to $6.6 billion in cash — enough to run the Los Angeles Unified School District or the Chicago Public Schools for a year, among many other things.
>
> For the first time, federal auditors are suggesting that some or all of the cash may have been stolen, not just mislaid in an accounting error. Stuart Bowen, special inspector general for Iraq reconstruction, an office created by Congress, said the missing $6.6 billion may be "the largest theft of funds in national history."[190]

Here's a rhetorical question for you. What would the reaction be if Obama "lost" $6 million? If there were strong suspicions that it was stolen? Does the word "impeachment" spring to mind?

Where is the outrage? In fairness, the outrage is not there because the public awareness is not there. And the public awareness is not there because the media hasn't pushed this story at least not to the massive extent it deserves. And, more irony here, Tea Party lunatics crow more and more about wanting fiscal responsibility.

Don't let anyone mollify you with the saying, "I'm not a Republican, I'm actually a conservative". They are the problem. The narrow-minded, anti-progress, Ayn Rand worshiping, materialistic conservatives have blocked everything good about our country.

Conservatives hated the idea of freeing the slaves. They were Democrats back then, but they loved states rights enough to kill and die for the right to own a slave. Their descendants continued the love affair with states rights, wishing for segregation to remain. Tea Partiers wish for the right to return to the system, in the name of freedom. Conservatives hated the idea of food inspections by the feds, as you saw in the last chapter. They currently hate the idea of clean air standards. They hated the idea of electricity in the south. And they will try to reassure you with the "Don't worry, I'm a conservative, not a Republican". We were a lot better off when there were enough Republicans that were not conservatives. They actually brought progress to our nation.

Conservative Republicans offer no hope today and only offer us a return to the bad old days for the masses and the good old days for the feudal lords. From whence will our salvation come?

The independents are our only hope. They don't label themselves or tie themselves to an extreme ideology. True believers are always the dangerous ones. They know the solution to every problem lies in their approach. This isn't unique to the right but the problem of right wing extremists is unique in America now. There is no real voice on the left and the extremists aren't taken seriously. But the extremists who believe in an inflexible laissez-faire world as a solution to everything are becoming more and more of a driving force in the Republican Party.

There is no significant extremist position on the left. President Obama has been smeared by the propagandists at Fox as a socialist but there is absolutely nothing he has proposed or endorsed that is more radical than any president in history, including Republicans Theodore Roosevelt, Dwight Eisenhower, Richard Nixon, and Ronald Reagan.

But the fear mongers play upon the lowest intellectual denominator, which is, not coincidentally, the people who believe one solution solves every problem. Simple explanations and solutions work best for them.

One of the good things about independents is that they are not tied to the zealotry of ideas in their purest form. But independents more often than not are uninspired, uneducated or flat out uninterested. The purpose of the book is to attempt to inspire, educate and interest those who need to rise up and stop this descent into feudalism.

What can you do? I am not asking much from you but it is everything you can do. I am asking you as a person to vote your conscience.

When all is said and done, we live in a world where so many things are beyond our control. We can do nothing about tornadoes, floods, stock market swings, or governments, be they foreign or domestic. But we owe it to ourselves and to what we believe in to stand up for those beliefs. It doesn't matter if the results are successful. It's great if they are but the rightness won't diminish because of a lack of success.

I wrote this book and formed a publishing company to publish and promote it based on one principle reflected in the name of my LLC: One Single Candle. It is better to light one single candle than to curse the darkness. I do not like the state of the world, and I fear for the direction we are moving. I feel the worst is yet to come because I believe that those who I warn about in this book, the army of Ayn Rand, will take power once again and the end result will be the aggregation of wealth and destruction of the middle class.

And one day it will tip and the tipping will be an overreaction. It won't just be the wealthy that suffer but also the middle class and the poor.

In order to save our system we have to reform it. The reforms aren't radical. They are reforms that we have had in place before but have systematically destroyed as an appeasement to Ayn Rand's gospel of greed.

I believe I have made the case, meticulously documented, showing the pervasiveness of Ayn Rand's new morality in our culture, our religion, our politics and how it is fueled and financed by the wealthiest, most powerful corporations. If I haven't convinced you, read it again. You may dispute my conclusions, as is your right, but you cannot dispute my facts.

The extreme right wing and those who identify themselves as conservatives will not heed my warnings or even acknowledge the factual nature of my examples. They know the answer before the question is asked. To them the universal answer is to be conservative which is defined as the destruction of government and the absolute protection of wealth.

Conservatives have voted out of their party all those who aren't "pure". They call them RINOs, shorthand for "Republicans In Name Only". If you disagree with any Republican policy; if you think that perhaps business needs to be restrained, that water should not be poisoned, that even the rich should pay for the privileges of our society at a higher rate than the middle class you are considered a traitor to conservatism and even to the notion of the Republican Party. Consequently, RINO's are almost an extinct breed.

The concept of RINO's isn't a new one. Back in 1884, the Republican purists had a different name for the RINO's of the day: Mugwumps.

James G. Blaine was the Republican nominee for president in 1884 against Democrat Grover Cleveland. Blaine was accused, not without justification, of being corrupt.

He was alleged to have been bought and paid for by big business, in this case the biggest business - the railroads. There were many principled Republicans that could not abide the thought of supporting such a tarnished candidate.

These Republicans threw their support behind the Democratic candidate rather than vote for a corrupt nominee. What's different today? As it was then, today big money has corrupted the Republican Party. Well, there is a major difference, today there aren't Mugwumps stepping up for integrity's sake.

For their trouble, the idealists of their day were branded as Mugwumps and ridiculed. Even then the ideological purists sacrificed integrity in order to serve the big money interests. The Mugwumps split the party, and President Grover Cleveland is remembered instead of President James G. Blaine.

Mark Twain commented on Mugwumps and the nature of blind loyalty and consistency in a lecture he gave in 1884 during the campaign, titled appropriately "Consistency". In his lecture, Twain speaks of the corruption of Blaine, how it is obvious to even those who support him, and marvels at the nature of consistency to the party even in the face of corruption. He cynically observes that even the principled man who defects to vote with the other side will later find himself chained to it out of consistency. The convert will never be able to change without any dishonor from those who celebrated him before.

Twain's comments on party loyalty suggest to me that his view of Tea Partiers and lifelong conservatives would not be favorable:

> "Is it possible for human wickedness to invent a
> doctrine more infernal and poisonous than this? Is there
> imaginable a baser servitude than it imposes? What slave is so
> degraded as the slave who is proud that he is a slave? What is
> the essential difference between a life-long Democrat and any
> other kind of life-long slave? Is it less humiliating to dance to
> the lash of one master than another?
>
> This atrocious doctrine of allegiance to party plays
> directly into the hands of politicians of the baser sort-and
> doubtless for that it was borrowed-or stolen-from the
> monarchical system. It enables them to foist upon the
> country officials whom no self-respecting man would vote for,
> if he could but come to understand that loyalty to himself is
> his first and highest duty, not loyalty to any party name...
>
> With the Daintiest and self-complacentest sarcasm
> the life-long loyalist scoffs at the Independent-or, as he calls
> him, with cutting irony, the Mugwump; makes himself too
> killingly funny for anything in this world about him.
>
> But-the Mugwump can stand it, for there is a great
> history at his back, stretching down the centuries, and he
> comes of a mighty ancestry. He knows that in the whole
> history of the race of men no single great and high and
> beneficent thing was ever done for the souls and bodies, the
> hearts and the brains, of the children of the world, but a
> Mugwump started it and Mugwumps carried it to victory.
>
> And their names are the stateliest in history;
> Washington, Garrison, Galileo, Luther, Christ. Loyalty to
> petrified opinions never yet broke a chain or freed a human
> soul in this world-and never will.
>
> To return to the starting point: I am persuaded that
> the world has been tricked into adopting some false and most
> pernicious notions about consistency-and to such a degree
> that the average man has turned the rights and wrongs of
> things entirely around, and is proud to be "consistent,"
> unchanging, immovable, fossilized, where it should be his
> humiliation that he is so."[91]

Consistency gives us tyranny. The status quo will
never self correct. Consistency in its purest form will watch
friends die leaving loved ones bankrupt just to maintain
purity. Consistency doesn't exist in nature, except in the
nature of little minds. Consistency will lead to a system
where millions vote themselves into servitude of the few,
rather than be called a RINO, a Mugwump, or, God
forbid, a liberal.

Don't vote the party. Don't vote the man. Vote
your conscience and vote for your values.

Do you want to have the system in place to help the next Tuscaloosa and Joplin? Do you wish to have opportunities in education for everyone? Do you wish to take back your right as a free citizen from the wealthiest men on the planet, to prohibit them from sending you to your death because safety is too expensive or even stop them from drawing a payoff when you die?

It won't be fixed with one election. It won't be fixed with one party. The Democrats can be corrupted as easily as Republicans. But we need balance and no Republican will even attempt to bring balance into the mix.

Do not be intimidated, scared, or ashamed to be angry at the behavior of the wealthy and powerful. You have a voice, and you have a vote. Use it.

If your value system is the same as what most Americans display in their everyday lives you will vote out the puppets of big business and you will defeat Ayn Rand's influence.

Does it offend you that selfishness is promoted as the highest virtue? Does it offend you that such a despicable person is promoted as a goddess of a new morality? Does the defense and enabling of forced sexual slavery in the Mariana Islands bother you at all? Does the deliberate pollution and poisoning of our water and air in the name of profit offend you? Where is your outrage at the super wealthy corporations making bets on lives of common men and women, and celebrating their deaths when they receive the payoffs on dead peasants? Do these things violate your core values? Prove it. You lie if you say you hate these things and then turn around and vote for those who wish more of the same on all of us.

One vote, which is all I ask for and that is what I wish from you.

I was a Republican for most of my adult life, but I will not vote for them now. Perhaps later, if they reform, but I shall not vote for them as long as Ayn Rand rules them.

Ayn doesn't rule me and she doesn't inspire my morality. I hope she doesn't inspire yours. We need you to vote your principles. The country depends upon the little guy, the poor and middle class, standing up to those who would enslave us.

I won't stand down, or become complacent. I'll vote my conscience and use every means possible to persuade anyone that will listen to me or read my words. Many of the things Ayn Rand has wished for are here, but my conscience is clear as I am opposing them with all the effort I can muster. If you aren't, your values aren't mine, and they aren't the values that made this country great

One vote. Light one candle. The darkness is upon us and it is getting darker.

SOURCES CONSULTED FOR CHAPTER 7

1 Wealth distribution chart available from
http://sociology.ucsc.edu/whorulesamerica/power/wealth.html

2 Ibid, P. 117.

3 Ibid, P. 113.

4 Ibid. P. 115.

5 Ibid. P. 124.

6 Summary of Russian Revolution available from
http://depts.washington.edu/baltic/papers/russianrevolution.htm

7 Alexander, Bevin "The Triumph of China" available from
http://bevinalexander.com/china/35-reds-create-peoples-republic.htm

8 Goodman, G.J.W. "The German Hyperinflation, 1923". ; Available from:
http://www.pbs.org/wgbh/commandingheights/shared/minitext/ess_german
hyperinflation.html

9 Ibid;

10 Shirer, W.L., "The Rise and Fall of the Third Reich". Seventeenth edition
1959, New York: Simon and Schuster. Pages 61-62

11 Ibid; p. 35.

12 Miller, S., The President and the Assassin 2011, New York: Random
House.
P. 36

13 Ibid; P. 301.

14 Ibid; P. 304

15 McMorris-Santoro, E. "Romney: America 'Inches Away From Ceasing To
Be A Free Market Economy'" June 2, 2011 TPM June 2, 2011; Available
from:
http://tpmdc.talkingpointsmemo.com/2011/06/romney-america-inches-away-
from-ceasing-to-be-a-capitalist-country.php?ref=fpa

16 Citibank Plutonomy Memo available from
http://jdeanicite.typepad.com/files/plutonomy-1.pdf

17 http://www.merriam-webster.com/dictionary/plutocracy

18 Citibank Plutonomy Memo available from
http://jdeanicite.typepad.com/files/plutonomy-1.pdf P. 8.

19 Ibid; P. 11.

20 Ibid; P. 14

21 Ibid; P. 15

22 Ibid, P. 17.

23 Ibid, P. 18.

24 Zeleny, J. "Romney: 'I'm Also Unemployed'" June 16, 2011 The Caucus
Blog June 16, 2011; Available from:
http://thecaucus.blogs.nytimes.com/2011/06/16/romney-im-also-unemployed/

25 Gavin, R. "As Bain Slashed Jobs, Romney Stayed To Side" Boston Globe
January 27, 2008 Available from:
http://www.boston.com/news/nation/articles/2008/01/27/as_bain_slashed_jobs_
romney_stayed_to_side/?page=full

26 "Romney Wealth As High As $250 Million". Date; Available from:
http://www.msnbc.msn.com/id/20251525/ns/politics-decision_08/t/romney-
wealth-high-million/#.To0HchX741Y

27 Mitt Romney's plan available from
http://www.mittromney.com/news/press/2011/09/fact-sheet-mitt-romneys-
plan-turn-around-economy

28 Okrent, D. "Wayne B. Wheeler: The Man Who Turned Off The Taps" Smithsonian Magazine May, 2010 Available from: http://www.smithsonianmag.com/history-archaeology/Wayne-B-Wheeler-The-Man-Who-Turned-Off-the-Taps.html

29 Ibid;

30 Ibid;

31 Ibid;

32 Ibid;

33 Ibid;

34 Horton, S. "The Failed Presidency of Karl Rove" Harpers Magazine August 13, 2007 Available from:http://harpers.org/archive/2007/08/hbc-90000877

35 Okrent, D. "Wayne B. Wheeler: The Man Who Turned Off The Taps"

36 Ibid;

37 Ibid;

38 Ibid;

39 Ibid;

40 Anderson, S., "Billy Sunday, Prophet or Charlatan?". The Overland Monthly, 1918. LXXI(January-June 1918). Page 78. Available from Google Books

41 Jane Addams biography available from http://www.iep.utm.edu/addamsj/

42 Okrent, D. "Wayne B. Wheeler: The Man Who Turned Off The Taps"

43 Ibid;

44 Fallows, J. "A Harsh Case Against Obama (And His Opponents)" September 3, 2011 Politics ; Available from: http://www.theatlantic.com/politics/archive/2011/09/a-harsh-case-against-obama-and-his-opponents/244512/

45 Double Indemnity quotes available from http://www.imdb.com/title/tt0036775/quotes

46 Lofgren, M. "Goodbye to All That: Reflections of a GOP Operative Who Left the Cult". Date September 2, 2011; Available from: http://www.truth-out.org/print/5901

47 Ibid;

48 Tanenhaus, S. "The Death Of Conservatism" 2009 Random House. P. 58

49 Krugman, P. "We Are Not Mirror Images" April 3, 2010 The Conscience of a Liberal April 3, 2010; Available from: http://krugman.blogs.nytimes.com/2010/04/03/we-are-not-mirror-images/

50 Lofgren, M. "Goodbye to All That: Reflections of a GOP Operative Who Left the Cult". Date September 2, 2011; Available from: http://www.truth-out.org/print/5901

51 Ibid;

52 Ibid;

53 Galloway, J. "Rand Paul and the Civil Rights Act of 1964" Political Insider with Jim Galloway; Available from: http://blogs.ajc.com/political-insider-jim-galloway/2010/05/20/rand-paul-and-the-civil-rights-act-of-1964/

54 Lawrence v Texas Decision 2003 Available from http://www.law.cornell.edu/supct/html/02-102.ZS.html

55 Dissent of Clarence Thomas Available from http://www.law.cornell.edu/supct/html/02-102.ZD1.html

56 Abraham Lincoln in Peoria, Illinois October 16, 1854 Available from http://quod.lib.umich.edu/cgi/t/text/text-idx?c=lincoln;cc=lincoln;type=simple;rgn=div1;q1=speech%20at%20peoria;view=text;subview=detail;sort=occur;idno=lincoln2;node=lincoln2%3A282

57 Ralph Waldo Emerson Available from http://www.bartleby.com/100/420.47.html

58 Bingham, A. "Tea Party Debate Audience Cheered Idea of Letting
   Uninsured Patients Die" September 13, 2011 Politics: The Note
   September 13, 2011; Available from:
   http://abcnews.go.com/blogs/politics/2011/09/tea-party-debate-audience-
   cheered-idea-of-letting-uninsured-patients-die/
59 Obituary for Kent Snyder, Wall Street Journal July 5, 2008. Available from
   http://online.wsj.com/article/SB121521859205329713.html?mod=todays_u
   s_page_one
60 Longbottom, W. "Dead at 49 Because He Couldn't Afford Health
   Insurance: Terrible Fate of Ron Paul Aide Emerges Hours After
   Republican Said State Shouldn't Afford Health Care" Daily Mail, UK
   September 15, 2011. Available from:
   http://www.dailymail.co.uk/news/article-2037330/Ron-Pauls-campaign-manager-
   died-pneumonia-afford-health-insurance.html
61 Estate tax rate chart available from
   http://wills.about.com/od/understandingestatetaxes/a/estatetaxchart.htm
62 Obituary Kent Snyder Available from
   http://online.wsj.com/article/SB121521859205329713.html?mod=todays_u
   s_page_one
63 D'Souza, D., Ronald Reagan: How an Ordinary Man Became an
   Extraordinary Leader 1997: Simon and Schuster. P. 80.
64 http://www.imdb.com/search/title?year=1950
65 http://www.imdb.com/search/title?year=1951
66 http://www.imdb.com/search/title?year=1952
67 http://www.imdb.com/search/title?year=1953
68 http://www.imdb.com/search/title?year=1954
69 http://www.imdb.com/search/title?year=1955
70 http://www.imdb.com/search/title?year=1956
71 http://www.imdb.com/search/title?year=1957
72 http://www.imdb.com/search/title?year=1958
73 http://www.imdb.com/search/title?year=1959
74 http://www.imdb.com/search/title?year=1960
75 Available from http://www.everythingisaremix.info/everything-is-a-remix-
   part-3-transcript/
76 Ibid;
77 Available from http://kottke.org/11/06/everything-is-a-remix-the-ideas-
   episode
78 Ames, Y.L.a.M. "Charles Koch to Friedrich Hayek: Use Social Security"
   The Nation October 17, 2011. Available from
   http://www.thenation.com/article/163672/charles-koch-friedrich-hayek-use-
   social-security
79 Ibid;
80 "BB&T touts Ayn Rand but takes taxpayer cash" October 28, 2008 Inside
   Philanthropy October 28, 2008.
   available from http://philanthropyjournal.blogspot.com/2008/10/bb-touts-ayn-
   rand-but-takes-taxpayer.html
81 Sauer, B.K. "10 Things You Didn't Know about Paul Ryan" U.S. News and
   World Report July 23, 2008 Available from:
   http://www.usnews.com/news/campaign-2008/articles/2008/07/23/10-
   things-you-didnt-know-about-paul-ryan
82 McConnell, S. "100 Voices: An Oral History of Ayn Rand " 2010 NAL
   Trade.
83 History of the Rural Electrification Administration available from
   http://eh.net/encyclopedia/article/malone.electrification.administration.rura
   l

84 History of the Rural Electrification Administration available from
  http://eh.net/encyclopedia/article/malone.electrification.administration.rura
  l
85 "The Economic Impact of the Interstate Highway System", 2006.
available from http://www.interstate50th.org/docs/techmemo2.pdf P. 50
86 The David R. Goode National Transportation Policy Conference Well
  Within Reach: America's New Transportation Agenda"
Bipartisan Conference led by Former Secretaries of Transportation Mineta and
  Skinner Available from http://millercenter.org/policy/transportation
87 Anderson, J.K.a.D., "Examining "Redistribution of Wealth" ". Available from
  http://www.lwv.org/AM/Template.cfm?Section=Home&CONTENTID=1
  7281&TEMPLATE=/CM/ContentDisplay.cfm
88 Longman, P. "Best Care Anywhere: Why VA Health Care Is Better Than
  Yours" 2010 Polipointpress. P. 2.
89 Ibid, P. 108.
90 Richter, P. "Missing Iraq money may have been stolen, auditors say" Los
  Angeles Time Available from:
  http://articles.latimes.com/print/2011/jun/13/world/la-fg-missing-billions-
  20110613
91 Mark Twain in a paper read at the Hartford Monday Evening Club
  following the Blaine Cleveland campaign 1884 accessed from Neider, C.,
  ed. "Consistency". The Complete Essays of Mark Twain"1963, De Capo
  Press Pages 576-583.

EPILOGUE: OZYMANDIAS

I *met a traveler from an antique land*
Who said: "Two vast and trunkless legs of stone
Stand in the desert. Near them on the sand,
Half sunk, a shattered visage lies, whose frown
And wrinkled lip and sneer of cold command
Tell that its sculptor well those passions read
Which yet survive, stamped on these lifeless things,
The hand that mocked them and the heart that fed.
And on the pedestal these words appear:
`My name is Ozymandias, King of Kings:
Look on my works, ye mighty, and despair!'
Nothing beside remains. Round the decay
Of that colossal wreck, boundless and bare,
The lone and level sands stretch far away".
percy bysshe shelley, 1818

I was in Tuscaloosa with my wife and stepchildren for The University of Alabama's Crimson Tide football team's first game of the 2011 season, which, coincidentally, was the first game, post tornado. As we drove down Fifteenth Street it was obvious even to my wife and the kids, who are not familiar with Tuscaloosa at all, that severe destruction had taken place.

The University had a very moving tribute both during the pre-game show and during half time for the first responders who worked so selflessly to rescue as many victims as possible immediately after the tornado struck.

In a video played on the four jumbo screens in Bryant-Denny Stadium, Coach Nick Saban is seen speaking to students, players, and citizens who are volunteering in the relief effort. In the particular scene shown they are apparently working on rebuilding a local business.

Coach Saban tells his audience that their contribution of time and energy is very much needed and will be remembered. He instructs the crowd in the video that whenever they pass by this location in the future they will be reminded of their contribution to this effort: "a legacy of their sacrifice for their fellow citizen will always be present in this building."

Besides being a very emotional moment intrinsically, the video was a poignant reminder of the difference between the values of Tuscaloosa, AL, Joplin, MO, and even America as a whole compared to the values of Ayn Rand and the Objectivists.

A crowd of approximately 100,000 cheered to honor the volunteers that day and I would wager that the realization of the randomness of the tragedy came upon most of us there. That is the "there but for the grace of God" it could, and can, be any of us. And all of us, not just any of us, should be grateful for the warm friendship, love, and sacrifice that our fellow Americans often show and which rises up immediately out of the debris of natural disasters to help with the healing and restoration process.

The instincts of the average citizen are this way. The average citizen's initial reaction is to offer help. And not in a conditional way suggested by the likes of Republican Eric Cantor who insists upon bargaining dollar for dollar cuts before it will be dispensed. The onslaught of compassion is antithetical to the dogma of Ayn Rand's doctrine of selfishness. In times such as these there is no virtue of selfishness when so many are dead, injured or missing through no fault of his or her own.

But this is not a unique phenomenon for Tuscaloosa or Joplin. It has occurred every time the alarm has sounded for tragedy and disaster. Americans have given till it has hurt for the hurting when the situation has demanded. Not just time or money either; lives have been sacrificed for strangers.

Look no further than the heroism of September 11th, 2001. Firefighters, policemen, and private citizens gave their lives knowingly to save others. Flight 93 famously crashed because the passengers believed that it was more important to die in a field than to sit back and have the government crippled. There were very few selfish pursuits that day, and these acts of heroism will always be a legacy we will honor.

The poem Ozymandias was written in 1818 by Percy Bysshe Shelley and serves as his literary legacy. This is particularly ironic given that one of the themes of the poem is the long term value of the legacy of the powerful. Shelley is the lesser-known member of the Shelley household. He was the husband of Mary Shelley, the author of "Frankenstein". But his sonnet "Ozymandias" conveys truth even today, almost two hundred years after its creation.

There was a real Ozymandias; he was a historical ruler of Egypt. However, Shelley embellished the part about the statue and disconnected feet. He drew inspiration from the first century Greek historian Diodorus Siculus - who recounted the story of the statue and the boastful inscription. Albeit Shelley phrased it differently in the poem due to poetic license. [1]

Notwithstanding the historical inaccuracies, the truth resonates. The mighty king Ozymandias ruled a powerful and large kingdom. He commissioned a statue to commemorate his power, his wealth, and his reach. His purpose was to immortalize himself as one of the greatest men of all time.

And yet by the time of Diodorus Siculus' writing, the first century, the legacy was reduced to dust and the inscribed boast mocks the king rather than offers tribute.

His works that were intended to bring despair upon the mighty were nothing but rubble and sand. The shattered face of the king lay in the sand and Shelley notes that its "*Frown and wrinkled lip and sneer of cold command tell that its sculptor well those passions read.*"

In other words, Shelley astutely notes that although the king postured himself as the great and powerful, the sculptor (and, by extension, all subjects of the king) knew the truth: the king was not so much powerful as he was cruel and merciless. One might rightly infer that the king never took away that lesson after the unveiling, preferring to bask in the realism of the sculpture and never realizing that the reality captured wasn't as flattering as he thought.

The inscription on the pedestal mocks the legacy even more: "*Look upon my works ye mighty and despair*", with the isolated appendages apparently ruling over nothing but desert sands.

Ayn Rand's worshippers could stand to read this poem; provided they could understand the metaphor. Although it is likely that, given their adoration of Ayn's crumbled literary monuments, one shouldn't expect that the true meaning of the sonnet would register with them.

On the off chance that an Objectivist has purchased this book thinking it a puff piece praising Ayn, I'll clarify: no refunds. Let the buyer beware, my self-interest prohibits me from giving refunds and I thank you for your purchase. A donation will be made in your name to the Democratic National Party.

With respect to man-made statues, monuments, and tributes, all are temporal. Enough money can be left in a trust to provide upkeep, but memories of the donation fade and eternal recognition is hollow. For those who have attended college, I daresay that almost every building on your campus bears the name of a long deceased donor.

I also venture a guess that most business students at the University of Alabama have not a clue as to who the Bidgood was that inspired the name of the business school's flagship building.

Bidgood has become a meaningless moniker, with no relevance to anyone other than the name of a landmark, save for the actual heirs of Mr. Bidgood. To answer the inevitable trivia question "Who was Bidgood?" I quote the University of Alabama's Culverhouse School of Business website - which carries the name Culverhouse because of a conditional bequest from the estate of Mr. Hugh Culverhouse, whose widow demanded his name be removed from the school. But that's another story. [2]

Lee Bidgood will be remembered for generations to come because he helped found the College of Commerce and Business Administration at The University of Alabama.

> *...Bidgood's reputation as a teacher and scholar in economics led to his appointment at The University of Alabama. With the support of President George H. Denny, Bidgood convinced the board to take action, and in January 1920, the School of Commerce and Business Administration came into being. Bidgood was chosen as Dean.*
>
> *...Under Bidgood's leadership, a building specifically designed for business programs was built in 1928.*
> [a]

For University of Alabama Business School graduates (including myself) who were unaware as to Mr. Bidgood's legacy do not despair because his name didn't register to you as more than a building positioned off of the Quad. This is the whole point. Legacies established with physical and material means will crumble, fade, grow obsolete or become forgotten. All man made monuments will fade away, no matter how important the inspiration had been during the dedication period. Which in no way implies any disrespect to Mr. Bidgood, this was precisely the point Percy Bysshe Shelley was making in "Ozymandias".

Everything about this life is temporal; it's a fleeting vapor.

If one fought defending the Alamo, they died that day. Everyone who walked the earth at that time that didn't participate in the battle of the Alamo is just as dead.

The Titanic carried on it some of the wealthiest men and women in the world. The aggregate wealth proved decisively ineffective in deflecting icebergs that day, and the names of the passengers are unknown to most Americans these days, except to the few Leonardo DiCaprio fans who live for the memorization of his movies.

Which raises an interesting point. Much emphasis has been placed in this book, the books of Ayn Rand, and in today's society on the subject of wealth. Is it corrupting? Or is it the ultimate benchmark of success, as the Randians believe it to be?

Don't read into this what I am not saying. Wealth does not in and of itself become evil. It is the love of money that is the root of all-evil according to the Bible. [4] How might one make the distinction between money and too much money; from stewardship to "a root of all kinds of evil"?

Compare the passengers of the Titanic with yourself or the average middle class or even poor American these days. Quality of life is superior in our age.

Consider John Jacob Astor, IV. He was the wealthiest person on the ship, and the wealthiest person to go down on the ship. He died at 48, but had lived a full and privileged life. His family was one of the most prestigious families in New York, or the world for that matter. He created the Astoria Hotel, which is now known as the Waldorf-Astoria. He had the ultimate rich man's perk: the much younger, trophy wife as his second wife. She was 18, and had been put in the family way by Mr. Astor and they were riding out the scandal overseas.

The Titanic was to be his triumphant return to the states. They checked into a first class suite, with a manservant, a maid, a nursemaid, and a dog named Kitty. The fare adjusted for 2011 prices was about $50,000 per night. [5]

Mr. Astor the IV was known to receive mail addressed to the "Richest Man in the World", [6] which was most likely an exaggeration, as John D. Rockefeller had by that point become the richest man. John Jacob Astor, IV need not feel self conscious, however. Some estimates have his net worth at the time of his death to be approximately $115 billion in current dollar amounts. Rockefeller was an overachiever; the same estimates have him at over $300 billion. For perspective, two of our more famous current billionaires, Warren Buffet and Bill Gates, have less than $120 billion...combined. [7] Whatever metric one chooses to use will show John Jacob Astor, IV as one of the wealthiest men of all time.

I will make a gutsy assumption and assume that none of my readers have that type of wealth. But what of the standard of living for me and the hundreds of thousands (let's think big) who are reading this now? I'd say it is pretty clear that all of us have a much better standard of living than everyone on the Titanic; including the richest man in the world.

We all have access to the internet, many of us on our phones. We get books transmitted over the airwaves into our hands without leaving the house, as this book can attest to this fact. I'm sure most of us have air conditioning, electric freezers and refrigerators, microwave ovens, and produce from all over the world available a short drive away. Speaking of driving, I of course mean driving in a climate-controlled car with lights for night, defrosters for winter, and wipers for rain.

We have no worries about polio, as the vaccine has benefited us all. We have access to better medical care and our life expectancy is much longer.

Those are just a few benefits we average Joes have which John Jacob Astor, IV could have never received, no matter what price he offered. A rising tide does lift all boats as technology and the marketplace bring progress and a higher standard of living to even the most common man.

The standard of living is not the measure of corrupting wealth. Houses are bigger for the wealthy, cars are more luxurious, and clothing more expensive. There is nothing inherently wrong with high-end goods being consumed by those who can afford it. Where in lies the abuse of wealth?

I can only offer my opinion and it is merely one of many philosophies worldwide. However it is one I share with one of the most respected theologian/philosophers of the 20th century, C.S. Lewis. Refer back to Chapter 4 and note his assessment of pride as the worst possible sin. Lewis correctly identifies the abuse of wealth and power that originates with pride. Quoting Lewis from his classic, "Mere Christianity":

> "Greed may drive men into competition if there is
> not enough to go round; but the proud man, even when he
> has got more than he can possibly want, will try to get still
> more just to assert his power. Nearly all those evils in the
> world which people put down to greed or selfishness are
> really far more the result of Pride.
>
> Take it with money. Greed will certainly make a
> man want money, for the sake of a better house, better
> holidays, better things to eat and drink. But only up to a
> point. What is it that makes a man with £10,000 a year
> anxious to get £20,000 a year?
> [Authors note: Do not be distracted by the
> ridiculously low threshold of wealth here, as this was written
> during World War II and applies to an England that was
> besieged by Nazi Germany. Put in $1,000,000 and
> $1,000,000,000 respectively. The same point applies, as
> there is only so much that can be consumed]
> It is not the greed for more pleasure. £10,000 will
> give all the luxuries that any man can really enjoy. It is Pride-
> the wish to be richer than some other rich man, and (still
> more) the wish for power. For, of course, power is what
> Pride really enjoys: there is nothing makes a man feel so
> superior to others as being able to move them about like toy
> soldiers. [8]

That's what it is about and it is the core issue - the
pride that motivates men to acquire not for comfort, not
for security, and not for the good of their family. It is about
acquisitions for the sake of acquisition. It is personified in
Don Blankenship of Massey Energy, the Koch Brothers, a
legion of hedge fund managers and CEO's and
Ozymandias.

To what end does this serve? Nothing more than
the fulfillment of the lust of power, to have enough wealth
to intimidate, to rule, to degrade other men into "moving
about like toy soldiers", to quote Lewis. Is the system in
place that facilitates the development of ruling families into
dynasties so sacred that it must be protected at any cost?

To Ayn Rand and her conservative commune that now dominate the discourse, it is. It is "freedom" manifest. But truly, it is not freedom for all but rather for the top one percent while the rest of us take marching orders from above. The orders are not from those who are better, more moral, or intellectually superior, but from many who were members of the "lucky sperm club". The genius of today's John Galt imitators is overstated. It is doubtful that we would perish without iPads, Facebook, or Brawny paper towels. Way back in the day, we lived without them.

Ayn Rand's message lives on today and her message appeals to the basest instinct of individuals: their pride. Those who embrace her celebrate the inversion of traditional morals, as up is now down, selfishness is now a virtue, and charity is nothing more than a waste of time. It is evil. If this be our ruling class, and it becomes more so with each election, what hope do Tuscaloosa and Joplin have? What chances do the poor, elderly, mentally retarded, disabled veterans, or cancer-suffering common men have?

John Jacob Astor, IV had all the wealth in the world, but was just as mortal as any poor immigrant on the Titanic. Does a luxury hotel which bears his name really matter as a legacy?

When it became apparent the Titanic was doomed, the spaces on the lifeboats became the most valuable real estate in the world of the passengers. The order went out to only load women and children. Astor's young wife was pregnant, and he escorted her into the boat, attempting to take a seat next to her. He was told that all spaces were reserved for women and children, and by all accounts he took this gracefully. He is reported to have given his gloves to his bride and lit a cigarette while awaiting the end. But there is more.

In 1981, a survivor of the Titanic, Louis Garrett, recounted the night. Louis Garrett was 12, his sister was 14, and neither could speak English, as they were immigrants from Lebanon. They were traveling without their parents, as the family could not afford complete passage for all at once, and they crossed the ocean in installments. Garrett recalled in 1981:

"What a sight! Most of the lifeboats were gone. The crew was permitting women and children only to board the lifeboats-there were not enough for everyone. We saw women crying, not wanting to leave their husbands; husbands begging their wives and children to hurry and get into the lifeboats. Amid this complete pandemonium and mass hysteria stood my sister and I, two immigrant children, unable to speak English, frightened beyond belief, crying and looking for help.

"The last lifeboat was being loaded. A middle-aged gentleman was with his very young, pregnant wife. He helped her into the lifeboat, then looked back to the deck and saw others wanting to get aboard. He kissed his wife good-bye, and, returning to the deck, grabbed the first person in his path. Fortunately, I was there in the right place at the right time and he put me into the lifeboat. I screamed for my sister who had frozen from fright. With the help of others, she also was pushed into the lifeboat. Who was the gallant man who performed this kind act? We were told he was John Jacob Astor IV."[9]

It appears in his last hours, the wealthiest man in the world gave his life to save two children without a dime; two children that could not speak one word of English.

No headlines or history book would have ever recorded their death, except in aggregate with the rest of the victims. Yet the most famous passenger stepped up and sacrificed for the least of these.

In Ayn Rand's world, he was a failure. For the rest of us, he left a more powerful and solid legacy than any material monument could do. Ozymandias' face reflected scorn, cruelty and contempt. Astor's image should be appreciated as a human one; one that displays the noblest qualities of humanity.

I misspoke in the title of the book. Ayn Rand doesn't hate Tuscaloosa. She hates America; the bulk of America that actually supports the economy, military, and real charity. This America bears the brunt of sacrifice in wars, depressions, budget cutbacks and natural disasters. This America rushes into burning buildings to save strangers, it braves inclement weather to restore power and communication for millions of citizens, and it prays earnestly for the well being of all of those who face life as its harshest.

Atlas held up the sky, but Atlas did not float in air. Atlas stood on firm ground shouldering his burden. The America hated by Ayn Rand and her disciples is that solid ground. We hold up Atlas. Let him shrug, we are strong enough where we will not be crushed.

Ayn hates America. That should be clear. What isn't clear is why America doesn't hate Ayn.

SOURCES CONSULTED FOR EPILOGUE

[1] Information on Diodorus Siculus available from
http://www.rc.umd.edu/rchs/diod.htm

[2] Reeves, J. "Widow Demands Return of Husband's Gift to School" Los
Angeles Times October 5, 1997 Available from:
http://articles.latimes.com/1997/oct/05/news/mn-39480

[3] About Lee Bidgood available from http://cba.ua.edu/about/hof/lee-bidgood

[4] 1 Timothy 6:10 For the love of money is a root of all kinds of evil. Some
people, eager for money, have wandered from the faith and pierced
themselves with many griefs.

[5] "John Jacob Astor, IV: The Richest Titantic Casulty" Ephemeral New
York; Available from
http://ephemeralnewyork.wordpress.com/2009/04/13/john-jacob-astor-iv-the-richest-titanic-casualty/

[6] Moshman, Robert L. "Celebrity Estates" FinacialCounsel.com Available
from
http://investor.financialcounsel.com/Articles/EstatePlanning/ARTEST0000
050-CelebrityEstates.asp

[7] "Top Ten Wealthiest Men of All Time" AskMen.com; Available from
http://www.askmen.com/top_10/entertainment/11b_top_10_list.html

[8] Lewis, C., *Mere Christianity*. *1952*. New York. P. 122.

[9] Nicola-Yarred, E., *'I Survived the Sinking of the Titanic'*, 1981. Available
from http://www.encyclopedia-titanica.org/i-survived-the-sinking-of-the-titanic.html

ABOUT THE AUTHOR...

George Kelley is a sometimes writer, halftime teacher, full time husband, part time dad to two wonderful stepchildren and long time political junkie living in Nashville, TN. He teaches political science courses at Cumberland University in Lebanon, TN. George has worked in previous times as a portfolio manager for a trust department, a restaurant manager, and served as an officer in the Alabama National Guard and Army Reserves.

George has studied, but not as much as he should have, at the University of Alabama, due in no small part to his pursuit of a good time. He participated in the "Major of the Month Club" as an undergraduate, trying out every field of study for a no risk thirty-day trial before settling on his degree program(s). By some accident he acquired a Bachelors of Science in Finance, a Masters of Arts in Finance, and a Masters of Arts in Political Science.

He has taught at the college level, courses in corporate finance, investment, American national government, international relations, American foreign policy, & state and local government.

George found his professional passion of writing, after he found his personal passion, his wife. He elected to devote his life to teaching via the written word in much the same style he tries to do with the spoken one.

George believes in lighting one single candle, rather than cursing the darkness. His books are candles lit, one at a time. It is hoped that these candles will be enjoyed and considered bright enough to be worthwhile.

393

George can found at the following locations:

WWW.OneSingleCandle.com
WWW.AynHatesAmerica.com (blog)
Twitter @AynHatesAmerica
Email george@aynhatesamerica.com
Facebook http://www.facebook.com/pages/Ayn-Rand-Hates-Tuscaloosa-And-You-Too-Joplin/130305840393295

AYN RAND HATES TUSCALOOSA...AND YOU TOO, JOPLIN!

www.ingramcontent.com/pod-product-compliance
Lightning Source LLC
Chambersburg PA
CBHW052028090426
42739CB00010B/1824